Railroading with AMERICAN FLYER

Developed at the GILBERT HALL OF SCIENCE

Greenberg's Price Guide

AMERICAN FLYER

S Gauge

Paul G. Yorkis, Ph.D.

James D. Walsh

Linda F. Greenberg

Bruce C. Greenberg, Ph.D.

This book is dedicated to present and
future generations of
Gilbert enthusiasts.

Copyright 1980

Greenberg Publishing Company
729 Oklahoma Road
Sykesville, MD 21784
301 - 795 - 7447

First Edition

Manufactured in the United States of America

Greenberg Publishing Company offers the world's largest selection of
model railroading, prototype railroading and collecting publications. A
year's subscription to our catalogue is available for $2.00. Greenberg
Publishing Company also sponsors the largest public train show in the
United States three times a year at Towson, Maryland. Contact us for
the next show date.

Greenberg Publishing Company distributes this book to the hobby
industry.

Van Nostrand Reinhold Company, distributes this book to the book
trade.

Van Nostrand Reinhold Company
Division of Litton Educational Publishing, Inc.
135 West 50th Street
New York, NY 10020, U.S.A.

Van Nostrand Reinhold Limited
1410 Birchmount Road
Scarborough, Ontario M1P 2E7, Canada

Van Nostrand Reinhold Australia Pty. Ltd.
17 Queen Street
Mitcham, Victoria 3132, Australia

Van Nostrand Reinhold Company Limited
Molly Millars Lane
Wokingham, Berkshire, England

1 3 5 7 9 11 13 15 16 14 12 10 8 6 4 2

Library of Congress Number 80-67942

ISBN 0-442-21209-7

ACKNOWLEDGEMENTS

The study of toy trains is at its best a collaborative mutually enlightening experience. As I have remarked in our earlier books, each Guide is the product of the collective expertise and interests of many train enthusiasts. The S Gauge Guide is true to this tradition and more so. Never have I worked with as many collectors with such intense appreciation of the trains they operate and collect.

The Guide in a sense "began" when Paul Yorkis approached me two years ago with a request--he wanted to write a book on American Flyer S Gauge trains. I said, "fine, but I'm not ready yet." Then about a year and a half ago Mike Newcomer came to me and said "You've done books on Lionel, lots of books on Lionel, you should do a book on Gilbert and I will help you do it." I said great. Late last fall Paul, Jack Radcliff, a photographer recommended by Paul and I met with Mike at his home in Dover, Pennsylvania and for two days we examined in detail and photographed Mike's collection. This was quite a feat since Mike's entire collection was in boxes and every box had to be unpacked and repacked. It was quite a strain on his household. About this time I heard from Jim Walsh for the first time. He had been studying Gilbert for several years and thinking of writing his own book. He had interviewed a number of people from Gilbert management and was very enthused about them and the story to be told. He had heard about this project and wanted to see if we could work out something jointly. I was delighted when he agreed to join the project. Several local friends, Jim Patterson, Walt Balint and Dave Hawkins with long standing interests in Gilbert joined the project. Ed Leonard, who I had met in my book selling travels expressed an interest in the project and offered to assist. I contacted Dan Olson because of his national reputation which is justly deserved and he graciously agreed to help. Leonard Welter, the owner of a fine hobby shop in Schenectady was very enthusiastic about the project and he and his friend Ted Rudzinski offered to review the manuscript. Leonard also produced several magnificent photographs, including the Union Pacific Passenger Set, the accessory illustration with the Mini-craft buildings and the rare box cars from the Walsh Collection. Warren Perrine offered to read the manuscript as did Ed Schneider, a long time enthusiast from Reading. Lou Bargeron, who had long advocated a Gilbert book, joined the project with gusto. Lou's passion for S Gauge goes back to his youth and he willingly shared his knowledge of and affection for Gilbert with us. Jim La Calle, Charles Simms, and Pete Petri graciously allowed us to review their fine collections. Ken Hein of Illinois wrote and offered his help. At the Timonium train show in March, while looking at some Gilbert products, I met Jim Sutter. He immediately clarified some misunderstandings and joined the project.

One big problem was to find a large collection near my house where I could easily go to review descriptions and learn more about variations. Fortunately, Don Caples lived nearby and welcomed my visits, which extended for more times and many more hours than either he or I ever anticipated. The hospitality of his family and the good lunches prepared by his wife Caroline are part of the pleasant associations of this book. In addition, Allen Passman brought his fine S Gauge collection to our offices so that we could review it in detail. His observations were most appreciated.

This book is set in seven and nine point Century in our office by two very able and talented typsetters, Mary Dresner and Mae Myers. Not only are they accurate and careful, but they have taken a personal interest in the meaning of the words and concepts describing Gilbert and frequently raised questions as to the sense or nonsense of a sentence. Their thoughtfulness helped significantly to make this a better book.

One day Dan Olson suggested that I contact Robert Stromberg. Several years ago Major Stromberg published his own price guide and listing of Gilbert production. His research efforts substantially advanced the knowledge of the field. I was delighted when in response to my letter Bob agreed to collaborate on the project. His critical reading of the draft manuscript greatly strengthened the entire Guide. His chapter covering cabooses represents the state of the art in the study of toy train variations and stands. It is a remarkable piece of scholarship and I am honored to have his contribution.

Jim Patterson of Silver Spring has had a long standing in American Flyer. He spent many, many hours in his basement writing comments, additions and corrections to this manuscript. His concern that the details be true and accurate are very appreciated. Walt Balint also has a keen eye and active concern for accuracy and clarity. When I was mystifed by a comment or observation of one of our reviewers I would call Walt and ask for clarification. And clarification I would get.

Ed Leonard specializes in the unusual and the rare. When a question arose about whether a "never made" was actually a "seldom seen," Ed would explain how the confusion arose. Ed is also an active buyer and seller of Gilbert equipment and provided accurate price evaluations.

Nat Polk, one of the fathers of the modern hobby industry was a most helpful informant. He personally knew both Cowan and Gilbert and their key staff members. His insights explained the personalities and styles of these men and the structure of the hobby marketplace and how it affected the type of trains produced. Much of the descriptions in this book about the model railroad and toy industry are based on concepts and ideas generated by Nat Polk.

Maury Romer was the Chief Engineer at the Gilbert plant for many years and he has graciously shared his wealth of knowledge. His explanations on the why and how of Flyer manufacturing helped make this a much more informative book. His lifetime of experience would fill several books and feeling the growing interest in American Flyer, Maury has underway his own book to explain what Gilbert did and why he did it.

Bruce Manson, the editor of the TCA Quarterly and the TCA Museum Director, is a long time Gilbert fan, in fact he used to make regular pilgrimages to the Gilbert Hall of Science. He kindly shared his love of Gilbert and his trove of information and lore. His comments and additions to the draft manuscript were very helpful.

Hank Degano, an expert on toy train prices and "the marketplace" generously shared his technical information.

Don Heimburger was very helpful and supportive. Don publishes the leading S Gauge magazine, appropriately called "The S Gaugian," which contains articles of interest to both scale-oriented S Gauge fans as well as S Gauge tin platers.

Jack Radcliff is a very talented photographer. Prior to our two day stand at Mike's house, he met with Paul and me at Paul's house to photograph a variety of test subjects. He carefully analyzed the developed photographs and reshot them. Again he analyzed his results and reshot those which did not meet his standards. Note the general absence of shadows and glare and the crispness of detail which characterize most of the color photographs (and certainly all of Jack's). Also note that there are no intrusive shelf brackets behind the glass shelves. That is because my good friend and Chief Engineer Joseph Riley designed a portable, light weight unit for photographing trains. Engineer Riley also lent some of his 1938-41 Gilbert iron steeds for our analysis. Lois Kindell, an advanced photography student working for Jack Radcliff, printed many of the fine black and white prints. Tom Freet of Blakeslee Lane Studios in Baltimore provided other photographs. The color separations were done by Graph Tec with the able assistance of Jim Ritz. The excellent printing is the product of our favorite Baltimore firm, Collins Lithography. Bob Greelee of Collins provided his usual superb coordinator services.

Pat DeMarco graciously permitted us to use his slide of the Silver Flash B unit and also provided a slide of the rare Peanut car from his collection. Reggie Carnes provided important information about very rare items from his collection. Gabe and Florence Monaco shared with Jim Walsh stories from their years at Gilbert. Herb Pierce talked with Jim Walsh about his role in Gilbert management of the forties and fifties. Frank Castiglione provided details about the great layouts built by him for Gilbert. Jerry Silvia shared his counsel and added a number of outstanding factory photographs including both external and interior views. Jim also talked with Marshall Frisbie, Maury Romer and Spike Fitzpatrick about their experiences as senior Gilbert managers. Other Gilbert people that Jim talked with are: Molly Wool, Bernie Goldbeck, Jack MacGrail, John Donahue, Al Repplier, Al Orsbee, Harry Gordon, Angus Gordon, Jr., Robert Berner, and Mike Crisola as well as a number of others. Al Scalingi, formerly of Keystone Camera, provided fascinating data about the Keystone-Gilbert relationship. We are most appreciative of the willingness of all of these people to share their experiences with us. They have added much to our understanding of Gilbert. In addition to his interviews Jim also read the manuscript carefully and made ongoing suggestions for its improvement.

Paul Yorkis did the initial drafts of the loco and diesel chapters as well as the first part of the Epilogue. He spent many, many hours looking at Gilbert trains and provided ongoing technical information.

Jan Rechenberg's counsel was appreciated -- he spent the better part of a day with me explaining the intricacies of Gilbert sets.

Early into the Guide, I learned that John Wickland had earlier compiled a list of Gilbert variations based on his extensive collection. In a subsequent conversation with John he offered to provide a copy of this list and other Flyer materials to guide me in examining Gilbert items. For example, he identified thin and thick shell passenger cars. Maury Romer then differentiated between the bakelite and injection molded plastics used in the passenger cars. I am most appreciative of John's willingness to assist me and this book is that much the richer for his contribution.

Lou Dell'Orfano spent two days with us while we photographed Michael's Collection. He assisted us in numerous ways from hauling trains to providing important background information. I much appreciate his assistance. Lee Gettel, Jr. and Lee Gettel, Sr. are ardent S Gaugians. Father and son provided several of the F-9s that are shown in this volume. Lee, Sr. is the secretary of the Central Pennsylvania "S" Gaugers and welcomes inquiries from fellow S Gauge fans. He may be contacted at 742 Florida Avenue, York, Pennsylvania, 17404. The Shughart family: Emory, Alan and Larry assisted by providing their Domino Sugar hopper for this volume.

My son Paul was an observant assistant. Together he and I spent many an evening peering at slides of Mike's collection to decipher lettering and numbers.

Linda, my wife, is the chief editor. She is also the principal draftsman of the introductory chapter. She is a skillful editor, particularly in pointing out ambiguous phrases as well as trying to invent diverse ways of conveying an often repeated description. This book was actively in progress for about seven months. Every day Linda and I would work on "the project." It became very trying on some days, but we are still best of friends.

In the course of our research for this book we gathered a substantial body of information which is not included because of time and financial constraints. Our plans, given sufficient interest, are to publish a Volume II which will delve into the production and distribution of Gilbert products. We hope that those of you who are interested in such a book will let us know and that those with information about items that we did not cover or did not cover adequately will fill us in on the missing data. In a work of this magnitude there are necessarily going to be errors. I would be most appreciative to learn of these so that we may correct these in future editions.

Bruce C. Greenberg
Sykesville, June 28, 1980

PREFACE

Purpose

The purpose of this book is to provide a comprehensive listing and description of Gilbert production from 1946 through 1966 and current Fundimension production, 1979-80. Current values are provided where available and background and historical material are included to enrich and extend the joys of collecting and operating Gilbert S Gauge.

How to Find the Car You Are Looking For

This book is organized to help you locate a particular item. Its chapters generally correspond to major categories of equipment. However, some groupings may be defined somewhat differently. Thus, the major categories which correspond to chapters are: steam locomotives; diesels and small self propelled units; passenger cars; cranes and floodlights; gondolas, hoppers and dump cars; cabooses and work cabooses; and accessories, track and transformers. In addition all rectangular box-shaped rolling stock are in the chapter called box cars, reefers and stock cars. Also included in this chapter are automatic box, cattle and related cars. Another composite chapter is called flat cars because it includes not only the usual flat cars with lumber, pipe or girder loads, but also specialized flats which carry autos and rockets, as well as operating and action cars that us the basic flat car base. Finally, the flat car chapter includes depressed center cars other than floodlight cars.

Within each chapter items are organized by ascending catalogue number. Since Gilbert produced some items without catalogue numbers or only with partial catalogue numbers, we list such items at the beginning of the chapter in order to refer the reader to its complete description later in the chapter.

Determining Values

Toy train values vary for a number of reasons. First, consider the **relative knowledge** of the buyer and seller. A seller may be unaware that he has a rare variation and sell it for the price of a common piece. Another source of price variation is **short-term fluctuation** which depends on what is being offered at a given train meet on a given day. If four 336s are for sale at a small meet, we would expect that supply would outpace demand and lead to a reduction in price. A related source of variation is the **season** of the year. The train market is slower in the summer and sellers may at this time be more inclined to reduce prices if they really want to move an item. Another important source of price variation is the relative strength of the seller's **desire to sell** and the buyer's eagerness to buy. Clearly a seller in economic distress will be more eager to strike a bargain. A final source of variation are the **personalities** of the seller and buyer. Some sellers like to quickly turn over items and, therefore, price their items to move; others seek a higher price and will bring an item to meet after meet until they find a willing buyer.

Train values in this book are based on prices obtained at large East Coast train meets during the spring of 1980. We have chosen East Coast meets since the greatest dollar volume of transactions appear there. The prices reported here represent a "ready sale," or a price perceived as a good value by the buyer. They may sometimes appear lower than those seen on trains at meets for two reasons. First, items that do sell often sell quickly in the first hour of a train meet and, therefore, are no longer visible. (We have observed that a good portion of the action at most meets occurs in the first hour.) The items that do not sell in the first hour have a higher price tag and this price, although not representing the sales price, is the price observed at the meet. A related source of discrepancy is the willingness of some sellers to bargain over price.

From our studies of train prices, it appears that mail order prices for used trains are generally higher than those obtained at Eastern train meets. This is quite appropriate considering the costs and efforts of producing and distributing a price list and packing and shipping items. Mail order items do sell at prices above those listed in this book. A final source of difference between observed prices and reported prices is region. Prices are clearly higher in the South and West where trains are less plentiful than along the East Coast.

Condition

For each item, we provide three categories: **Good, Very Good and Excellent.** The Train Collectors Association (TCA) defines condition as:

FAIR - Well-scratched, chipped, dented, rusted or warped

GOOD - Scratches, small dents, dirty

VERY GOOD - Few scratches, exceptionally clean, no dents or rust

EXCELLENT - Minute scratches or nicks, no dents or rust

MINT - Brand new, absolutely unmarred, all original and unused

In the toy train field there is a great deal of concern with exterior appearance and less concern with operation. If operation is important to you, then ask the seller whether the train runs. If the seller indicates that he does not know whether the equipment operates, you should test it. Most train meets have test track provided for that purpose.

We do not show a value for Fair or Mint. Fair items are valued substantially below Good. Pre-1970 Mint items usually bring a substantial premium over Excellent. Truly Mint items are extremely scarce. Many items are offered as Mint which do not meet the exacting requirements of this condition. Mint means absolutely unused and unrun. An item must have the original box to be considered Mint. It may have been removed from the box and replaced in it but it should show no evidence of handling. A piece is not Mint if it has any scratches, fingerprints or evidence of discoloration. We have not included 'Restored' because such items are not a major portion of the market for postwar trains. As a rough guide, we expect that Restored items will bring prices equivalent to Good or Very Good.

As we indicated, prices in this book were derived from large train meets or shows. If you have trains to sell and you sell them to a person planning to resell them at another train meet, you will not obtain the prices reported in this book. Rather, you may expect to achieve about fifty percent of these prices. Basically, for your items to be of interest to a buyer who plans to resell them, he must purchase them for considerably less than the prices listed here. We receive continual inquiries as to whether or not a particular piece is a "good value." This book will help you answer that question; but, there is NO substitute for experience in the marketplace. WE STRONGLY RECOMMEND THAT NOVICES DO NOT MAKE MAJOR PURCHASES WITHOUT THE ASSISTANCE OF FRIENDS WHO HAVE EXPERIENCE IN BUYING AND SELLING TRAINS. If you are at a train meet and do not know who to ask about a train's value, look for the people running the meet and discuss with them your need for assistance. Usually they can refer you to an experienced collector who will be willing to examine the piece and offer his opinion.

The Gilbert News

VOL. 1, NO. 6   PUBLISHED BY THE A. C. GILBERT CO.   DECEMBER, 1941

Merry Christmas

This is the front cover of the December, 1941 Gilbert News showing the plant. Note that the two new wings shown in the later picture in the Caboose Chapter are not present. Walsh Collection.

TABLE OF CONTENTS

Acknowledgements iii

Preface v

Chapter I Overview 9

Chapter II Diesels and Motorized Units 24

Chapter III Locomotives 38

Chapter IV Cabooses by Robert N. Stromberg 62

Chapter V Gondolas 71

Chapter VI Catalogues 75

Chapter VII Trucks 77

Chapter VIII Box Cars: Operating, Non-Operating, Reefers and Stock Cars 78

Chapter IX Accessories 96

Chapter X Tank Cars 119

Chapter XI Flat Cars: Operating, Non-Operating and Depressed Centers 125

Chapter XII Cranes and Floodlights 138

Chapter XIII Passenger Cars 147

Chapter XIV Hoppers and Dump Cars 167

Chapter XV Transformers 172

Epilogue 174

Color Plates

Alco PA Diesels 25

Missouri Pacific Set 28

Union Pacific Set 29

EMD F-9S 32

Steam Engine Prototypes 60

Colorful Steam Engines 61

Cabooses 64

Box Cars 81

Box Cars 84

Box Cars 85

Rare Box Cars 89

Prototype Box Cars 93

Accessories 96

Baggage Loader 113

Tank Cars 121

Flat Cars 125

Flat Cars 128

CHAPTER I
OVERVIEW

INTRODUCTION

Once upon a time a man by the name of Alfred Carlton Gilbert determined to find a better way to sell magical tricks. In 1909 he set himself up in business in a rented shed near New Haven and began to manufacture and sell boxed magical tricks in earnest. From these humble beginnings the Mysto Manufacturing Company was born and A.C. Gilbert was launched into business. Throughout his career A.C. Gilbert sought to win first place by using his natural ability and perseverence to prove himself the better man. He was successful, and his peers considered him able to marshall technological innovation, personal commitment and showmanship to more effectively compete in the American marketplace.

In many ways Gilbert's story reads like that of Horatio Alger. "A.C." -- as he was popularly known -- worked diligently, treated people fairly, strove for competence and self-sufficiency and won praise for the toys he made and the kind of man he was. His story is exemplary and thus intriguing; the demise of the company that much harder to explain. By 1961 when Gilbert died his name was associated with a prestigious, established toy business and he owned a six hundred acre estate in Paradise (Connecticut) with its own game preserve, kennel and stocked lake. A.C. was a gregarious, public spirited man; a man of standards and business acumen. He knew, in the best sense, the rewards of combining business interests, consumer solicitousness and philanthropy.

"Gilbert the Great"

A.C. was born in 1884 in Salem, Oregon.[1] By the time he was in elementary school he was captivated by magic and began to teach himself how to perform magic tricks. He was also a very active, energetic child and sports fan. His enthusiasm led him to form the Moscow Athletic Club when he was about 12.[2] The club was popular with the local boys even though A.C. was the winner in most of the contests. A.C.'s athletic program was rigorous, his regime successful. He became an expert gymnast, a good wrestler and a super bag puncher. After Gilbert completed preparatory school he went on to the affiliated Pacific University in Forest Grove, Oregon, where he gained renown for organizing and becoming captain of the school's first track team.[3]

In 1904, after promising his father that he would work summers as a field hand in the northwest and at Yale to earn money, he enrolled at Yale University (after completing only one year at Pacific University) with the purpose of becoming a physical education director. His planned course of study was not sports or gymnastics but medicine. He knew the importance of physical stamina and prowess in athletic competition. His choice was influenced by his summer athletic activities at the Chautauqua, New York, School of Physical Education. Here he met Dr. Seaver, Director of the Yale Gymnasium and head of the Chautauqua School and Dr. W.G. Anderson who was a member of the Yale faculty. Both doctors recommended that A.C. go to Yale and that he study medicine to prepare for a career as physical education director.[4] At Yale he became an expert pole vaulter and even designed a better pole, a spikeless bamboo pole, which relied on a box is the ground, rather than a spike, to hold the pole steady. With the spikeless pole he literally soared to new heights and in 1908 was a participant in the Olympic Games in London. Here, according to a New Yorker article from December 1952, he and another American broke the world's record for pole vaulting.[5] In other accounts of this event Gilbert is usually described as having been the sole record breaker. Apparently Gilbert's Olympic experience was grueling. To begin with the Olympic judges required Gilbert to use the older, spiked pole with which he was no longer familiar, and then another American was deemed to have done as well as he, although both were credited with breaking the existing world's record. Gilbert felt that he was returning home in defeat and this event soured him to the Olympics and athletics.[6]

---

[1] A.C. was the middle child. He had an older brother Harold who Gilbert describes as pious, serious and hard-working. His younger brother Frank Wellington, eight years his junior, eventually went to work for the New Haven company. A.C. describes himself as a leader in devising pranks and general tomfoolery. A.C. Gilbert, with Marshall McClintock, **The Man Who Lives in Paradise**, 1954, Rinehart & Co., New York, page 50.

[2] **Ibid.**, page 29.

[3] "He Supplies Santa Claus," by Dillon Roberts, Saga, 1950, page 56.

In 1909 Gilbert graduated from Yale University with an M.D. in Medicine. He never practiced medicine, even though several Yale physicians urged him to become a surgeon because his hands were so nimble, nor did he work as a physical education director. Rather his extracurricular activities to earn money became the avenue for his professional interests. One of his moneymaking activities at Yale was to give magic demonstrations at parties and clubs in New Haven, Boston and New York. As a result of these performances many persons asked him to teach them sleight of hand manipulations. When he tried to teach others magic he found that most were not willing to devote enough time to learn the art. Eventually he put together a package of quite simple tricks for his friends and these he thought the more casual enthusiast could learn how to perform. His friends bought his kits and buoyed by these sales he decided to go into business for himself, he would package magic kits and sell them.[7] As this tale unfolds we will see a recurring pattern -- Gilbert instinctively recognizes the popular appeal of a concept or product (sleight of hand or scale model trains) and transforms a rather sophisticated item into a price competitive mass marketed product, such as magic kits or Flyer S Gauge.

The Mysto Manufacturing Company was created in 1909 with A.C. as president and John Petrie, a mechanic handyman, as partner. Together they devoted their energies to the boxed trick business or the selling of Mysto Magic Sets. A.C. believed the venture would be profitable because of the inherent interest of all boys in performing magic and because the kits allowed him to reach an untold number of children. It was not long before the limitations of this logic became apparent. Not all children or adults were mesmerized by magic; magic was more easily sold when aptly demonstrated and most store retailers were not able to perform the tricks in the kits; when magicians were hired to perform they usually let Gilbert down as they were undependable and frequently incoherent; besides, the toy business was a difficult nut to crack. Money was made only in the Christmas season, Christmas sales had to carry you for the rest of the year and getting a store or department store to carry a new line often required inordinate work, good luck and sometimes payoffs. But A.C. was industrious and persuasive and during his cross country selling tours he opened one account after another. Thus, by 1911 Mysto Magic had grossed $37,000, although it only had a net profit of $360.[8]

Erector Sets on the other had were tangible, self-selling toys. Erector Sets made their debut during the 1912 Christmas season. The inspiration for Erector is a frequently told story. One night while Gilbert was riding home from New York City on the New York, New Haven & Hartford Railroad he was looking out at the steel girders and towers which were being put up to support the new electric power lines (since the railroad was converting from steam to electricity). As he marveled at these large but basic structures he though how every boy would like to be an engineer and build such structures. It would be an

educational and entertaining experience; as a toy it would be a sturdy, tangible and enduring plaything.[9] It would also provide a needed complement to the Mysto magic line. Shortly thereafter Gilbert bought out his partner, moved to more substantial quarters in New Haven and hired Al Richmond for sales and Charles W. Hoyt for advertising. Gilbert's approach to advertising was that of a personal, man-to-man or man-to-boy appeal. It was direct and friendly.

By 1915 Erector and Mysto had grossed three-quarter of a million dollars and had earned a net profit of $100,000. This auspicious increase in sales reflected Gilbert's marketing ingenuity and the instantaneous appeal of Erector sets. In 1916 the firm's name was changed to the A.C. Gilbert Company and A.C. continued to add new lines to the business.[10] Chemistry sets were added and a new building was built that year; Gilbert had decided to become the largest toy manufacturer in the United States.[11]

Even though Erector sets sold well Gilbert still faced the problem of seasonal work flow. In 1915 to alleviate this problem he took on fan and appliance manufacturing. Retailing at $5.00 his Polar Cub fans were the "world's first low-priced fans."[12] One of the reasons they were less expensive was that Gilbert was the first to use enameled wire in a fan's armature winding and to substitute automatic machine wire winding for hand winding. He was particularly proud of this accomplishment because everyone said it couldn't be done. Eventually his appliance line included power tools, kitchen appliances, hair dryers and fountain mixers.

[4] **Op. cit.**, Gilbert, pages 61-62.

[5] "American Boy," **The New Yorker**, December 20, 1952, pages 36, 38 and 40.

[6] **Ibid.**, page 40.

[7] **Ibid.**, page 42.

[8] **Ibid.**, pages 42 and 45.

[9] **Ibid.**, page 45. Note that this is the story Molly Wood relates. There were other Erector type toys being manufactured before 1912 such as Richter Anchor Block and Meccano.

[10] At this time Louis Marx, who would become the largest toy manufacturer in the thirties, was a commissioned toy salesman. Lionel Cowen was seriously challenging Ives' dominance of the U.S. train market. American Flyer, under Coleman, Sr., was in the number three position. For the Marx story see **Greenberg's Guide to Marx Trains.**

[11] "Riding the Tinplate Rails The Boy Who Made $1,000,000," **Collecting Model Trains** by Louis Hertz, Simmons-Boardman Publishing Corporation, New York, 1956, page 116. In 1928 Gilbert bought out Meccano. In 1930 it closed their Elizabeth, New Jersey plant and moved Meccano production to New Haven.

[12] **Op. cit.**, Saga, page 83.

[13] **Op. cit.**, Gilbert, page 141.

1916 was a notable year for the company. It expanded, moved into the building on what is now Erector Square, spent $144,746 on advertising, earned over $1,000,000 and instituted the Gilbert Institute of Engineering. The Institute did not feature faculty or a campus, but it gave diplomas to boys for their ingenuity and inventiveness in making Erector models. Local "Institutes" supported by the Miller Hardware Company were started all over the country. Erector was the big profit maker for the year.[14]

Also in 1916 A.C.'s younger brother Wellington joined the firm.[15] The year before Herman L. Trisch had joined the firm as a salesman. By 1917 Molly Wool, an endearing and faithful employee, estimated that 1,000 people were employed at the A.C. Gilbert Company and that it was a happy "family" of workers.[16]

Gilbert early articulated the interests of the toy industry on which his livelihood depended. He and Harry Ives helped to found the Toy Manufacturers Association and in 1916 Gilbert became the new organization's first president (and Ives its vice president). Its goals were to assist and protect the American toy industry from an inundation of inexpensive European imports (particularly German toys). In 1921, for example, he and an ample supply of toys went to Washington, D.C., to convince the House Ways and Means Committee that American toy tariffs -- then at 35 percent -- should be raised to 60 percent so that American toys would not be undercut by the less expensive imports. To make his point Gilbert passed his playthings around for all to appreciate (and knowingly he forgot to collect them). Thus, although Gilbert returned to New Haven empty-handed, the Committee had been won over by his presentation and passed a tariff of 70 percent.[17]

American Flyer enthusiasts understandably have great admiration for A.C. He evokes the best of the free enterprise system and the quality and features of American Flyer trains dramatically improved under his leadership. However, to understand American Flyer production and the final chapter of the A.C. Gilbert story we must look to the other men who actually imagined, designed, manufactured and sold S Gauge equipment to toy train buyers across the country. Theirs is a story of toy tinkerers, model builders and innovative businessmen who collectively built the American Flyer "Empire."

The story itself is based on a series of interviews taped by Jim Walsh from 1978 through 1980 as well as supplemental research, newspaper and magazine articles. It is not exhaustive but it does explain the reasons why many production decisions were made, who made them and the idiosyncrasies and constancies of AF production from 1946-1966.

Marshall Frisbie

Marshall Frisbie was one of the first people interviewed by Jim Walsh. Frisbie had worked with A.C. before Chicago Flyer came to New Haven. In describing why he went to work for A.C., Frisbie explained that his father had been president of the New Haven bank and that A.C. had eventually become a member of its board of directors. But, he recalls, in 1938 when he was a teenager looking for a summer job, he hadn't tried the bank, he had gone to Gilbert's and worked in their model shop doing odd jobs. At that time Frisbie estimated that Gilbert was not the biggest New Haven business, but it was perhaps third or fourth in size; Winchester guns were number one. Marshall preferred working with the other "toy tinkerers" to pursuing a banking career, much to his father's chagrin. Nevertheless, he toed the traditional business line after high school until business prospects became bleak in 1935 and A.C. offered him a job at $35.00 a week as a model maker in the model shop of the engineering department. Marshall accepted the offer having concluded that in spite of the depression people never seemed to stop buying toys. Marshall worked for A.C. through 1955 and summed up his years with Gilbert by saying, "I never enjoyed myself as much in my life as I did working for the A.C. Gilbert Company."[18]

Frisbie tried out or tested electric engine models produced for toys and appliances for about a year and was then promoted to chief engineer. In this position he supervised six model makers and one draftsman. His men upgraded microscopes or chemistry sets, added a piece of chrome here or a gizmo there to make this year's model different from and better than last year's.

Frisbie well remembers the purchase of American Flyer.

Wellington and the role he played at the Gilbert Company. There is also scant personal information about Herman Trisch. Trisch also rose quickly in the company. He joined it in 1915 as a salesman and in 1924 became a sales manager in New Haven; in 1930 he became a director; in 1940 a vice president, in 1944 first vice president and in 1948 an executive vice president. He retired in 1961 after having been with the company for 42 years.

[16]Wool Tape (1980).

[17]Op. cit., Saga, page 83.

[14]Ibid., page 143.

[15]During the twenties he became factory manager, in 1928 a vice president, in 1929 a director and in 1944 he resigned to go into business for himself. There is a dearth of information about

He thought it not a surprising decision because A.C. had always been a toy train enthusiast, although never a practicing hobbyist. A.C.'s files in fact contained Lionel, Ives, and Dorfan catalogues with detailed notes on each manufacturer. Before the purchase there was considerable debate among the senior staff at their weekly management meetings. It was projected that thirty percent of Gilbert's business would be in American Flyer trains. This seemed a reasonable figure because Flyer was an established volume operation which would complement the existing Gilbert toy line. The icing on the cake was the fact that there was no immediate cash payment required for the sale. Rather a percentage or royalty, perhaps Mr. Romer estimates, from one-and-a-half to three percent of the sales for a ten year period, was to be eventually paid to Coleman. The unstated problem with the venture was any competitor's ability to outdo Lionel. Lionel was a hard act to follow and, as we shall see, Gilbert chose to lay his own (S Gauge) rail rather than follow in Lionel's track.

Maury Romer

Maury Romer who had worked for Chicago Flyer before joining the Gilbert staff recalls the immediate events around the Chicago Flyer sale this way. At the 1937 Toy Manufacturing Association meeting A.C. surprised W.O. Coleman Jr., (son of the founder of Flyer trains), then president of Flyer, by saying that he (A.C.) was going to be a competitor of Coleman's, that he was going to bring out a line of trains. Coleman's rejoinder was, "Why start a new line, why not take over American Flyer?" In Romer's estimation Coleman's proposal was well-timed. Romer had felt for some time that Coleman was involved in too wide a range of projects and that he was too busy to really control Flyer management or its train production. Romer blamed management with doing a lackadaisical job because they did not maintain quality controls, consequently Flyer was losing its market position and subsequent sales and money. [19]

Another article notes that when Flyer trains were purchased by Gilbert, Coleman was in ill health and that Flyer sales had sagged considerably, a situation which was soon turned around by A.C. Gilbert. It was turned around because A.C. was inventive, demanded that standards be adhered to and brought in equipment which was second only to Lionel's. [20] Although not mentioned in the article the quickening pace of the economy also helped because in 1938 and 1939 the Gilbert people were just beginning to learn how to manufacture and market toy trains efficiently.

According to A.C.'s account of the transaction, it was on a visit to Gilbert's in Connecticut when both men were out doing some shooting that Coleman (there's no mention of a "Jr." or a "Sr.," but simply the former president of the Toy Manufacturers Association) proposed that A.C. take over American Flyer trains. A.C. was intrigued with the proposition, but figured that he could never swing the deal financially, until Coleman proposed a royalty basis for the sale. That so altered Gilbert's assessment of his financial

requirements that he began to immediately pursue closure of the deal. [21]

For better or for worse A.C. was into trains. The 1938 through 1940 Gilbert catalogues dramatically reveal the extent of Flyer changes and establish the direction which American Flyer would take for the next thirty years. The 1938 catalogue is smaller, has a different format and broke with traditional Chicago Flyer design. Gilbert trains appear more realistic, less toy-like and show much greater surface detail. And, the first trains shown were H0 Tru Model Gilbert designed sets. Opening the catalogue one is greeted on the left by a standing figure of A.C. and his dog with a message for all boys and a close-up photo on the right of a #3000 boiler front with a large sized checklist of AF features. In 1939 the H0 line is relegated to the rear of the catalogue and it is interesting to note that the cheapest H0 set is almost three times as expensive as the cheapest 0 Gauge set which probably explains why H0 was such a slow seller. Along with the continuation of traditional Flyer equipment, Gilbert brought dramatic innovation: 3/16 scale equipment appears in 1939, it is offered in the top-of-the-line sets such as the New York Central die-cast Hudson and the remarkable Union Pacific 4-8-4 Challenger 806. (It is actually a Northern, since a Challenger is a 4-6-6-4!) The Challenger, as its name implies, is the first eight-wheel 0 Gauge locomotive built in America and it challenged the toy-like steamers of earlier days. In addition Gilbert produced a line of die-cast 3/16 scale freight and passenger cars whose basic designs are carried (with adaptations) through the 1960s. In 1940, innovation continues with the Pennsylvania K-5 locomotive and tender and the Baltimore & Ohio Royal Blue. 3/16th scale cars in sheet metal are also introduced to complement the existing die-cast cars. The sheet metal cars are less expensive to manufacture and operate better than the die-cast ones because of their lighter weight. At the same time A.C. extended the highly detailed scale die-cast locos to the popularly priced sets. Thus, by the close of 1941 Gilbert had retooled and produced new dies to create a new American Flyer image. [22]

[18]Frisbie Tape. Frisbie's assessment seems astute in retrospect. Gilbert operated in the red in 1932 and 1933 only. By 1934 it showed a small profit; by 1936 it rang up $2,000,000 in total sales. In 1940 it went over the $3,000,000 mark and in 1941 the firm set a new record with an increase of total sales of nearly one million, volume was up to $4,335,000. **Op. cit.**, Gilbert, pages 263-264.

[19]Romer Tapes.

[20]**Op. cit.**, Saga, page 84.

[21]**Op. cit.**, Gilbert, pages 268-269.

[22]Lionel's scale model realism of 1938-42 focuses on several models: the 0-6-0 Pennsy switcher, the New York Central Hudson and two streamliners, the City of Portland and the Hiawatha. The rest of the Lionel line of this period loosely interpret real locomotives. Gilbert did Lionel one better beginning in 1938 -- year by year the existing locos were replaced until by 1941 all the locos from the least to the most expensive are scale models.

The question might well be asked, what then did A.C. buy from Coleman and the answer would seem to be first and foremost the Flyer name and access to its professional staff, buy only limited use of its machinery and dies. Coleman, Jr., died in 1939 so his influence was minimal. In terms of professional staff Guy Schumacher and Maury Romer were two key Chicago people who joined the New Haven staff. Guy Schumacher had been factory manager in Chicago. Maury Romer had been head of the service department there. Schumacher became superintendent of Gilbert's American Flyer Division, 1938-1944; in 1944 he became works manager for the entire factory; in 1945 an elected director of the company, and finally vice president in 1949. [23] Romer had been head of the Chicago service department and it was the need for an equivalent department that brought him east. When his temporary position became a permanent one he was given responsibility for the service department and assisted in production from 1938 to 1941; from 1945 to 1958 he was engineer in charge of the train line; from 1958 to 1963 he was sales engineer and from then to his retirement in 1967 he was sales promotional manager. The Chicago machinery was moved to New Haven and put into a new wing of the Gilbert plant. [24]

Coleman did prepare a list of recommendations for A.C. to help the latter merchandise trains. Copies of some early 1938 office memos from Romer's Archives, reprinted in "The Collector," provide a pragmatic glimpse of W.O. Coleman, Jr. "The Collector" is concerned with prewar American Flyer production and is edited by the well known Frank Hare. ("The Collector," Volume 2, Number 3.) [25]

Gilbert's objectives as Coleman interpreted them -- and he seems well tuned to his friend's preferences -- were to (1) first and above all establish a quality line that would (eventually) be second-to-none; (2) merchandise trains as a continuing hobby item which could be added onto year after year -- not as a one shot play experience; and (3) attract new train buyers by pricing the equipment to compete with other trains and other toys. He reminds Gilbert that H0 is still an unknown quantity, both in its sales potential and its adaptability to 0 Gauge accessories. As we have seen, Coleman's concern was not heeded in 1938, but in 1939 H0 is moved to the rear of the catalogue, most likely because its sales were unspectacular. Coleman also advised Gilbert to compete in the higher priced bracket and better grade stores. In other words, Flyer should leave the low priced end of the train market to Louis Marx and concentrate on the lucrative, quality concerned buyer. In another memo he shows his knowledge of "the enemy" -- under the heading "Lionel Competition," he writes... "They are fighters. Don't underestimate them." (He knew the lengths that Lionel would go to to deal with competition.)

Romer played a vital role in easing the Chicago to New Haven transition. He was the link between the two. Mr. Romer's history with Chicago Flyer went back to the twenties when he first worked in the display department. In those days he nailed small displays together, then he worked on department store display orders, later he was promoted

to designing displays and finally he was sent out to trouble shoot or solve display-layout problems (under Schumacher's direction). In 1927 he was put in charge of the service department, although he continued to be responsible for displays, such as the big one he designed for Wanamaker's.

In those days, he recalled, when you were given a job you worked on it until it was completed. If you had to work overtime, you worked overtime; there were no unions to limit hours or productivity. In the early thirties, he explained, display men and salesmen worked together hand-in-glove. Department store and retail store displays were the primary sales medium for toy trains and toys. There were no discount stores or self-service stores and no television. Toy salesmen depended on store displays to sell their products and display men relied on the salesmen to bring in their work. Romer remembered always trying to get as much space as possible for Flyer trains and to design displays that forcefully showed off the line, just as today Bachman and Tyco salesmen vie for prime space in the railroad department at Toys R' Us. Romer visited a great many stores and hobby departments in department stores in the midwest before Christmas to make sure that Flyer's holiday merchandise operated smoothly and was well presented.

After Gilbert bought Chicago Flyer Maury Romer was sent east, in 1938, to set up their service department; that is to train the men and women in how to repair and handle toy trains and equipment. In addition, when he arrived in New Haven he became involved in production decisions. He well recalls his first glimpse of A.C. It was awhile before he was formally introduced, although in retrospect he realized that he had seen A.C. around the factory before, but had never guessed that this was the boss because he looked so unprepossessing. He dressed very casually, as if he had spent the day fishing, but from their first meeting he considered A.C. a down-to-earth, unusually involved and caring employer. [26]

In production he was in charge of building cars and tracks. He liked 3/16th equipment and approved of its more accurate, realistic scale, particularly because it reflected his own toy train preferences. In the factory at this time one conveyor ran cars, two ran locomotives and each had a supervisor (as did tool set-up). There were foremen and assistant foremen and Romer's job was to give advice as it was needed.

War Years

As he recalls sometime in late 1941 or 1942 production came to a halt because of the war. A few train items continued to be produced in limited quantities by a small family

[23]**Ibid**, Gilbert, page 270.

[24]**Ibid**, page 269.

[25]Frank Hare, P.O. Box 216, Bethel Park, PA 15102.

[26]Romer Tape.

factory to which work was sublet. When possible bits and pieces of train parts were assembled in New Haven. Magic and chemistry set production did not suffer as acutely as did trains or Erector because the latter two depended on metal, copper wire and zinc.

Herbert Pierce, another senior staff member, estimated that during the war 95 percent of Gilbert's effort was devoted to war contracts and five percent to toys. From about 1942 to 1945 Romer was chief inspector for government contracts and supervised the manufacture of nylon parachutes, flares, electric motors for airplanes, flutters and the making of booby traps. At the same time, he, Frisbie, William Russell Smith (Smitty) and A.C. continued to meet to plan how to win the market once the war was over. They talked about scale detailing, about smoke, choo-choo and two rail track. It was an exciting dialogue. The war gave them the time to plan for the future and to determine how to introduce two rail track.

Even though these innovative ideas had to wait to be carried out, Gilbert knew the importance of keeping American Flyer trains before the public. He had the fore-thought to keep the Gilbert Hall of Science open so that Gilbert products --American Flyer trains, Erector, chemistry and magic sets -- were always on display before all who passed the corner of Fifth Avenue and 25th Street in New York City.

The Gilbert Hall of Science was in a smartly rennovated six story building. Its displays were intended to impress and entice the on-looker.[27] The building had been dedicated to the children and people of New York City by A.C. himself. It soon became a model promotional vehicle and was emulated in other cities. It offered a showroom with a magnificent train display, a sales office and company sales rooms. Soon less pretentious versions appeared in Chicago, Washington, D.C., and Miami, but none topped the lavishness of the New York Hall. One display on the first floor featured a GG-1 nose and behind its windshield an H0 layout with a miniature New Haven plant.[28] On the second floor was the biggest layout imaginable -- it was 80 feet with "miles of track, nine different lines connected by switches, mountains, waterfalls, a lake, towns, crossings, sidings and every accessory dreamed up to date by A.C. Gilbert and his engineers" -- and not open to the public except by special permission.[29] On the third floor were Erector toys, on the fourth appliances, on the fifth displays and on the sixth various offices.

When the war ended everyone was eager to get back to normal: to buy toys and trains. Erector, chemistry and microscope sets, all were ready to gear up, but the real excitement centered around the new train line. Flyer felt that it had never been in such a strong position; its prototype realism and scale equipment would outrun Lionel's still toy-like trains any day. Flyer's 3/16th scale and soon to be announced two rail track would make it second to none. Gilbert's re-entry into toy train production was, however, a full model year behind that of Lionel's. Unforeseen problems arose in converting to peace time production. Removing government machinery was the first problem, taking Flyer's machinery out of mothballs and overhauling it

★ RAILROAD LINGO ★

Battleship	Large Locomotive	Highball Artist	
Bend the Iron or Bend the Rail			Engineer noted for fast running
	Change the position of a switch	High Iron, Main Iron or Main Stem	
Big Hook	Wrecking Crane		Main line track
Black Snake	Train of coal cars	Highliner	
Brass Pounder, Lightning Slinger			Main line passenger express train
or Op.	Telegraph Operator	Hit the dirt	
Captain, Brains or Skipper	Conductor		To jump or fall off moving train
Cinder Cruncher, Dolly Flapper		Hog, Pig, Smoker	Locomotive
or Snake	Switchman	Hole	Siding into which train pulls
Club Winder, Ground Hog			to let another pass
or Shack	Brakeman	Hot Shot	Fast passenger or freight train
Clown Wagon, Crummy, Dog-House,		King	Freight conductor or yardmaster
Hack, Monkey House, Shanty		Liner	Passenger Train
	Caboose	Mtys	Empty cars
Cornfield Meet	Head-on collision	Paddle	Semaphore signal
between two trains on same main track		Peddler	Local Freight
Cut	Several cars coupled together	Pike	Railroad system
	or attached to engine	Plug	Locomotive throttle
Detainer	Train Dispatcher	Pound Her	Work locomotive to capacity
Diamond	Track crossover	Rattler	Freight Train
Dinger	Yardmaster	Red Ball	Fast Freight
Drag	A slow freight train	Shuffle the Deck	To switch cars on
Eagle Eye, Hogger, Hoghead, Pig			house tracks at every station
Mauler or Whistle Pig	Engineer	String	Several cars coupled together
Flimsy	Written train order	Tank	Locomotive tender
Garden	Freight yard	Varnish	Passenger cars or train
Gate	Switch	Washout	Quick stop signal
Glory	String of empty cars	Whale Belly	Steel coal car
Gon	Gondola car	Wheel	
Highball	Signal for clear track, mean-		To drive locomotive at high speed
	ing go ahead at high speed		

In his 1940 catalogue Gilbert provided his youthful engineers with railroad lingo to go with their realistic trains.

without access to frequently needed parts was the second problem and dealing with unexpected labor grievances was the third. Still, in 1946, Flyer broke new ground by earning over $6 million.[30]

Two Rail Track

Finally on January 1, 1945 Romer was taken off war contracts and promoted to engineer in charge of the train line with responsibility for developing the S Gauge line. Romer well knew Chicago Flyer's arguments for converting to two rail track. The reason for not converting had been one of timing; what did you do with existing three rail track and equipment while promoting two rail? And, could you keep or win over three rail operators to two rail? The war seemed to solve this problem by providing a hiatus between sale of the old and the new. After all, everyone wanted to return to peace time pursuits and if trains were your hobby, two rail track carrying S Gauge equipment would be the most realistic and best crafted equipment ever. That was something to come home to.

Romer and Phil Connell favored two rail track for its prototypical authenticity. It was felt, too, that the growing acceptance of H0 by model railroaders would help legitimize Flyer's new system. Two rail might disturb the toy train memories of some dads and grandfathers, but if grandma, auntie or mother did the shopping, it was assumed that they would not notice the difference. On the other hand, if mother brought home an S Gauge outfit and dad's track was 0 Gauge how could he run his trains unless he bought all new

[27]Op. cit., Hertz, page 117.

[28]Castiglione Tape.

[29]Op. cit., Gilbert, page 261.

[30]Ibid, page 328.

are not consistent), only some cars are listed with five digit codes. All the sets from page 1 through 19 have cars without any numbers. This omission is a substantial departure from a long-standing Gilbert custom to give all components an item number as well as a description. Then on page 20, the mystery numbers begin. If an item ran more than one year, that is if the item appeared in 1958 or later, it turns up with a five digit code shown originally in 1957! If the item ran only in 1957, it is very difficult to find with its 1957 catalogue number on its side. It is also remarkable that not a single illustration in the 1957 catalogue shows a five digit number, rather all show three digit numbers. There are however frequent reports of 1957 boxes marked with five digit numbers containing items marked with three digit numbers. This finding provides a clue to unravel one mystery, the missing 1957 numbers.

The hypothesis is: the introduction of the inventory record system came too late to change the numbers on the car sides. Obviously, it is easier to change the numbers in the catalogue and on the box ends than to change the numbers on the production run itself. The partially changed catalogue suggests that either the whole catalogue was changed and then rechanged which seems unlikely, or the staff "correcting" the catalogue copy for some reason started at the back and worked forward or started at the midpoint and worked back! Supporting our explanation is the fact that three prominent steam engines catalogued in 1957 have not been found with the new numbers. However, they have been found with their 1956 three digit numbers with 1957 sets. The question that the hypothesis does not answer is whether the boxes that came with these locos were stamped with the 1957 five digit numbers. Hopefully our readers can assist in answering this question.

The 1957 Mystery Roll

21016 4-6-2 Pacific steamer (with bell above boiler front), alias 283.

21059 4-6-4 Hudson steamer, alias 326.

21069 4-8-4 Northern steamer, alias 336.

1957 produces other surprises for Gilbert enthusiasts. Not only did the Gilbert catalogues list items carrying numbers that were not produced, but Gilbert also gave the same item two **different** catalogue numbers. The dual numbering system was part of a sophisticated cost accounting system which considered the item's packaging and merchandising costs. Hence an item that is packaged as part of a set has a different cost basis than an item sold as a separate item. Among others, the dual numbering system is used for the aluminum finished plastic streamlined passenger cars with red stripes. These cars come with the SUPER CHIEF set and are numbered and lettered "24773 COLUMBUS 24773" "24793 JEFFERSON 24793" "24813 HAMILTON 24813" and "24833 WASHINGTON 24833." These cars appear with these numbers. The same four cars are also available for sale separately in the catalogue and are then listed as "24776" (Columbus), "24796" (Jefferson), "24816" (Hamilton) and "24836" (Washington). Cars with red stripes have not been found with these numbers on their

sides, although they are seen with orange side stripes. There may be boxes marked 24776, 24796, 24816 and 24836 with red striped cars marked with the usual 1957 numbers: 24773, 24793, 24813 and 24833. Hopefully our readers may shed light on this puzzle.

Usually when Gilbert changed an item's number, the item changed in some way. Of course the fun is in finding the change since Gilbert is not always explicit in the catalogue! When the streamlined aluminum finished plastic passenger cars went from the three digit 960s to five digits in 1957 Gilbert makes several changes in the cars themselves. First, consistent with the overall cost control objective, they simplify the cars. The 960s have a metal plate showing the number, name and number in that order (i.e. 962 HAMILTON 962) riveted to the car side. The rivets are inserted into holes on the car side. With the five digit system the number and name are directly imprinted on the car. However, car dies were not immediately changed and some five digit cars are found with rivet holes and the information printed on the side.

The second change is the substitution of six pins or rivets to fasten the base to the shell of the 960s instead of its six screws on the five digit cars. Neither of these changes made the cars less attractive and both contributed to Gilbert's profitability in a very competitive market.

A QUALITY LINE

Gilbert enthusiasts often complain about the decline of Flyer quality starting in the mid-fifties and progressively accelerating to 1966. This book, in fact, explicates how Gilbert engineers learned how to make things more economically, whether it be Atlantic engines, box cars or trucks. "Economical activities" can be seen as efficacious or as the cheapening of standards; as an intellectual challenge or as a casting aside of a craftsman's norms. The changes however evaluated should be understood in the context of the toy industry. Toy manufacturing has traditionally been one of the most competitive of American industries. For Gilbert, then, price competition was an on-going concern. Flyer was flanked on one side by Marx, the world's largest producer of cheap toys, and on the other by Lionel, an established and well-recognized quality line. Yet, at the same time Lionel produced cheap sets and Marx produced better grade ones. So although each had a clear market position, each continually tested the waters to see where they could nudge out the competition and gain a percentage or two of the market. Marx would bring out a top grade set in the low-to-medium price range and Lionel and Gilbert would stir the waters by bringing out cheap sets.

Price was also strongly influenced by the large national catalogue retailers such as Sears, Penney and Ward. The toy buyers from these catalogue houses could make or break a toy manufacturer. Without these volume orders, Gilbert, Lionel and Marx could not turn on their machines. When Gilbert or Lionel management complained about a $19.95 price point for the beginner set because of its implications for quality and reliability, Sears or Ward had a reasonable answer. They explained that they knew their markets, they knew who bought from their catalogues. They knew that they had many, many more buyers for a $19.95 train set than for one costing $39.95. "We have to cater to the mass public who are our customers," they argued. Implicit in this analysis, but usually unstated was the threat that if Lionel or Gilbert could not meet their price guidelines they could find someone who could. The threat of a potential competitor provided a compelling incentive to meet price ceilings. In our view, Sears and Montgomery Ward correctly assessed their markets. They also knew that if they did not carry inexpensive trains another retailer would. At the same time, Lionel and Gilbert were correct about the dismal long term implications of cheaper trains.

A related aspect of the decline of the toy train company is their focus on volume. The belief prevalent among American manufacturers in many fields in the 1950s and 1960s was that profitability was inexorably linked to ever increasing sales volume and that sales volume was linked to low prices. The lower the price, the more you sold; low prices meant a continual focus on cost reduction. The leadership of Lionel under Cohen and Gilbert under Isaacson shared these views. Nat Polk's reaction to all of this was a well-seasoned skepticism, after all he recently commented, "these people acted as if they believed that if they sold enough, even at a loss, they still made a profit." Nat confessed that he could never understand this reasoning.

The development of the Atlantic, the change in the way box car shells fastened to the frame and the development of the 800 series freight car line are indicative of unbridled market competition. Cost reduction measures formed part of Gilbert's answer to Lionel's Scout sets and to Marx's better electric sets. Later, we discuss changes in the Atlantic and in the methods of fastening shells to frames. According to Maury Romer, the 800 series was intended to be the cheap complement to the 600 and 900 series. The cars were to have an inexpensive metal truck without journal boxes and a single color unpainted plastic body. Although a coat of paint costs only pennies, a three cent increase in cost increases the ultimate retail cost by fifteen cents, and three cents when multiplied by hundreds of thousands of units suddenly becomes a significant figure.

Hence in the competition at the cheap end those pennies are crucial. The cars were to be unadorned, without brakewheels, journal boxes and the like. Box car doors would not open. However, as the concept was turned into a production run, Gilbert management had second thoughts. The line would create internal problems, adding a third line meant more costly warehousing and inventory. Second, marketing a more complicated rather than a less complicated line was hard and expensive work.

Many collectors and enthusiasts fail to realize the intensity of market economics -- price competition -- in forcing manufacturers to substitute one manufacturing process or material for another one. They forget that although toy trains bring eternal joy and are wreathed in a halo of family happiness, the business end of the hobby has a deadly edge. It's a do or die proposition, and you either do or die in the sixty days from November 15 to January 15.

THE END

The demise of A.C. Gilbert was a bitter pill for S Gauge enthusiasts to swallow; it was as well an unexpected blow to the hobby industry and business forecasters. A current market analyst, Professor Robert F. Hartley of The Cleveland State University, found the Gilbert debacle an interesting case of how a marketing mistake, or series of mistakes, could cause a company's failure. His analysis, which is summarized below, is insightful. [40]

Gilbert was ill-prepared for the 1960s. The 1960s began (and ended) glowing with prosperity, and the toy market shared in the boom. But the market was changing. Television and one-shot fad toys like Batmobiles or hula hoops captivated the consumer. Animated toys shown on TV during Saturday morning kiddie programs became the main thrust of manufacturing promotions. New toys were demonstrated and their packaging shown in a hard sell, visually dynamic approach. The high cost of TV promotions required a higher sales volume and a higher breakeven point, yet the item could not be inordinately expensive since the consumer was to go to the cheapest outlet (usually a Toys R' Us or Kiddie City or the like) to buy the toy. The purchase was made without the assistance of sales clerks (since these stores had limited help) and was based only on package recognition (derived from its TV promotion). A toy had a 90 day season only. At the end of a 90 day cycle remaining inventory would be moved out at cost or sometimes for less, so that the merchant would be able to buy the next 90 day wonder.

Contrast the toy marketplace of the sixties with that of the late forties and early fifties. In the forties toys were sold primarily by family-owned small scale toy stores and by large toy departments in department stores. The same basic toys were carried year after year with only annual cosmetic changes: building blocks, American bricks, Lincoln logs, Tinker toys, Erector sets, chemistry sets and board games; large steel trucks and smaller die-cast cars; or brightly colored tin windup toys. The challenge had been to get space from the retailer and once secured to assist him in promoting the goods. Trains were ideally suited to this mode since Lionel and Gilbert had large, well-staffed display departments. Display departments built elaborate Christmas train layouts in coordination with the stores. One expected to see a new Christmas layout and to add some new accessories or rolling stock each year to the home layout. The catalogue functioned as an adjunct to the store promotion, it indicated the range of goods available and thus encouraged the retailer to carry the entire line since the catalogue would generate demand for all items. Continuity of both the type of promotion and the merchandise created a different selling

[40] Robert F. Hartley, **Marketing Mistakes**, Copyright Grid, Inc., Ohio, 1976, pages 111 - 119.

environment. If the inventory was not depleted by the end of the sales season it was regrettable but not a calamity because it could be sold next year or run as a store special.

Department stores and family-owned toy stores of the fifties employed more sales staff then do current retailers. It is hard for those of us under 40 to remember how well staffed stores were. We have become accustomed to finding goods without help, and certainly without informed help, at a K-Mart or Korvettes. Today even the department store and traditional merchants have reduced their staffing. Part of this change is economical. As retailer margins decrease managers believe that modestly reduced staff will reduce costs but not materially reduce sales. To some extent this is true. But beyond a certain point the consumer's unanswered question is an impediment to making a purchase. The train market in particular was affected by declining staffing. Trains are complex. Although many of this book's readers think that installing a track terminal or track clip and running wires from the transformer to the track terminal are so elementary as to require no explanations, our retail experience says just the opposite. Newcomers to trains need step-by-step guidance and reassurance so that they will look forward to the challenge of full scale operations. It is the human touch, the interaction between the knowledgeable clerk and the uncertain and slightly anxious buyer that dramatically affect the first and all future purchases. High volume supermarket style stores and discount stores cannot give the personal touch necessary.

To put the problem boldly, in 1961 Gilbert's sales had dropped to $11,600,000 from $12,600,00 in 1960. (In the 1950s sales had exceeded 17 million dollars.) [41] In 1961 its profits only amounted to $20,011. Also in this year A.C., Sr., died and Al, Jr., became chairman of the board. In early 1962 the company became attractive to Jack Wrather, president of a west coast holding company that owned the "Lassie" and "Lone Ranger" television programs, the Disneyland Hotel and the Muzak Corporation. Wrather acquired a 52% interest in Gilbert for the sum of $4,000,000 and then replaced their senior staff with his own men, at the same time Al, Jr.'s power was substantially curbed.

The poor showing of A.F. in 1961 was attributed to too few new products and to too little advertising. The sales staff, therefore, was increased by fifty percent so that the men could make more frequent and more persuasive contacts with retailers. A new general sales manager and a director of international sales were appointed.

But in 1962 sales dropped to $10,900,000 with a loss of $281,000. The loss was attributed to preparing an expanded line for 1963 and to the scrapping of obsolete equipment. In 1963 there were over **307** items for sale including fifty new ones. One million dollars was spent on repackaging the entire line. But sales slid again to $10,700,000 and this time there was a loss of $5,700,000 (mostly from supermarket returns for toys shipped on a guaranteed sales basis). After Christmas Gilbert had an inventory of almost 3,500,000 unsold toys.

Reviewing his dilemma Jack Wrather fired most of the recently hired top management people and A.C. Gilbert, Jr., was made president. Anson Isaacson, former vice president of Ideal Toy Company, was brought in as chief operating officer and chairman of the executive committee. Isaacson began a stringent economy drive. He fired company salesmen and hired manufacturers' representatives in a drastic attempt to cut sales costs. Although the manufacturers' representatives were less expensive employees, Gilbert also had less control over them. [42] Then factory personnel cuts were made to cut administrative and operating expenses from $10,000,000 to $4,700,000 in 1964. Then, another blow, in June, Al, Jr., died. Wrather became chairman of the board and Isaacson became president.

Things seem to brighten, sales picked up to $11,400,000, but there was a loss of $1,900,000 because Isaacson fearing that he would get stuck with unsold inventory dumped the excess. If the tide was not turned creditors would no longer agree to wait out these rough times. In 1965 the product line was again revamped, television advertising was increased dramatically -- $2,000,000 was budgeted and a Saturday morning cartoon show was to give prime exposure.

1965 sales did total $14.9 million dollars which represented a thirty percent increase over 1964, but losses were up to $2,900,000, mostly from the heavy returns of an 007 racing auto set. Although Wrather managed to raise money to keep the company's head above water, these loans were dependent on the company's earning a profit in 1966. Otherwise it was all over. The Gilbert Company did not make a profit. Its losses totalled $12,872,000 and it did indeed go out of business in 1967. [43]

In retrospect Hartley enumerates the problem as follows:

First, slow recognition that there was a fiscal/marketing problem. Slow recognition of the changing marketplace in which slot-car auto racing sets were outselling toy trains and, consequently, little innovation in the Gilbert line. When Herbert Pierce was asked about the company's demise his reaction was that if he had been making the decisions he would have placed more emphasis on what people were asking for, i.e., stock car racers, and less emphasis on trains. He felt that even by the mid-fifties trains were becoming less important to the company.

Furthermore, he points out that A.C. was 71 in 1955 and not as able to vigorously lead in the competition with the new firms like Revel and Mattel. The latter two had sprung up like weeds but their multi-million dollar volume indicated that they were staunch contenders for prime toy business sales. On the other hand, Pierce never would have sold the

[41] **Ibid.**, page 111.

[42] A manufacturer's representative (rep) is an independent businessman who carries a number of different lines and works strictly on commission. He generally has a specific geographic territory and sells primarily to distributors and large merchants.

[43] **Op. cit.**, Hartley, page 112.

company to Wrather for whose management he had little respect. Somehow he would have hung on. He and the other former Gilbert executives (interviewed) shared this same feeling. They hated to see the firm fall apart. They all agreed, too, that although Al, Jr., was a most intelligent, likeable and concerned boss, he was not A.C., and he had no pretentions that he was. Al, Jr., did not have the drive, purpose or ambition that had made the difference for his dad. What Pierce could not understand was why none of the remaining family showed any interest in preserving the records or heritage that was A.C. Gilbert. [44]

Romer recalled at the end how busily everyone worked, everyone was producing things that could **not** sell, would never operate and for this they were paying time and a half. Who would believe that the company was on the verge of bankruptcy? It was a shame, here they were, working at breakneck speed to produce toys which Gilbert salesmen would never sell. [45]

Second, Hartley lists Gilbert's frantic efforts to recoup the now obvious losses. Too many new items were added at one time; most did not build on the company's strengths of quality and good design but were gimmicky and ineffectual, a disappointment to stalwart Flyer customers. In an effort, for example, to sell a girl's toy they came out with a doll series but it, too, was overpriced, poorly made and without several outfits (at a time when all dolls had to be merchandised with several outfits).

Third, timing -- a sure-to-be-a-success spy line did not arrive until after Christmas Day in 1965.

Fourth, marketing judgments which sought to save money created new problems; manufacturers' reps could not provide service for Flyer trains; guaranteeing sales should not have been a condition for selling goods in discount type stores; and alloting so much of Gilbert's hard earned money to television advertising just did not make sense. All of the Wrather era marketing decisions were rash, none built on the company's past practices or offered gradual changes. [46]

In Nat Polk's view, Flyer's All Aboard train sets should have been a winner, after all Nat considered them one of the greatest concepts ever devised in model railroading. They circumvented the limitations of past, packaged train sets. Previously, stores displayed trains on elaborately decorated layouts. The layout helped to sell the trains. When the customer returned home, however, and set up the train set on the floor, there was only one circle of track, a transformer and a train. Missing were all the extras, the buildings and scenery which increased the verisimilitude of the train set. The customer was understandably disappointed. In the All Aboard System, scenery, buildings, wiring and interesting track plans were included and were as well designed to plug together for quick assembly (and to unplug for convenient storage).

Spike Fitzpatrick, the Gilbert sales manager, sold the concept of the All Aboard System to Montgomery Ward. Ward gave it great play on several of its catalogue pages. Gilbert staff expected the All Aboard System to be a ninety day winner. When the sets did not achieve instantaneous acclaim, they gave up. After their admission of defeat Ward cooled to the idea too. In Polk's view they gave up too easily. The system had enormous potential but would take at least five seasons to be understood and accepted. Gilbert, of course, could not wait.

One reason why the All Aboard System would take five seasons to catch on was that "the age of marketing a face without a voice" had arrived. As Nat explains it, although the trains were handsomely packaged, there was no voice or person to show (and thereby sell) the product to a potential buyer. The discount store rack had no voice and department stores were devoting less of their space to trains.

It is a sad conclusion, a sad ending to the story of such hope and optimism. A.C. Gilbert was such an appealing and energetic man that it was hard to imagine the world without him. Perhaps, that was the flaw. Without him, there was no prime mover.

* * * *

How to conclude the story? There is much that has not been told and that will be told in the future. A.C. Gilbert was a fascinating person, a man with great vision, who created a two rail S Gauge railroad empire second-to-none.

In fact the Gilbert Company's products have such a devoted following that today Fundimensions is successfully making S Gauge again. This testament of great devotion and enthusiasm speaks well for the future and for our hope that as long as there are model trains there will be Gilbert S Gaugians!

[44]Pierce Tape.

[45]Romer Tape.

[46]**Op. cit.,** Hartley, pages 116 - 118.

The New York showroom, the Hall of Science, had distinctive port hole type windows. Note the large station and behind it the double shed. The layout is L shaped.

The New York Gilbert layout. The push buttons along the edge activates the cattle loader in the farm scene. The next push button activates the oil drum loader. There is also a lumber scene. Outside on 5th Avenue there is a winter scene! [The pole outside the front window reads 5th AVE.]

Chapter II
DIESEL AND ELECTRIC ENGINES AND
MOTORIZED UNITS

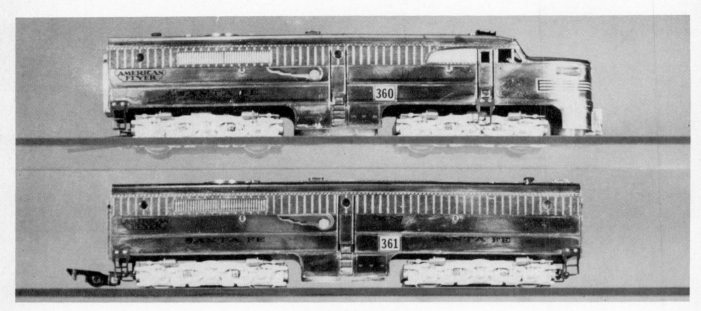

360, 361 Santa Fe Alcos
In Chrome Without the Red, Yellow and Black War Bonnet,
Newcomer Collection

Gilbert's diesel line consists of top-of-the-line Alco PA and PBs, the General Motors GP-7s, the Baldwin switchers and the F-9s. The PAs are undoubtedly Gilbert's most successful and longest running diesels, from 1950 through 1964. They were introduced to compete with Lionel's F-3s. Gilbert wisely chose a different diesel prototype. It has a particularly dramatic, sculptured facade; although the Santa Fe's red, silver and black war bonnet paint scheme gives such a vivid and pleasing appearance that it is retained. The design is seen so frequently by collectors, because it sold so well, that its dramatic qualities are unfortunately lost on many. Newcomers to the field, however, find it irresistible. Gilbert also uses the Alco PAs and matching PBs for other bright and attractive designs. The 405 Silver Streak is finished in chrome with a red or yellow stripe; the 466 and 467 Comets come in chrome or silver with blue-green areas trimmed in yellow; the Rockets (474,475 and 476) are found in forest green with gold and chrome or gold and silver. The Silver Flash units (477,478,479,480 and 481) feature a chocolate brown, orange and silver finish. The Northern Pacifics came in a very attractive dark/light green combination. The New Haven is found in a distinctive orange, black and white scheme, while the Missouri Pacific covers the rail in a silver and blue scheme. The Union Pacific appears in gray, yellow and red. The accompanying color

plates show the excitement and radiance of these paint schemes. Today, the Northern Pacific, Missouri Pacific and Union Pacific PA versions are the most sought after and command the highest prices. The Santa Fe was perennially popular and is offered every year from 1950 through 1962, except for 1959! Although the Santa Fe was issued primarily in the war bonnet color scheme, it was also produced in the blue, gold and black freight livery as 484, 485, 486 and 21910, 21910-1 and 21910-2. The deluxe PAs came with two motors in one unit, and in some sets as a magnificent A, B, A combination.

In 1955, Gilbert offers several matching B units for separate sale. These were made in very limited quantities because of a very modest response to them at the Toy Fair. The Comet and Rocket B units are exceedingly rare and have the highest values of any Gilbert equipment, other than box cars. The Silver Flash B unit, although rare, does not fall into the super rare category.

The other Gilbert diesel first issued in 1950 is the GP-7. It was first produced in the GMC demonstrator colors (as a 370), but with large AMERICAN FLYER lettering. It is later offered in the same livery as a 371 and 375. GP-7s also came with Union Pacific lettering (obviously a Gilbert favorite since it is used on the Alco PA and the 4-8-4 steam locos). Geeps also came with T & P markings with large

466

470

474

477

497

21561

499

25

"AMERICAN FLYER LINES" and a rare version with large lettered "TEXAS & PACIFIC." And for C & O fans, there is a five digit catalogued Geep, 21234, bearing only the number "234" on the side. The C & O made in 1961-62 was Gilbert's last GP-7.

The third Gilbert diesel, based on the Baldwin switcher, is introduced in 1956 as a 355 in Chicago Northwestern Lines livery. In 1958 it is offered as a 21801 and then as a pair consisting of 21801 and 21801-1. Gilbert also produces a hand reversing version, a 21808, and a Minneapolis and St. Louis 21918 version. A second double unit set is offered in Seaboard colors - 21918 and 21918-1. In 1959 Texas and Pacific markings appear on the (21)812 Baldwin, although only the "812" appears on its side. In 1960 the Baldwins are offered for the last time in the T & P 21(812) version.

The fourth and last Gilbert diesel is the F-9. It marks the end of scale realism as the F-9 is a much foreshortened and more interpretive piece. It is designed to run on the tighter curves of Pike Master track and is offered in Rio Grande, Boston & Maine, Santa Fe, Great Northern, Burlington and Union Pacific livery.

355 CHICAGO NORTHWESTERN LINES 1956, Baldwin switcher, headlight, knuckle coupler at each end, Pull-mor power. Yellow silk-screened "ROUTE OF THE '400'" on green shell with red, white and black "CHICAGO NORTHWESTERN SYSTEM" logo and white "355" on cab, black plastic decorative horn, with F-N-R-N reverse; also reported with F-R-F and DPDT switch; confirmation requested. All Baldwin diesels have black plastic side frame four-wheel trucks, are reported to run poorly and should be checked for screw hole damage where top meets frame.

		Good	Very Good	Excel
(A)	Unpainted green plastic	25	35	55
(B)	Green painted plastic	30	40	60

360/361 or 360/364 SANTA FE 1950-52, Alco PA and PB units connected by fiber drawbar. Different types of drawbars have been observed. PA unit has two double worm drive motors, lights, four-position reverse unit and black plastic roof mounted decorative horn which is often broken; however horn replacements are available. Number boards on PAs are solid and do not have numbers. PA unit does not have coupler on front. PB unit has link coupler on rear and fiber bar on other end. Both PA and PB units each have one black metal stud on roof in rear. Both units have black painted sheet metal two step units affixed to the ends of each side by rivets. (The step units are sometimes broken but replacements are available.) Two clear plastic portholes on each side of the PAs and three on the PBs. PA sides show wrap around yellow and black stripes from nose, "360" in black on yellow block, small red, yellow and black Indian chief decal, "SANTA FE" in black and "AMERICAN FLYER" in black lettering within black outline.

PBs' sides show "AMERICAN FLYER" in black in black outline at both ends, "SANTA FE" in black over each truck, small red, yellow and black Indian chief decal with or without lettering and black "364" on yellow black towards center. "361" PB unit has what Gilbert described as "Air Chime Electronic horn." "SANTA FE" lettering on sides come with large bold face, medium regular face and small regular face, all with serifs. In a

similar way "AMERICAN FLYER" in black border is found in light and bold faces with serifs. Since only the lighter faces have been observed to-date in the 470/471 units, we may assume that the lighter face 360/361 and 360/364 are later units.

(A) 360/361, 1950, silver finished shell with red, yellow and black Santa Fe war bonnet design, "Santa Fe" Indian Chief decal on PA and PB sides, silver finished simulated six-wheel trucks, PA and PB combined length of 23 7/8".

    45 70 85

(B) 360/361, 1951, Chrome finished shell with red, yellow and black Santa Fe war bonnet design. Chrome tends to chip off and flake with age.

    40 60 80

(C) 360/361, all chrome finished white plastic shell without red, yellow and black design. Only decoration is black/yellow stripes on nose, "360" yellow and black number on PA, "361" on PB unit; both with Indian Chief decal on side without "Santa Fe" or "Chief" lettering. "AMERICAN FLYER" in heavy, black serif lettering outlined in black; "SANTA FE" in heavy, black serif lettering; fiber linkage unit between PA and PB; PA unit with T-shaped hole in base behind reverse unit lever; two rivets hold each sheet metal step unit; Caples Collection.

    75 110 150

(D) 360/364, 1951 silver finished shell with red, yellow and black Santa Fe war bonnet design, silver finished trucks. 364 PB unit contains air chime whistle; three rivet hole sheet metal steps held in place by two rivets; "SANTA FE" on Indian Chief decal on side, "AMERICAN FLYER" and "SANTA FE" on 360 side are very bold; Newcomer Collection.

    45 70 90

(E) 360/364, 1961. chrome finished shell with red, yellow and black Santa Fe war bonnet design, silver finished simulated six-wheel trucks, 364 unit and 364 PB contain, air chime whistles. 364 PB unit with air chime rare.

    No Reported Sales

(F) Same as (C) but one rivet steps and wire handrails.

    75 110 150

370 GM AMERICAN FLYER, 1950-53, GP-7 road switcher, coupler bar on both ends to accept link couplers, sheet metal frame, headlight, rear light, illuminated number boards, one double worm drive motor, four-position reverse unit, silver finished four-wheel die-cast trucks; silver shell with red and yellow GM logo decal, and blue decal band on side with "AMERICAN FLYER" in yellow letters, 10 1/2" long.

(A)	Without "Built by Gilbert," Newcomer Collection.	30	45	70
(B)	With "Built by Gilbert."	30	50	80

371 GM AMERICAN FLYER, 1954, GP-7 road switcher, knuckle couplers at both ends, Pull-mor power, four-position reverse unit, headlight, rear light, illuminated number boards, aluminum finish four-wheel die-cast trucks, silver shell with red and yellow GM logo decal; blue and yellow trim, sheet metal frame, Newcomer Collection.   **32 55 80**

372 UNION PACIFIC, 1955-57, GP-7 road switcher, knuckle couplers at both ends, headlight, rear light, illuminated number boards; die-cast four-wheel trucks, four-position reverse unit, Pull-mor power, yellow and gray shell with red trim and red lettered "UNION PACIFIC" and "SERVES ALL THE WEST", die-cast frame.

(A) Yellow and light gray shell with red lettered "BUILT BY GILBERT" on hood side in front of cab; light gray finished four-wheel trucks, gray frame, Newcomer Collection.

    50 70 95

(B) Yellow and dark gray shell, red lettered "MADE BY AMERICAN FLYER," dark gray finished four-wheel trucks.   **60 90 125**

GP-7s

370

371

372

374

375

[21]234

Plate by Jack Radcliff, from the Newcomer Collection.

21920

21920-1

24856

24863

24859

24866

Plate by Leonard Welter, from the Walsh Collection

The Union Pacific Set

21925

21925-1

24837

24839

24838

24840

The rare GM 375, Walsh Collection

374/375 T & P 1955, GP-7 road switcher, orange and black body with black stripes at ends, yellow and white T & P diamond decal beneath cab window, "AMERICAN FLYER LINES" in black letters on side of hood, black finished four-wheel die-cast trucks. Both units lighted front and rear, have lighted number boards and knuckle couplers. 374 is powered with Pull-mor power, four-position reverse unit and built-in diesel horn; 375 is dummy unit; combined length is 21". Combination available only in sets.

(A)	Sheet metal frame.	70	95	140
(B)	Die-cast frame.	70	95	140

375 GM AMERICAN FLYER 1953, GP-7 road switcher, silver finished shell with blue decal on side band, yellow lettered "AMERICAN FLYER," red and yellow GM decal beneath cab window; knuckle couplers on both ends; single motor, four-position reverse unit, air chime whistle, lights at both ends, illuminated number boards, four-wheel silver finished die-cast trucks, sheet metal frame, 10 1/2" long. Catalogued as separate item rather than as part of set. Very rare. Extreme care is recommended when purchasing this item. The date stamped inside the cab will determine its authenticity; Walsh Collection.
$\qquad$ **250 300 400**

377/378 T & P 1956-57, GP-7 road switcher, orange and black finished shell with red and yellow "T & P" diamond decal beneath cab window, and "AMERICAN FLYER LINES" in black letters on side. 377 motor with Pull-mor power and four-position reverse unit. 378 with built-in electronic horn and diesel roar. Lighted front and rear, illuminated number boards and black finished four-wheel die-cast trucks, available only in sets. **80 100 150**

379 T & P, 1956, GP-7 road switcher, orange and black finished shell with red and yellow "T & P" diamond decal beneath cab window and "TEXAS AND PACIFIC" in black letters on side with small "AMERICAN FLYER LINES" beneath it. Pull-mor traction tires, four position reverse unit, lighted front and rear, illuminated number boards and black finished four-wheel die-cast trucks, Carnes Collection. **No Reported Sales**

405 Silver Streak 1952, Alco PA, chrome finished with red or yellow stripe, no front coupler, link coupler on rear, two step sheet metal unit with three rivets attached to each side of shell, two portholes with clear plastic windows; black plastic decorative horns, simulated six-wheel gray finished die-cast truck; number does not appear on engine, air chime whistle, four-position reverse unit.

(A)	White lettered "AMERICAN FLYER" and "Silver Streak" in red stripe, Newcomer Collection.	30	50	75
(B)	Yellow stripe, very rare.			**No Reported Sales**
(C)	Same as (A) but dull chrome finish, very rare.			**No Reported Sales**

466 COMET 1953-55, Alco PA, chrome or silver painted shell with blue-green areas trimmed by yellow lines; yellow decal lettered "AMERICAN FLYER LINES 466" without serifs and "COMET." "COMET" lettering over star on nose decal. Knuckle couplers on both ends, two sets of sheet metal steps attached to each side with two rivets, two clear plastic portholes on each side, silver finished simulated six-wheel die-cast trucks, black decorative horns on roof, black stud on rear roof, headlight, four-position reverse unit.

(A)	Chrome painted shell, 1953, Newcomer Collection.	25	45	55
(B)	Silver painted shell, 1954-55.	30	45	60

467 COMET 1955, Alco PB, silver painted shell with blue-green areas trimmed by yellow lines, yellow decal letter "COMET" and "AMERICAN FLYER LINES 467," knuckle couplers at both ends, with controller, simulated six-wheel trucks. One of the first units with diesel roar and horn; catalogued as separate unit, matches 466; very rare. **No Reported Sales**

470/471/473 SANTA FE 1953, PA, PB and PA units together; chrome or silver shell with red, yellow and black war bonnet Santa Fe design. All three units with knuckle couplers front and rear and silver finished simulated six-wheel die-cast trucks. The 360 body shell mold was substantially modified to accept the new front couplers. Three tubes added for mounting screws on the 470s (compared with the 360s). 470s come with either one or two rivet step units. All observed 360s have two rivets holding steps in place. The 470s with single rivet type steps have a modified step on the plastic shell so that the metal step will not swivel. Note that the number boards on the Alco PA units are solid in contrast to the GP-7s on which numbers show. 470 contains two double worm drive motors, and four-position reverse unit (A and B variations); 471 contains air chime whistle and 473 is a dummy unit. Both 470 and 473 are lighted and both have black plastic decorative horns on the cab roof.

(A) Chrome finished shell with "CHIEF" nose decal and "CHIEF" lettered Indian head decal on side. "AMERICAN FLYER LINES" in black lettering on lower rear of PAs, 1953. **55 75 140**

(B) Silver finished shell with "CHIEF" nose decal and "CHIEF" lettered Indian head decal on side. "AMERICAN FLYER LINES" in black lettering on lower rear of PAs.
$\qquad$ **60 90 150**

(C) Silver finished PA shells with "SANTA FE" nose decal on PAs and "BUILT BY GILBERT" in black letters on rear side, "Santa Fe" cross logo decal under cab window and small "CHIEF" Indian head decal on center of side. Single rivet holds black sheet metal steps, clear plastic porthole windows, two-position reverse unit, Newcomer Collection.
$\qquad$ **60 90 150**

The Rare 480 Silver Flash, from the DeMarco Collection

472   **SANTA FE**, 1956, Alco PA only, silver, red, yellow and black war bonnet Santa Fe design. "SANTA FE" nose decal, black "BUILT BY GILBERT" on rear side, "Santa Fe" cross decal under cab window. Single motor with Pull-mor traction tires, one year only with the El Capitan Set, No. 5640TBH.

30   45   60

474/475   ROCKET 1953-55, Alco PA. PA is forest green, gold and chrome or silver design. 474 contains headlight and two double worm drive motors, four-position reverse unit with knuckle couplers at both ends; 475 contains either diesel horn or air chime whistle and headlight. Both units with decorative black plastic horns, portholes with clear plastic windows, metal stud in rear roof, two rivets hold sheet metal steps on loco shell, green and yellow "ROCKET" decal on nose, white lettered "AMERICAN FLYER LINES" on rear side, silver finished simulated six-wheel die-cast trucks.

(A)   Chrome finish, more desirable than (B), 1953, Newcomer Collection.   55   80   105
(B)   Silver finish, 1954, air chime whistle.   50   70   90
(C)   Silver finish, 1955, diesel horn.

476   ROCKET 1955, Alco PB, matches 474(B), forest green, gold and silver finish, knuckle couplers at both ends, two rivets hold sheet metal steps, yellow lettered "ROCKET" decal, and white lettered "AMERICAN FLYER LINES 476" also on side, silver finished simulated six-wheel die-cast trucks, with diesel roar. Only available as a separate unit and then only for one year, it was one of the first to feature the new diesel roar, 12 1/4" long; very rare.   **No Reported Sales**

477/478   SILVER FLASH, 1953-54, Alco PA and PB, chocolate brown, orange and chrome or silver finish. 477 PA unit has two double worm drive motors, four-position reverse unit and headlight, black plastic decorative horns and two clear plastic portholes. 478 PB unit has air chime whistle. Both units with knuckle couplers at both ends, metal stud on roof, two rivets hold each sheet metal step unit, silver finished simulated six-wheel die-cast trucks, "SILVER FLASH" in orange, "vibrating" letters, and "AMERICAN FLYER" in orange letters. Maine Central green tree motif on nose of PA. Units together are 24 1/2" long.

(A)   Chrome finish, 1953.   80   120   180
(B)   Silver finish, 1954, Newcomer Collection.   80   120   180

479   SILVER FLASH 1955, Alco PA, chocolate brown, orange and silver finish; "SILVER FLASH" in vibrating letters, "AMERICAN FLYER" in gold letters, Main Central green tree on nose, lighted, metal stud on rear roof, single rivet fastens sheet metal steps, silver finished trucks, clear plastic portholes, black plastic decorative horns, single motor, four-position reverse unit, diesel horn, Pull-mor power, knuckle couplers at both ends.   40   60   85

480   SILVER FLASH 1955, Alco PB, matches 479, chocolate brown, orange and silver finish, "AMERICAN FLYER SILVER 480 FLASH AMERICAN FLYER" on side; diesel roar and diesel horn, 14 1/2" long. Offered as a separate unit only and then only for one year. One of the first units with diesel roar and diesel horn.   175   250   350

481   SILVER FLASH 1956, Alco PA, chocolate brown, orange and silver finish, "481 SILVER FLASH AMERICAN FLYER" on side, Maine Central green tree on nose, lighted, diesel roar, electronic horn, single motor, Pull-mor power, clear plastic portholes, black plastic decorative horns, knuckle couplers at both ends, one rivet holds each black sheet metal step unit, metal stud on roof, silver finished simulated six-wheel die-cast trucks, 12 1/4" long. The only Alco PA unit with a single Pull-mor motor, electronic horn, four-position reverse unit, headlight and diesel roar.   40   60   90

484/485/486   SANTA FE 1955-57, Alco PA, PB and PA, blue and yellow with black roof; PA with "SANTA FE" yellow and black nose decal and yellow and black wrap around stripes. 484 PA unit has two worm drive motors with four-position reverse unit. All units have knuckle couplers at both ends, silver finished simulated six-wheel die-cast trucks, one or two rivets hold each sheet metal step unit, clear plastic portholes. All three units with yellow "BUILT BY GILBERT" in sans serif and "SANTA FE" in Railroad Roman with serifs; 485 PB units contain diesel roar and electronic horn, 486 PA dummy unit has light.

(A)   One rivet holds each sheet metal step unit, Caples Collection.   130   180   230
(B)   Two rivets hold each sheet metal step unit, Newcomer Collection.   130   180   230

EMD F-9 Diesels

21210

21205 21205-1

21207 21207-1

21206 21206-1

L2004

Plate by Jack Radcliff, from the Newcomer Collection

32

Preproduction, Sample of 499 New Haven. Note the rivet holes beneath the doors, Walsh Collection.

490/491/493 NORTHERN PACIFIC 1956, Alco PA, PB and PA, dark green roof and upper side; light green lower side, white line separates light green and dark green; also white line along top of side. 490 PA unit has headlight, two double worm drive motors with Pull-mor power and four-position reverse unit; 491 PB unit has diesel roar and electronic horn; 493 PA is dummy unit with light. Both PA units have black decorative plastic horns on cab roofs and "NORTHERN PACIFIC" and red and black yin /yang decal on nose; "Main Street of the Northwest" in white lettered script on sides and red and black yin /yang decal on cab beneath and slightly in front of windows on side. All three units have "BUILT BY GILBERT" in white sans serif letter on sides. 491 PB unit has "NORTHERN PACIFIC" in white serif letters, flanked on each side by red and black yin /yang decals. All three units have silver finished die-cast trucks, knuckle couplers at each end; single rivets hold sheet metal step units, a metal stud on roof, and portholes with clear plastic windows. Total length of three units is 36 3/4". These three units along with the five matching passenger cars is one of the most desirable and longest of the S gauge passenger sets. **200 300 450**

497 NEW HAVEN, 1957, Alco PA, black body with orange band from cab window to rear, white and orange areas on side of hood, white "NEW HAVEN" with serifs and "BUILT BY GILBERT" without serifs. (The 21561, the uncatalogued 1958 version, has lettering that is similar but more vertical.) Single double worm drive motor and headlight, knuckle couplers front and rear, silver finished simulated six-wheel trucks, two portholes with clear plastic window, white large "N" and orange large "H," one rivet holds on each set of metal steps, stud on rear roof, black plastic decorative horn on roof, 12.25" long, Newcomer Collection. **45 65 90**

499 NEW HAVEN, 1956, GE Electric, two operating pantographs, black body with orange and white bands on side and orange and white areas on black nose, rectifier box on roof, light gray finished simulated six-wheel die-cast trucks, white lettered "BUILT BY GILBERT" in short sans serif letters, white "499," large white "N" and large orange "H" in block serifs, "NEW HAVEN" in white serif lettering, four-step (F-N-R-N) reverse unit, single motor with Pull-mor power (traction tires) and electronic whistle, 12 1/2" long.
(A) Light gray finished trucks, Newcomer Collection.
  100 125 160
(B) Black finished trucks, prototype, Olson Collection.
  No Reported Sales

(C) Silver finished trucks, rivet hole for steps on one side only, no steps, preproduction sample, Walsh Collection.
  No Reported Sales

812 See (21)812.

L2004 Rio Grande, 1962, EMD F-9, red plastic shell, white roof with white decorative horns and white outlined louvers, two white outlined solid portholes; white line on side along base broken by two doors, each door has pierced window; two windows on cab side in front of cab door, white script "Rio Grande" on side, white "L2004" on side beneath cab, "AMERICAN FLYER LINES" in small sans serif letters along side in rear; single worm drive motor with reverse unit, black plastic side frame on four-wheel trucks, two traction tires, no front coupler, knuckle coupler on rear, 12 1/4" long, Newcomer Collection. **30 50 80**

L2004-1 Rio Grande, 1962, EMD F-9, dummy, matches L2004 above but without motor and with two couplers, very rare.
  No Reported Sales

21205/ 21205-1 BOSTON and MAINE, 1961, EMD F-9, both units have blue plastic shells and blue decorative horns on cab roof, white outlined louvers on sides, two white outlined solid portholes on sides, large white outlined "B" and large solid white "M" on cab side, large white "BOSTON and MAINE" on sides, small white sans serif lettered "AMERICAN FLYER LINES" on sides in rear, black plastic side frame four-wheel trucks, two doors on each side with pierced windows, two windows on cab sides in front of cab door. 21205 with single worm drive motor with Pull-mor power (two traction tires), three-position (F-R-F) reverse unit, no front coupler, knuckle coupler on rear. 21205-1 is dummy with front and rear knuckle couplers. No operating headlights on either unit, both units total 24 1/2", Newcomer Collection. **40 60 80**

21206/ 21206-1 SANTA FE, 1962, uncatalogued, EMD F-9, both units have red plastic shells and red decorative horns on cab roof, white outlined louvers on sides, two white outlined solid portholes on sides, white Santa Fe cross inside circle logo on cab side beneath window, "21206" or "21206-1" in white beneath logo, large white "SANTA FE" with serifs on sides, small white sans serif "AMERICAN FLYER LINES" on sides in rear, black plastic side frame, four-wheel trucks, two doors on each side with pierced windows, two windows on cab sides in front of cab door; both units total 24 1/2". 21206 with single worm drive motor, Pull-mor power (two traction tires), reverse unit attached to top of rear truck, stud through roof, no front coupler, knuckle coupler on rear. 21206-1 is dummy unit with knuckle couplers front and rear. These units came with a special yellow box car in a set made only for White's Discount Store, Newcomer Collection.　　　　　　　　　　　　**50　70　90**

21207/ GREAT NORTHERN, 1963-64, EMD F-9, both units have
21207-1 orange plastic shells and dark green roofs with dark green decorative horns, Great Northern logo beneath cab window in dark green, "21207" or "21207-1" beneath logo in green, green outlined louvers on sides, two green outlined solid portholes on each side, "GREAT NORTHERN" in large dark green modern sans serif face, heavy dark green line along base broken by two doors, each door has pierced windows, two pierced cab windows on cab side in front of cab door, small dark green sans serif "AMERICAN FLYER LINES" on side at rear. Both units total 24 1/2" and have Pull-mor power (two traction tires). 21207 has single worm drive motor, three-position (F-R-F) reverse unit located on top of rear truck, black plastic side frame, four-wheel trucks, no coupler on front, knuckle coupler on rear. 21207-1 is dummy unit with knuckle couplers front and rear, Newcomer Collection.　　　　　　　　　　　**50　70　90**

21210 BURLINGTON, 1961, EMD F-9, red plastic shell has large white stripe across side, large white "21210" beneath cab windows and white stripe, large white sans serif lettered "BURLINGTON" on side, small white sans serif "AMERICAN FLYER LINES" on rear at end; white outlined solid portholes, two doors with pierced windows, two pierced cab windows on side in front of cab door; operating headlight, single motor, Pull-mor power (two traction tires), three-position (F-R-F) reverse unit located on top of rear trucks, knuckle couplers front and rear.　**35　55　70**

21215/ UNION PACIFIC, 1961-62, EMD F-9, both units have yellow
21215-1 plastic shells with gray roofs, and trim; decorative horns, large red sans serif "UNION PACIFIC" on sides, red numbers beneath cab window; "21215" or "21215-1" in small red sans serif letters at rear of side "AMERICAN FLYER LINES," red line along base of side broken by two doors; door with pierced windows, two pierced windows on cab side in front of cab door; 21215 has motor with Pull-mor power (two traction tires), three-position (F-R-F) reverse unit on top of rear truck, knuckle couplers front and rear and operating headlight. 21215-1 is dummy with knuckle couplers front and rear.
(A) Yellow-orange shell.　　　　　　　**50　75　100**
(B) Yellow shell.　　　　　　　　　　**50　75　100**

[21]234 CHESAPEAKE & OHIO, 1961-62, GP-7, blue shell has large yellow "C & O" on side of short hood, large yellow "234" under cab window, yellow serif "CHESAPEAKE & OHIO" on side of long hood, large yellow "C & O" logo on side of long hood near end; lights and lighted number boards at both ends with "234" appearing in number boards; aluminum finished four-wheel truck side frames, yellow painted die-cast frame with yellow painted stamped steel handrails on sides and ends; bell operates continuously at slow speeds, knuckle couplers at both ends, single worm drive motor with Pull-mor power (traction tires), two-position reverse unit. Collectors should determine if the chassis is original; an original chassis tends to suffer from chipped paint.

(A) Long step units at each end, Newcomer Collection.
　　　　　　　　　　　　　　　　95　115　150
(B) Short step units at each end -- the steps were altered to fit the tighter curves of Pikemaster track.　**100　135　175**

21551 (NORTHERN PACIFIC), 1958, Alco PA, dark green roof, black plastic decorative horn, white stripe along roof line, dark green upper side section, white line through center of side, medium green lower side; ying/yang red and blue decal on side beneath cab windows, white script "Main Street of the Northwest," white block sans serif lettered "BUILT BY GILBERT" and "21551," solid portholes integral to shell, knuckle couplers front and rear, single double worm drive motor, operating headlight, stud on rear roof, simulated silver finished six-wheel trucks.
(A) Sheet metal steps fastened to body by single rivet; plastic shell modified so that step will not swivel.　**70　100　140**
(B) Steps integral to plastic body, Newcomer Collection.
　　　　　　　　　　　　　　　　60　90　110

21561 NEW HAVEN, uncatalogued, 1958, Alco PA, dull black body with orange band from cab window to rear and white and orange areas on side of hood, white lettered "NEW HAVEN" with serifs and "BUILT BY GILBERT" without serifs. One double worm drive motor and headlight, knuckle couplers front and rear, silver finished simulated six-wheel trucks, two simulated portholes integral to body, white large "N" and orange large "H," steps integral part of plastic shell, no stud on roof, black plastic decorative horn on roof, 12 1/4" long.
(A) One rivet metal steps, pierced portholes without plastic inserts, Walsh Collection.　　　　　**75　110　150**
(B) Plastic steps integral to body, porthole integral to body with body color.　　　　　　　　　**40　60　85**

21571 NEW HAVEN, 1957, GE Electric. Catalogued as "21571" but actually comes with "499" on side, probably in a box numbered "21571." Confirmation of the box number requested.
　　　　　　　　　　　　　　　No Reported Sales

21573 NEW HAVEN, 1958-59, GE Electric, two operating pantographs, black body with orange and white bands on side and orange and white areas on black nose, rectifier box on roof, light gray finished simulated six-wheel die-cast trucks, white lettered "BUILT BY GILBERT" in short sans serif letters, white "21573," large white "N" and large orange "H" in block serifs, "NEW HAVEN" in white serif lettering, two step reverse unit, single motor with Pull-mor traction tires.　　**100　125　160**

21720 SANTA FE, 1958, uncatalogued, Alco PB, black roof, yellow band through portholes and louvers, blue lower body section with yellow stripe along bottom edge; "BUILT BY GILBERT" in small yellow sans serif face at one end and large yellow "SANTA FE" with serifs along bottom edge. Contains diesel roar and horn. Knuckle couplers front and rear, metal stud on rear roof, with metal steps, clear plastic windows, "21720" on side along lower edge; simulated six-wheel die-cast trucks with aluminum finish. Very scarce.　　　　　　**200　300　400**

[21821] UNION PACIFIC, 1957, GP-7, gray roof and gray top side, red
372   stripe across side, bottom two-thirds of side in yellow, red stripe
along bottom, gray frame, gray stamped handrails along side and
at ends, knuckle couplers at both ends, gray finished four-wheel
trucks, operating headlights and number boards at both ends,
red lettered "BUILT BY GILBERT" in front of cab on side, red
sans serif "SERVES ALL THE WEST AND" beneath cab
window and red lettered sans serif "UNION PACIFIC" on side of
hood, single worm drive motor, 11 1/4" long. Possibly never
made, confirmation requested.   **No Reported Sales**

21831 TEXAS & PACIFIC, 1958, GP-7, black hood roof, black cab,
lower two-thirds of side in orange with black stripes at ends of
sides and black diagonal stripes on end, black frame and railings
on sides and at ends, red and yellow T&P decal beneath cab
windows, black side frames on die-cast four-wheel trucks,
headlights and lighted number boards at both ends, single worm
drive motor with Pull-mor power (traction tires), two-position
reverse unit.
(A) "AMERICAN FLYER LINES" in black sans serif letters
     on sides.   **55   70   95**
(B) "TEXAS & PACIFIC" in thin black sans serif letters on
     sides.   **90 130 175**
(C) "TEXAS & PACIFIC" in thick black sans serif letters on
     side, uncommon.   **100 150 200**

21902   SANTA FE, 1957-58, Alco PA, PB and PA units, silver finished
21902-1 PA units with red, yellow and black war bonnet design, 21902-1
21902-2 PB unit in silver finish with black lettered "AMERICAN FLYER
LINES" appearing two times on each side along lower edge,
small red, yellow and black Indian Chief decal on side; PA units
have small black and white "Santa FE" decal on cab beneath
windows. All units with simulated six-wheel die-cast trucks with
silver finished sides and black single rivet steps. Two clear
plastic portholes on PA units and three portholes on PB unit; all
units with knuckle couplers at both ends; 21902 PA with
operating headlight, two double worm drive motors with
Pull-mor power and four-position reverse unit; 21902-1 PB with
diesel roar and electronic horn; 21902-2 PA unit is dummy; all
three units total 36 3/4" long, considered very desirable.
                                       200 300 400

[21908] T & P, AMERICAN FLYER LINES, 1957, GP-7 units, black roof
377/378 and hood roof, black band along top of side and black cab with
orange sides with black stripes at both ends of sides and black
diagonal stripes on ends; 377 has operating headlight, lighted
number boards and single worm drive motor with Pull-mor
power and four-position reverse unit; 378 with diesel roar and
electronic horn; red and yellow "T & P" decal beneath cab
windows on both units (T & P stands for Texas and Pacific).
"AMERICAN FLYER LINES" in black sans serif lettering on
sides of both units; "377" and "378" found on number boards of
respective units; black finished four-wheel trucks; both units
total 21 3/4"; knuckle couplers on both ends of both units; rare.
(It is not clear how to distinguish a 377 from a 21908?
Information requested.)   **No Reported Sales**

21910   SANTA FE, 1957-58, Alco PA, PB and PA units, black roof,
21910-1 yellow band across top of side passing through cab front and side
21910-2 windows, blue sides with yellow stripe along bottom, black and
yellow "SANTA FE" logo on PA front ends, two clear plastic
portholes in PA units on each side, and three on each side of PB
unit. Yellow serif lettered "SANTA FE" on the lower side of
each unit; small yellow sans serif "BUILT BY GILBERT" on the
side at the end of each unit; two rivets hold sheet metal steps on
each unit; simulated six-wheel die-cast trucks with aluminum
finished sides; metal stud on the roof of each unit; 21910 PA unit

with two worm drive motors and operating headlight; 21910-1
PB unit with diesel roar and electronic horn; 21910-2 PA unit is a
dummy; all units with knuckle couplers front and rear; three
units total 36 3/4"; units numbered "21910," "21910-1" and
"21910-2" respectively on sides.   **150 225 350**

21918   SEABOARD, 1958, Baldwin switcher, both units with black hood
21918-1 and cab roofs, headlights slightly raised above hood line, three
small stacks on hood roof, predominantly black sides with three
red stripes on side front, and red area encompassing cab sides;
white "SEABOARD" on side, small white sans serif lettered
"BUILT BY GILBERT" in front of cab; Seaboard logo on
adhesive label and unit number "21918" or "21918-1" beneath cab
window; yellow and black stripes along frame edge, black air
tanks hang below frame; four-wheel trucks with black plastic
side frames, knuckle couplers at both ends, black decorative
horns on hood. Usually 21918 has single motor and operating
headlight and 21918-1 is dummy, however, in the units
photographed, the cabs are reversed, Newcomer Collection.
                                       125 200 285

21920   MISSOURI PACIFIC, 1958, 1963-64, Alco PA, PA, silver roof,
21920-1 silver and blue bands on sides with yellow stripes outlining the
silver areas, black decorative horns on cab roofs, metal stud on
rear roofs, white "MISSOURI PACIFIC" on lower sides, "21920"
or "21920-1" on side, very small sans serif "BUILT BY
GILBERT" beneath cab window, Missouri Pacific logo on nose,
knuckle couplers at both ends; 21920-1 with electronic horn.
(A) 1958, two portholes with clear plastic windows, metal steps
     with single rivet and modified plastic shell to prevent steps
     from swiveling; 21920 with two worm drive motors with
     Pull-mor power (traction tires) and operating headlight.
                                       150 200 300
(B) 1963-64, simulated portholes integral to body shell with
     body color, plastic steps integral to body shell; 21920 with
     one worm drive motor with Pull-mor power (traction tires)
     and operating headlight.   **60   90 150**

21922   MISSOURI PACIFIC, 1959, Alco PA, PA, silver roof, silver and
21922-1 blue bands on sides with yellow stripes separating the blue and
silver areas; black plastic decorative horns on cab roofs, metal
stud on rear roofs, white "MISSOURI PACIFIC" on lower sides,
"21922" or "21922-1" on side, very small sans serif "BUILT BY
GILBERT" beneath cab window, red and white "MISSOURI
PACIFIC LINES" decal logo with eagle on nose, knuckle
couplers at both ends, simulated portholes integral to body shell
with body color. Observed with plastic steps integral to body
shell, however, the 1959 catalogue shows unit with metal steps.
The catalogue version has not been confirmed. 21922 with two
worm drive motors, Pull-mor power (traction tires) and
operating headlight. 21922-1 with bell that automatically tolled
at low speed, Newcomer Collection.   **150 200 250**

21925   UNION PACIFIC, 1959-60, Alco PA, PA, gray roof, yellow body
21925-1 with red line separating side and roof and red line along bottom
of side above gray frame; red large "UNION PACIFIC" and
"21925" or "21925-1." Stud on rear roof, gray finished simulated
six-wheel die-cast trucks. Simulated portholes integral to body
shell with body color, steps integral to body shell; knuckle
couplers at both ends. 21925 with two worm drive motors with
Pull-mor power (traction tires), reverse unit (F-R-F sequence)
and operating headlight. 21925-1 with automatic operating bell
that sounds when unit is moving slowly. Came as part of the top
of the line "PONY EXPRESS" passenger set including four
passenger cars for $67.50 in 1959 and $69.98 in 1960, Walsh
Collection.   **150 225 300**

35

The Baldwins

355

21801-1   21808

21[812]

21918   21918-1

21813

21801   (CHICAGO &) NORTHWESTERN, 1958, Baldwin, with green cab, cab roof and hood top, yellow sides, green and yellow diagonal stripes on lower side, green lettered "ROUTE OF THE" and yellow "400" in green box, knuckle couplers front and rear, single worm drive motor with two or three-position (F-N-R) remote control reverse unit, four-wheel black plastic truck side frames black decorative plastic horn on hood; red, white and black "NORTHWESTERN" decal and "21801" on cab, light.
25   45   55

21801-1 (CHICAGO &) NORTHWESTERN, 1958, Baldwin, uncatalogued, matches 21801, but dummy without light, knuckle couplers front and rear, Newcomer Collection.   **20   30   45**

21808   (CHICAGO &) NORTHWESTERN, 1958, Baldwin, uncatalogued, matches design and appearance of 21801, single worm drive motor, manual reverse unit, knuckle couplers front and rear, Newcomer Collection.   **25   35   45**

[21]812 TEXAS & PACIFIC, 1959-60, Baldwin, black cab and cab roof, black hood top, orange sides, orange and black diagonal stripes along base, knuckle couplers front and rear, operating headlight slightly raised above hood line, decorative plastic horn on hood top, black fuel tank, black lettered "TEXAS & PACIFIC" on hood side, and light orange "812" on cab side beneath window, single worm drive motor, four-wheel trucks with black plastic side frames.   **30   45   85**

21813   M·St L, 1958   uncatalogued, Baldwin, red body with white and red diagonal stripes along base, white stripes on nose, knuckle couplers front and rear, decorative plastic horn on hood top, non-operating headlight slightly raised above hood line, large white "M·St L" beneath cab windows representing Minneapolis and St. Louis Railroad, white "PEORIA GATE-WAY" without serifs, red fuel tank beneath frame, "21813" in white letters on side slightly in front of cab, four-wheel trucks with black plastic side frames, Newcomer Collection.
100   150   200

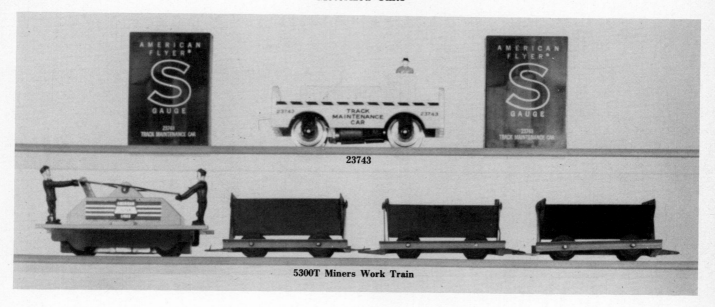

23743

5300T Miners Work Train

21927 SANTA FE, 1960-62, Alco PA, silver finished body with red, yellow and black war bonnet design; "SANTA FE" Indian Chief decal on side, "SANTA FE" lettering on lower rear side, small "BUILT BY GILBERT" on rear side. Black decorative horns on cab roof, operating headlight, one worm drive motor with Pull-mor power (two traction tires), four-position reverse unit, simulated six-wheel trucks with silver finished die-cast side frames, knuckle couplers front and rear, solid portholes integral to body and plastic steps integral to body. Note that catalogue copy shows two rivet metal steps rather than plastic steps, not confirmed; stud on roof in rear. Came with the Chief -- top of the line passenger set including three passenger cars in 1961-1963 and the complete set retailed for $44.98.　　**50　70　95**

..... (BOSTON & MAINE), ... Alco PA, blue body with black band from cab window to rear end of side, blue decorative horns on cab roof, large white "B" and large black "M" on side, two portholes with clear plastic inserts, silver finished simulated six-wheel trucks, stud on rear roof, one knuckle coupler on front, two rivets hold metal steps to plastic body, prototype, Walsh Collection.　　**No Reported Sales**

MOTORIZED UNITS

740　**HANDCAR** Four-wheel powered unit, two hard working men pump unceasingly; black plastic frame holds metal motor chassis, orange plastic superstructure; men with black pants, blue shirts, blue jackets, flesh colored faces, blue hats, two red lanterns; reproductions of men, lanterns and decals are available from Dan Olson, a contributor to this book. Black metal pumping bar connects to motor through lever - the men do not actually do the work. Tony Gonzalez reports that the metal chassis comes in two varieties -- one has the end cut out to provide room for the drawbar of the tipple car.
(A)　"AMERICAN FLYER LINES" in black lettering on side, no decals, no vent holes, 1952 (early version). **9　12　18**

(B)　Red, white and blue decal with stripes, shield in center, lettering on shield reads "AMERICAN" in white letters, "FLYER" in blue letters and "LINES" in white letters, 1952, Newcomer Collection.　　**15　20　25**
(C)　Red, white and blue shield without stripes with white "AMERICAN," blue "FLYER" and red "LINES," with vent holes.　　**15　20　25**

741　**HANDCAR and SHED** A set consisting of a 740 Handcar, version (B), and TOOL SHED. The tool shed differs from a regular 585 shed in that its base is cut out to allow track to enter; the remaining base is basically U shaped, 1953.　**25　40　75**

5300T　**MINERS WORK TRAIN** A special set consisting of a 740 Handcar, version (B), with the end of the chassis cut out for the drawbar of the tipple car; three tipple cars with tuscan, blue and green bins respectively. The tipples have gray painted sheet metal bases and four wheels, 1953-54, Newcomer Collection.
　　35　50　70

[742]　**HANDCAR** With reversing mechanism. When the car hits a solid object, it reverses direction.
(A)　Red, white and blue decal with stripes, shield in center, lettering on shield reads "AMERICAN" in white,"FLYER" in blue and "LINES" in white letters, 1955.　**15　25　40**
(B)　Red, white and blue decal with shield but without stripes; lettering on shield reads "AMERICAN" in white,"FLYER" in blue and "LINES" in white letters, confirmation requested.　　**10　15　20**

743　See (23)743.

[23]743　**TRACK MAINTENANCE CAR** Yellow plastic body with "743 TRACK MAINTENANCE CAR 743" in black on side, black safety stripe along top of side, operator with turquoise shirt, flesh colored face and brown hat; has inexpensive Japanese motor with an operating maximum of 9 volts. This is the less common car, the next entry is the more common. **15　22　40**

23743　**TRACK MAINTENANCE CAR** Same as (23)743 but reads "23744 TRACK MAINTENANCE CAR 23743."　**10　15　20**

Chapter III
STEAM LOCOMOTIVES

The development of steam locomotives is complex. Although general principles characterize Flyer's locomotive evolution there are exceptions to the rule. First, in the late forties -- 1946-48 -- it was apparently the Gilbert Company's intention to devise a numbering system to easily identify each of the locomotive types and their features. Their system classifies the five locomotive types into five series: the 300 series which are 4-4-2 Atlantics, the 310 series which are Pennsylvania K-5 Pacifics, the 320 series which are 4-6-4 Hudsons, the 330 series which are 4-8-4 Northerns (which Gilbert called "Challengers") and lastly the 340 series which are the 0-8-0 Nickel Plate switchers.

The last digit of the number code indicates engine features. When the last number is a zero the engine has no special feature, i.e., no smoke or choo-choo. If the last number is a "1" the engine has choo-choo only; "2" indicates smoke and choo-choo. It was originally planned, as the catalogues reveal, that each of the five series would come in three versions: either without features, with choo-choo only or with smoke and choo-choo. Thus, an Atlantic without any features could come as a 300; with choo-choo only it would come as a 301, and with smoke and choo-choo it would come as a 302. In spite of these intentions, however, the three versions were produced only for the 300 Atlantic series and the 320 Hudson series. There are: 300, 301 and 302 in the Atlantic series and a 320, 321 and 322 in the Hudson series. The Pennsylvania K-5 was produced only in the 310 and 312 versions, although it is catalogued as a 311 in 1946. The Northern 330 series is only offered in the deluxe 332 version with smoke and choo-choo. Likewise, the Nickel Plate switcher is only offered as a 342.[1]

The first postwar locomotives from 1946 are composed of four pieces: a boiler, steam chest, pilot and boiler front. These locomotives have wire handrails along the boilers and the boiler fronts are removable so that the headlamp socket, which is mounted on the motor chassis, is easily accessible for servicing. The crosshead guides, a one piece steel channel fastened only to the steam chest, tend to loosen with use and create an operating problem. The four position reverse unit is mounted horizontally in the locomotive with a lever protruding through the boiler top. Tenders have prototype roadnames only, such as Reading, PENNSYLVANIA, NICKEL PLATE, UNION PACIFIC and NEW YORK CENTRAL. The smoke unit and bellows type choo-choo, when present, are mounted in the tender and are driven by a separate motor. A rubber hose carries smoke from the tender to the locomotive stack. There are hollow spaces in the Atlantic and K-5 locomotive chassis and two spring-loaded brass buttons on the underside of the chassis on all models. The trailing truck is separate from the drawbar. Silver rather than white lettering is found on the

New 1948 crosshead guide design with rear of guide fastened by screw to boiler.

loco and tender. Engines with smoke have a filler cap on top of the tender, and the valve gear and drive rod rivets have round heads. Tenders have link couplers with thin shanks, embossed with "PAT. NO 2240137" and no coupler weights.

The 1946 designs continue in 1947 with a few notable changes. Tenders are lettered "AMERICAN FLYER LINES" and the prototype roadnames appear as heralds in a smaller size near the front of the tender side. Hex head rivets replace roundhead rivets on the valve gear and the link coupler on the tender rear now has a thick shank, but not a coupler weight.

1948 was a year of profound design change. The most important change was relocation of the choo-choo and smoke mechanisms in the locomotive. The choo-choo and smoke mechanisms are redesigned to be driven by the same motor that powers the wheels, thus eliminating the need for a second motor. To make room for the choo-choo and smoke mechanisms, the reverse unit is moved to the tender; the reverse unit lever protrudes through the tender floor (except on some Atlantics where the reverse unit remains in the engine). The location of the choo-choo/smoke unit in the engine creates the opportunity for synchronized smoke and driver action. Gilbert, of course, avails himself of this opportunity. Since the reverse unit lever no longer penetrates the boiler (except on Atlantics), the boiler slot is eliminated in the boiler dies. Smoke fluid is now added through the locomotive stack and the hole in the tender casting where smoke fluid was formerly added is closed. The troublesome crosshead guide is improved by a new L shaped design. The new design required boiler changes. The boiler was extended to provide a place to fasten the rear of the new crosshead guide with a screw.

Additional boiler redesign occurs because of changes in the method of boiler front closure and structural support. In

[1] With the exception of a 340 now in the Carnes Collection.

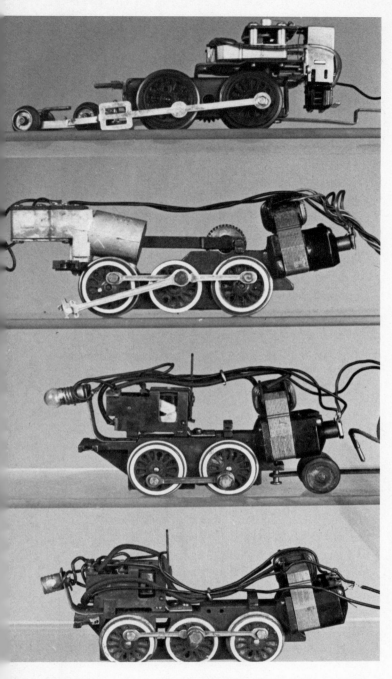

Top Shelf: Casey Jones chassis with vertical armature shaft; Second Shelf: Pacific chassis with choo-choo and smoke unit. Third Shelf: Atlantic chassis with reverse unit and lamp socket bracket affixed to chassis. Bottom Shelf: K-5 Pacific chassis with reverse unit and lamp socket bracket affixed to chassis.

1948 Gilbert discontinued use of the two long brass springs to hold the boiler front in place. In its place the company introduced a new rivet on the right side of the boiler front to provide a snug fit between the boiler front and the boiler. At the same time, the headlight socket is moved from the motor chassis to the boiler front which places the lamp closer to the

Lucite lens. The structure of the boiler bottom is also changed: two ridges now run the length of the boiler and the lip is removed that formerly crossed the boiler opening. To summarize 1948 changes it is clear that Gilbert conducted an enormous retooling effort involving all five engines. The results were worthwhile. There was a dramatic reduction in manufacturing costs since one motor was eliminated and the synchronized smoke was an exciting sales feature. Also this year, Gilbert solved a coupler problem. It was a big job well done. Under certain conditions the latch coupler would unlatch and leave a most embarrassed engineer with half a train. Gilbert's solution: add a brass weight to the link.

Another 1948 cost reduction for K-5s and Atlantics is the combined drawbar and trailing truck assembly. Formerly the drawbar was separated from the die-cast trailing truck. The trailing truck looses its die-cast side frames and the axle is held by a stamped steel frame that is riveted to the drawbar.

Many of the features introduced in 1948 were successful and appear in the line year after year. Some are adapted in new engines that join the line. The smoke/choo-choo relocation in the boiler, the reverse unit's location in the tender, the change in boiler bottom structure and the L shaped crosshead guide characterize K-5, Hudson, Northern and 0-8-0 production for many years. The combined drawbar-trailing truck unit was successful and in modified form was used on Atlantics and New Haven and Chicago North Western Pacifics. Not all changes worked and the rivet type boiler front was not successful, but that is another story.

1948 was a hard year to measure up to and the rate of innovation visibly tapered off in 1949. The next change in the boiler front occurs either in 1949 or 1950 when a one piece brass spring is substituted for the rivet to hold the boiler front to the boiler. The new brass spring has two ends, each 7/8" long (compared to the first 1946-47 springs which are each 1 3/16" long). At the same time, Gilbert engineers found a way to eliminate a construction step; the headlamp socket fastens to the boiler front with the same rivet that holds the spring in place!

1949 saw the first new addition to the locomotive roster since 1941 -- the die-cast 290 Pacific. The 290, with its distinctive feedwater heater above the boiler is based on a New Haven design. It is the first Gilbert engine expressly designed for a 3/16 two rail system. It has a sleek appearance in part because it is narrower than the earlier engines. It also shows the wave of the future in its one piece die-cast boiler with integral pilot, boiler front and steam cylinder. Also introduced (with the 1949 Atlantic) is the simplified slide action crosshead guide. Over the years variations of this simpler crosshead appear in other engines. It is interesting that Gilbert did not redesign the tender, but offers the basic sheet metal Atlantic tender (originally designed for 0 Gauge track) with this sleek new engine. The 290 also adapted the simpler drawbar-trailing truck combination introduced a year earlier. Again cost considerations would eventually cause this design to be utilized in the higher priced models across the line. 1949 also brings in the much tooted whistle in the 314AW tender. This whistle, powered by a separate motor and activated by a D.C. relay, is a close cousin of Lionel's successful whistles. In spite of its familial resemblance Gilbert management did not believe that the design infringed on Lionel's patent and were to say the least very surprised when the court's ruling (a consequence of Lionel's suit) went against them!

The most important steam innovation in 1950 is the new electronic whistle in the Hudson and Northern. Substantial innovation was occuring in the diesel line as well, but that story is told elsewhere in this book.

Atlantics

We have chosen Atlantics for a detailed analysis because they are inexpensive, easy to find, fun to study and show the richness and the complexity of Gilbert's locomotive development. When Gilbert's overall locomotive development is compared to that of Lionel's, Gilbert's always presents greater design change. It appears that Gilbert management was always experimenting in how to build it better or at least to build it as well for less! The Atlantics studied here represent the Atlantic types in the collections of Norman Passman, Bruce Greenberg, Don Caples and the Railroad Emporium. Their diversity and variation is Gilbert's creativity. The units, gathered more or less randomly, differ in one or more ways other than their numbers. We are looking forward to hearing from you about your variations!

The analysis begins with an overview of major locomotive body differences, then proceeds to differentiate crosshead guide construction, boiler fronts, trailing trucks and drawbars.

Locomotives fall into three big categories: four piece die-cast locos, one piece die-cast locos and one piece plastic locos. Each of these categories most likely has two or more subcategories. The four piece die-cast loco is so described because it is composed of four separate die-cast pieces: a boiler, a one piece set of steam cylinders, a boiler front and a pilot (cowcatcher). (We have not examined these pieces to identify their parts numbers, although such scrutiny would undoubtedly produce some very interesting information).

We have identified three different four piece locomotives. The first, which we call Type I has three sets of wire handrails. A set consists of one handrail on each side and it runs the length of the boiler and is fastened by five cotter pins on each side. A second set of handrails links the pilot (cowcatcher) with the boiler. The third set graces the rear of the cab. The four part locomotive has a simulated coupler integral to the pilot casting and also has two large air compressors on the left engine side. (These simulated compressors are larger than those found on the one piece die-cast locomotive and the one piece plastic locomotive. We will have more to say about these later.)

The characteristics just described have also been observed on Types II and III four part locomotives. Type I locomotives have a slot on the top of the boiler for the reverse unit and a lip across the boiler opening at the bottom. This lip is visible when the boiler front is removed. Type I locos also have a partially completed round opening on the side which is centered between the drivers near the bottom edge of the boiler casting. This most likely has a definite purpose but we have still to discover what it is. This opening is visible in the Atlantic illustrations in the 1946-48 Gilbert catalogues and on the 1941 565 3/16" 0 Gauge production. The channel type crosshead guide is fastened only to the rear of the steam cylinders and not to the boiler. In fact the boiler casting slopes away and up from the crosshead guide.

The second version of the four part locomotive -- Type II -- is quite similar to Type I except that the boiler casting is extended for the length of the crosshead guide to provide room for a sheet metal screw to pass through the L shaped crosshead guide into the frame. This change prevents the new type crosshead guide from wobbling and is a nice solution to an operating problem. Type II locos also differ from Type I in that there are two small ridges running lengthwise along the boiler bottom that are visible when the boiler front is removed. The lip which formerly ran across the boiler opening is gone. These are the major differences that we have observed between Types I and II four part locomotives, exclusive of those differences in motors, trucks and boiler fronts. We welcome your comments and observations.

The third version of the four part locomotive, Type III, differs from both I and II in that the slot in the boiler top for the reverse unit is no longer present. Type III has the same longitudinal ridges we observed in Type II plus a headlamp socket mounted on the back of the boiler front. However, contrary to our expectations, the crosshead guide is not supported on the rear by a metal screw as with Type II, but rather has the same configuration as on Type I, namely the boiler side slopes away and up from the rear of the crosshead guide. This is unexpected since we assumed that Type III was later than Types I and II and that the improvements to the crosshead guide assembly would necessarily appear in Type III. Now we have a dating mystery to solve for the next edition.*

In 1951 the electronic whistle is redesigned and renamed; it is now air chime whistle. The air chime whistle utilizes a controller powered by transformer output (15 volts) rather than house current (110 volts) used for the electronic whistle. Gilbert's claim about the realism and fidelity of their equipment is a bit overdrawn, but given the circumstances, its inability to use a D.C. relay as an activator because Lionel had preempted the field, their substitution was creative and a pragmatic solution.

The major change affecting the steam line in 1952 is the introduction of a new knuckle coupler for the top-of-the-line Hudson and Northern sets. These sets, prefaced with "K" in their set numbers, include the new sintered iron truck frame

*Gilbert usually dates locomotives in the inside of the boiler. Learning these dates should permit us to clarify the chronology of Types I, II and III.

21105 Atlantic without Whistle on Boiler Top

21160 Atlantic with Whistle on Boiler Top

282 CNW Type Pacific

283 CNW Type Pacific

289 CNW Type Pacific

21085 CNW Type Pacific

290 NH Type Pacific with Feedwater Heater

Compare the 21105 and 21160. Note the difference in whistles and the two wires that go from the loco to plug into the tender. The 282 has a metal Atlantic type tender, while the 283, on the next shelf, has a plastic tender superstructure. The 282 has cloth covered wires between the loco and tender, while

sides on their cars (but not their tenders). The tenders continue their die-cast sides but with new knuckle couplers. The sintered iron truck sides are a substantial improvement in realism when compared to the sheet metal trucks which date back to the late thirties. The other major addition that year is another engine at the low priced end of the line. The CNW Pacifics -- 282 and 285 -- with a small bell above the boiler front are the first engines ever introduced with a one piece plastic shell. This is indicative of Flyer's success with plastics in terms of realism, detail, wear characteristics and cost reduction. At the same time that the plastic 282 and 285 appear the Atlantic makes its debut in plastic. The growing importance of plastic superstructures is underscored by the redesign of the old faithful Atlantic tender (dating to 1941) in plastic both for some of the new CNW Pacifics and some of the Atlantics. In fact 1952 also sees the redesign of the streamlined passenger cars: the extruded aluminum cars used in 1951 and 1950 are replaced with plastic. Clearly, plastic is becoming strongly associated with modern, appealing, fun to operate Flyer train design. This is particularly interesting since the 1952 changes represent Gilbert's second major commitment to plastics. The first efforts in 1946 to utilize the little understood and new materials had been a disaster. Fortunately, history was not repeated.

In 1953 Gilbert introduces trucks with sintered iron sides and knuckle couplers. The lower priced diesel and steam sets ($36.00 or less) retain the sheet metal trucks and link couplers while sets costing more (from $38.75 and up) are equipped with Flyer's newest feature. Gilbert also continues to offer almost all of its rolling stock in two forms -- with the new sintered iron trucks and knuckle couplers as 900 series cars or with the traditional sheet metal trucks and link couplers as 600 series cars.

"Pull-mor Power" is the headliner in 1953. Pull-mor Power was introduced partially to counter Lionel's magnetraction. Lionel used permanently magnetized axles to dramatically increase the pulling power of its equipment and to reduce derailments at high speed on its sharp curves. Lionel's "technical advance" became a great marketing ploy and Gilbert realized that he would have to dramatically promote Flyer's power to pull ahead of Lionel sales. Gilbert's ad copy writer was unleashed: "With the remarkable 'PULL-MOR' feature American Flyer steam locos can haul FORTY or more freight or passenger cars - or climb grades like a mountain goat." The claim of forty cars is true although the analogy to nimble mountain goats is harder to test out since Gilbert does not explain how Pull-mor accomplishes this remarkable feat. Of course, the Flyer method is elegant in its simplicity. Pull-mor traction power is achieved by bonding a set of rubber tires to one set of wheels in the motor. Pull-mor power did not come with all 1953 sets. In fact Gilbert's decision to include or exclude Pull-mor power depends on the cost of the set. If it cost $36.00 or less, Pull-mor was excluded, if you made the extra effort and spent $38.75 or more you became the happy owner of the newest and best Gilbert features. Many a boy persuaded many a willing father to do just this.

An Atlantic type metal tender with a hole in lower side and an Atlantic type plastic tender.

Type IV represents a redesigned Atlantic engine. It becomes a one piece die-cast unit and keeps only the general outline and details of its former self. The boiler, boiler front, pilot and steam cylinders are now one die-cast unit. As one piece, the time required to clean off the flashing on each of the exterior surfaces of the four pieces (with close tolerances) is dramatically reduced. Assembly line time is likewise reduced. These economy measures are particularly important since it is a long standing maxim in the toy train industry that the low priced sets are not profitable. In fact, according to Nat Polk, the least expensive starter sets cost Lionel and Gilbert much more than they yielded in revenue and selling an inexpensive set was the equivalent of packing a $5.00 bill in the box. This situation resembles that of the U.S. auto industry which finds that a stripped down, economy model is not profitable and only the more expensive cars generate a profit. Considering these cost factors Gilbert's continued thrust to produce a less costly Atlantic, its lowest price steam engine, is much more understandable.

The new one piece Atlantic casting differs from the older model in that the steam cylinder is about one inch high while those on Types I-III boilers are ¾". The partially completed opening which appears along the center of the side of the older models, and whose purpose we do not know, disappears with the new Atlantic model. In a very clever design change, the pilot truck is fastened to a sheet metal bracket which also forms the crosshead guide. (This is the Type III crosshead guide.)

The Type IV boiler has an integral cast railing along the length of the boiler which replaces the separate handrail

A side view of a four piece Atlantic showing the partial hole on the lower side and part of the L shaped crosshead guide.

found on Types I-III. The simulated coupler which appears on the pilot of Types I-III is not present on the new casting. The slot on the top of the boiler for the reverse lever is still present; and the metal bell and whistle still grace the top of the boiler.

Type V is the twin to Type IV except that the slot for the reverse unit disappears. The reverse unit is relocated in the tender and the space now available in the engine is usually used for a choo-choo and smoke unit.

A side view of a one piece 300AC Atlantic showing that the hole on the side has disappeared. Note the metal whistle, bell and the reverse slot on the boiler top.

Although use of a one piece die-casting is clearly more cost efficient than a four piece die-casting Gilbert continued to look for ways to reduce production costs. In 1952 Gilbert again revises the Atlantic engine to create a one piece black plastic engine which we call Type VI. The art of plastic injection molding had reached some sophistication by this time and the plastic engines are highly detailed and very durable. The black plastic engine did not require additional painting and its cleanup time was minimal when compared to that of the die-cast model. Furthermore, shipping costs went down substantially with the lighter weight plastic boilers. Gilbert

thus achieved another edge in competing with the Lionel and Marx low cost sets.

When Gilbert switches from the four piece to the one piece Atlantic casting, only the engine's general characteristics are carried on. When Gilbert changes from the one piece Type IV die-cast engine to the plastic Type VI, the Type IV design is closely mirrored in Type VI, although some differences occur. Some of the important characteristics are: a slot on the top of the boiler, handrails that run the length of the boiler which are part of the plastic body, no simulated coupler on the front pilot and steam cylinders about 1" high.

Type VII should be no surprise to Gilbert watchers. Remove the slot from a one piece black plastic Type VI, move the reverse unit back to the tender and that's Type VII. This unit has a metal bell and whistle on the top of the boiler as well as a Lucite headlight lens as on Types I - VI.

Type VIII represents Gilbert's most drastic cost cutting effort for the Atlantic. The basic Type VI plastic body is utilized but with no slot in the boiler top, the bell and whistle on the boiler top are now plastic. The reverse unit is now only a toggle switch with a forward and reverse mode mounted in the rear of the cab.

Atlantic Boilers

Atlantic boiler fronts show a sequence of development that is generally similar to that of other Gilbert steam engines, but that takes some distinctive turns because of the Atlantic's position as the low priced leader in the line. The 1946 Atlantic is the same as the prewar four piece engine with its separate and removable boiler front. The boiler front is held in place by two brass clips, each 1 3/16" long. The headlamp socket is mounted on the motor chassis. About 1948, Gilbert creates a less costly boiler front fastener consisting of a brass rivet mounted on the right side of the boiler front. This rivet holds the boiler front securely to the boiler. At the same time, the headlamp socket is relocated from the motor chassis to the rear of the boiler front. These changes occur at the same time on the K-5s, the Hudsons, the Northerns and the 0-8-0s.

Apparently the rivet fastener was not satisfactory and Gilbert engineers consequently modified and improved the brass clip fastener. It becomes a Type III boiler front with a single brass spring mounted on the boiler front, with two ends, each 7/8" long. The headlamp socket is also mounted on the boiler front using the same rivet which holds the brass spring. This arrangement proves satisfactory in terms of cost and operations and continues as long as the separate front is retained on Gilbert locos.

As we have already indicated, price competition between Lionel and Gilbert, particularly for dollars for low end sets, was fierce. Gilbert engineers had to find a way to reduce costs to effectively compete with Lionel's one piece cast Scout 2-4-2 loco. The Gilbert solution was to develop a one piece engine, an innovation which did away with the separate boiler front. The one piece engine gives us, therefore, a Type IV boiler front and a relocated headlamp socket on the motor chassis. The change to a one piece metal engine is clearly a step in the right direction.

But Lionel moved fast and in 1950 it adopted a one piece plastic boiler for one of its low price locos, the 1130 and the path was clear. In 1952, Gilbert replaces its one piece die-cast engine with a one piece plastic engine. The Atlantic boiler front story now enters its fifth and last stage with the change to plastic. It retains the lamp socket bracket mounting on the underside of the pilot. As price competition intensifies in the late 50s, the headlamp's socket completely disappears from some models.

The Atlantic's trailing trucks show a parallel development with other loco components. The 1946 Atlantics carry over the general details of the prewar trailing truck design which is adapted for S Gauge track. The truck consists of a metal bracket which is attached to the motor chassis at one end and floats against a stretcher bar across the rear of the cab. There is a separate, short nickeled drawbar between the loco and the tender which has several bends; it bends down, goes across and then bends up. The tender frame is notched to accept the drawbar.

In the second stage of trailing truck - drawbar development, Gilbert engineers find a way to substantially reduce costs by combining the drawbar and trailing truck. This concept is also adopted in several of the other Gilbert models. A single black painted bar now links the engine and tender. The bar has an upside down U shaped bend to sufficiently raise the bar so that the trailing truck assembly has sufficient clearance. The trailing truck assembly swivels on a brass rivet that is fastened at the top of the U shaped bend. The tender frame is no longer notched since the redesigned drawbar clears the tender frame. In the sample examined, the stretcher bar still spans the rear although it no longer has a specific function.

Gilbert next changes the drawbar from a black finish to a shiny metal one. Since a black finish is more realistic, it is likely that the change to shiny metal resulted in savings, probably only pennies but still a savings.

Gilbert's fourth stage of Atlantic drawbar-truck trailing truck development changes the drawbar-to-tender connection. The drawbar is now connected to the leading truck on the tender and is 3½" long. The fifth stage is similar to the fourth stage but the drawbar is made about ¼" shorter to provide close loco-tender coupling. In the sixth and last stage, Gilbert introduces a straight drawbar without the U channel bend of the previous five types and thereby reduces the manufacturing cost by eliminating one step in the process. This drawbar, unlike all the other postwar versions, has a large hole and is detachable from the tender, which brings Gilbert back to its prewar detachable design.

The Atlantic crosshead guide has an interesting history. As with many of the 1946 Atlantic characteristics, the crosshead guide is carried over from 1941 production. The first crosshead guide has a steel channel in which the main rod slides back and forth. As we have earlier mentioned this

The simplified U shaped crosshead guide which is part of a stamping which provides support for the leading truck.

does not prove satisfactory and in 1948 it is replaced by an L shaped crosshead guide with a slot on the top. The third Atlantic crosshead guide has a U shape with the base of the U headed towards the train rear. This version is called the sliding crosshead guide. The boiler is modified to accept this type which is partially held on by tabs inside and outside of the boiler. The sliding crosshead guide differs from the earlier Types I and II in that it is part of the sheet metal stamping that supports the leading truck. The U shaped crosshead guide and leading truck support stamping is very similar to that used by Lionel in its 249 and other inexpensive locos. The four piece main rod-side rod-valve gear combination that appears in Types I and II is replaced by a simpler two piece assembly in Type III.

Type IV continues the U channel found in Type III. It is the most economical drive rod assembly Gilbert produced. The end of the main rod is formed into a T, as viewed from the side, and has a bent over tab.

Introduction To The Pennsylvania K5 Series

The 310-312 series evolves from the 559 and 561 K-5s, from 1940 and 1941. In outward appearance the four part castings appear quite similar since both the 559 and 561 do not smoke and have the same plugged stacks as do the later 310s. The handrail trim on the engine appears to be the same on the 559 as on the 310 and early 312. The prewar crosshead guide is the same channel type found on the 1946 postwar K-5. The prewar main rod, side rod, eccentric rod and control rod mechanisms are carried over to 1946 production. The prewar locos do not have brass buttons on the bottom of the motor chassis. Rather there are two sliding shoes for center rail pickup. The die-cast leading truck frame is wider than that appearing on the postwar version. Since the axles are longer; the trailing truck is also similar to those found on the first postwar K-5s with a die-cast frame but are appropriately wider to fit 0 Gauge track. The 1939-41 locos have larger diameter wheels than those found on the postwar K-5s. The prewar boiler front is held in place by two long brass springs, a feature which is carried over into 1946 production. The slot in the boiler top for the reverse lever is

Top Shelf: 1947 K-5 with rubber hose from tender to loco, reverse unit lever through boiler top, channel type crosshead guide, only two wires from tender to loco; Bottom Shelf: 1948 K-5 with cloth covering four wires from tender to loco, reverse lever now through tender frame, combined trailing truck and drawbar.

also carried over to 1946. The basis boiler casting is carried over and is very noticeable because its width is substantially greater than that of the two rail motor. This size difference implies that the wide boilers are not true 3/16 scale. 1939-41 equipment has black side walls but in 1946 Gilbert innovates by introducing white side walls.

The locos and tenders in the late thirties have detachable drawbars. No wires join them together. Some tenders come with choo-choo mechanisms. In the immediate postwar years, Gilbert permanently fastens the locos and tenders and uses the tenders for current pickup. The current picked up by the tender is then carried by wires to the locomotive.

Following the prewar practice of locating the chugger in the tender and the reverse unit in the boiler, with a reverse lever appearing through the boiler top, Gilbert in 1946, put the new choo-choo/smoke unit in the tender and so the smoke is carried by a black rubber tube to the loco stack. The reverse unit continues to be in the boiler with its lever through the boiler top.

1948 was a year of great change for the 312. The boiler is redesigned to support the new L shaped crosshead guide. The boiler front is redesigned for the new rivet fastening. The structure of the bottom of the boiler is changed and longitudinal ridges added. The reverse unit is moved to the tender, the slot for the reverse lever which once pierced the boiler top disappears and a new slot is provided through the tender floor. With the reverse unit in the tender more complex wiring is needed to join the loco and tender and four wires in a cloth covered wrapping replace the two wires that previously joined the loco and tender. With the space now available in the loco the choo-choo and smoke mechanisms are located in the boiler. This ends the need for a separate motor to drive the choo-choo/smoke mechanism in the tender and paves the way to synchronize the choo-choo sound with the action of the drivers. The

headlamp socket moves from the motor chassis where is has been since 1941 to the boiler front.

1949 sees the replacement of the rivet fastening the boiler front with a boiler front held in place by a one piece brass spring with two ends, each 7/8" long. 1949 also brings the addition of a motor-powered whistle to the tender of one K-5 model. This is a short lived innovation since Lionel's suit for patent infringement was successful. Whistles are an important sales tool which Gilbert does not want to forfeit. In 1950 an electronic whistle is designed without a motor and the company thus successfully circumvents Lionel's patent. The new electronic whistle and its subsequent modification appear in most K-5 tenders from then on. In 1953 Gilbert introduces knuckle couplers and with the K-5's sintered iron sides the tender's new features replace the truck and coupler designs originating in 1940. The new couplers and trucks are added to most of the Gilbert line in 1953 having been available only on the top-of-the-line Hudson and Northern 1952 sets. 1953 also marks the addition of traction tires to the K-5 as part of the general program to equip Gilbert engines with Pull-mor power.

The 21115, the last version of the K-5, manufactured in 1958, has smoke and choo-choo in the engine, traction tires on the rear drivers and a die-cast trailing truck. The drawbar is now mounted on the same stud in the loco that holds the die-cast trailing truck. Features that continue to characterize the K-5 are: the L shaped crosshead guides, the boiler casting with longitudinal ridges along its length and the boiler front held in place by a one piece brass spring with two ends, each 7/8" long. However, the engine sports a new motor with a drum type commutator designed to work with the new two position reverse unit mounted on the rear of the motor. Since the reverse unit is mounted in the rear, only two wires are needed to carry current from the tender pickup to the loco. The tender has a highly detailed plastic superstructure replacing the die-cast one.

Washington See 21089

88 See 21088.

263 0-6-0, 1957 only, switcher, black plastic engine, smoke, light, choo-choo, and Pull-mor power. White "PRR" in Keystone and "AMERICAN FLYER LINES" silk-screened on eight-wheel slope back plastic tender with rear light and knuckle couplers. It is believed that only a very small number, if any, of the early versions of the loco were actually numbered 263. Uncatalogued number is 21004 and catalogued number is 21005. Two wires between engine and tender with plug and socket, 13 7/8". Considered highly accurate model of PRR B6sb. **200 350 500**

282 4-6-2, 1952-53, CNW Pacific with small bell above boiler, one piece black plastic engine, with handrailings integral to boiler, with smoke and choo-choo in boiler and reverse unit in tender. White "282" on cab beneath windows; link couplers in 1952 and knuckle coupler and traction tires in 1953. Engine and tender total 17 ¾".
(A) Black painted Atlantic type sheet metal tender with "AMERICAN FLYER" in white and "CHICAGO NORTH WESTERN LINE" herald, tender has small hole on lower side and one round hole with rubber grommet on side facing engine, Type D sheet metal trucks, black coupler weight, link coupler, 1952. Example shown for Newcomer Collection has replacement knuckle coupler.
12 18 25
(B) Same as (A) but black plastic Atlantic type tender, 1952.
12 18 25
(C) Red plastic insert in stack produces red glow in smoke, black plastic Atlantic type tender with same lettering as (A), sintered iron truck side frames, knuckle coupler, traction tires, 1953, Balint Collection. **14 20 30**

283 4-6-2, 1954-57, CNW Pacific with small bell above boiler front, one piece black plastic engine with handrailings integral to boiler; with smoke and choo-choo in boiler; Pull-mor traction tires on front drivers; combined trailing truck and drawbar; slide action crosshead guide; four wires which do not unplug between loco and tender, headlight socket bracket is screwed to underside of pilot; Atlantic type highly detailed plastic tender with "AMERICAN FLYER LINES" in white sans serif face and "CHICAGO NORTH WESTERN LINE" herald towards front of tender side; sintered iron truck side frames with concave ovals and knuckle couplers, Newcomer Collection. **18 25 35**

285 4-6-2, 1952, CNW Pacific with small bell above boiler front, one piece black plastic engine with handrailings integral to boiler; with smoke and choo-choo in boiler, combined trailing truck and drawbar; slide action crosshead guide; Atlantic type metal tender with "AMERICAN FLYER" in white and "CHICAGO NORTH WESTERN LINE" herald in white towards front of tender side; air chime whistle; sheet metal trucks, link coupler, black coupler weight, Caples Collection. **25 45 60**

287 4-6-2, 1954, CNW Pacific with small bell above boiler front, one piece black plastic engine, Pull-mor traction tires, no smoke or choo-choo; white "287" on loco cab beneath window; tender with "AMERICAN FLYER LINES" in sans serif white letters and "CHICAGO NORTH WESTERN LINE" herald towards front of tender; tender with sintered iron truck side frames and knuckle couplers. This is the stripped version of the 283 and comes with either the low priced K5421T freight set or with a low priced K5411T passenger set. The sets were priced at $27.95 each. The loco was not available for separate sale. **15 22 30**

289 4-6-2, 1956, CNW Pacific with small bell above boiler front, one piece black plastic engine, Pull-mor traction tires, whistle, no smoke or choo-choo; white "289" on loco cab beneath window; tender with "AMERICAN FLYER LINES" in sans serif white letters and a "CHICAGO NORTH WESTERN LINE" herald towards the front of the tender. Black plastic highly detailed Atlantic type tender with sintered iron truck side frames with concave ovals and knuckle couplers. The 289 is an uncommon engine and came with a low priced uncatalogued set, Newcomer Collection. **60 90 125**

**Top Shelf: Atlantic type tender with stoker;
Bottom Shelf: K-5 type tender.**

290 4-6-2, 1949-51, Pacific, with feedwater heater above boiler front, black one piece die-cast engine, handrails integral to boiler, combined trailing truck and drawbar, headlight, smoke and choo-choo in engine, white "290" on loco cab beneath window, sheet metal Atlantic type tender with link couplers; example shown has had its coupler changed.
(A) Tender lettered "AMERICAN FLYER" in white sans serif face; "Reading Lines" diamond does not appear on tender, black coupler weight, Type C trucks, hole in lower side of tender, one hole with rubber grommet at end facing engine, Caples Collection. **20 30 40**
(B) Tender lettered "AMERICAN FLYER" in sans serif face, "Reading Lines" in diamond outline , three holes on tender end facing loco, Type D nine spring trucks, no hole on lower side of tender, three holes on tender end facing engine, Caples and Newcomer Collections. **20 30 40**

293 4-6-2, 1953-58, Pacific with feedwater heater above boiler front, black one piece die-cast engine, die-cast trailing truck, smoke with red plastic insert in stack for red glow, choo-choo, die-cast trailing truck, Pull-mor traction tires, "293" in white on cab beneath windows, white "AMERICAN FLYER LINES" with serif and "The New York New Haven and Hartford Railroad Co" in semi-script on plastic Atlantic type tender with stoker;

A 300AC Atlantic with the long B & O type tender frame and the regular Atlantic type sheet metal tender with the hole in the side. The tender has "AMERICAN FLYER" in sans serif face. Also note the two different versions of Type D [nine-spring] trucks on the tender. The

sintered iron truck side frames, knuckle coupler; four wires between loco and tender; total length 17¾". Considered an outstanding representation of the New Haven 1-4 Pacific.

(A) Reverse unit in tender, 1953-57.   **22   30   45**

(B) Reverse unit in loco, no choo-choo or smoke; uncatalogued 1957 special version.   **35   45   70**

(C) Two position reverse unit mounted on the rear of engine, Pull-mor traction tires, smoke, choo-choo and whistle. Available for separatae sale at $39.95 in 1958.
    35   45   70

295   4-6-2, 1951, Pacific with feedwater heater above boiler front, one piece black die-cast engine with choo-choo and smoke in boiler, air chime whistle in tender. White "295" on engine cab beneath window and white "AMERICAN FLYER" on black sheet metal Atlantic type tender. Tender has sheet metal trucks with black coupler weight, link coupler and spring-loaded pickup to provide better contact for air chime whistle and to reduce speaker static. Engine and tender are 17¾" long, Newcomer Collection.
    35   50   75

296   4-6-2, 1955, Pacific with feedwater heater above boiler front, uncatalogued; one piece black die-cast engine with smoke and choo-choo in boiler and traction tires. Black plastic Atlantic type tender with stoker, air chime whistle, sintered iron truck side frames and knuckle coupler.   **50   80   135**

299   4-4-2, 1954, Atlantic, one piece black plastic engine with operating headlight. Plug and jack wiring between loco and tender, no choo-choo or smoke. Tender has sheet metal trucks and link coupler which makes it the only link coupler engine produced in 1954.

(A) Atlantic type black sheet metal tender containing reverse unit.   **45   75   100**

(B) Atlantic type black plastic tender containing reverse unit.
    35   60   80

300   4-4-2, 1946-47 and 1952, Atlantic.

(A) Four piece die-cast body with wire handrails, no smoke or choo-choo, direct wiring between loco and tender, reverse unit in loco with lever protruding through boiler top, headlight socket mounted on motor chassis, hollow spaces in locomotive chassis, two spring loaded small brass buttons on underside of motor chassis, round head rivets on valve gear, die-cast trailing truck is separate from drawbar; silver lettering on loco and tender. Tender is lettered "READING" only in embossed area on side; has thin shank link coupler and no coupler weight, 1946.   **15   25   40**

(B) Same as (A) but without hollow spaces in chassis and brass buttons, hex head rivets on valve gear, tender lettered "AMERICAN FLYER" in white and "READING LINES" inside of white outlined diamond, tender with thick shank link coupler and no coupler weight, 1947.   **10   15   20**

front truck has no slots while the rear truck has two slots. Only two wires go from the tender to the loco because the reverse unit is in the loco. Note the single hole with the rubber grommet protecting the wires on the tender side facing the loco.

(C) One piece die-cast locomotive body, no smoke or choo-choo, reverse unit in loco with lever protruding through boiler, headlight socket mounted on locomotive boiler front, L type crosshead guide have a solid rear and are screwed to the steam chests. Sheet metal tender lettered "AMER-ICAN FLYER" and in white outlined diamond "Reading Lines," link couplers with thick shank, black coupler weight. This model as well as (D) and (E) are unusual in that they retain the reverse unit in the loco long after it has been placed in the tenders of other models, 1952.
    10   15   20

(D) Black plastic boiler with slot for reverse unit and reverse unit in loco; metal simulated bell and whistle units, sliding action type valve gear. Type IV combined drawbar and trailing truck, two wires from the loco plug into the tender's fiberboard, Atlantic type metal tender without hole in lower side, white "Reading Lines" in white diamond with white "AMERICAN FLYER" in sans serif lettering, Type D trucks, link coupler, black weight, three holes on tender side facing engine. Of the tenders we have examined that have a small hole on the lower side, nearly all have only one hole on the tender side facing the locomotive; circa 1952, Caples Collection.   **10   15   20**

(E) 1953, same as (C) but one piece plastic locomotive body and plastic Atlantic type tender body.   **10   15   20**

300 AC   4-4-2, 1949-50, Atlantic, black die-cast locomotive, no smoke or choo-choo, reverse unit in loco with lever protruding through the boiler. In 1950 the 300 AC comes as part of the 5001T Farm Set. The set consists of four freight cars and cardboard cutouts to make five farm buildings and two vehicles. The cutouts are very scarce and as a group bring over $100.

(A) 1949-50, four part die-cast locomotive with wire handrails, removable boiler front; some locos have silver but most have white lettering; sheet metal Atlantic type tender with white "AMERICAN FLYER" in sans serif face and "Reading Lines" in white diamond outline.   **15   20   35**

(B) 1950, black one piece die-cast locomotive body with slot in boiler top for engine mounted reverse unit, metal simulated bell and whistle on boiler top, boiler length handrails integral to casting, slide action crosshead guide and valve gear; headlight bracket screws to pilot underside; trailing truck mounted on Type IV drawbar, two wires from tender plug into fiber panel on loco cab rear, white "300 AC" in two lines on cab beneath window. The tender frame extends approximately ¾" beyond the tender's superstructure which is a regular Atlantic type sheet metal unit. The frame is either from the B & O or the Circus type tender. Two types of tender "set backs" have been observed: some have the superstructure set back from the front; others have it set back from the rear. The tender superstructure has a small hole centered on the

295 New Haven Type Pacific

293 New Haven Type Pacific with Stoker Tender

21099 New Haven Type Pacific with Stoker Tender

312 K-5 from 1947

312 K-5 from 1948

The ill fated 314AW with Whistle

315 K-5

lower side; there are also three round holes on the side facing the engine. White "AMERICAN FLYER" in heavy sans serif face and white "Reading Lines" in white diamond on tender side. Type D front tender truck and Type B rear tender truck, link coupler, black coupler weight; shiny metal ladder on tender rear, Caples and Bargeron Collections.   **10 15 25**

301 4-4-2, Atlantic.
  (A) Four piece die-cast engine with "READING" on tender, catalogued in 1946, but not believed to have been manufactured.
  (B) Four piece die-cast engine with "AMERICAN FLYER LINES" and "Reading Lines" inside of diamond on tender, catalogued in 1947, but not believed to have been manufactured.
  (C) Shiny black one piece plastic boiler, boiler without slot on top, with metal simulated whistle and bell on boiler top; slide action crosshead guide valve gear, four prong plug in wire from loco to tender, choo-choo only in boiler, Type IV headlamp socket fastens to underside of pilot, Type IV combined trailing truck and drawbar unit. Drawbar fastens to leading tender truck. Black shiny plastic tender with white "Reading Lines" inside of white diamond and white "AMERICAN FLYER LINES" in sans serif lettering, reverse unit in tender with reverse lever protruding through slot in tender floor, Type D nine spring sheet metal trucks, link coupler, black coupler weight, 1953, Caples Collection.   **10 15 20**

302 4-4-2, Atlantic.
  (A) 1948, four part die-cast locomotive body, removable boiler front, reverse unit in loco with lever protruding through boiler, smoke and choo-choo unit in tender with rubber hose carrying smoke from tender to loco stack, long drawbar incorporates trailing truck, tender with link coupler and brass coupler weight, Degano Collection.   **10 15 20**
  (B) Same as (A) but short drawbar and separate trailing truck, Passman Collection.   **10 15 20**
  (C) 1952, one piece plastic boiler, non-removable boiler front, choo-choo and smoke in boiler, white "302" on cab beneath window, metal simulated bell and whistle on top of boiler, die-cast front truck frame, slide action crosshead guide, headlamp socket screwed to underside of pilot with a small tank on top of pilot holding and hiding screw point; long shiny finished metal drawbar incorporates loco trailing truck, four black wires run from tender to a fiber plate which plugs into a matching plate on the loco's rear, the fifth black wire is for constant lighting and is soldered to rear of loco. Black sheet metal Atlantic tender is lettered "AMERICAN FLYER" in silver with serifs and in silver outlined diamond "Reading Lines," tender does not have hole on lower side and has only one large hole fitted with rubber grommet on side facing loco. Tender has Type A sheet metal trucks and a link coupler with a black coupler weight, Greenberg and Caples Collection.   **10 15 20**
  (D) 1953, similar to (C) but with plastic Atlantic type tender, Caples Collection.   **10 15 20**

302AC 4-4-2, Atlantic with smoke and choo-choo.
  (A) Black painted die-cast boiler with metal handrails along boiler, L crosshead guides with better valve gear, metal simulated bell and whistle on boiler top, choo-choo and smoke in engine; sheet metal tender; "AMERICAN FLYER" in white letters and "Reading Lines" in white diamond outline, Caples Collection.   **10 15 20**
  (B) Black painted one piece die-cast locomotive body with simulated handrails along the side, metal simulated bell and

whistle on boiler top; the screw fastening the headlamp socket to the underside of the pilot comes through the top surface of the pilot, (Note that on 302(C) this problem is eliminated.) Slide action crosshead guide and valve gear, choo-choo and smoke in engine, Type IV trailing truck and drawbar unit, four prong fiber panel plug from loco to tender. Sheet metal tender with hole in lower side, white "Reading Lines" in white diamond, white "AMERICAN FLYER" in sans serif letters, one round hole on tender side facing loco with rubber grommet, shiny metal ladder on tender rear, Type C trucks on tender (worn out die), black coupler weight, Degano Collection.   **10 15 20**
  (C) One piece black plastic locomotive, handrails integral to casting, slide action crosshead guide and valve gear, long drawbar with incorporated trailing truck, Atlantic type sheet metal tender with white sans serif "AMERICAN FLYER" and white "Reading Lines" in white diamond outline, link coupler, black coupler weight, Newcomer Collection.   **10 15 20**

303 4-4-2, Atlantic, 1954-57, one piece black plastic engine, smoke and choo-choo in boiler, Pull-mor traction tires, slide action crosshead guide and valve gear, red plastic insert in stack gives red glow to smoke, headlight socket bracket fastens to underside of pilot, plastic Atlantic type highly detailed tender lettered "AMERICAN FLYER LINES" in white sans serif face and "Reading Lines" in white outlined diamond, sintered iron truck side frames and knuckle coupler, Balint Collection.   **10 15 20**

305 4-4-2, 1951, Atlantic, black die-cast engine, smoke, air chime whistle and choo-choo. "305" rubber stamped on engine and "Reading Lines" in diamond and "AMERICAN FLYER LINES" in white on black sheet metal tender. Extremely rare, Carnes Collection.   **No Reported Sales**

307 4-4-2, 1954-55, Atlantic, black one piece plastic engine with operating headlight and Pull-mor traction tires on the front drivers, no smoke or choo-choo, combined drawbar and trailing truck, metal simulated bell and whistle on top of boiler, front truck with sheet metal frame, slide action crosshead guide, "307" in white on cab beneath windows, direct wiring between loco and tender, Atlantic type plastic tender with white "AMERICAN FLYER LINES" in sans serif face and white "Reading Lines" inside of white diamond, four wires (two gray, one black and one green) which cannot be disconnected go from tender to loco, reverse unit in tender with lever protruding through floor, sintered iron truck side frames with concave ovals, knuckle coupler, Balint Collection.   **7 10 15**

308 4-4-2, Atlantic, 1956, black one piece plastic engine with operating headlight, choo-choo in engine, Pull-mor traction tires on front drivers, combined drawbar and trailing truck, slide action crosshead guide, "308" in white on cab beneath windows, direct wiring between loco and tender, Atlantic type plastic tender with white "AMERICAN FLYER LINES" in sans serif face and white "Reading Lines" inside of white diamond; reverse unit in tender with lever protruding through floor, sintered iron truck side frames, knuckle coupler, Degano Collection.   **10 15 20**

310 4-6-2, 1946-47, K-5, four piece black die-cast engine, no smoke or choo-choo, reverse unit in loco with reverse lever through a slot through boiler top; separate trailing truck with die-cast frame; this truck "floats" from a spreader bar across the back of the cab, short drawbar approximately 1¾" long, channel shaped crosshead fastened only to steam cylinder and not fastened at rear, with or without brass buttons on locomotive motor bottom, open space between the first and second set of drivers, boiler front opening has lip across bottom, boiler front held to boiler by two

316 K-5 with U Shaped Drawbar

21115 K-5, the Last in the Line

322AC with U Shaped Crosshead Guide

21130 Hudson with "American Flyer Lines" in Serif Face on tender

21139 Northern with Sintered Iron Drivers

21140 Northern with Nylon Drivers

21165 Casey Jones with "Chicago Milwaukee St. Paul" Herald

Photo by Jack Radcliff, from the Newcomer Collection

long brass springs. "310" in silver on cab beneath window. The 310 has a full compliment of handrails: one on the pilot, two from the pilot to the boiler front, one around and over the top of the boiler, one on each side of the boiler, two at the rear of the cab. The tender has a sheet metal frame, a die-cast superstructure and front and rear steps that are integral to the casting. There are four shiny handrails on the tender with one on each corner. There is a black ladder on the rear of the tender with a small handrail at the top of the ladder. The tender has Type A trucks with a link coupler with no weight and a thin shank link, embossed "PAT. NO. 2240137." Two separate wires with male plugs go from the tender to a fiber panel with female receptacles on the loco cab rear.

(A) Tender is lettered "PENNSYLVANIA" in silver. Engine has two brass spring loaded buttons on the underside of the motor, 1946.   **30 45 75**

(B) Tender has "AMERICAN FLYER LINES" in silver with serifs and silver "PRR" in Keystone; no buttons on motor, 1947, Caples Collection.   **20 30 50**

311 4-6-2, K-5, 1946, similar to 310(A), but with choo-choo, not manufactured.

312 4-6-2, 1946, 1948 and 1951, K-5, black four piece die-cast locomotive.

(A) Smoke and choo-choo in tender, black rubber hose goes from tender through engine to stack, reverse unit in loco with reverse lever through slot in boiler top, separate trailing truck with die-cast frame, short drawbar approximately 1¾" long, channel shaped crosshead guide fastened to steam cylinder but not to boiler at rear, two spring loaded brass buttons on underside of motor chassis, open space in motor chassis between the first and second set of drivers, boiler front opening has lip across the bottom. The boiler front has two long springs (1 3/16") that hold the boiler front to the boiler, the headlamp socket is mounted on the motor chassis, with a die-cast leading truck frame and full compliment of shiny handrails and marker lights.[1] The tender has a metal frame and die-cast superstructure, four shiny handrails, one at each corner, and four steps which are integral to the superstructure casting. There is a hole in the tender coal pile casting for smoke fluid; with a black painted brass round cap with a flat top and serrated edges; ladder with handrail on tender rear. Tender has Type A trucks with a thin shank link coupler embossed "PAT NO. 2240137," no weight; two separate wires with male plugs go from tender to loco. Tender has silver "PENNSYLVANIA" on side, loco has silver "312" beneath cab windows, brass wheels on one side of each tender truck, shiny lever protrudes through tender floor and turns choo-choo off and on, 1946, Balint and Caples Collections.   **30 45 70**

(B) Same as (A) but does not have two buttons on motor nor open space in chassis between the first and second set of drivers; tender lettered "AMERICAN FLYER LINES" in silver with serifs and "PRR" in Keystone; Type A truck with a link coupler and thick shank, no coupler weight, 1947, Newcomer Collection.   **20 30 40**

(C) Smoke and choo-choo in engine driven by main motor, reverse unit in tender with lever protruding through tender floor; trailing truck wheels incorporated with 3½" drawbar; drawbar is connected to leading tender truck, L shaped crosshead guide fastened in front to steam cylinder in rear to boiler; boiler front has rivet on right side to hold it snugly to boiler, the headlamp socket is mounted on boiler front, the leading truck of the loco has a die-cast frame, the tender has a sheet metal frame and a die-cast superstructure with integral step castings front and rear;

there are black finished handrails on the front corners and shiny metal handrails on the rear corners; with two marker lights on tender rear; tender has white "PRR" in white Keystone and white "AMERICAN FLYER LINES" in serif face; the tender has a ladder on rear with a handrail at the top of the ladder. A four prong fiber plate goes from the tender to plug into a matching plate on rear of the loco; the loco is handsomely decorated with shiny handrails from the pilot to the boiler, around and over the boiler front, along the length of the boiler and at the rear of the cab. An additional piece of dark finished piping runs up the left side of the boiler. Inside the boiler opening, at the bottom, there are two ridges which run back into the boiler; there is no lip across the front. The tender has Type B sheet metal trucks with a brass weight and a thick shank link coupler, there is no hole in the tender coal pile; 1948, Newcomer and Caples Collections.   **20 30 40**

(D) Similar to (C) but tender lettered "AMERICAN FLYER" and "PRR" in Keystone in white, the boiler front is fastened by a one piece brass spring with two ends each 7/8" long, the headlamp socket is mounted on the rear of the boiler front, black sheet metal trucks, black coupler weight, thick shank link coupler, 1951.   **20 30 40**

312AC 4-6-2, 1949-51, K-5, black four piece die-cast locomotive, smoke and choo-choo in engine, reverse unit in tender, trailing truck wheels incorporated with drawbar, drawbar connects to leading tender truck, L shaped crosshead guide fastens in rear to loco boiler, headlamp socket is mounted on boiler front; the locomotive comes with a full compliment of handrails and jewels.[1] The K type tender has a sheet metal frame and a die-cast superstructure with integral step castings rear and front.

(A) Tender lettered "AMERICAN FLYER LINES" in white with serifs and "PRR" in Keystone, 1949.   **25 35 50**

(B) Tender lettered "AMERICAN FLYER" in white without serifs, "PRR" in Keystone, 1950-51.   **25 35 50**

313 4-6-2, 1955-57, K-5, black four piece die-cast locomotive, smoke and choo-choo in engine, red plastic insert in stack gives red glow to smoke, Pull-mor traction tires, die-cast trailing truck and separate drawbar, small armature motor with ½" wide field laminations in 1955 but large armature motor with ¾" wide field laminations in 1956-57, reverse unit in K-5 type tender.

(A) Tender with "AMERICAN FLYER LINES" in white and "PRR" in white Keystone.   **30 40 50**

(B) Tender with "AMERICAN FLYER" in white and "PRR" in white Keystone.   **30 40 50**

314AW 4-6-2, 1949-50, K-5 black four piece die-cast engine, smoke and choo-choo in loco are driven by motor, in the tender the motor-driven whistle is activated by a D.C. relay in a similar fashion to Lionel's. Trailing truck wheels are incorporated with a long 3½" drawbar; drawbar connects to leading tender truck, L shaped crosshead guide fastens in rear to loco boiler, boiler front has rivet on one side to make snug fit with boiler; headlamp socket is mounted on boiler front, the loco's leading truck has a die-cast frame. Tender has a sheet metal frame and a die-cast

[1] The K-5 comes with a magnificent set of handrails and jewels. Handrails include: one on the pilot, two from the pilot to the boiler, one over the boiler front, two along the length of the boiler and two at the rear of the cab. The jewels, also called marker lights actually are small pieces of cut glass or plastic. There are two jewels on the pilot, two flank the boiler and two grace the rear of the tender. The tender also has handrails: one in each of the four corners, and a handrail on the top of the sheet metal ladder found on the rear.

342DC

343

343 with plastic curtain

346

21155   21158

302AC

21100

superstructure with integral step castings rear and front, black finished handrails on each corner of the tender, black finished separate ladder and two marker lights on tender rear. Tender has white "PRR" in white Keystone and "AMERICAN FLYER" in white sans serif face. The tender contains American Flyer's best sounding whistle; which had a short life span because it infringed on a Lionel whistle patent. The Flyer whistle requires a full 15 volts to operate, comes with a special whistle controller and is easily overpowered by the choo-choo. The locomotive is handsomely decorated with handrails: from the pilot to the boiler, over the boiler at the front and along the length of each side of the boiler, on the rear of the cab and has a pipe in a dark finish over one side of the boiler and a spreader bar across the back of the cab. "5698" is embossed on the boiler front. The tender has a Type C truck made from a worn die and a black coupler weight with no hole in the tender coal pile casting, Caples Collection. **60   70   100**

315   4-6-2, 1952, K-5, black die-cast engine, smoke, choo-choo and air chime whistle. Die-cast K-5 type tender with link coupler, 17¾". "PRR" in Keystone and "AMERICAN FLYER" silk-screened on tender; catalogued in 1951, but not produced until 1952.

30   40   55

316   4-6-2, 1953-54, K-5, four piece black die-cast engine, smoke and choo-choo in engine, red plastic insert in stack gives red glow to smoke, Pull-mor traction tires on rear drivers, die-cast trailing truck with separate drawbar, no slot in boiler top, short 1¾" long drawbar. L shaped crosshead guide fastens to steam cylinder at one end and to side of boiler at other, removable boiler front; boiler bottom has two grooves that are visible when the boiler front is removed, one piece brass spring on the back of the boiler front with two ends each 7/8" long; lamp socket mounted on rear of boiler front; die-cast leading truck frame, loco with full compliment of shiny handrails.[1] Tender has sheet metal frame and die-cast superstructure without hole in coal pile, four wires fasten to fiberboard and go from tender to plug into matching board in rear of loco's cab; fifth wire provides more constant current for headlight; tender has full compliment of handrails all of which are darkened. There is a darkened ladder on the rear of the tender with a handrail at the top of the ladder. Tender has air chime whistle and "PRR" in white inside of white Keystone and either "AMERICAN FLYER LINES" or "AMERICAN FLYER" on side; sintered iron truck side frames, knuckle couplers.
(A)   "AMERICAN FLYER LINES" in white with serifs on tender, flat ovals on trucks, Caples and Newcomer Collections. **40   60   80**
(B)   "AMERICAN FLYER" in white on tender. **40   60   80**

317   4-6-2, K-5, four piece black die-cast engine, reverse unit in engine, large armature motor, extraordinarily rare, Carnes Collection. **No Reported Sales**

320   4-6-4, 1946-47, Hudson, black four piece die-cast engine with New York Central type tender, sheet metal frame and die-cast superstructure with link coupler, no smoke or choo-choo.
(A)   Locomotive with spring loaded brass buttons on motor underside, channel type crosshead guide, round head valve gear rivets, boiler front held to boiler by two brass springs 1 3/16" long, lip across bottom of boiler visible when boiler front is removed; headlamp socket mounted on motor chassis; no hollow space on motor chassis when viewed from side; "320" in silver on loco cab beneath window. The tender is lettered "NEW YORK CENTRAL" in silver and has die-cast six-wheel trucks with three axles and six wheels; three wheels on one side of each truck are brass; two wires go from tender and plug into loco, thin shank link coupler embossed "PAT. NO. 2240137," no coupler weight, Patterson Collection. **40   60   80**

(B)   Locomotive does not have brass buttons on motor underside, channel type crosshead guide, hex head valve gear rivets, boiler front with two brass springs 1 3/16" long, with lip across bottom of boiler, headlamp socket mounted on motor chassis, no hollow spaces in motor, "320" in silver on loco cab beneath window. The tender is lettered "AMERICAN FLYER LINES" and "NEW YORK CENTRAL SYSTEM" in silver inside a silver oval, die-cast six-wheel trucks with three axles and six wheels; three brass wheels on one side of each truck, thick shank link coupler and no coupler weight. **40   60   80**

321   4-6-4, 1946-47, Hudson, mentioned as a version of the 322 in the catalogue but not specifically cited with a number, black die-cast four piece engine with New York Central tender with die-cast superstructure. Reported with or without smoke and choo-choo. Tender with link coupler.
(A)   Locomotive with spring-loaded brass buttons on motor underside, channel type crosshead guide, round head valve gear rivets, boiler front with two brass springs 1 3/16" long, reverse unit in engine with lever protruding through a slot in the boiler top, lip across bottom of boiler, silver "321" on cab side beneath window, headlight socket mounted on motor chassis; there are no hollow spaces in the motor chassis. Tender is lettered with silver "NEW YORK CENTRAL" and has die-cast six-wheel trucks with three axles and six wheels. Each truck has three brass wheels on one side. Choo-choo and smoke units if present are located in the tender. In the sample examined, the choo-choo/smoke unit is held in place by two screws from inside the tender; there is a small lever protruding through the tender floor which turns the choo-choo motor off and on. Two wires run from the tender and plug into the rear of the loco, with link coupler with thin shank embossed "PAT. NO. 2240137," no coupler weight, Patterson Collection.

100   150   200
(B)   Same as (A) but loco does not have brass buttons on the motor underside; with hex head valve gear rivets; tender is lettered on side "NEW YORK CENTRAL SYSTEM" in silver, in silver oval, and "AMERICAN FLYER LINES" in silver; thick shank link coupler, no coupler weight.

75   100   150
322   4-6-4, 1946-50, Hudson, black four part die-cast locomotive, four-wheel die-cast trailing truck, full compliment of handrails,[2] tender with sheet metal frame and die-cast superstructure with six-wheel die-cast trucks and link couplers.
(A)   Reverse unit lever protrudes through slot in the top of the boiler, channel shaped crosshead guide fastens to steam cylinder but not to boiler, two spring loaded brass buttons on underside of motor chassis; boiler opening has lip across the bottom; the boiler front has two brass springs each 1 3/16" long which hold the boiler front to the boiler, round head valve gear rivets, silver "322" on cab beneath window. The headlamp socket is mounted on the motor chassis; the tender is lettered "NEW YORK CENTRAL" in silver and contains a small motor which drives the bellows type choo-choo and smoke generator. The smoke is carried from the tender to the loco stack by a rubber hose. Because the bellows is driven by a separate motor, smoke is produced while the engine is in neutral; a thin shank link coupler embossed "PA 2240137" is found on the tender rear, there is no coupler weight, 1946. **75   100   150**

[2]The Hudson comes with a pair of handrails from the pilot to the boiler and running the length of the boiler, there is a pair of handrails along the rear of the cab. There are three pipes mounted on the boiler, there are railings on each of the tender corners and a railing on the rear tender deck.

(B) Same as (A) but no brass buttons with hex head valve gear rivets, tender has silver lettered "AMERICAN FLYER LINES" and "NEW YORK CENTRAL SYSTEM" in silver oval; thick shank link coupler without embossed letters, no coupler weight, 1947. **60 80 120**

(C) No slot in boiler top, L shaped crosshead guide fastens to steam cylinder and to boiler, no buttons on motor chassis, boiler has two ridges which run longitudinally along the base of the boiler back towards the rear, the boiler front has a brass rivet on the right side which causes the boiler front to fit snugly in the boiler; hex head valve gear rivets, white "322" on cab beneath window, the headlamp socket is mounted on the rear of the boiler front; there is a hollow space in the motor chassis behind the first set of drivers; the piston type choo-choo and smoke are located in the boiler and held in place by a screw from the bottom of the motor chassis. The tender is lettered in white with serifs "AMERICAN FLYER LINES" and in white oval "NEW YORK CENTRAL SYSTEM." The reverse unit is mounted in the tender and its lever protrudes through the tender floor; the reverse unit is held in place by three screws behind the lever through the tender floor; there are four wires running from the tender to the loco in a cloth covered wire, they are mounted on a fiber panel which plugs into a matching panel on the rear of the loco, 1948, Patterson Collection. **50 75 100**

322AC 4-6-4, 1949-50, Hudson, black four piece die-cast engine with New York Central type tender with sheet metal frame and die-cast superstructure; reverse unit in tender with lever protruding through tender floor; smoke and choo-choo in boiler; a full compliment of handrails on the loco and tender. [2]

(A) Boiler front is held in place by a rivet on one side of boiler front, lamp socket is mounted on the back of the boiler front, regular size numbers "322AC" in white below cab window, thicker stanchions on pilot, two black boiler bands, tender is lettered "AMERICAN FLYER LINES" in white serif face and "NEW YORK CENTRAL SYSTEM" in white inside white oval, link coupler with brass weight. Tender has slot for reverse unit lever; behind slot in tender floor are two shiny screws that hold reverse unit, long rivet on crossbar on car rear holds tender drawbar, Degano Collection. **30 45 70**

(B) Boiler front held in by separate brass springs each 7/8" long, headlamp socket is mounted on back of boiler front, "322AC" in thick white numbers below cab window, thinner stanchions on pilot, one nickel and one black finished boiler band. Tender is lettered "AMERICAN FLYER" in heavy sans serif white letters and "NEW YORK CENTRAL SYSTEM" in oval, link coupler with black coupler weight; through tender floor in front of reverse slot are two bent over tabs that hold reverse unit in place, short rivet on crossbar on cab rear holds tender drawbar, Passman Collection. **30 45 70**

324AC 4-6-4, 1950, Hudson four piece black die-cast loco with tender with sheet metal frame and die-cast superstructure. The boiler front is fastened to the boiler by a one piece brass spring with two short ends, each 7/8". The headlamp socket is mounted on the rear of the boiler front with the same rivets that mount the brass spring. Two longitudinal ridges run from the boiler front along the boiler bottom towards the rear; there is an open space behind the first set of drivers; the choo-choo and smoke units are located in the boiler and fasten by one bottom screw; there are L shaped crosshead guides and hex head valve gear rivets. Four wires from the tender are encased in a cloth cover and attached to a fiber panel with four prongs. This panel plugs into a matching female panel on the rear of the loco. "324 AC" is found on the loco cab beneath the windows in one line in white. The

tender is lettered in white on side "AMERICAN FLYER" with serifs and "NEW YORK CENTRAL SYSTEMS" inside of a white oval. The reverse unit is located in the tender, its lever protrudes through the tender floor; it is held in place by two bent over prongs in front of the lever and one screw behind the lever. The tender has simulated six-wheel trucks with the center axle and wheels missing. In place of the axle is one nickel finished cylinder with a spring-loaded plunger with a flat surface that contacts the rail. There is an electronic whistle in the tender which requires a special controller that plugs into 110-120 house current (includes two adjustment screws on the bottom). There is a link coupler with a thick shank and a black weight, Patterson Collection. **40 60 80**

325 4-6-4, 1951, Hudson, four piece black die-cast loco with New York Central type tender with sheet metal frame and die-cast superstructure. Catalogued in 1951 but probably not manufactured, although the 325AC was made. See next entry.

325AC 4-6-4, 1951, Hudson, four piece black die-cast loco with New York Central type tender with sheet metal frame and die-cast superstructure. The boiler front is fastened to the boiler by a one piece brass spring with two short ends, each 7/8". The headlamp socket is mounted on the rear of the boiler front with the same rivets that mount the brass spring. Two longitudinal ridges run from the boiler front along the boiler bottom towards the rear, the choo-choo and smoke units are located in the boiler, there are L shaped crosshead guides and hex head valve gear rivets. "325AC" is found on the loco cab beneath the windows. The tender is lettered "NEW YORK CENTRAL SYSTEMS" inside of a white oval and "AMERICAN FLYER" in white serif face; the reverse unit is located in the tender and its lever protrudes through the tender floor; there is an air chime whistle in the tender that is operated by a special controller hooked up to the transformer. The controller generates an electric signal that is carried to the track by wires and sounds something like a whistle when amplified by the speaker in the tender; with a link coupler with thick shank and black coupler weight on tender rear. **30 45 60**

K325 4-6-4, 1952, Hudson, four piece black die-cast loco with New York Central type tender with sheet metal frame and die-cast superstructure. The boiler front is fastened to the boiler with a one piece brass spring with two short ends each 7/8". The headlight socket is mounted on the rear of the boiler front with the same rivets that mount the brass spring. Two longitudinal ridges run from the boiler front along the boiler bottom towards the rear; the choo-choo and smoke units are located in the boiler; there are L shaped crosshead guides and hex head valve gear rivets. "K325" is found in white on the loco cab beneath the windows. A clear plastic insert is found in the stack which directs light upward into the smoke. The tender's side is lettered in white "AMERICAN FLYER LINES" and in white oval "NEW YORK CENTRAL SYSTEMS," the reverse unit is in the tender and its lever protrudes through the tender floor; there is an air chime whistle in the tender that is operated by a special controller hooked up to the transformer and to the track. This is one of the first two engines to come with a knuckle coupler; it is part of set K5206W, Balint Collection. **30 45 60**

326 4-6-4, 1953-56, Hudson, four piece black die-cast loco with New York Central type tender with sheet metal frame and die-cast superstructure. The boiler front is fastened to the boiler by a single brass spring with two short ends each 7/8" long; the headlamp socket is fastened to the rear of the boiler front with the same rivets that mount the brass spring. Two longitudinal ridges run from the boiler front along the bottom of the boiler towards rear; there is no open space behind the first set of drivers; the choo-choo and smoke units are in the boiler; there are L shaped crosshead guides and hex head valve gear rivets; the motor has a large armature and its field laminations are ¾" wide (compared with the ½" field laminations on small armature motors). The motor has Pull-mor traction tires on the rear set of drivers, there is a white "326" on the cab beneath the windows, the inside of the stack is painted white and there is a red plastic insert in the stack to give a red glow to the smoke. Five wires go from the tender to the loco, four wires (two gray, one green and one black) in a square design are non-disconnecting from the loco, the fifth, a separate black wire, provides continuous headlight illumination. The reverse unit is in tender, its lever protrudes through the tender floor; two bent over prongs in front of the lever and one screw behind the lever hold the reverse unit to the floor, there is an air chime whistle in the tender; the tender has six-wheel die-cast trucks with three axles, its center wheels are plastic, it has an operating knuckle coupler, with white lettered "NEW YORK CENTRAL SYSTEM" in white oval and "AMERICAN FLYER LINES" with serifs, on side, Patterson Collection.   **30   45   60**

332   4-8-4, 1946-1949, NORTHERN, black four piece die-cast locomotive has Union Pacific type tender with sheet metal frame and die-cast superstructure, combined loco-tender length is 21½", full compliment of loco and tender handrailings, turbo generator on left side of boiler. Called a Challenger by Gilbert the 332 is actually a Northern since a Challenger has a 4-6-6-4 wheel arrangement.

(A)   Reverse unit in boiler with lever protruding through a slot in boiler top, channel shaped crosshead guide fastens to steam cylinder but not boiler, two spring loaded brass buttons on underside of motor chassis, boiler front has two brass springs each 1 3/16" long which hold the boiler front to the boiler, boiler opening has a lip with center groove, round head valve gear rivets, silver "332" on cab beneath window and on number boards and headlamp socket mounts on motor chassis. Tender is lettered "UNION PACIFIC" in silver sans serif face; it contains a small motor which drives the bellows type choo-choo and smoke generator; smoke is carried by a rubber hose to the loco stack; since the bellows is driven by a separate motor, smoke is produced while the loco is in neutral; link coupler with thin shank embossed "PAT. NO. 2240137" and no coupler weight; six-wheel trucks with die-cast sides, 1946, Jones Collection.   **400 600 1000**

(B)   No reverse unit, no brass buttons, with hex head valve gear rivets; tender has silver lettered "AMERICAN FLYER LINES" and "UNION PACIFIC" on shield, thick shank link coupler without embossed letters, no coupler weight; D.C. motor, with permanent magnet field, without laminated field and field winding, Caples Collection.

                                               75 100 125

(C)   No reverse unit, L shaped crosshead guide fastens to steam cylinder and to boiler, no brass buttons, boiler front with rivet on right side that fits snugly against boiler sides; lamp socket mounted on boiler front rear, boiler opening shows ridges along the boiler bottom that run longitudinally; boiler front has Lucite lens, two simulated lenses and bell casting, hex head valve gear rivets, "332" in white on cab beneath window and on number board, smoke and choo-choo mechanisms in loco, D.C. motor with permanent magnet field rather than laminated field with windings. The tender reads "AMERICAN FLYER LINES" in white face towards rear and "UNION PACIFIC" in white shield towards front, six-wheel die-cast trucks, link coupler with brass coupler weight, two male leads from tender plug into fiber board on loco cab rear, Caples Collection.

                                               65 100 125

332AC   4-8-4, 1950-51, Northern, black four part die-cast locomotive, choo-choo and smoke in engine, L shaped crosshead guide

fastens at one end to steam cylinders and at other to boiler, "332AC" rubber stamped in white on loco cab beneath windows and "332" white rubber stamped on marker boards at the front, full compliment of railings on loco and tender, removable boiler front with one piece brass spring with two ends, each end 7/8" long; headlamp socket mounted on the rear of the boiler front. The tender has a sheet metal frame and a die-cast superstructure. White "UNION PACIFIC" shield towards front end of tender and "AMERICAN FLYER" in white without serifs towards the back, four wires inside of covering, the four wires fasten to male plugs in fiber board which plug into and carry circuit from tender to matching female plugs on fiber board at loco rear. Tender has six-wheel trucks with three axles and six wheels; link coupler on tender with thick shank and black coupler weight; combined length of loco and tender is 21½". Loco has white stripes along the length of boiler walkway and along cab bottom edge; boiler front has headlight with Lucite lens plus two smaller simulated round lenses and die-cast bell, turbo generator piece on left boiler side towards back is often missing. Reverse unit is in tender and lever protrudes through floor, Caples Collection.   **50   75 125**
334AC
4-8-4, 1950, Northern, black four part die-cast locomotive, extraordinarily rare, Carnes Collection.   **No Reported Sales**
334DC, 1950, Northern, black four part die-cast engine, smoke and choo-choo in engine, remote control electronic whistle in tender, L type crosshead guide fastens at one end to steam cylinder and at other to boiler, "334DC" rubber stamped in white on loco cab beneath window, full compliment of railings on loco and tender, 2 removable boiler front with one piece brass spring with two ends, each 7/8" long, headlamp socket mounts on boiler front. No reverse unit because there is a D.C. motor. D.C. motor has permanent magnet field rather than wound field with laminations. Tender with sheet metal frame and die-cast superstructure; white "UNION PACIFIC" shield towards front of tender and white "AMERICAN FLYER" towards rear; tender has link coupler with black coupler weight. It is reported that towards the end of 1950, the 332 without whistle and the 337 Whistling Billboard were substituted in sets for the 334DC.

                                               75 125 175
335
4-8-4, 1951, Northern, black die-cast engine. The 1951 catalogue shows on page 12 a Union Pacific numbered 335 but the description is for a 332AC . No Listing for a 335 appears in the 1951 price list. Probably it was never made.

                                         No Reported Sales
K335
4-8-4, 1952, Northern, black die-cast engine, red glowing smoke, choo-choo and air chime whistle. White "K 335" rubber stamped on engine. White rubber stamped "UNION PACIFIC" in shield and "AMERICAN FLYER" without serifs on die-cast U.P. type tender with simulated die-cast six-wheel trucks and knuckle coupler, 21½". White stripe along engine walkway. Five wires between engine and tender. Wire handrails on engine and tender. "335" on number boards on loco front. Note that the 1952 catalogue shows a 332 rather than K335. Degano Collection.

                                               60   90 125
336
4-8-4, 1953-56, Northern, black four part die-cast locomotive, choo-choo and smoke in boiler, remote control air chime whistle in tender, Pull-mor traction tires on rear drivers, L type crosshead guide fastens at one end to steam cylinder and at other to boiler, "336" rubber stamped in white on loco cab beneath windows and on marker boards at the front, full compliment of railings on loco and tender, 2 removable boiler front with one piece brass spring with two ends each 7/8" long, headlamp socket mounted on boiler front, metal bell over boiler front. Tender with sheet metal frame and die-cast superstructure;

white "UNION PACIFIC" shield at front on tender side and "AMERICAN FLYER LINES" in sans serif face; four wires between loco and tender with no disconnect device or with fiber plate with plugs; tender has simulated six-wheel trucks with no center axle on trucks, knuckle coupler on tender, combined loco-tender length is 21½". Loco has white stripe along edge of boiler walkway and along bottom edge of cab; boiler front has headlight with Lucite lens plus two smaller round lenses and die-cast bell, turbo generator piece on left boiler side towards back is often missing.   **75   100   125**

340   0-8-0, switcher, black die-cast engine, "340" on loco cab beneath window, bunker tender with bunker walls set back from tender sides, extraordinarily rare, (see 342 for more background), Carnes Collection.   **No Reported Sales**

342   0-8-0, 1946-48 and 1952, switcher, black die-cast engine, white or silver "342" on loco cab beneath window, bunker tender with bunker walls set back from tender sides. This engine is based on Gilbert's highly innovative 1941 0-8-0 Nickel Plate switcher, 574 and 575. In the view of many collectors, the 342 is the most sophisticated and handsome Gilbert locomotive. Its intricate detailing and in particular the valve gear assembly which consists of a main rod, side rod, eccentric rod and reversing rod lever make this a joy to watch in action. It features remarkable pulling power because of its eight wheels and properly proportioned weight distribution. Other important embellishments are: a front crossbar for coupling purposes, a railing across the pilot, handrailings linking the pilot and the walkways along the boiler, railings the length of the boiler, railings above the cab windows and behind the cab. On the tender there are railings along the front edges above the steps, there is a rear ladder with a handrail at the top and a light on the back of the deck.

(A)   1946, smoke and choo-choo in tender, hence the 342 could puff smoke while in neutral because of its separate motor in the tender; reverse unit in loco, direct wiring between loco and tender, tender lettered "NICKEL PLATE ROAD," brass buttons on chassis bottom, valve gear with round head rivets. Tender has link coupler with thin shank and no coupler weights; rare.   **400 600 800**

(B)   1947, smoke and choo-choo in tender, reverse unit in loco, direct wiring between loco and tender, tender lettered "AMERICAN FLYER LINES" and "NICKEL PLATE ROAD" in smaller letters in upper corner; no brass buttons on chassis bottom, valve gear with hex head rivets, loco wiring plugs into tender, A.C. motor. Tender has link coupler with thick shank and no coupler weight.
                    100 150 225

(C)   Same as (B) but D.C. version comes without a reverse unit and the motor has a permanent magnet rather than a field coil.   **100 150 225**

(D)   1948, smoke and choo-choo in loco driven by motor; reverse unit in tender, loco wiring plugs into tender, tender lettered "AMERICAN FLYER LINES" and "NICKEL PLATE ROAD" in smaller letters in upper corner, no brass buttons on chassis bottom, valve gear with hex head rivets, link coupler with brass coupler weight.   **40 60 85**

(E)   1952, smoke and choo-choo in loco, boiler front held in by one piece brass spring with two ends each 7/8" long, headlamp socket mounted on the rear of boiler front, red plastic liner inside of stack. Tender contains reverse unit with lever protruding through floor and is lettered "AMERICAN FLYER" in sans serif face and "NICKEL PLATE ROAD" inside of white box outline, Type D nine spring trucks, link coupler with black coupler weight, Passman Collection.   **40 60 85**

342AC   0-8-0, 1949-51, Nickel Plate switcher, black four piece die-cast engine with smoke and choo-choo in boiler, reverse unit in

tender; white "342 AC" in large or small white rubber stamping beneath cab window; "NICKEL PLATE ROAD" in white outlined box, and sans serif "AMERICAN FLYER" on tender, die-cast bunker tender with raised set back, rectangular sides on forward half, drawbar on front of engine and link coupler on tender rear; wire handrails on engine.

(A)   1949, "342AC" in large type, Type B trucks.   **40   65   80**
(B)   1950, "342AC" in small type, Type B trucks.   **40   65   80**
(C)   1951, "342AC" in small type, Type D nine spring trucks.
                    40   65   80

342DC   0-8-0, 1948-50, Nickel Plate switcher, black die-cast engine, smoke, choo-choo, DC motor with permanent magnet field; no reverse unit, silver or white "342DC" in small or large letters, rivet type boiler front clip or spring type boiler front clip, brass or black coupler weight, 14¾" long.

(A)   1948, silver "342DC" in large thin letters on loco cab, tender lettered "AMERICAN FLYER LINES" and in smaller letters "NICKEL PLATE ROAD," rivet type boiler front clip. Tender has link coupler, brass coupler weight.   **40   65   80**

(B)   1948, silver "342DC" in thick very large letters, tender lettered "AMERICAN FLYER LINES" and in smaller letters "NICKEL PLATE ROAD," rivet type boiler front clip, then tender with link coupler and brass coupler weight.   **40   65   80**

(C)   1949, white "342DC" in thick, very large letters, tender lettered "AMERICAN FLYER" in sans serif face and "NICKEL PLATE ROAD" inside of white box outline, rivet type boiler front clip; tender with link coupler and black coupler weight.   **40   65   80**

(D)   1950, white "342DC" in smaller thick letters, tender lettered "AMERICAN FLYER" in sans serif face and "NICKEL PLATE ROAD" inside of white box outline, one piece spring boiler front clip with two ends each 7/8" long. Tender has link coupler and black coupler weight.
                    40   65   80

343   0-8-0, 1953-54, Nickel Plate switcher, black die-cast engine, red glowing smoke, choo-choo and Pull-mor motor. White "343" rubber stamped on engine; eight-wheel die-cast tender with rear light, 14¾". Front of engine and rear of tender have knuckle couplers. Reverse unit in tender except for (C).

(A)   1953, tender silk-screened "AMERICAN FLYER LINES" without serif and "NICKEL PLATE ROAD" in square.
                    50   65   90
(B)   1954, tender silk-screened "AMERICAN FLYER" and in square "NICKEL PLATE ROAD."   **40   70   95**
(C)   1956, tender lettered "AMERICAN FLYER LINES" in white and "NICKEL PLATE ROAD" white herald; four step reverse unit in rear of cab, plastic curtain covers reverse unit, Newcomer Collection.   **55   75   100**

346   0-8-0, 1955, Nickel Plate switcher, black die-cast engine, red flowing smoke, choo-choo, Pull-mor power and air chime whistle. White "346" rubber stamped on engine and "NICKEL PLATE ROAD" in square and "AMERICAN FLYER LINES" silk-screened on die-cast bunker type eight-wheel tender with light and knuckle coupler 14¾". This was the only switcher with a whistle. Early 346s had four-position reverse unit mount on rear of motor in engine cab. It proved unsatisfactory and later switchers were manufactured with a two-position unit, Newcomer Collection.   **80 120 150**

350   4-6-2, 1948-50, Pacific, royal blue die-cast torpedo nose engine with light; "THE ROYAL BLUE" and "350" rubber stamped in white on engine tender with link coupler, wire handrails, black coal load; engine and tender 17½" long; two wires between engine and tender. The boiler and tender are basically the same as the prewar 0 versions; reverse unit in engine.

(A) 1948, tender embossed in area that is lettered "AMERI-CAN FLYER LINES" with serifs; tender drawbar connected to a brace across the back of the cab; B&O herald found both forward and rear of "AMERICAN FLYER LINES," wire handrails.   **35   50   75**

(B) 1948, same as (A) but tender drawbar and engine trailing truck as single unit, cast on handrails.   **30   45   70**

(C) 1950, tender not embossed in lettered area; tender lettered "AMERICAN FLYER" in heavy black sans serif lettering; engine lettered "THE ROYAL BLUE" in heavy block lettering; engine and tender are lighter shade of blue than (A) or (B); tender drawbar and engine trailing truck are single unit; no handrails on loco front, black coupler weight on tender, railing on tender rear, Caples Collection.   **20   35   50**

(D) Tender not embossed in lettered area, tender rubber stamped "AMERICAN FLYER LINES" in serif lettering; B&O emblem in front of other tender lettering, tender trucks have black sheet metal side frames with two embossed areas with limited detail; loco and tender are darker blue than (C); railing on tender rear; black coupler weight, Caples Collection.   **20   35   50**

(E) Same as (D) but slots in truck side frames, brass coupler weights, Caples Collection.   **20   35   50**

(F) Same as (C) but handrails on loco front, Walsh Collection.   **20   35   50**

353 4-6-2, 1950-51, Pacific, brilliant circus red die-cast torpedo nose engine. Yellow "353" and "AMERICAN FLYER CIRCUS" rubber stamped on engine; eight-wheel sheet metal tender with nickel journals and black coal load, 17 5/8". Two wires between engine and tender, reverse unit in engine.   **40   60   85**

354 4-6-2, 1954, Pacific, satin silver finish plastic torpedo nose engine, red glowing smoke, choo-choo and headlight. Red, white and blue American Flyer decal shield on cow catcher, silver and blue Silver Bullet decal on engine; sheet metal satin silver finish eight-wheel knuckle coupler tender.   **30   45   60**

355 4-6-2, 1950-51, Pacific, brilliant circus red torpedo nose engine, eight-wheel sheet metal tender.

(A) Die-cast body, wire handrails, extremely rare, Carnes Collection.   **No Reported Sales**

(B) Plastic body, extremely rare, Carnes Collection.   **No Reported Sales**

356 4-6-2, Pacific, chrome or silver finished black plastic torpedo nose engine, smoke, choo-choo in engine; red, white and blue "AMERICAN FLYER LINES" decal shield on pilot, gold and blue "SILVER BULLET" decal on engine side, headlamp socket screws to underside of pilot, main rod and value eccentric rod slide back and forth in small metal brackets that are fastened on the inside of the steam cylinders; "356" in blue on yellow background decal beneath cab window, spreader bar across cab rear, combination trailing truck and drawbar; tender has black painted sheet metal frame, silver or chrome plated superstructure; sheet metal ladder on tender rear, tender has reverse unit fastened by two bent prongs in front of reverse lever which protrudes through floor, black painted coal pile and rear deck, gold and blue "SILVER BULLET" decal on tender side; five wires (yellow, green, red and two black) that do not disconnect between engine and tender; type D trucks (nine spring), thick shank link coupler with black coupler weight, chrome finish does not wear well and often chips, hence, a substantial premium is paid for pieces in truly excellent condition.

(A) Bright chrome finish.   **30   45   100**

(B) Dull silver finish.   **25   35   50**

L2001 4-4-0, 1963, "Casey Jones" style one piece black plastic engine, no reversing unit; "L2001" in white in recessed area under cab windows, black plastic cab windows have white parallel diagonal lines, one piece main rod, black plastic drivers, Atlantic type tender with metal frame and detailed plastic superstructure. Tender has "GAME TRAIN" logo and "CASEY JONES" in white. This engine came as part of set 20800 with a green "BUFFALO HUNT" gondola, a "FREIGHT AHEAD" caboose, a game board and enough pieces for three different games. The set did not set well and is consequently rare and brings a substantial premium. Value for the engine only.   **10   20   30**

L2002 4-4-0, 1963, "Casey Jones" style one piece black plastic engine, no reversing unit, Pull-mor traction tires on the front drivers; "L2002" in white in recessed area under cab windows, black plastic cab windows with white parallel diagonal lines, black plastic drivers. Atlantic type tender with metal frame and detailed plastic superstructure.

(A) Black tender with both "Burlington Route" logo and "AMERICAN FLYER LINES" in white.   **125 160 200**

(B) Tender with "Burlington Route" logo in black on white background and "AMERICAN FLYER LINES" in white.   **125 160 200**

(C) Tender with "ERIE" logo and "AMERICAN FLYER LINES" in white.   **100 140 175**

21004 0-6-0, 1957, uncatalogued, switcher, black plastic engine, smoke, choo-choo, light and Pull-mor power. White "21004" rubber stamped on engine and "PRR" in Keystone and "AMERICAN FLYER LINES" silk-screened on slope back eight-wheel plastic tender with operating rear light, 13 7/8". Knuckle coupler on front of engine and rear of tender; two-step reverse unit (F-R-F). on rear of loco with plastic curtain cover. Two wires between engine and tender. Considered a highly accurate model of PRR B6sb.   **80 120 150**

21005 0-6-0, 1958, switcher, black plastic engine, smoke, choo-choo, light, and Pull-mor power, two-position reverse unit with plastic curtain on rear of loco cab. White "21005" rubber stamped and white painted stripe on engine; "PRR" in Keystone and "AMERICAN FLYER LINES" silk-screened on slope back plastic eight-wheel tender with non-operating rear light. Knuckle coupler on front of engine and rear of tender, 13 7/8". Two wires between engine and tender. Engine numbered as "263" or "21005" in catalogue. Considered highly accurate model of PRR B6sb, a popular loco, it is rearer than 21004.   **100 150 190**

21015 4-6-2, 1957, Pacific, black plastic engine, smoke, choo-choo, light, and Pull-mor power. White "21015" rubber stamped on engine and "Chicago Northwestern Line" in logo and "AMERICAN FLYER LINES" silk-screened on plastic eight-wheel tender with knuckle coupler, 17 3/4". Questionable existence.   **No Reported Sales**

21045 4-6-2, 1957, Pacific, black die-cast engine, smoke, choo-choo, light and Pull-mor power. White "21045" rubber stamped on engine and "PRR" in Keystone and "AMERICAN FLYER LINES" silk-screened on eight-wheel plastic tender. There are conflicting reports concerning the existence of this engine. It is clear that boxes are found with "21045" on their ends containing 313 K-5s.   **No Reported Sales**

21059 4-6-4, 1957, Hudson, black die-cast engine, smoke, choo-choo, light, whistle, Pull-mor power and die-cast trailing truck. White "21059" rubber stamped on engine and "NEW YORK CENTRAL SYSTEM" in oval and "AMERICAN FLYER LINES" silk-screened on black die-cast bunker type tender with simulated six-wheel trucks and knuckle coupler, 19". Questionable existence.   **No Reported Sales**

21069 4-8-4, 1957, Northern, black die-cast engine, smoke, choo-choo, light, whistle, Pull-mor power and die-cast trailing truck. White "21069" rubber stamped on engine and "UNION PACIFIC" in shield and "AMERICAN FLYER" without serif silk-screened on die-cast bunker type tender with knuckle coupler and simulated six-wheel trucks, 21 1/2". Questionable existence.

No Reported Sales

21075 0-8-0, 1957, switcher, black plastic engine, smoke, choo-choo, light and Pull-mor power. White "21075" rubber stamped on engine and "NICKEL PLATE ROAD" in square and "AMERICAN FLYER LINES" with serif and eight-wheel plastic bunker type tender with operating light. Knuckle coupler on front of engine and rear of tender, 14 3/4". Questionable existence.

No Reported Sales

21084 4-6-2, 1957, uncatalogued, Pacific, black plastic engine, smoke, choo-choo, light and Pull-mor power. White "21084" rubber stamped on engine and "Chicago Northwestern Line" in logo and "AMERICAN FLYER LINES" silk-screened on plastic bunker type eight-wheel tender with knuckle coupler, 17 3/4".

30   45   65

21085 4-6-2, 1962-63, 1965, Pacific, black plastic engine, smoke, choo-choo, light, and Pull-mor power, standard or narrow white wall drive wheels, white "21085" rubber stamped on engine. Plastic eight-wheel tender with knuckle coupler or Pike Master trucks and coupler, loco has plastic drive wheels.
- (A) "CHICAGO NORTHWESTERN LINE" in logo and "AMERICAN FLYER LINES" without serifs on tender, Newcomer Collection.   20   30   40
- (B) "Chicago, Milwaukee, St. Paul and Pacific" in rectangle and "AMERICAN FLYER LINES" without serif on tender, 1963.   20   25   35
- (C) 1965, same as (B) except black wall drive wheels.

20   25   35

[210]88 4-4-0, 1959, Franklin, green, black, red and yellow, black plastic funnel stack engine with smoke and Pull-mor power with traction tires on two rear drivers, two position reverse unit in tender, and no pickups on engine. "F.Y.88 & P." paper trim printed in red and yellow on tender and "FRANKLIN" on paper trim printed in red and yellow on engine. Four wires between engine and tender.
- (A) Tender lettered "ONE OF THE FIRST FIFTY," Leonard Collection.   **No Reported Sales**
- (B) Not lettered as (A).   30   40   55

[21089] 4-4-0, 1960-61, Washington blue and gold plastic funnel stack engine with smoke, Pull-mor power with traction tires on two rear drivers, two position reverse unit in tender, and no pickups on engine. "Washington" across shield on engine and "F.Y. & P.R.R." on tender. Catalogue shows balloon stack engine, but never made. Number does not appear on engine or tender.

50   75   100

21095 4-6-2, 1957, Pacific, black die-cast engine, smoke, choo-choo, light. Pull-mor power and white wall driving wheels. White "21095" rubber stamped on engine with silk-screened "The New York New Haven and Hartford Railroad Co." and "AMERICAN FLYER LINES" on plastic eight-wheel tender with knuckle coupler, rare, Olson Collection.   300   400   500

21099 4-6-2, 1958, Pacific, black die-cast engine, smoke, choo-choo, light, air chime whistle, Pull-mor power and white wall driving wheels. White "21099" rubber stamped on engine and white stripe on engine with silk-screened "The New York New Haven and Hartford Railroad Co." and "AMERICAN FLYER LINES" on plastic eight-wheel tender with knuckle coupler, Newcomer Collection.   75   125   150

21100 4-4-2, 1957 (uncatalogued), Atlantic, black plastic engine, smoke, choo-choo, light, Pull-mor power and white wall driving wheels. White "21100" rubber stamped on engine with silk-screened "Reading Lines" in diamond and "AMERICAN FLYER LINES" without serif on eight-wheel plastic bunker type tender with knuckle coupler. This unit featured the plug and socket connection between the engine and tender.   7   10   18

21105 4-4-2, 1957-58, Atlantic, black plastic engine, smoke, choo-choo, light, Pull-mor power and white wall driving wheels. White "21105" rubber stamped on engine with silk-screened "Reading Lines" in diamond and "AMERICAN FLYER LINES" without serif on eight-wheel plastic tender with knuckle coupler. Also 1960, Newcomer Collection.   7   10   20

21106 4-4-2, 1964 (uncatalogued), Atlantic, black plastic engine, smoke, choo-choo, light, Pull-mor power and white wall driving wheels. White "21106" rubber stamped on engine and "Reading Lines" in diamond and "AMERICAN FLYER LINES" without serif and "MADE FOR SEARS" on black plastic bunker type eight-wheel tender with knuckle coupler. Also, 1959.   12   20   35

21107 4-4-2, 1964 (uncatalogued), Atlantic, black plastic engine, smoke, choo-choo, light, Pull-mor power and white wall driving wheels. White "21107" rubber stamped on engine and black plastic eight-wheel tender with knuckle coupler.
- (A) 1964, white wall driving wheels, "Burlington Route" in logo and "AMERICAN FLYER LINES" silk-screened on tender.   11   20   35
- (B) 1964, black wall driving wheels and "PRR" in Keystone and "AMERICAN FLYER LINES" silk-screened on tender.   7   15   20
- (C) 1965, white wall drivers, "Reading Lines" in diamond and "AMERICAN FLYER LINES" silk-screened on tender.   7   15   20

21115 4-6-2, 1958, K-5, four piece black die-cast engine, smoke and choo-choo in engine, red plastic insert in white painted stack gives red glow to smoke, Pull-mor traction tires on rear drivers, die-cast trailing truck, separate flat, black drawbar, no slot in boiler top, drawbar and trailing truck held by same shoulder screw on loco; drawbar may be disconnected from tender truck, L shaped crosshead guide fastens to steam cylinder at one end and boiler at other; removable boiler front, boiler has two longitudinal ridges that run along the bottom towards rear, one piece brass spring on boiler front with two ends each 7/8" long, "21115" in white beneath cab window; lamp socket mounted on boiler front rear, die-cast leading truck frame, open space on motor chassis between first and second drivers, new motor design with drum type commutator designed to work with reverse unit mounted on motor rear, full compliment of handrails -- shiny ones on engine and black finished on tender. Tender has sheet metal frame and plastic superstructure without hole in coal pile; two wires from rear of engine, one green and one black with two prong plastic plug, that plug into tender, uncovered two step reverse unit mounted on rear of motor, sintered iron truck side frames with concave ovals with four wheels, knuckle coupler; tender is lettered "PRR" in Keystone and "AMERICAN FLYER LINES" with serifs, ladder is molded plastic; marker boxes on the boiler front, pilot, and tender rear do not have green jewels. This is the only five digit Pennsy K-5 locomotive made by Gilbert and is the last of the line that began in 1940, Balint Collection.   100   175   250

21129 4-6-4, 1958, Hudson, black die-cast engine, smoke, choo-choo, light, Pull-mor power, air chime whistle and white wall driving wheels, two step reverse unit; white "21129" rubber stamped on engine and "NEW YORK CENTRAL SYSTEM" in oval and "AMERICAN FLYER LINES" with serif on plastic tender with simulated six-wheel trucks and knuckle coupler. Wire handrails on engine and tender, Balint Collection.   90   150   200

21130 4-6-4, 1959-60, 62-63, black four piece die-cast loco with New York Central type plastic tender with sheet metal frame, the boiler front is fastened to the boiler by a single brass spring with two short ends, each 7/8" long, the headlamp socket is fastened to the rear of the boiler front with the same rivets that mount the brass spring; there is open space between the first and second set of drivers when viewed from the side, the choo-choo and smoke are located in the boiler; U shaped crosshead guides fasten to the steam cylinder at one end and by an extension to the boiler at the end; nylon wheels with metal tires, some with white walls, some with black walls. Pull-mor traction tires on rear drivers, hex head valve gear rivets, redesigned motor with drum shaped commutator (as compared with flat shaped commutator on earlier motors), brushes can be serviced without removing reverse unit although boiler must be removed, white "21130" on cab beneath window, red plastic insert inside of boiler stack, however boiler stack is not painted white, two wires, one green and one black go from loco to tender, black plastic plug inserts into tender, two position reverse unit is mounted on motor rear in cab, silver finished shiny metal oblong reverse lever protrudes from the bottom of reverse unit; turned off or on by pushing up or down, drawbar and trailing truck are separate units but share the same shoulder screw on loco; the drawbar may be disconnected from the tender truck on 62 and later models. The loco trailing truck has four wheels and die-cast sides. Plastic tender is lettered "NEW YORK CENTRAL SYSTEM" in white oval and "AMERICAN FLYER LINES" in white face with serifs; the tender is molded plastic. **70 100 140**

21139 4-8-4, 1958, Northern, black four part die-cast locomotive, Union Pacific type tender with sheet metal frame and die-cast superstructure, choo-choo and smoke in boiler, remote control air chime whistle in tender, Pull-mor traction tires on rear drivers, L type crosshead guide fastens at one end to steam cylinder and at the other to boiler, "21139" rubber stamped in white on loco cab beneath windows and on marker boards at the front; full compliment of railings on loco and tender; removable boiler front with metal simulated bell over boiler front; boiler front held in place by a one piece brass spring with two ends, each 7/8" long; headlamp socket mounted on boiler front with same rivet that holds retaining spring, turbo generator piece on left boiler side back towards cab; boiler front has Lucite headlight lens plus two small simulated lenses called "jewels," two jewels on pilot, regular three piece white wall driver; two wires, one green and one black, between loco and tender, black plastic plug inserts into tender, new style motor with drum type commutator, two position reverse unit mounted on motor rear, four-wheel die-cast trailing truck on loco; drawbar shares same shoulder screw used by trailing truck, drawbar can be disconnected from leading truck screw. Tender has simulated six-wheel trucks with a diesel type pickup shoe where the middle axle would be on each truck, steel colored handrails except for the two long handrails that run from the coal pile to the rear, brass/copper color pickup wheels on tender; has "UNION PACIFIC" shield and is lettered "AMERICAN FLYER," also possibly "AMERICAN FLYER LINES," Newcomer and Balint Collections. **90 130 180**

21140 4-8-4, 1959, Northern, black die-cast engine, smoke, choo-choo, light, Pull-mor power, new nylon driving wheels with metal tires. White "21140" rubber stamped on engine and "UNION PACIFIC" in shield and "AMERICAN FLYER LINES" on plastic tender with simulated six-wheel trucks and knuckle coupler. Two step reverse unit mounted on rear of motor. Very rare, Balint and Newcomer Collections. **100 160 250**

21145 0-8-0, 1958, switcher, black die-cast engine, light, Pull-mor power and small white wall driving wheels. White "21145" rubber stamped on engine and "NICKEL PLATE ROAD" in square and

"AMERICAN FLYER LINES" on eight-wheel die-cast tender with knuckle coupler. Wire handrails on engine. Two step reverse unit mounted on rear of motor with reverse unit cover, Balint Collection. **90 150 180**

21155 0-6-0, 1958, Docksider switcher, black plastic engine, smoke, choo-choo, no light, Pull-mor power and six small white wall drivers. "21155" rubber stamped on engine with knuckle coupler front and rear, Balint Collection. **70 100 140**

21156 0-6-0, 1959, Docksider switcher, black plastic engine, Pull-mor power and six small white wall drivers. "21156" rubber stamped on engine with knuckle coupler front and rear; yellow stripes on steam chest and white stripes on side. **60 90 150**

21157 0-6-0, Docksider switcher, black plastic engine, six small black driving wheels, "21157" on engine, operating knuckle couplers, hand reverse, extremely rare, Carnes Collection. **No Reported Sales**

21158 0-6-0, 1960, Docksider switcher, uncatalogued, blue plastic engine, six small black driving wheels, "21158" in white on engine, non-opening knuckle couplers, no reverse unit, Newcomer Collection. **35 50 75**

21160 Black plastic one piece Atlantic locomotive body with no slot on boiler, metal bell is replaced by integral plastic bell, metal whistle is gone and not replaced by plastic molding, headlight lens is present but without socket assembly; Type III slide action valve gear with separate crosshead, Type VI drawbar-trailing truck assembly can be detached from tender. Loco does not have a remote reverse unit, but has a toggle switch mounted on the cab rear to change direction, traction tires on front drivers, white side wall drivers, smoke and choo-choo in boiler. A plastic/metal plug assembly goes from the loco into tender. Black plastic highly detailed Atlantic tender, white "Reading Lines" inside white diamond, white "AMERICAN FLYER LINES" in sans serif face, plastic ladder on tender rear integral to casting, female plug holes on tender side facing loco, sintered iron truck side frames, concave ovals, knuckle coupler, Degano Collection. **10 15 25**

21161 4-4-2, 1960 (uncatalogued), Atlantic, black plastic engine with no reverse unit and plastic drive wheels with metal tires. "21161" silk-screened on engine, no light or lens.
(A) Tender silk-screened "Reading Lines" in diamond and "AMERICAN FLYER" silk-screened on eight-wheel plastic tender with knuckle coupler. **7 11 20**
(B) Tender silk-screened "Reading Lines" in diamond and "AMERICAN FLYER" and "PRESTONE CAR CARE EXPRESS," solid knuckle. **30 45 70**

21165 4-4-0, 1961-62, "Casey Jones" style one-piece black plastic engine, two position remote control reverse unit mounted in the rear of loco cab, not lighted, Pull-mor traction tires on front drivers, "21165" in white in recessed area under cab windows, black plastic cab windows with white parallel diagonal lines, only one driver rod on each side links rear driver to slot in steam cylinder; black plastic drivers, Atlantic type tender with metal frame and highly detailed plastic superstructure; tender with sintered iron truck side frames and operating knuckle coupler or all plastic truck with fixed coupler.
(A) Tender lettered "ERIE" in logo and "AMERICAN FLYER LINES" in white letters, Balint Collection. **7 8 12**
(B) Tender lettered "CHICAGO MILWAUKEE ST. PAUL" in herald and "AMERICAN FLYER LINES" in sans serif white face, Newcomer Collection. **No Reported Sales**

21166 4-4-0, 1963, "Casey Jones" style black one piece plastic engine; two position remote control reverse unit mounted in loco cab,

Pull-mor traction tires on front drivers, "21166" in white in recessed area under cab windows, black plastic cab windows have white parallel diagonal lines, no headlight, only one drive rod on each side links rear driver to slot in steam cylinder, black plastic drivers; Atlantic type tender with metal frame and detailed plastic superstructure; tender with "AMERICAN FLYER LINES" in white sans serif face and "Burlington Route" in double outlined box, two non-disconnecting wires link loco and tender; Pike Master trucks and coupler. Tender has three slots on the rear of the coal bunker. There are no holes in the rectangles on the of the rear deck in the rear corners.

(A) "Burlington Route" in white letters.   4   6   10
(B) "Burlington Route" in black letters on white field.
                                                        80 140 175

21168   4-4-0, 1961-63, "Casey Jones" style black one piece plastic engine, two position remote control reverse unit mounted in rear of loco cab, smoke and choo-choo in engine, Pull-mor traction tires on front drivers, "21168" in white in recessed area under cab windows, black plastic cab windows have white parallel diagonal lines, operating headlight, two piece rod assembly with side and main rod, black plastic drivers, Atlantic type tender with metal frame and detailed plastic superstructure. Tender lettered "AMERICAN FLYER LINES" in white without serifs, and "SR THE SOUTHERN SERVES THE SOUTH." This is the only Gilbert steam engine carrying the Southern logo.   10   15   18

Four factory prototypes including the Franklin Old Timer, the New Haven electric, and the Docksider.

The Olson Collection

21088 Franklin

350 Royal Blue

353 American Flyer Circus

356 Silver Bullet with Chrome Finish

354 Silver Bullet with Silver Finish

21158 Dockside   21155 Dockside

Chapter IV
CABOOSES

ALWAYS LAST IN LINE -
AMERICAN FLYER CABOOSES

BY MAJOR ROBERT STROMBERG

We all remember our first train and when we received it. My first train arrived for Christmas in 1948. My dad, life member #110 of N.M.R.A., was enjoying the prosperity (??) of a sergeant in the postwar army. He decided to celebrate by spending more than one month's rent on a toy train for his four year old son. Dad was a died-in-the-wool scaler, so Lionel received little consideration. Only American Flyer with its tru-scale, two rail operation would do for his son. Thus, that Christmas morning our house was filled with the sounds of a choo-chooing 342. To this very day, Christmas isn't complete without the smell of American Flyer smoke fluid.

Oh, the consist was ordinary enough. There was the chunky little 0-8-0 switcher that seemed to me to be a high stepping road loco. The green 631 Gondola, brown 642 Box Car, and black 625 Shell Tank Car all seemed drab; but trains - REAL trains - were supposed to be drab. Of course, their drabness paled in the light of the star of my railroad - the 634 Searchlight Car. Ah yes, that was the car that illuminated the work of the graveyard shift as they toiled to right an errant box car or a tipsy loco. That was the car that probed the midnight skies for enemy warplanes and locked on to them while ack-ack guns sent them to their just rewards. Why, even a mom would turn off the living room lights to better observe the piercing shaft of light from that little beauty.

But what's this? Am I forgetting the most important car of all? To be certain, box cars, gondolas and tank cars are important. But not every train has every one of them. That's what that switch was for - to make a siding. And a siding was useless if not occupied by at least one car. Even the star - yes even the search-light car had to while away its daylight hours on the siding. There was one car, however, whose wheels never polished a rail on the siding. For only a fool would run any train without the caboose. Even high speed, no load testing of the engine required a caboose.

Of course, I spent hours pouring over the slick pages of the catalogues. I dreamed of the vast fleet I would amass. There would be rows of locomotives, lines of box cars across the horizon, and passenger trains dispatched to all the exotic places important enough to be pictured in the encyclopedia. But alas, my father did not believe in an allowance, and there were few jobs around for four year olds. It was to be two-and-a-half long years before my net worth approached the purchase price of a bright red cattle car. In fact, that cattle car was to be my only acquisition until 1972. At the age of twenty-seven I decided I could not afford any of my adult fantasies, so I chose to bankroll my childhood dreams. Harsh economic realities led me to believe that even childhood dreams might prove to be night-mares.

Once again, Dear-Old-Dad saved the day. "Why not," said he, "collect cabooses?" Of course! Nobody else wants them, so they are cheap. And only I secretly know the true value of cabooses. Why, cabooses were those funny little red cars that every train had to have! "And," said D-O-D, "since you're a career army officer – you ought to collect something that's always last in line!" That did it – cabooses it would be!

As my collection of cabooses expanded, I found it increasingly difficult to remember what I had at home. A list of numbers helped, but when one has ten or twelve variations of a 630, the permutations and combinations get fuzzy. My second aid was a stack of 3 x 5 cards, one per caboose. However, as the stack approached an inch in thickness it became cumbersome. When I dropped the stack at a York meet, I walked away and left it spread all over the blue hall. It was then that I hit upon the coding system that is the purpose of this chapter.

Any caboose could be represented by a code consisting of nine numerical digits. Soon, however, the number of key variations exceeded ten. Thus, I developed my latest code featuring eight alpha characters. Theoretically, that means I can uniquely identify nearly five-and-one-half trillion combinations of variations. I think I have it all covered this time!

The 1946 caboose with warped roof. Note the slots in the truck side frames.

There were more trains later - circus cars, heavyweight beauties of the lacquer era, streamlined lightweights, long, sleek 4-8-4s and Hudsons; but that humble little road switcher and its five car consist still sit on the **top** shelf in my train room. They sit, in fact, right next to the classic elegance of a Northern Pacific A-B-A with five cars. Anyone who has ever been a Flyer Collector would spot the Northern Pacific as the star of my collection. But anyone who has ever been a little boy would spot that freight, from chunky loco to bright red caboose, as a super nova - the kind seen only by a four year old on Christmas morning.

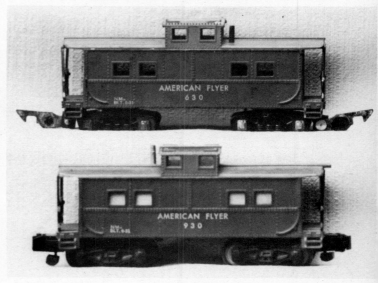

How many differences can you find between the top and bottom? 630 vs. 930; letter thickness; color of chimney, presence of window material, type of truck, type of coupler, other?

The code consists of three groups of letters of three-two and three characters. The first group of three relate to super-structure and windows. The second group of two describes the roadname and other lettering, and the final group of three covers the frame, trucks, couplers, lights and brakewheels. An X describes any variation that I cannot determine. For instance, if a caboose has been converted from link to knuckle couplers, I cannot determine what kind of link couplers it had. I have even obtained some cabooses on which the entire frame has obviously been switched. Though cabooses, by their similarity, lend themselves to this sort of system; it could also be used with other types of cars. This then is my code:

Note the difference in the "M" of AMERICAN. The top row has a straight sided M while the bottom row has a slant sided M.

CABOOSE CODE

First Character - Color and type of Plastic
(A) Red celluloid plastic, unpainted. There are many shades of red. Most shades were caused by the fading of unstable dyes. Some "rare" orange 630s have been offered for sale. However, every one that I have examined, has had a brighter underside or inside. I feel the orange is really extremely faded red.
(B) Red styrene plastic, unpainted. All except (A) are styrene plastic.
(C) Light red plastic, unpainted. This is an even coloration and is not due to fading.
(D) Red paint on white plastic.
(E) Red paint on clear plastic.
(F) Red paint on black plastic.
(G) Red paint on red plastic.
(H) Brown paint on red plastic.
(I) Brown paint on black plastic.
(J) Brown paint on gray plastic.
(K) Not used.
(L) Shiny yellow paint, silver top and ends, red-orange stripe and grab-irons.
(M) Same as (L) but maroon stripe and grab irons.
(N) Same as L, but dull paint; (L), (M) and (N) all are on black plastic.
(O) Not used.
(P) Silver paint on black plastic.

Second Character - Window Coverings
(A) Fogged plastic, bottom side windows only, no paper diffuser.
(B) Fogged plastic, all windows, no paper diffuser.
(C) Fogged plastic, all windows, brown waxed paper diffuser.
(D) Fogged plastic, all windows, white paper diffuser.
(E) Clear plastic, all windows, white paper diffuser.
(F) Clear plastic, all windows, no paper diffuser.
(G) Rigid, opaque, plastic insert.
(O) No window coverings.
(X) Unknown, window coverings apparently removed.

Third Character - Body Casting
(A) Center cupola, four rivet mounting of frame, long step, left-hand door knob.
(B) Same as (A) except short step and righthand knob.
(C) Same as (B) except on one side the upper right end step is partially filled and the catwalk on the same end has a rounded corner. This was apparently due to a deteriorating mold.
(D) Center cupola, no rivets, small hole in bottom of each door for snap fit frame; short step and righthand knob.
(E) Same as (D) except both upper steps on one side are filled in.
(F) Bay window.
(G) Same as (D) except on one side righthand upper step is filled in.
(H) Same as (G) except step is only partially filled.

Fourth Character - Roadname
(A) READING, silver lettering.
(B) READING, white lettering.
(C) Not used.
(D) AMERICAN FLYER LINES, sans serif, slope-sided M, white 5/32" high letters.
(E) Same as (D) except 1/3" high letters.
(F) Same as (E) except silver letters.
(G) Not used.
(H) AMERICAN FLYER LINES, sans serif, straight-sided M, 1/8" high letters, 3/32" high numbers.
(I) Same as (H) except 1/8" letters and 1/16" numbers.
(J) Same as (H) except 3/16" letters, 3/32" numbers and "M" has pointed tops.
(K) Same as (J) except M has flat tops.
(L) Same as (K) except 7/32" letters and 3/32" numbers.
(M) Same as (H) except 5/32" letters and 1/8" numbers.
(N) AMERICAN FLYER LINES, small lettering on bay window cabooses.
(O) Not used.
(P) Freight Ahead.
(Q) Not used.
(R) AMERICAN FLYER, sans serif, slope-sided M.
(S) AMERICAN FLYER, serif, 5/32" high by 2 3/16" long.
(T) AMERICAN FLYER, serif, 1/8" high by 2" long.

Fifth Character - Other Lettering
(A) NM$_H$ BLT. 6-31.
(B) NM$_H$ BLT. 6-3, "BLT. 6-3" is 13/32" long.
(C) NM$_H$ BLT. 6-3, "BLT. 6-3" is 15/32" long.
(D) NM$_H$ BLT 6-51, No "." after BLT.
(E) NMH BLT 6-51.
(F) NMH BLT6-51, no space between "T" and "6."
(G) WT. 48000 NEW 9-54.

630   638   638

806   904   930

930   934   938

935   979

977   977   24610

24603   24627   24631

24626   24636   24636

Note that the left truck has flat ovals while the right truck has concave ovals

(H) WT 43000 NEW 3-54 Radio Equipped.
(I) WT 43000 NEW 9-54 Radio Equipped.
(J) Radio Equipped.
(K) NMH BLT6-51 Radio Equipped, no space between "T" "6."
(L) Game Train Shield.
(O) No other lettering besides number.
(P) No other lettering.

Three different bases. Top row: sheet metal held by four rivets, one in each corner, with conversion knuckle couplers. Middle row: a die-cast base. Bottom row: a plastic base that is glued to the superstructure. Note the warping on the sides and the thin shank on the coupler.

Sixth Character - Frame, Light and Brakewheel

(A) Red plastic frame, no light, brass railing, two piece brakewheel, reported to exist, confirmation requested.
(B) Red plastic frame, light with silver socket, brass railings, two piece brakewheel; all lights have silver sockets except where noted.
(C) Black plastic, no light, brass railing, two piece brakewheel.
(D) Black plastic, lighted, brass railing, two piece brakewheel.
(E) Die-cast metal frame, light with silver socket, brass railing, two piece brakewheel, frame fastened with #2 sheet metal screws.
(F) Die-cast metal, light with black socket, brass railing, two piece brakewheel, frame fastened with rivets.
(G) Sheet metal frame, lighted, brass railing, two piece brakewheel.
(H) Sheet metal, lighted, brass railing, one piece brakewheel.
(I) Sheet metal, no light, but hole in frame for socket, brass railing, no brakewheel.
(J) Sheet metal, no light and no hole for socket, brass railing, no brakewheel.
(K) Same as (E) except fastened with rivets.
(L) Sheet metal frame with integral railings, no light, brakewheel mounting plates with holes on opposite corners of car; mounting plates are on the left looking at the end of the car.
(M) Same as (L) except no holes on mounting plates.
(N) Same as (M) except mounting plates are on the same side of the car, i.e., plate on one end is on the right and on the other is on the left.
(O) Bay window, sheet metal frame, bronze pickup wheels, lighted, rubber man.
(P) Bay window, bronze wheels, lighted, no man.
(Q) Bay window, steel wheels, lighted, no man.
(R) Bay window, all plastic wheels, no light, no man.
(S) Same as (K) except 1/16" line across top of tool boxes.
(T) Sheet metal 977 frame, one piece brakewheel, rubber man, plastic insulation on wire for light.
(U) Same as (T) except braided insulation.
(V) Sheet metal 977 frame, one piece brakewheel, metal man with facial features painted on and braided insulation.
(W) Same as (V) except no facial features and patent number stamped on frame.

Note: Plastic frames have holes for rivets but no rivets. They are apparently glued in.

How many differences can you find among the four cabooses?

Seventh Character - Trucks
(A) Sheet metal, six spring (undifferentiated springs - bad die?), no slots in side frame, stamped journals.
(B) Sheet metal, six spring, one horizontal slot in each side frame, cast journals.
(C) Same as (B) except stamped journals.
(D) Sheet metal, six spring, no slots, stamped journals.
(E) Sheet metal, nine spring, no slots, stamped journals.
(F) Sheet metal, nine spring, two vertical slots on one side of each truck, stamped journals.
(G) One type C truck and one type D truck.
(H) Type D truck without journals; very careful examination is required to insure that journals were never installed.
(I) Not used.
(J) Not used.
(K) Sintered metal side frames with flat-centered triangles.
(L) Same as (K) except concave-centered triangles.
(M) One K truck and one L truck.
(N) Same as (L) except concave center is deeper and back side of side frame has horizontal slot indentation.
(O) Same as K except horizontal slot indentation on back side.
(P) Pike Master trucks without pickups.
(Q) Pike Master trucks with pickups.
(X) Unknown, trucks missing or obviously changed.

Eighth Character - Couplers
(A) Link, no weight, thin shank, black rivet.
(B) Link, no weight, thin shank, silver rivet.
(C) Link, no weight, thick shank, silver rivet.
(D) Link, brass weight, silver rivet.
(E) Link, black weight, silver rivet.
(F) Not used.
(G) Knuckle, operating, with holes in shanks.
(H) Knuckle, operating, without holes in shanks.
(I) Knuckle, operating, with split shanks.
(J) One G coupler and one H coupler.
(K) Not used.
(L) Knuckle, non-operating, no holes.
(M) Bobtail type L coupler.
(N) Bobtail type G coupler.
(O) Bobtail type H coupler.
(P) Pike Master.
(X) Unknown, couplers missing or obviously changed.

Car Number[1]	Color & Type of Plastic	Window Coverings	Body Casting	Roadname	Other Lettering	Frame, Light & Brakewheel	Trucks	Couplers	Good	Very Good	Excellent
---	B	O	D	P	L	L	P	P	3	5	7
630	A	B	A	A	A	B	C	A	3	5	7
630	A	B	A	A	A	B	B	B	3	5	7
630	A	A	A	A	A	C	C	A	3	5	6
630	A	B	A	B	A	D	B	B	3	5	7
630	A	B	A	A	A	D	B	B	3	5	7
630	A	B	A	A	A	E	C	C	3	4	5
630	A	B	A	B	A	E	C	C	3	4	5
630	A	B	A	B	A	K	C	C	3	4	5
630	A	D	A	B	A	K	D	D	3	4	5
630	A	C	A	B	A	K	C	D	3	4	5
630	A	B	A	B	A	E	C	D	3	4	5
630	A	D	A	B	A	K	C	D	3	4	5
630	A	D	A	B	A	F	C	D	3	4	5
630	A	D	A	B	A	S	C	D	3	4	5
630	A	D	A	B	A	K	G	D	3	4	5
630	A	E	A	B	A	S	A	E	3	4	5
630	A	E	A	B	A	G	D	E	3	4	5
630	A	E	A	B	A	G	E	E	3	4	5
630	A	E	A	B	B	G	D	E	3	4	5
630[2]	D	E	A	B	C	G	D	E	3	4	5
630[2]	D	E	A	B	C	G	D	E	3	4	5
630	F	E	C	D	D	G	F	E	4	5	6
630	E	E	B	E	D	H	D	E	4	5	6
630	F	E	C	H	O	G	A	E	10	20	30
630	F	E	B	R	A	G	D	E	7	11	15
630	F	E	B	R	A	G	F	E	7	11	15

Car Number[1]	Color & Type of Plastic	Window Coverings	Body Casting	Roadname	Other Lettering	Frame, Light & Brakewheel	Trucks	Couplers	Good	Very Good	Excellent
638	E	O	B	F	D	J	E	E	3	4	5
638	E	O	B	E	D	J	E	E	3	4	5
638	F	O	C	E	D	J	D	E	3	4	5
638	F	O	B	E	D	J	D	E	3	4	5
638	F	O	A	E	D	J	E	E	3	4	5
638	A	O	A	S	O	J	A	E	2	3	4
638	A	O	A	S	O	I	A	E	2	3	4
638	A	O	A	S	O	I	A	D	2	3	4
638	A	O	A	S	O	J	H	E	2	3	4
638	F	O	A	S	O	J	F	E	2	3	4
638	F	O	A	S	O	J	D	E	2	3	4
638	F	O	B	S	O	J	D	E	2	3	4
638	F	O	B	S	O	J	F	E	2	3	4
638	F	O	A	S	O	I	D	E	2	3	4
638	A	O	A	T	O	I	A	E	9	15	22
806	B	O	D	D	D	N	L	G	2	3	4
806	B	O	D	E	D	N	L	H	2	3	4
806	B	O	D	D	D	L	P	P	2	3	4
904	F	F	A	E	D	I	L	I	3	5	7
904	F	F	A	E	D	J	L	J	3	5	7
930	F	E	A	R	A	G	N	H	9	15	22
930	H	E	A	E	D	G	N	J	3	5	7
930	I	E	A	E	D	G	K	H	3	5	7
930	I	E	B	E	D	H	K	G	3	5	7
930	J	E	B	E	D	G	O	G	3	5	7
930	I	E	B	E	D	H	N	I	3	5	7
930	I	E	C	E	D	G	O	G	3	5	7

[1] This listing does not include work cabooses - see next section.

[2] These two are the same except the paint on one side of one is so thin that it can be seen through.

Car Number[1]	Color & Type of Plastic	Window Coverings	Body Casting	Roadname	Other Lettering	Frame, Light & Brakewheel	Trucks	Couplers	Good	Very Good	Excellent
934	F	O	A	E	D	J	N	G	10	15	20
934	F	O	B	E	D	J	L	H	10	15	20
935	I	G	F	N	G	P	L	G	8	12	16
935	I	G	F	N	G	P	N	G	8	12	16
938	F	O	B	E	D	J	L	N	2	3	4
938	F	O	B	E	D	J	L	G	2	3	4
938	F	O	B	E	D	J	M	N	2	3	4
938	F	O	A	E	D	J	L	O	2	3	4
938	D	O	B	E	D	J	K	G	2	3	4
977	I	E	B	E	D	W	L	G	9	14	18
977	I	E	B	E	D	V	K	G	8	12	16
977	I	E	B	E	D	V	L	G	8	12	16
977	I	E	A	E	D	T	L	G	9	14	18
977	I	E	A	E	D	U	L	G	9	14	18
979	I	G	F	N	G	O	L	J	10	15	20
24603	B	O	D	E	D	L	L	L	1	2	3
24603	B	O	D	E	D	L	L	G	2	3	4
24610	B	O	D	H	D	L	L	L	1	2	3
24610	B	O	D	H	D	N	L	H	2	3	4
24619	I	G	F	N	G	P	N	G	10	15	20
24626	L	F	D	I	J	L	L	G	3	5	7
24626	L	O	D	I	J	L	L	G	3	5	7
24626	M	F	D	I	J	L	L	G	3	5	7
24627	B	O	D	H	E	L	L	N	2	3	4
24627	G	O	D	H	E	L	L	N	2	3	4
24630	B	O	D	H	E	L	L	N	1	2	3
24631	L	O	D	I	J	L	L	G	3	5	7
24631	L	O	G	I	J	M	P	P	3	5	7
24631	M	O	D	I	J	M	P	P	3	5	7
24632	L	O	D	I	J	L	L	N	15	25	35
24633	P	G	F	N	H	P	Q	P	10	15	20
24634	F	G	F	N	I	P	Q	P	8	12	16
(24634)	F	O	F	N	P	R	P	P	10	15	20
24636	B	O	E	H	F	M	P	P	1	2	3
24636	B	O	E	M	F	M	P	P	1	2	3
24636	B	O	D	H	F	M	P	P	1	2	3
24636	B	O	H	H	F	M	P	P	1	2	3
24636	B	O	D	L	F	L	P	P	1	2	3
24636	B	O	D	K	F	L	P	P	1	2	3
24636	B	O	D	J	K	L	P	P	1	2	3
24636	C	O	D	J	K	M	P	P	1	2	3
24636*	L	X	D	H	F	X	X	X	200	250	300
24638	P	G	F	N	H	P	Q	P	8	12	16
25052	P	G	F	N	I	O	N	G	12	18	25

*I do not have this, but I have seen one. Lettering is **white**!

68

24619   24633

25052   907

24546   945

645

This plate shows three bay window cabooses with cupola and four work cabooses.

WORK CABOOSES

607   **AMERICAN FLYER LINES** Gray painted sheet metal frame, "AMERICAN FLYER LINES 607" in black on frame side; brown painted black plastic shed with solid metal stack, "607" on shed side in white, red painted wood tool box, one four-wheel Type B or D truck is the load which is riveted to the frame; Type B or D sheet metal trucks, black coupler weights; part of the lower priced 1953 work set, 5317T, with the 370 GP-7 diesel, Stromberg and Caples Collections. Note that the sheet metal frames on the 607 and 907 are revivals of the prewar 0 Gauge 3/16 frame and that they are too wide for the 3/16 inch to a foot measure because the trucks are substantially set-in from the frame. The reuse of the sheet metal frame die is an effective cost control measure.   **5   7   10**

645   **AMERICAN FLYER** Gray painted die-cast frame with "AMERICAN FLYER" in black letters, red plastic shed with chimney and rear railing, "645" in white on shed side, yellow or brown plastic "stake" sides, two-piece brakewheel, Type B trucks, black coupler weights, 1950.
(A)   Yellow plastic stake sides, Newcomer and Stromberg Collections.   **7   11   14**
(B)   Brown plastic stake sides, Newcomer Collection.
     7   11   14

645A   **AMERICAN FLYER** Gray painted die-cast frame with "AMERICAN FLYER LINES" in black letters, red or brown plastic shed with chimney and rear railing, "645A" in white on shed side, yellow or brown "stake" sides, Type B trucks, black coupler weights, 1951-53.
(A)   Red shed, yellow stakes, Newcomer Collection.
     6   9   12
(B)   Brown shed, yellow stakes, Yorkis and Stromberg Collections.   **6   9   12**
(C)   Brown shed, yellow stakes, Greenberg Collection.
     6   9   12

907   **AMERICAN FLYER LINES** Gray painted sheet metal frame, "AMERICAN FLYER LINES 907" on frame in black, "907" in white on shed, tuscan painted black or gray plastic shed with solid metal stud chimney, brass rear railing with brakewheel, red painted wood tool box; one four-wheel sintered iron side frame truck is the load which is riveted on the frame; car has sintered iron side trucks with knuckle couplers and is part of a 1954 lower priced work train set, K417T, with an AMERICAN FLYER 371 diesel.
(A)   Tuscan painted --this paint appears darker than (B)-- with black plastic shed; rubber stamped frame with heavier lettering than on (B), truck is load and has flat ovals while trucks on car have concave ovals. Caples and Stromberg Collections.   **6   9   12**

(B) Tuscan painted --this paint appears lighter than (A)-- with gray plastic shed, trucks on car and truck which is load have concave ovals, rubber stamped lettering on frame is lighter than on (A), Caples Collection. 6 9 12

945 **AMERICAN FLYER LINES** Gray painted die-cast or plastic frame with "AMERICAN FLYER LINES" in black sans serif, tuscan painted black plastic shed with plastic windows, solid metal studs for chimney on roof, two brown plastic fences embossed "PA 11198," red painted wooden tool box, brass railings with brakewheel, white "945" on sintered iron truck side frames, knuckle couplers, 1953-57.

(A) Die-cast frame embossed "PA-9952 AMERICAN FLYER MFD. BY THE A.C. GILBERT CO. NEW HAVEN, CONN.

U.S.A.," flat ovals on trucks, Caples and Stromberg Collections. 6 9 12

(B) Plastic frame catalogued in 1957 as 24526. 6 9 12

24526 **AMERICAN FLYER** Tool and boom car, catalogued as 24526 with this number probably printed on its box; car probably came with "945" on side, 1957, confirmation requested.

No Reported Sales

24546 **AMERICAN FLYER** Gray painted black plastic base, tuscan shed with rear railing, ladder and chimney, "24546" on shed side in white, "AMERICAN FLYER" on frame side in black, tuscan painted black plastic tool box, yellow and brown plastic stake sides, sintered iron truck side frames, knuckle couplers, 1958-64, Stromberg Collection. 6 9 12

The A.C. Gilbert factory in New Haven
Note the New Haven tracks in the rear and the Erector
tower in the left corner. Walsh Collection.

Chapter V

GONDOLAS

Gilbert uses one basic gondola body. All bodies are plastic; some are unpainted plastic, some are painted, but all come with little ornamentation, and little if any visible warping. All observed bodies are embossed "PA-9986" on the underside. The gondolas show less development than do the other cars. Trucks progress from sheet metal to die-cast side frames and finally to Pike Master. Gondolas come with various types of link, knuckle, Pike Master and one piece fixed knuckle couplers. We do not find gondolas with labels or decals and applied lettering is often designed to fit around the rivet rows on the side.

All observed gondolas to date come with molded brake units on the underside and corrugated ends. Some carry truck weights which make for better running. Jan Rechenberg reports that one or more of the 24000 series gondolas has been seen with fixed knuckle couplers. According to Robert Stromberg, fixed knuckle couplers come generally with a special set put out for Sears. All the cars in the Sears set have a zero as the last digit. The cars are: 24110 PRR Gondola, 24320 Deep Rock Tank and 24610 American Flyer Lines Caboose. However the fixed knuckles show up on other cars, including 24000 series gondolas, as production control was not a major concern of A.C. Gilbert.

The most difficult gondola to find is the 641 dark gray T & P. Other hard-to-find items are the 641 American Flyer in gray and the 24109 C & O. The C & O is reportedly owned by only one of the contributors to this book.

Fundimension production is listed following Gilbert production.

	Good	Very Good	Excel
PENNSYLVANIA See (24130).			

BUFFALO HUNT Green unpainted plastic body, large sans serif "BUFFALO HUNT" and Game Train logo, "CAPY 100000 LD LMT 110000 LD WGT 39800" in white, 1963, comes as part of an unusual set known as "the Game Train," Stromberg and Schneider Collections.

| | 3 | 5 | 8 |

620 SOUTHERN Black painted or unpainted plastic body; "SOUTHERN" in white sans serif face; "CAP 130000 LD LMT 124200 LT WT 50000 BLT 4-50 CU FT 4000" in white, 1953, Type D sheet metal trucks, link couplers, black coupler weights, Balint and Patterson Collections.

| | 4 | 6 | 8 |

631 T & P Red, green or gray plastic body; "T & P TEXAS & PACIFIC 631" in three lines with white line over and under lettering; "CAPACITY 100000 LBS. LOAD LIMIT 123500 LBS. LT.WT. 45500 NEW 4-28" in white, "PA-9986" embossed on underside of body, link couplers, 1946-53.

(A) Dark green unpainted body, Type C trucks, brass coupler weights, truck weight with embossed "PA 11304," Sutter and Newcomer Collections. | 2 | 3 | 5
(B) Dark gray unpainted body, Type B trucks. | 30 | 50 | 75
(C) Red painted plastic body, Type B trucks. | 25 | 35 | 45

	Good	Very Good	Excel

(D) Dark green painted body, Type D trucks, black coupler weights, Sutter Collection. | 2 | 3 | 5
(E) Same as (D) except Type B trucks, Sutter Collection. | 2 | 3 | 5
(F) Same as (A), no truck weights, Bargeron Collection. | 2 | 3 | 5

641 AMERICAN FLYER Red or green plastic body, white sans serif lettering spaced to fit between rivet rows "AM ERI CAN FL YER 641," link couplers, 1949-51.

(A) Red unpainted plastic, Type D trucks, black coupler weights, Sutter Collection. | 5 | 7 | 10
(B) Green unpainted plastic. | 10 | 15 | 20
(C) Same as (A) but Type C trucks, Sutter Collection. | 5 | 7 | 10
(D) Red painted white plastic body, Type B trucks, black coupler weights, Sutter Collection. | 5 | 7 | 10
(E) Gray unpainted plastic body, Type A trucks, brass coupler weights. | 30 | 50 | 75

641 FRISCO Brown painted black plastic body, "FRISCO LINES" in tuscan, "SL SF 941" in white in two lines with white line above and below; "CAPY 110000 LD LMT 126800 LT WT 42200 NEW 4-50 CU FT 4000" in white, Type B or D trucks, link couplers, black coupler weights, 1953; Stromberg, Patterson and Petri Collections. | 10 | 15 | 20

804 N & W Shiny black unpainted plastic body, "N & W 804" in white with lines above and below, "CAPY 110000 LD.LMT. 126300 LT.WT. 42700 NEW 12-40 BLT 12-40 IL41-6 CU FT 1765" in white, black sintered iron truck side frames, knuckle couplers, 1956-57, Patterson, Newcomer and Sutter Collections. | 5 | 7 | 9

805 PENNSYLVANIA Tuscan unpainted or painted plastic body, "PENNSYLVANIA 805" in white with line above and below, spaced to fit between car struts, white and tuscan PRR Keystone logo inside white circle, white technical data "CAPY 140000 LD LMT 127400 LT WT 52700," sintered iron black truck side frames, knuckle couplers, also "IL40-3 CU FT 4318," 1956-57.

(A) Tuscan unpainted plastic, Newcomer Collection. | 3 | 5 | 8
(B) Tuscan painted black plastic, Smith Collection. | 6 | 9 | 12

911 C & O Black painted or unpainted plastic body, white lettering fits between struts: "CHES APEA KE & OHIO;" "C & O FOR PROGRESS" logo, six silver or brown pipes, sintered iron truck side frames, knuckle couplers, pipes sit in yellow plastic braces, 1955-57. There are two 911 variations: 911 with serifs on the top and bottom of the 1s and with serifs on the top of the 1s only. Brown pipes bring a premium over silver pipes.

(A) Black painted black plastic body, Newcomer Collection. | 5 | 7 | 11
(B) Black painted red plastic body, Balint and Schneider Collections. | 5 | 7 | 11
(C) Black unpainted plastic body, Patterson Collection. | 5 | 7 | 11

24125

24125

24127

C2009

916 **D & H** Light tuscan painted black plastic body, "The D H" in white script, white D & H logo with "A CENTURY OF SERVICE." There are two versions of the "D & H," one with sans serif face and the other with serif face. Five canisters lettered "DELAWARE AND HUDSON" with logo and "THE LCL CORPORATION AIR ACTIVATED CONTAINER." Car reads "CAPY 140000 LD LMT 127400 LT WT 52900 NEW 4-42 BLT 6-42 IL 40-30 CU FT 4318," black sintered iron truck side frames, knuckle couplers, 1955-57; Patterson, Degano and Stromberg Collections.   5   7   10

920 **SOUTHERN** Black painted black or black unpainted plastic body, "SOUTHERN" in white letters fits in bwetween struts, white technical data "CAPY 130000 LD. LMT 124200 LT. WT. 50000 BLT 4-50 CU.FT. 4000;" black sintered iron truck side frames, knuckle couplers 1953-57, Petri, Balint and Sutter Collections.   4   7   9

931 **T & P** Green painted or unpainted plastic body, "T & P TEXAS & PACIFIC 931" in white on three lines with white line above and below; "CAPACITY 100000LB. LOAD LMT. 123500 LB. LT. WT. 45500 NEW 4-28," sintered iron truck side frames, knuckle couplers; Patterson, Sutter and Schneider Collections.
(A)   Dark green painted black plastic.   3   5   7
(B)   Medium green painted black plastic, Bargeron Collection.   3   5   7
(C)   Medium green unpainted plastic.   3   5   7

941 **FRISCO LINES** Light tuscan painted black or white plastic body, white logo with "FRISCO LINES" in tuscan; also "SL SF 941" in white on two lines with white line above and below; sintered iron truck side frames, knuckle couplers, 1953-57.
(A)   Light tuscan painted black plastic body, Patterson and Newcomer Collections.   4   6   8
(B)   Light tuscan painted white plastic body, Schneider Collection.   4   6   8

C2009 **TEXAS & PACIFIC** Light green unpainted plastic body, "TEXAS & PACIFIC" in large white serif face, "T & P" and "C2009," "CAPY." "CAPY. 100000 LD LMT 111000 LT WT 39800" in small white face; Pike Master trucks and couplers, Patterson and Newcomer Collections.   5   7   10

24103 **N & W** Unpainted black plastic body, large white lettering "N & W," in large face "NORFOLK AND WESTERN" and "N & W 24103" in medium white face on two lines with white line above and below; white technical data "NEW 12-40" and "BLT 12-40," "CAPY 111000 LD LMT 126300 LT WT 42700 IL 41-6 CU FT. 1765," sintered iron truck side frames, knuckle couplers, Patterson and Newcomer Collections.   5   7   10

24106 **PENNSYLVANIA** Dark tuscan unpainted plastic, white circle with tuscan keystone logo with "PRR" in white, white lettering spaced between rivet rows: "PEN NSY LVA NIA" and "24106" in two lines with white line above and below "CAPY 140000 LD LMT 127400 LT WT 52700 IL 40-3 CU FT. 4318" in white; sintered iron truck side frames, knuckle couplers, 1960, Newcomer and Patterson Collections.   4   6   8

24109 **C & O** Unpainted black plastic, dull yellow lettered "C & O 24109 CAPY 100000 LD LMT 36700 LT WT 42300 NEW 4-48" "C & O For Progress" logo, pipes supported by three yellow plastic supports and held down by three silver metal ties, 1957-60, Patterson Collection. Also found with flat black painted shiny plastic body, Manson Collection.
(A)   Silver plastic pipes.   6   7   10
(B)   Silver cardboard pipes.   6   7   10
(C)   Brown plastic pipes.   6   7   10

24110 **PENNSYLVANIA** Very dark tuscan unpainted plastic, white circle with tuscan keystone logo with "PRR" in white; white lettering spaced between rivet rows: "PEN NSY LVA NIA" and "24110" in two lines with white line above and below; also "CAPY 140000 LD LMT 127400 LT WT 52700 IL 40-3 CU FT. 4318," sintered iron truck side frames, knuckle couplers or one piece fixed knuckle couplers, Patterson and Newcomer Collections.   3   5   6

24113 **D & H** Brown painted black plastic, "D&H" in white script, sintered iron trucks, knuckle couplers, silver and gray plastic containers with "LCL Corporation Air Activated," 1957-59, Manson, Petri and Balint Collections.   5   7   10

24116 **SOUTHERN** Black unpainted plastic with white lettering spaced between rivet rows: "S OU TH ER N" and "CAPY 130000 LD LMT 124200 LT WT 50000 BLT 4-50 CU. FT. 40000" in white; sintered iron truck side frames, knuckle couplers, 1958-60, Patterson, Schneider and Newcomer Collections.
                                                10   15   20

24120 **T & P** Dark green unpainted plastic body, white lettering "T&P 24120 CAPY 1807 CU FT LD RMT 10000 LT WT 48900," Pike Master trucks and couplers, 1960, Schneider, Manson, Balint and Patterson Collections.   10   15   20

24123 **FRISCO** Catalogued as 24123 in 1957 but probably issued with "941" on side, box probably marked "24123" on end. Confirmation requested.   **No Reported Sales**

24124 **BOSTON AND MAINE** Light blue or dark blue plastic with white lettering spaced between rivet rows: "B O S T O N A N D

72

631

641

804

805

911

916

920

931

941

24103

24106

24110

24116

24124

M A I N E," "24124" in white with white line under it; Pike Master trucks and couplers, 1963-64.

(A) Light blue unpainted plastic, Bargeron, Sutter and Balint Collections.   3   4   5

(B) Dark blue painted blue plastic, Patterson and Balint Collections.   7   10   15

(C) Dark blue painted black plastic.   9   12   18

24125 **BETHELEHEM STEEL** Light or medium gray plastic, dark red lettering spaced between rivet rows: "B ET HL EHEM ST EE L;" dark red I beam logo "BETHELEHEM STEEL;" sintered iron truck side frames with knuckle couplers or Pike Master trucks and couplers, 1960-65.

(A) Light gray unpainted plastic without load, maroon lettering, Pike Master trucks and couplers, Sutter and Balint Collections.   5   8   10

(B) Medium gray painted black plastic with load; two small metal rail holders supported by buttresses inside car; four T rails, 10" long, red lettering, sintered iron truck side frames, Sutter Collection.   6   9   12

(C) Same as (A) except orange lettering, Sutter Collection.   6   9   12

(D) Same as (A) but red lettering, Manson Collection.   5   8   10

(E) Light gray painted black plastic with load, sintered iron truck side frames, knuckle couplers, Bargeron Collection.   6   9   12

24126 **FRISCO** Unpainted tuscan plastic body, Pike Master trucks and couplers, lettered "FRISCO LINES" in tuscan, "SL SF 24126" in white, "FRISCO" logo in white, Balint Collection.   20   30   40

24127 **MONON** Light gray unpainted plastic, dark large red "MONON" and dark red small "MON 24127" with line above and below; dark red logo with "M" and tree inside circle, sintered iron truck side frames and knuckle couplers or Pike Master trucks and couplers, 1961-65.

(A) Sintered iron truck side frames, knuckle couplers, Newcomer and Sutter Collections.   5   7   10

(B) Pike Master trucks and couplers, Balint Collection.   5   7   10

[24130] **PENNSYLVANIA** Brown unpainted plastic, lettered "PEN NSY LVA NIA" in white, tuscan keystone logo, catalogue number does not appear on car, Pike Master trucks and couplers, or sintered iron truck side frames and fixed knuckles, 1960.

(A) Pike Master trucks and couplers, Sutter and Balint Collections.   4   6   8

(B) Sintered iron truck side frames and fixed knuckles, Balint Collection.   4   6   8

FUNDIMENSIONS PRODUCTION

9300 **BURLINGTON** Fundimensions 1980 production, green body, "CAPY... LD LMT.... BLT 1-80 LIONEL C B & Q 9300" in white face.   8   12   15

The layout at the New York Hall of Science.
Note the famous portholes on the side of the building. Walsh Collection.

Chapter VI
CATALOGUES & INSTRUCTION BOOKLETS

GILBERT CATALOGUES AND OTHER PRINTED MATERIAL IN THE "D" SERIES

		Good	Very Good	Excel

1946 D1451 32 pages, 14½ w. x 10¼ h., full color throughout, Consumer Catalogue. **20 30 40**

D1451 Same as above but plastic red end binder. **100 150 200**

D1455 Dealer, pages not marked. **25 35 40**

D1458 Service Station Appointment Card. **50c 1 1.50**

1947 D1473 32 pages, 14½ w. x 10¼ h., full color throughout, Consumer Catalogue. **20 30 40**

D1482 4 pages, Dealer. **10 15 20**

D1502 16 pages, black and blue, Advance Catalogue, 9 x 12", reproduction available, 16 pages. **10 15 20**

D1495 16 pages, What Retail Stores Should Know. **1 2 3**

D1496 16 pages, Display Suggestions. **1 2 3**

1948 D1505 15 pages, 9 x 12", red and black, Advance Catalogue for the Trade. **6 10 12**

D1507 32 pages, 14½ w. x 10¼ h., full color throughout, Consumer Catalogue. **20 30 40**

D1508 32 pages, 8½ w. x 5½ h., full color throughout, Superman at the Gilbert Hall of Science. **10 15 25**

D1508 20 pages, 11¼ w. x 8 h., full color, Consumer Catalogue. **10 15 25**

1949 D1525 16 pages, 9 w. x 12 h., Bang Bang Torpedo on cover. **50 75 100**

D1530 16 pages, 9 w. x 12 h., blue and black, Advance Catalogue for the Trade. **10 15 20**

D1536 40 pages, 11¼ w. x 7 15/16 h., full color throughout, Consumer Catalogue. **10 15 25**

D1552 25 pages, How to Sell American Flyer. **1 2 3**

1950 D1578 32 pages, 12 w. x 9 h., red and black, Dealer Catalogue. **7 12 20**

D1579 Gilbert Toys. **6 8 16**

D1604 56 pages, 11 3/16 w. x 7 15/16 h., full color throughout, Consumer Catalogue. **10 15 20**

1951 D1637 28 pages, 8½ w. x 11 1/16 h., black and blue, Dealer Catalogue. **10 15 20**

D1637A 28 pages, 8½ w. x 11 h., blue and black, Advance. **8 13 18**

D1640 48 pages, 11½ w. x 8 h., full color throughout, Consumer Catalogue. **5 10 15**

D1660 16 pages, Gilbert Electric Eye. **3 4 6**

D1656 8 pages, A.F. and Toys. **3 4 6**

1952 D1667 40 pages, 8½ w. x 11 h., orange and black, Advance, Silver Streak lettered "Burlington". **10 15 20**

D1667A 40 pages, 8½ w. x 11 h., orange and black, Advance. **10 15 20**

		Good	Very Good	Excel

D1677 48 pages, 11¼ w. x 8 h., full color throughout, Consumer Catalogue. **5 10 15**

D1678 24 pages, 5 w. x 6¾ h., brown and black, Facts About American Flyer Trains. **5 7 10**

1953 D1703 16 pages, Erector and Other Toys. **3 4 6**

D1704 36 pages, 8½ w. x 11 h., orange and black, Dealer Catalogue, coated paper. **8 13 16**

D1714 52 pages, 11¼ w. x 8 h., full color and black and white Dealer Catalogue, pulp paper. **5 10 15**

D1714 52 pages, 11¼ w. x 8 h., full color and black and white, Dealer Catalogue, coated paper. **6 12 18**

D1715 52 pages, 11¼ w. x 8 h., full color throughout, Consumer Catalogue. **5 10 15**

D1728 12 pages, Tips on Erector. **1 2 3**

1954 D1740 12 pages, Erector and Gilbert Toys. **1 3 5**

D1744 A.F. and Erector Ad Program. **50c 1 2**

D1746 32 pages, 8½ w. x 11 h., dull color, vellum finish paper, Consumer Catalogue. **3 7 10**

D1748 32 pages, 8½ w. x 11 h., dull color, vellum finish paper, Consumer Catalogue. **3 7 10**

D1749 32 pages, 8½ w. x 11 h., dull color, pulp paper, Consumer Catalogue. **4 8 12**

D1760 48 pages, 1¼ w. x 8 h., full color, vellum finish paper, Consumer Catalogue. **5 8 12**

D1761 48 pages, 11½ w. x 8 h., full color, Consumer Catalogue. **10 15 20**

D1769 6 pages, Read All About Ad Campaign. **1 2 3**

D1782 11¼ w. x 8 h., color cover, black and white interior, vellum finish, Dealer Catalogue. **6 12 18**

1955 D1801 44 pages, 11 5/16 w. x 7 15/16 h., full color throughout, Consumer Catalogue. **6 9 12**

D1802 44 pages, 11 15/16 w. x 7 15/16 h., full color throughout, Western Consumer Catalogue. **8 12 16**

D1816 36 pages, 11¼ w. x 8 h., full color throughout, Dealer Catalogue. **10 15 20**

D1820 H0. **1 2 3**

D1835 Tips For Selling Erector. **1 2 3**

1956 D1866 52 pages, 11¼ w. x 8 h., full color, slick cover, Consumer Catalogue. **4 7 9**

D1867 52 pages, 11¼ w. x 8 h., full color throughout, Western Consumer Catalogue. **3 5 8**

D1879 24 pages, Erector and Gilbert Toys. **1 3 7**

D1904 28 pages, 9¼ w. x 6 3/16 h., full color cover, red and black interior, H0 Trains Consumer Catalogue. **1 2 3**

D1882 12 pages, A.F. and Erector Displays. **1 3 7**

D1907 black and white, Dealer. **15 20 25**

D1922 52 pages 5 3/8 w. x 7 3/8 h., full color and black and white, shiny finish, Miniature Catalogue. **2 4 6**

1957 D1937 48 pages, 11¼ w. x 8 h., full color, Consumer Catalogue. **7 12 15**

D1973 12 pages, Erector and Other Toys. **1** **2** **3**

D2006 48 pages, 11 3/8 w. x 7 7/8 h., full color throughout, Consumer Catalogue. **5** **8** **10**

D2007 48 pages 11 3/8 w. x 7 7/8 h., full color throughout, Western Consumer Catalogue. **6** **9** **12**

D2008 12 pages, Erector and Toys. **1** **2** **3**

1958 D2047 48 pages, 11¼ w. x 8 h., full color throughout, "AMERICAN FLYER by GILBERT Consumer Catalogue. **15** **20** **25**

D2048 48 pages, 11½ w. x 8 h., same as D12047 but Western US prices. **15** **20** **25**

D2058 12 pages, Erector and Toys. **50c** **1** **2**

D2073 10 pages, Advance Catalogue. **3** **5** **10**

D2080 1 page, 8½ w. x 11 h., Smoking Caboose. **15** **20** **25**

D2086 Folder 8½ w. x 4½ h., opens to 17 w. x 34¾ h., full color throughout, Consumer Catalogue. **1** **2** **3**

D4106 H0 Catalogue, numbering error. **1** **2** **3**

1959 D2115 24 pages, 8 7/16 w. x 10 15/16 h., four color cover, red and black interior, Dealer Catalogue. **3** **6** **10**

D2120 10 pages, Science Toys. **1** **2** **4**

D2132 4 page folder, Gilbert H0 **2** **3** **6**

D2146 Folder, 17 w. x 34½ h., full color throughout, Consumer Catalogue. **1** **2** **4**

D2148 Folder, 17 w. x 26 h., full color throughout, Consumer Catalogue H0 only. **1** **2** **3**

D2179 Promotional Sheet, Franklin Set. **1** **2** **3**

D2180 14 pages, Gilbert Science Toys. **1** **2** **3**

1960 D2192 20 pages, 8½ w. x 11 h., green and black, Dealer Catalogue. **6** **9** **12**

D2193 12 pages, 8½ w. x 11 h., blue and black, H0 Advance Catalogue. **2** **3** **4**

D2205 24 pages, Gilbert Toys. **1** **2** **3**

D2224 Folder, 9 w. x 12 h., gold and black, Consumber Catalogue, 1960-61. **1** **2** **4**

D2225 Folder, H0. **1** **2** **3**

D2230 20 pages, 8½ w. x 11 h., orange and black, "AMERICAN FLYER TRAINS FOR 1960" Consumer Catalogue. **5** **7** **10**

D2231 Folder, H0. **1** **2** **3**

1961 D2239 36 pages, 8½ w. x 11 h., green and black, Consumer Catalogue 1961-62. **3** **6** **10**

D2242 REV, Auto Rama Catalogue. **50c** **1** **2**

D2255 4 pages, 1961-62 Retail Display. **50c** **1** **2**

D2267 24 pages, 8½ w. x 11 h., red and black, Consumer Catalogue. **1** **3** **5**

D2268 Folder, Auto Rama Folder. **50c** **1** **2**

1962 D2278R 36 pages, 8½ w. x 11 h., full color cover, green and black interior, Consumer Catalogue. **2** **4** **6**

D2310 36 pages, 8½ w. x 11 h., full color cover, green and black interior, Consumer Catalogue. **1** **2** **3**

D2321 Dealer Catalogue. **2** **3** **5**

D2321R 48 pages, 8½ w. x 11 h., Revised Dealer Catalogue. **2** **3** **5**

1963 D2321 REV 48 pages, 8½ w. x 11 h., full color Dealer Catalogue. **1** **2** **5**

X863-3 32 pages, 8½ w. x 10 7/8 h., full color throughout, Consumer Catalogue. **2** **4** **6**

1964 X-264-6 40 pages, 8½ w. x 11 h., orange and black, "GILBERT TOYS AND TRANSPORTATION 1964" Consumer Catalogue. **1** **2** **4**

1965 X156-12REV 20 pages, 8½ w. x 11 h., full color throughout, "65 THE YEAR TO GO GILBERT" Dealer Catalogue. **5** **7** **10**

1966 X-466-1 24 pages, 8½ w. x 11 h., full color throughout, Gilbert Toys, Consumer Catalogue. **2** **4** **8**

T166-7 full color throughout, Gilbert Action Toys. **1** **2** **3**

T166-6 Gilbert Toys, 1966. **3** **6** **9**

1967 No identification number, four page folder, 8½ w. x 11 h., black, American Flyer Industries (reproduction has been made). **1** **2** **3**

AMERICAN FLYER INSTRUCTION BOOKS ["M" Series]

1947 M2502 48 pages, yellow and red cover, 5 3/8 w. x 8 5/8" h. **2** **3** **4**

1949 M2690 65 pages, yellow and blue cover, 5 3/8 w. x 8 1/2" h. **2** **3** **4**

M2690 65 pages, white cover. **2** **3** **4**

1952 M2978 30 pages, black and blue cover, American Flyer Model Railroad Handbook. **2** **3** **4**

M2984 64 pages, yellow and blue cover, 5 3/8 w. x 8 3/8" h. **1** **2** **3**

1954 M3290 72 pages. **1** **2** **3**

1956 M3450 44 pages, 5 3/8 w. x 8 3/8". **1** **2** **3**

1957 M3817 24 pages, H0. **1** **2** **3**

1960 M4195 folder, 18 w. x 23 h., best described as an accessory catalogue. **2** **4** **6**

1966 M6788 "ALL ABOARD" Instructions for train panels. **2** **4** **6**

Chapter VII
TRUCKS

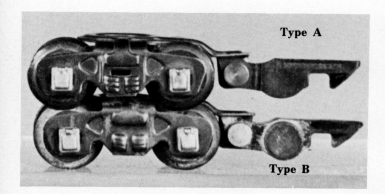

Type A

Type B

Type D

Type A has a slot above its six springs. Type B does not have the slot.
Type B is found with six clearly defined springs and also with less
defined springs as the die wore out. When the spring definition is lost,
we call this a Type C truck. The Type B truck illustrated above is almost
a Type C.

Note the slots on the top truck and the absence of slots on the bottom
truck.

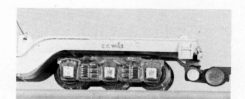

The Special Six Wheel Trucks
Found on the 636 Depressed
Center Car

Chapter VIII
BOX CARS

Type I uses a combination of our plastic studs and four rivets to hold the frame to the body. Note that the body has four plastic studs and a place at each corner to hold the rivet. The frame required the most labor to produce because of its four rivets.

Type II uses a screw hole at one end and a metal plate that fits through a slot in one end of the car to hold the frame to the body. The four holes for the plastic studs are present although the holes for the rivets (at the ends) have disappeared. The two larger holes on the car's longitudinal center axis are still present. This frame is found on the 807 car and 24419.

Type III uses one slot through each body side and one slot at one end. Extensions of the frame which we call plates fit into these slots. The four holes for the plastic studs are gone and only the two other larger holes remain. Type III is found on five digit cars.

Type IV uses four plastic studs and four rivets to hold the shell to the frame. It is found on the 976 cattle car and other cars. There are three other holes in the frame in addition to those for the trucks.

Type V uses a screw hole at one end and a plate at the other to fasten the shell to the frame. In addition holes for rivets are provided at the four corners. In addition three oval holes are found on the base.

American Flyer bodies fall into six major categories: a box car with opening door, a box car with plug door, reefer with opening door, reefer with plug door, operating box car with two doors on one side and (usually) a plug door on the other and the Frontiersman box car.

Each of these six types has one or more subcategories. For example, box cars with opening doors come with (1) no screw holes or slots and fit Type I frames; (2) a screw hole at one end and a slot at the other to fit Type II sheet metal frames; (3) two slots on each side to fit Type III frames or (4) one slot on each side and a slot at one end and a screw hole at the other end. This versatile body will fit either Type II or Type III sheet metal frames.

Plug door box cars are designed to fit Type I sheet metal frames and have no screw hole or slots. Their shells were also made to fit Type II sheet metal frames with a screw hole at one end and a slot at the other. Plug door bodies are also found with two slots on each side to fit Type III sheet metal frames.

Bruce Manson has reported that Plug door box car bodies also vary in another way. Some shells are found with a simulated reinforcing rivet plate in each of the four lower side corners while others only show the usual L shaped reinforcing. The rivet plate has been observed on 24039 D R G W, 24047 GN in red, 24058 POST CEREAL, 24019 SEABOARD and 24066 L & N.

Link Coupler Types

I No weights, thin shank, embossed "PAT NO...," short rivet 1946.
II No weights, thick shank, no embossed lettering, long rivet, 1947.
III Same as II but brass weights, 1948.
IV Same as II but black weights, 1949-53.

On the top shelf is a Type I shell with no slots or end holes to fit a Type I frame. Note the holes in the corners to receive the rivets. On the second row is the Type I shell shown from the underside. Note the four plastic studs coming through the floor. On the third row is a box car with a plastic frame. The frame is glued to the body. Warping is visible in the picture.

COUPLERS

Gilbert began the transition from link to knuckle couplers in 1952 in its two top of the lines sets: The K5206W Hudson Set and the K5210W Challenger Set. (The "K" in the set numbers stands for "knuckle coupler.") The Hudson set features a 325 Hudson, 929 MP Cattle Car, 931 T&P Gondola, 925 Gulf Tank and 930 Caboose. However, in the catalogues the cars are illustrated with their old "link numbers:" 629, 631, 625 and 630. The Challenger Set came with a K335 loco (which has a Northern wheel arrangement), a 931 T&P Gondola, 928 C & NW Log Car, 944 Industrial Brownhoist Crane and 945A Work Caboose. Again the cars illustrated are the earlier link coupler versions: 631, 628, 644 and 645.

There is evidence that some 600 series cars were available in 1952 and 1953 from the factory with knuckle couplers. The first support for this proposition is that too many cars, particularly 647s, have turned up with knuckle couplers and sintered iron side frame trucks to be explained by post manufacture truck changes. Second, a truck change would have required removing a riveted link coupler truck and replacing it with a new style truck and coupler. Such a change usually leaves some little scratches. Also, Gilbert provided a kit to change just the link for the sake of compatibility. Third, a change of bases to change the trucks attached to the bases would also have left tell tale signs. Small brass pins hold the frames to the shells and removing their pins requires a pair of pliers with serrated edges. The serrated edges of the pliers would leave marks on the softer pins if removed and reinserted.

G. Fox & Co.   One of the rarest of the Gilbert box cars. From the Olson Collection

SHEET METAL FRAME TYPES

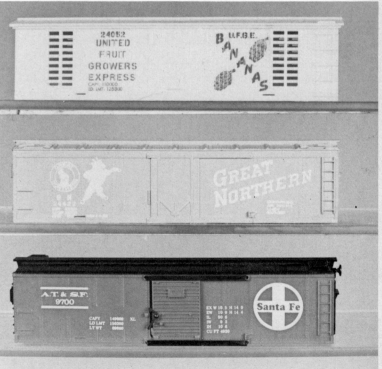

Three types of frames: on the top shelf is a Type III frame with two plates on each side and Pike Master couplers. This frame goes with the 24052 Banana Box. On the middle shelf is a frame with one plate on each side and a plate at one end and a screw hole at the other. It is a modification of a Type II frame and fits the 24422 Great Northern shown on the companion illustration. The bottom row illustrates the frames used in the 1979 Fundimensions production. The frame has one plate on each side, a plate at one end and a screw hole at the other.

On the top shelf is a Civil War type box car used for a modern purpose -- carrying bananas. Note that this box shell has two slots on the plugged door side and fits a Type III frame. On the middle shelf is a 2442 Great Northern plugged door reefer shell with a slot on each side and a screw hole at one end and a slot at the other. On the bottom shelf is a 1979 Fundimensions shell which has a slot on each side and screw hole at one end.

BOX CARS

55 See (24055) Gold Belt.

KEYSTONE See 24067.

SIMMONS See 24420.

G. FOX & CO. See next entry.

G. FOX & CO. Brown painted cream plastic box car body with opening door; white lettered "G. FOX & CO. SERVES CONNECTICUT" to left of door and "The New York, New Haven and Hartford....." to right of door; black metal door guides fastened by rivets, black latch with shiny rivet on door, two part metal brakewheel [2] at one end, Type B [1] six spring trucks, link coupler with weights; one of the rarest S gauge cars; Olson Collection.

	Good	Very Good	Excel
(A) Metal frame.	1000	1200	1500
(B) Plastic frame.	1000	1200	1500

613 GREAT NORTHERN Box, white lettering and logo, brown painted yellow plastic doors, Type I black painted sheet metal frame, opening door, black door guides fastened with rivets.

(A) Brown paint over yellow paint on clear plastic shell, nickel door latch, two piece metal brakewheel, link coupler with black weight, Type D truck side frames with nine springs, Caples Collection.   7   12   15

(B) Brown paint on clear plastic shell, black door latch, one piece plastic brakewheel, knuckle coupler, sintered iron truck side frames, Balint Collection.   7   12   15

622 GAEX Box, yellow lettering and logo, Type I sheet metal frame, link couplers, black weights, opening door, black door guides fastened by four rivets, black latch, two piece metal brakewheel, 1953.   7   12   15

623 ILLINOIS CENTRAL reefer, orange painted black clear plastic shell with plug door, dark green lettered "IC 623" with lines above and below; "ILLINOIS CENTRAL" diamond logo with Type I black sheet metal frame, link coupler with black weight, Type D trucks with nine springs, no brakewheel as hole is plugged, no end slot or screw hole in body.

(A) Orange painted black plastic, Caples Collection.   7   12   15

(B) Orange painted clear plastic, Petri Collection. 7   12   15

629 MISSOURI PACIFIC Stock, comes with open or closed slots.

(A) Type I plastic frame with embossed lettering "PA-9982," solid red plastic shell with silver lettered "MISSOURI PACIFIC with Missouri Pacific logo, opening door, black door latches, black door guides, Type A trucks, two piece brakewheel, Petri Collection.   7   12   15

(B) Same as (A) but Type II die-cast frame, La Calle Collection.   7   10   15

(C) Same as (A) except Type I sheet metal frame, Type B trucks, red painted yellow plastic doors, white plastic shell, Yorkis Collection.   7   10   15

633 BALTIMORE & OHIO Box, 1948-53, two piece brakewheel, no slot or screw hole on ends, Type I sheet metal frames or Type I or II die-cast frames or plastic frames. Because of the numerous 633 variations each is listed by shell type (box or reefer) and color of sides.

633 White Sided Box Cars

(A) White sides, brown ends and roof, black lettering and logo, plastic frame, link couplers, white opening doors, black door guides fastened by four rivets, black latches, 1946.   7   10   15

(B) Same as (A) but Type I die-cast frame, 1948. 7   10   15

(C) Same as (A) but Type I sheet metal frame, Type A trucks.   7   12   15

(D) Same as (A) but Type I sheet metal frame, Type B six-spring trucks, Balint Collection.   7   10   15

(E) Same as (A) but Type I sheet metal frame, Type D nine-spring trucks, white painted clear plastic doors, Degano Collection.   7   10   15

(F) Clear plastic shell with white painted sides, brown painted roof and ends, black lettering and logo, black metal door guides and door latch, Caples Collection.   7   10   15

(G) White plastic body with unpainted shiny white sides, brown roof and ends, die-cast metal frame with two piece brakewheel, black metal door guides fastened by four rivets, black door latch, Type A trucks but springs are undifferentiated as in Type C, Caples Collection. 7   10   15

(H-M) Reserved for future varieties of white box cars.

633 Brown Sided Box Cars

(N) Brown painted white plastic box shell, white lettering and logo, "EH 12-9," die-cast frame, opening door, black door guides fastened by rivets, black door latch, Type A trucks, link coupler with "PAT. NO." and no weights.   7   10   15

(O) Brown painted black plastic shell, white lettering and logo, "EH 12-6." Type I sheet metal frame, link couplers, black weights, opening doors, black door guides, black latches, Type A trucks, 1949.   7   10   15

(P-T) Reserved for future varieties of brown box cars.

633 Red Unpainted Sides Box Cars

(AA) Deep red unpainted plastic shell, white lettering and logo "EH 12-9," Type II die-cast frame, link couplers, brass weights, opening door, black door guides, black latches, two piece brakewheel, Type A truck, "633" underscored, Schneider Collection.   7   10   15

(A) Same as (AA) but "EH 12-6" and bright red unpainted shell, Type III die-cast frame, Type C trucks, two piece brakewheel.   7   10   15

(AC) Same as (AA) but "EH 12-6."   7   10   15

(AD) Same as (AA) but "EH 12-6," bright red unpainted shell.   7   10   15

(AE) Bright red unpainted plastic shell, white lettering and logo, "EH 12-6," Type II die-cast frame, Type A trucks, black coupler weight, two piece brakewheel, link coupler, opening door, black door guides, black latch. 6   19   12

(AF) Same as (AE) but Type B trucks.   6   9   12

(AG) Red unpainted plastic shell, white lettering and logo, "633" underscored, "EH 12-6," Type I sheet metal frame, link couplers, black coupler weight, opening door, black door guides, black latches, two piece brakewheels, Type A sheet metal trucks, 1949.   7   10   15

(AH) Same as (AG), Type B sheet metal trucks.   7   10   15

633 Red Painted Sides Box Cars

(AM) Red painted cream plastic shell, white lettering and logo "EH 12-6," "633" underscored, Type I black sheet metal frame, link couplers, brass weights, opening door, black door guides, black latches, two piece brakewheel, Type B black sheet metal truck sides, Schneider Collection.   7   10   12

(AN) Same as (AM) but red painted yellow plastic. 7   10   12

[1] **TRUCK TYPES**

(A) Six springs and slot.

(B) Six springs, no slot.

(C) Undifferentiated springs.

(D) Nine springs.

[2] **BRAKEWHEELS**

(A) Two piece with shiny metal shift and die-cast wheels.

(B) One piece black plastic.

642 reefer

803

807

913

922

933

937

942

980

981

982

983

984

985

633 **Red Sided Reefers**
    (BA) Unpainted red plastic sides, Type I frame, Type B trucks, link couplers.   20   25   35
    (BB) Same as (BA) but Type C trucks.   20   25   35

633 **Brown Sided Reefers**
    (CA) Brown painted plastic sides, Type I frame, Type B trucks, link couplers.   25   37   50

637 **MKT** All yellow or yellow with brown roof and ends, black lettering and logo "The Katy SERVES THE SOUTHWEST," link coupler, black door guides, black latches, 7 13/16" long, 1949-53.
    (A) Yellow and brown painted black plastic shell, black painted ladder on side, Type I die-cast frame, black coupler weights, Type B trucks.   4   7   10
    (B) Translucent all yellow unpainted plastic shell, Type I sheet metal frame, Type B trucks, black weights, black painted ladders, Schneider and Stromberg Collections.   4   7   10
    (C) Bright all yellow painted shell with translucent yellow doors, Type I sheet metal frame, Type B trucks, black coupler weights; Schneider Collection.   4   7   10
    (D) Deep all yellow painted brown shell, Type I sheet metal frame, Type B trucks, black coupler weights, two piece brakewheel; Welter Collection.   4   7   10
    (E) Lemon yellow painted body, one piece brakewheel, black painted ladders; Stromberg Collection.   4   7   10

639 **AMERICAN FLYER** Box or reefer usually yellow with logo: "AMERICAN FLYER" in black, block sans serif lettering, "639" in Flyer shield, plug door, link couplers.

639 **Reefers**

    (A) Dark yellow painted white plastic shell, Type I sheet metal frame fastened to body with four rivets, Type C trucks, black coupler weights, no brakewheel.   4   7   10
    (B) Dark yellow unpainted shell, Type I yellow plastic frame, Type B trucks, one piece black plastic brakewheel; Schneider Collection.   4   7   10
    (C) Dark yellow unpainted shell, Type I sheet metal frame, Type B trucks, black coupler weights, no brakewheel but hole goes through; Stromberg Collection.   4   7   10
    (D) Lemon yellow painted shell, Type I sheet metal frame, Type B trucks, black coupler weights, no brakewheel, brakewheel hole is plugged, Stromberg Collection.   4   7   10
    (E) Cream unpainted shell, Type I sheet metal frame, Type C trucks, frame fastened to shell by four rivets, black coupler weights; Bargeron and Manson Collections.   20   30   40

639 **Box**
    (A) Bright yellow unpainted plastic shell, Type I sheet metal frame, Type A trucks, black coupler weights, no brakewheel, rivet row separates "AMERICAN FLYER," shield straddles rivet row; Welter Collection.   5   8   11
    (B) Yellow painted white plastic shell, Type I sheet metal frame, Type B trucks, black weights, no brakewheel, Welter Collection.   5   8   11
    (C) Mustard painted white plastic shell, Type I sheet metal frame, no brakewheel.   5   8   11
    (D) Lemon yellow painted black shell, Type I sheet metal frame, Type B trucks with black weights, no brakewheel, plugged hole; Stromberg Collection.   5   8   11
    (E) Same as (D) but yellow shell, Stromberg Collection.   5   8   11
    (F) Same as (D) but bright yellow unpainted plastic; Stromberg Collection.   5   8   11

    (G) Brown painted yellow plastic shell, white lettering, Type I sheet metal frame, Type B trucks, black coupler weights, no brakewheel, with plugged hole; Stromberg Collection.   5   8   11
    (H) Same as (G) but Type A trucks; Welter Collection.   5   8   11
    (I) Yellow painted black plastic shell, Type I sheet metal frame, Type B trucks, black coupler weights, no brakewheel; Welter Collection.   5   8   11

642 **SEABOARD** Light brown painted clear plastic box car shell with plug door, simulated door guides integral to shell, white lettered "Route of the Silver Meteor," white technical data, Type D nine spring trucks, lettering has a washed out appearance; Type I black sheet metal frame, one piece or no brakewheel, white circular "SEABOARD RAILROAD" logo "THROUGH THE HEART OF THE SOUTH" in a white outlined head.
    (A) Flat light brown painted clear plastic shell, Caples Collection.   6   9   15
    (B) Shinier light brown painted clear plastic shell, Caples Collection.   5   8   11
    (C) Flat light brown painted black plastic shell, one piece brakewheel, Stromberg Collection.   5   8   11

642 **AMERICAN FLYER** Reefer or box, brown or red car, plug door, white lettered "AMERICAN FLYER" in black sans serif face, white "642" in white outlined shield, link couplers, black coupler weights, no brakewheel, shell does not have screw-hole and slot at ends.

642 **Reefers** Reefers have doors with triangular bottom section and vertical rivet row.
    (A) Red orange unpainted shell, Type I sheet metal frame, Type B trucks, 1952.   7   11   13
    (B) Dark red painted white shell, Type I sheet metal frame, Type B trucks, 1952.   6   10   12
    (C) Brown painted black shell, Type I sheet metal frame, Type D trucks.   7   10   14
    (D) Same as (C) but Type B trucks, Stromberg Collection.   7   10   14
    (E) Same as (C) but Type A trucks.   7   10   14
    (F) Brown painted white shell, Type I sheet metal frame, Type D trucks.   7   10   14
    (G) Red painted cream shell, Type I sheet metal frame, Type B trucks.   7   10   14

642 **Box Cars** Box cars have doors with horizontal ridges and letterboard.
    (A) Red painted white shell, Type I sheet metal frame, Type B trucks.   7   11   13
    (B) Brown painted white shell, Type I sheet metal frame, Type B trucks.   7   11   13
    (C) Red orange unpainted shell, Type I sheet metal frame, Type C trucks, Yorkis Collection.   7   11   13
    (D) Brown painted yellow shell, Type I sheet metal frame, Type C trucks, Stromberg Collection.   7   11   13
    (E) Red unpainted shell, Type I sheet metal frame, Type C trucks, Stromberg Collection.   7   11   13
    (F) Dark red unpainted shell, Type I sheet metal frames, Type A trucks, Welter Collection.   7   11   13

647 **NORTHERN PACIFIC** Reefer with orange sides and tuscan roof and ends painted on black, gray-white, or green plastic shell, opening door, link or knuckle couplers, stamped steel or sintered iron truck side frames, one or two piece brakewheel, black lettered: "NORTHERN PACIFIC" and "Main Street of the Northwest" in script.
    (A) Black plastic shell, Type B trucks, link couplers, black

970 Seaboard Operating Box Car with Smitty

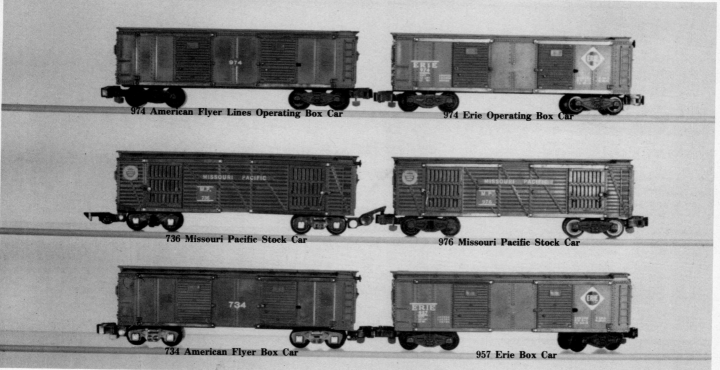

974 American Flyer Lines Operating Box Car   974 Erie Operating Box Car

736 Missouri Pacific Stock Car   976 Missouri Pacific Stock Car

734 American Flyer Box Car   957 Erie Box Car

coupler weights, two piece brakewheel, 1952-53, Patterson, Schneider and Balint Collections.   5   10   15

(B) Gray-white plastic shell, sintered iron truck side frames with concave oval, knuckle couplers, one piece brakewheel, circa 1952, Stromberg Collection.   10   15   20

(C) Green plastic shell, Type B trucks, link couplers, black coupler weights, two piece brakewheel, Welter Collection.   5   10   15

734 AMERICAN FLYER Red, tuscan red or brown on various color plastic shells, two opening doors on one side and one plug door on other side; two sets of black metal door guides fastened to shell by rivets on one side and no door guides on other side, two piece brakewheel, white "734" only on side with two doors; no other lettering on this side. Other side reads: "AMERICAN FLYER" and "734." Note that on the side with the two doors, the rivet row ends to leave space for the number. All reported with link couplers, 1950-54.

(A) Tuscan red painted olive green plastic body, Type A trucks, Balint Collection.   10   15   20

(B) Light brown painted white plastic, lettered "AMERICAN FLYER," one pick up shoe truck, one Type B truck, black coupler weights, Stromberg Collection.   10   15   20

(C) Red unpainted plastic shell, lettered "AMERICAN FLYER," one pick up shoe truck, one Type C truck, black coupler weights, Stromberg Collection.   10   15   20

(D) Brown painted black plastic, lettered "AMERICAN FLY-

ER LINES," one pick up shoe truck, one Type D truck, black coupler weights, Stromberg Collection. 10   15   20

736 MISSOURI PACIFIC Red tuscan painted plastic stock car with two opening doors on Side A; two sets of black door guides fastened to the shell with rivets on Side A; Side B is either open door with door glued in place or opening door; "M.P.736" in white with lines above and below; white and red "MISSOURI PACIFIC LINES" logo, two piece brakewheel, link couplers with black weights, 1954.

(A) Opening door with black metal door guides fastened to the shell by rivets on Side B, Type A trucks, two piece brakewheel, La Calle Collection.   7   11   15

(B) Open door with door glued in place on Side B, Type A trucks, two piece brakewheel, Stromberg Collection.   7   11   15

(C) Same as (B) but Type D trucks, one piece brakewheel, Stromberg Collection.   7   11   15

802 ILLINOIS CENTRAL Unpainted orange plastic reefer shell with dark green "ILLINOIS CENTRAL" in serif face, Illinois Central diamond, dimensions and capacity information, Type II sheet metal frame, shell fastened to frame by slot at one end and screw at other, plug door, one piece or no brakewheel, knuckle couplers, sintered iron truck side frames, 1956-57.

(A) One piece brakewheel, Balint Collection, 1956-57.

  6   8   14

984 985

24030 24043

24047 24048

24052 24054

[240]55[A] [240]55[B]

24057 24058

24065 24066

623 reefer

642 reefer

947

988

989

24403

24413

24419

24422

929

929

994

24076

24077

The top row shows a 623 Illinois Central plug door reefer and a 642 American Flyer plug door reefer. The second row displays a 947 Northern Pacific reefer and a 988 A.R.T. reefer both with opening doors. The third row features a 989 Northwestern Refrigerator with opening door and a 24403 Illinois Central plug door reefer, the fourth row shows a 24413 A.R.T. and a 24419 Canadian National both reefers with opening doors; the fifth row displays a 24422 Great Northern plug door reefer with incorrect trucks and 929 Missouri Pacific stock car. Row seven features a 929 Missouri Pacific and a 994 Union Pacific, both stock cars. The bottom row has two more stock cars: 24076 Union Pacific and 24077 Northern Pacific.

(B) No brakewheel, Stromberg, Bargeron and Patterson Collections.   6   8   14

803 **A.T.S.F.** Box car with plug door, tuscan unpainted plastic shell with white "The Chief," "FAMOUS DAILY STREAMLINER West," "803," and black and white paper lable with "Santa Fe" on cross, one piece plastic brakewheel, Type I or II sheet metal frames, knuckle couplers, sintered iron truck side frames, simulated door guides integral to shell, 1956.
(A) Type I frame, concave oval on truck side frames, Stromberg Collection.   6   10   15
(B) Type II frame, Balint and Schneider Collections.   6   10   15

807 **RIO GRANDE** White unpainted plastic box shell with plug or opening door, black "Rio Grande" and "INSULATED BAKERY GOODS D & R G W," "807," and red "Cookie Box," simulated door guides integral to shell. Black painted Type I or II sheet metal frames, one piece plastic brakewheel, black finished sintered iron truck side frames, knuckle couplers, known as "Cookie Box Car," 1957.
(A) Plug door, Balint Collection.   10   15   20
(B) Opening door, Taylor observation.   200   300   500

913 **GREAT NORTHERN** Box car with opening doors, tuscan painted white plastic shell, white "GREAT NORTHERN," "913," two black door guides fastened by four rivets, black door latch, Type I or II sheet metal frame, knuckle couplers, black sintered iron truck side frames, one piece brakewheel, 1953-56.
(A) Silk-screened "GREAT NORTHERN" goat, Type I sheet metal frame, shell fastened to frame by four pins, one at each corner, flat ovals on truck side frames, Schneider, Manson and Stromberg Collections.   10   15   20
(B) Decaled fat "GREAT NORTHERN" goat, Type I sheet metal frame, shell fastened to frame by four pins one at each corner, Schneider and Manson Collections.   10   15   20
(C) Skinny goat, tall "GREAT NORTHERN" letters, Type I sheet metal frame, shell fastened to frame by four pins, one at each corner, Manson Collection.   10   15   20
(D) Skinny goat, short "GREAT NORTHERN" letters, Type I sheet metal frame, shell fastened to frame by four pins, one at each corner, Manson Collection.   10   15   20

922 **GAEX** Box with opening door, green painted black plastic shell with yellow trim, black door latch, black door guides fastened with rivets; type I sheet metal frame, one or two piece brakewheel, sintered iron truck side frames, knuckle couplers, 1953-56.
(A) Silk-screened stripe, no brakewheel, shell fastened to frame by four pins, one at each corner.   10   15   20
(B) Silk-screened stripe, two piece brakewheel, shell fastened to frame by four pins, one at each corner; concave ovals on on truck side frames, Schneider, La Calle and Stromberg Collections.   10   15   20
(C) Flat green sides, decal stripe, two piece brakewheel, shell fastened to frame by four pins, one at each corner, flat ovals on truck side frames, Stromberg Collection.   10   15   20
(D) Shiny green sides, decal stripe, one piece brakewheel, shell fastened to frame by four pins, one at each corner, Schneider and Balint Collections.   10   15   20

923 **ILLINOIS CENTRAL** Plug door reefer, orange painted or unpainted plastic shell, no brakewheel, dark green lettered "IC 923" with line above and below; black sintered iron, concave oval truck side frames with knuckle couplers, Type I frame, 1954-55.

(A) Orange painted black plastic shell, Stromberg Collection.   7   11   15
(B) Orange unpainted plastic shell, Balint Collection.   7   11   15

929 **MISSOURI PACIFIC** Red or tuscan painted plastic stock car, white lettering with white bar over and under "M.P. 929," "MISSOURI PACIFIC LINES" circular logo on letterboard, black metal door guides fastened with rivets, red or tuscan painted white plastic opening doors with black door latch, black sintered iron truck side frames, knuckle couplers, one or two piece brakewheels, Type I sheet metal frame, 1953-56.
(A) Red painted black plastic shell, two piece brakewheel, Newcomer Collection.   7   11   15
(B) Tuscan painted black plastic shell, one piece brakewheel, Newcomer Collection.   8   12   16
(C) Tuscan painted white plastic shell, two piece brakewheel, Welter Collection.   8   12   16

933 **BALTIMORE AND OHIO** White painted sides, brown painted roof and ends on either clear or brown plastic box car shell; opening doors, one or two piece brakewheel, "BALTIMORE & OHIO" in black sans serif face and B & O Capital dome logo on other side of door; black underscored "933," white painted clear plastic door, black metal door guides fastened to shell with rivets, black door handle, black sintered iron truck side frames, knuckle couplers, Type I frame, 1953-54.
(A) White and brown painted clear plastic shell, two piece brakewheel, Newcomer Collection.   8   10   16
(B) White and brown painted brown plastic shell, two piece brakewheel, Patterson Collection.   8   10   16
(C) Same as (A) but one piece brakewheel, Welter Collection.   8   10   16

937 **M K T** All yellow or yellow and brown painted box car with opening door. "The Katy SERVES THE SOUTHWEST" in black, black technical data, black metal door guides held on by rivets, black door latch, sintered iron truck side frames, knuckle couplers, one piece black plastic brakewheel, 1953-55.
(A) Yellow painted side and brown painted roof and ends on black plastic shell, yellow painted black plastic door, Type I frame, body fastened to shell by four pins, concave oval truck side frames, Stromberg and Newcomer Collections.   7   11   15
(B) All yellow painted sides, roof and ends on clear plastic shell, yellow painted clear plastic doors, Type I frame, body fastened to frame by four pins, flat oval truck side frames, La Calle Collection.   7   11   15

942 **SEABOARD** Plug door box car, tuscan painted white or black plastic shell with faded white "ROUTE OF THE Silver Meteor," white logo "SEABOARD RAILROAD THROUGH THE HEART OF THE SOUTH" with white outlined heart, Type I frame, no brakewheel, black sintered iron, concave oval truck side frames, knuckle couplers, shell does not have slot or screw-hole at ends, 1954.
(A) Tuscan painted white plastic shell, Newcomer Collection.   7   11   15
(B) Tuscan painted black plastic shell, Balint and Stromberg Collections.   7   11   15

947 **NORTHERN PACIFIC** Reefer, orange painted sides and brown painted roof and ends on black or white plastic reefer shell with opening door. Type I sheet metal frame, black lettered "NORTHERN PACIFIC" "Main Street of the Northwest" in script, white "NORTHERN PACIFIC" logo decal with red and black yin yang, black door guides held on by rivets, orange painted black, white or clear plastic door with black trim and lettering; usually one piece brakewheel, black sintered iron truck side frames, knuckle couplers; car shell usually does not have slot or screw-hole at end, 1953-56.

(A) Black plastic shell, black plastic door, one piece brakewheel, Petri Collection.   10   15   20

(B) Black plastic shell, white plastic door, one piece brakewheel, Petri Collection.   10   15   20

(C) Black plastic shell, clear plastic door, one piece brakewheel.   10   15   20

(D) Same as (A) but slot at one end and screw hole at other, one piece brakewheel, Balint Collection.   10   15   20

(E) White plastic shell, white plastic door, two piece brakewheel, flat oval truck side frames, La Calle Collection.   10   15   20

(F) White plastic shell, white plastic door, one piece brakewheel, La Calle Collection.   10   15   20

(G) Black plastic shell, gray plastic door, one piece brakewheel, concave oval truck side frames, Taylor Collection.   10   15   20

957   **ERIE** Tuscan painted black plastic body with two opening doors with two sets of black metal door guides fastened to shell by rivets on one side; on other side is one plug door, one piece brakewheel, "ERIE 957" in white with line above and below, "ERIE" diamond logo paper label; dark gray sintered iron truck side frames, knuckle couplers, shell fastened to frame by four pins; lights; came with button lettered "957 ACTION CAR," aluminum barrels, Balint Collection.   20   40   50

970   **SEABOARD** Operating box car with Smitty, the walking brakeman; tuscan painted black plastic box car shell with plug door, one piece brakewheel; Smitty, the brakeman on roof has blue pants, shirt and hat, red bandana, flesh colored arms and face and walks back and forth controlled by adjustment screw on car end. White "ROUTE OF THE Silver Meteor," Type I frame, sintered iron, concave oval truck side frames, knuckle couplers, clear plastic adhesive on the back of the Seaboard logo, replacement brakemen available, Petrie and Patterson Collections.   10   15   20

973 Gilbert Operating Milk Car, with milkman who tirelessly delivered milk cans, 1956

973   **GILBERT OPERATING MILK CAR** White painted black plastic box, 1956, shell with two opening doors; black milkman with white suit delivers milk cans, four or five milk cans with rounded bases as well as a stand and base came with car, black metal door guides fastened with rivets, white painted sheet metal stand, special frame to accomodate internal mechanism, body fastened to frame with four rivets, concave ovals on sintered iron truck side frames, milk cans are plastic with round metal bottoms to be self righting, Balint, Schneider and Stromberg Collections.
    14   18   30

974   **AMERICAN FLYER LINES** Operating box car, road name only on non-operating side, tuscan painted black plastic box car with two opening doors with two sets of black door guides fastened to the shell with rivets on one side, only lettering on two door side is white numbers "947" on side center. Note that the rivet row

ends to allow space for this number. The car takes crates in through the left door and the blue suited man pushes them out of the right door. This car was made to be used with the K775 baggage loader; the loader, however is not included in the price. One piece brakewheel, "AMERICAN FLYER LINES" in white and plug door on non-operating side. Black sintered iron truck side frames with flat ovals on one truck. The pick up shoe truck has a flat oval on one side and the concave oval on the side where the shoe sticks out, 1953-54, Stromberg and Newcomer Collections.   20   30   40

974   **ERIE** Tuscan painted black plastic box car with two opening doors on one side, two sets of black door guides fastened to shell with rivets; car takes crates or milk cans in through left door and blue or white suited man pushes them out of right door. It was made to be used with K755 baggage loader; loader also used with baggage cars, loader not included in price, sintered iron truck side frames and knuckle couplers. "ERIE 974" in white letters with white lines above and below; "ERIE" diamond logo on white and black paper label; one piece brakewheel. Note that rivet row on center of car side with two doors ends to provide space for lettering but no lettering applied. The pick up shoe truck has a flat oval on one side and a concave oval on the side where the shoe sticks out; The other truck has flat ovals on both sides, 1955, Stromberg Collection.   15   20   35

976   **MISSOURI PACIFIC** Tuscan painted black plastic stock car shell with two opening doors on one side and one opening door glued to other side; also seen with door with guides on second side; two sets of black door guides fastened to the shell with rivets on two door side, black door latch, "M.P.976" in white with line above and below, white and red "MISSOURI PACIFIC LINES" logo, black plastic one piece brakewheel, black sintered iron truck side frames with concave ovals, knuckle couplers, Type IV sheet metal frame, silk-screened MPL logo.

(A) On one door side, a separate door is glued to car side, Stromberg Collectioin.   10   15   20

(B) On one door side, an opening door with door guides, Petri Collection.   10   15   20

980   **BALTIMORE & OHIO** Blue painted black plastic box car shell, orange narrowing band on side, white paper decal; "B & O TIME-SAVER SERVICE LESS-CARLOAD FREIGHT" in blue, "T-S" in orange, black metal door guides, black latch, sintered iron truck side frames, knuckle couplers, Type I sheet metal frame, one piece brakewheel, 1956, replacement stickers available, Newcomer Collection.   20   30   40

981   **CENTRAL OF GEORGIA** Box, black plastic painted with black paint and silver oval on sides and roof; black lettered "The RIGHT WAY" and "C.G. 981," white lettering for technical data, yellow paper label with black "CENTRAL OF GEORGIA," knuckle couplers with black sintered iron side frames, one piece brakewheel, silver painted operating door with black door guides and black latch, double row or rivets, 1956.

(A) Shiny black paint, Type II black sheet metal frame, shell not fastened to frame with slot and screw hole at ends, Newcomer Collection.   20   30   40

(B) Dull black paint, Type I sheet metal frame with four pins at corner, Balint Collection.   25   40   50

(C) Same as (A) but Type I sheet metal frame, concave ovals on truck side frames, Stromberg Collection.   20   30   40

982   **STATE OF MAINE** Blue, white and red painted black plastic box car shell with slot and screw hole; opening door, black metal door guides fastened with rivets, black door latch with Type I sheet metal frame, knuckle couplers, one piece brake wheel. White "STATE OF MAINE PRODUCTS," blue "BAR 982 BANGOR AND AROOSTOOK," 1956.

(A) Light white lettering, concave ovals on truck side frames, Caples Collection. 15 25 35

(B) Heavy white lettering with slightly rough to-the-touch finish, Caples Collection. 15 25 35

983 M.P. Black plastic box shell with slot at one end and screw hole at other painted with two blue bands on side with gray band in middle, gray ends and roof, black plastic opening door painted with yellow bands top and bottom and gray band, black metal door guides held on by four rivets, blue "Eagle MERCHANDISE SERVICE," on gray band, Type I metal frame, white lettering for technical specifications; red pressure sensitive MP sticker; knuckle couplers, one piece brakewheel, 1956, Manson and Newcomer Collections. 15 22 30

984 NEW HAVEN Clear or black plastic box shell with slot at one end and screw hole at other, painted orange with "NEW HAVEN" in white serif letters, "N" in black and "H" in white; black metal door guides, fastened with rivets, black plastic opening door painted orange, black door latch, one piece brakewheel, knuckle couplers, Type I frame fastened to shell by four rivets, one at each corner through frame, sintered iron truck side frames with concave ovals, 1956.
(A) Clear plastic shell, Newcomer Collection. 15 20 30
(B) Black plastic shell with slot and screw hole, Petri Collection. 15 20 30

985 B M Box with opening door, blue painted black plastic slot and screw hole shell, black metal door guides fastened with rivets, black door latch, large white "B" and large black "M" outlined in white; Type I frame, black plastic one piece brakewheel, sintered iron truck side frames with concave ovals and knuckle couplers, catalogued as 24036 in 1957, may have come in 1957 box numbered "24036," Newcomer and Balint Collections.
15 22 30

988 AMERICAN REFRIGERATION TRANSIT CO. Black plastic reefer shell with slot at one end and screw hole at other with orange painted sides and silver painted roof and ends, black "A.R.T. 988" with lines below and above, three paper decals on each side, red, white and blue shield for Union Pacific but no lettering, red cog wheel with white "MISSOURI PACIFIC LINES," red, white and blue "WABASH" flag with staff printed on car in black, no tassels, Type I sheet metal frame; body shell has slot at one end and screw hole at other although not used to fasten shell to frame; knuckle couplers with sintered iron truck side frames with concave ovals, one piece brakewheel, orange painted black plastic opening door with black painted lettering, cross bar simulated latching device; Patterson, Balint and Stromberg Collections. 12 17 25

989 NORTHWESTERN Reefer, black plastic shell painted dark green with yellow side band; black "NORTHWESTERN REFRIGERATION LINES COMPANY 989" and adhesive backed paper label with yellow or orange background with red, black and white "NORTHWESTERN" logo. Opening doors, one piece brakewheel, sintered iron truck side frames, knuckle couplers, black door guides, Type I frame; shell fastened to body by four pins or rivets, on at each corner.
(A) Yellow background, Olson and Balint Collections.
20 30 45
(B) Orange background, Stromberg Collection. 20 30 45

994 UNION PACIFIC Stock car with open slots and opening door; yellow painted black plastic shell with silver painted roof and one piece brakewheel; black metal door guides fastened to shell by four rivets, black door latch, red or maroon sans serif lettered "UNION PACIFIC," red or maroon "U.P. 944" with red line above and below; red or maroon technical data; dark gray

sintered iron truck side frames with knuckle couplers, Type II frame shell with slot at one end and screw hole at other, or Type I frame with four pins, yellow painted black plastic door, 1957, Newcomer and Balint Collections. 20 30 40

C1001 WSX Box with plug door, yellow unpainted plastic body, "SOUTHWEST GREATEST DISCOUNT CENTER" in red and "WHITE'S" in yellow, one piece brakewheel, Type III frame with plate through slot on each car slot and through slot at one end, Pike Master trucks and couplers, 1962, Walsh Collection.
250 400 600

C2001 POST White unpainted plastic Civil War style box car shell, Type III frame with and without hayjector mechanism, sintered iron truck side frames with concave ovals, knuckle couplers, or Pike Master trucks and couplers; orange "POST" logos - large logo on left and small logo on right; under large logo "Breakfast Cereals" and specification information; under small logo "C20001." On ejector side there are small and large logos in reversed position. The small logo is partially blocked by the simulated open door, no brakewheels; no door guides, the shell is fastened to the frame by side slots; the same car shell came with Washington sets, 1962.
(A) With hayjector mechanism, sintered iron truck side frames, concave ovals, knuckle couplers, Stromberg Collection. 20 30 40
(B) Without hayjector mechanism, Pike Master trucks and couplers. 20 30 40

9700 A.T.&S.F. See Fundimensions production at end of this section.

24003 A.T.S.F. Plug door box car, tuscan unpainted shell, one piece brakewheel, white lettered "A.T.S.F. 24003" and "The Chief Famous Daily Streamliner West" with paper label, Santa Fe cross, Type I frame, sintered iron truck side frames with concave ovals, knuckle couplers, shell with screw hole at one end and slot at other although frame fastened to shell by four rivets one at each corner, Balint, Stromberg and Mason Collections.
10 15 20

24006 GREAT NORTHERN Box car with opening doors, tuscan painted white plastic shell, white "GREAT NORTHERN" and "24006" in white, two black door guides fastened by four rivets, black door latch, Type I sheet metal frame, knuckle couplers, black sintered iron truck side frames, one piece brakewheel, 1957, Carnes Collection. No Reported Sales

24009 GAEX Box car with opening doors, green painted plastic shell with yellow trim, black door latch, black door guides fastened with rivets, Type I sheet metal frame, brakewheel, sintered iron truck side frames, knuckle couplers; 1957, Carnes Collection. No Reported Sales

24016 M K T Yellow painted sides and brown painted roof on black plastic shell, "The Katy SERVES THE SOUTHWEST" in black, black technical data slightly larger than on 937. Type II frame, shell fastened to frame by slot at one end and screw at other. Opening door with black metal door guides fastened by four pins on each side. One piece brakewheel, "24016" on car side, sintered iron trucks side frames with knuckle couplers, 1958, Welter

Collection. For another MKT see next entry. 150 200 300

24016 M K T All yellow car, sintered iron truck side frames, knuckle couplers, 1961. For a much rarer MKT see previous entry.
10 15 20

24016 SEABOARD brown painted sides and roof, sintered iron truck side frames, knuckle couplers, 1958. 20 30 40

On the top row is the B & M PA prototype that was not put into production. Row 2 features two prototype box cars the 00000 Rio Grande and the 240000 Mounds. The prototypes are described in the text following the last regular production box cars. The Mounds was issued as 24057 using the Civil War type body and is illustrated on another color plate. Row 3 shows the 24067 Keystone Camera car and the 24018 Katy box. On the fourth row are two more rare cars: the C1001 White's Discount Center and the [24420] Simmons Box reefer. The fifth row contains a 24426 Rath Packing Co. reefer with the Indian Head sticker and the 24425 B A R reefer. The bottom shelf has a rare Texas and Pacific GP-7 with "TEXAS & PACIFIC" on the side

24018 **MKT** Yellow sides, tuscan ends and roof, black plastic shell, Type II frame, shell fastened to frame by screw at one end and slot at other; opening doors, one piece black plastic brakewheel, sintered iron truck side frames, knuckle couplers; "The Katy SERVES THE SOUTHWEST" and technical data in black, black metal door guides fastened by rivets, Patterson Collection.

               300 500 700

24019 **SEABOARD** Tuscan painted black plug door box car shell, no brakewheel, "Silver Meteor" and Seaboard logo in white, Type I or II frame, shell fastened to body by four pins or slot and screw, uncatalogued, sintered iron truck side frames with concave ovals, knuckle couplers, Balint, Manson and Schneider Collections.   20 30 40

24023 **BALTIMORE & OHIO** Dark blue painted black plastic box car shell, orange painted narrowing band on side, blue lettering on label reads "B & O TIME-SAVER SERVICE LESS CARLOAD FREIGHT," and orange "T-S," shell fastened to frame by slot and screw, Type II frame, black metal door guides fastened by rivets; opening doors, one piece brakewheel, sintered iron truck side frames, knuckle couplers, comes in boxes numbered either "980" or "24024," 1957-59, Balint, Patterson and Schneider Collections.   10 15 25

24026 **CENTRAL OF GEORGIA** Shiny or dull black painted black plastic shell, silver oval with "C.G." with bar top and bottom and "The Right Way" in script in silver area; yellow and black adhesive paper label, silver painted roof, one piece plastic brakewheel, Type I frame fastened to shell by four rivets, one at each corner; black door guides with black latch, shell with slot at one end and screw hole at other, sintered iron truck side frames with concave ovals, 1957-58, Balint, Walsh, and Stromberg Collections.   35 45 60

24029 **STATE OF MAINE** Red, white and blue sides, black plastic shell, Type I, II, or III frames, "STATE OF MAINE PRODUCTS" in white "BAR 24029 BANGOR AND AROOSTOOK" in blue, black door guides fastened by four pins or by tabs on ends of guide inserted and bent back; opening doors, one piece brakewheel, 1957-60.

(A) Type II frame with shell fastened to frame by slot and screw, sintered iron truck side frames, knuckle couplers, door guides fastened by four pins, Balint and Schneider Collections.   35 48 60

(B) Type III frame with shell fastened to frame by slots on sides, Pike Master trucks and couplers, door guides fastened by tabs, Walsh and Stromberg Collections.

               100 200 300

(C) Type I frame, with shell fastened to frame by four rivets one in each corner; sintered iron truck side frames with concave ovals; knuckle couplers; door guides fastened by pins, Patterson Collection.   30 45 60

24030 **MKT** Yellow painted or unpainted plastic plug door box car, "The Katy SERVES THE SOUTHWEST" in black, Type III frame, no brakewheel, Pike Master plastic trucks and couplers, uncatalotued, production year not currently known.

(A) Unpainted yellow plastic, Newcomer Collection.

               10 15 20

(B) Yellow painted clear plastic shell, Balint Collection.

               100 200 300

24033 **MISSOURI PACIFIC** Box, black plastic shell with gray painted roof and ends, blue and gray sides; yellow and gray painted doors, black door guides and latches, Type II or III frames, knuckle coupler with black sintered iron side frames, shells have slot at one end and screw hole at other, 1958, Balint Collection.   20 30 45

24036 **NEW HAVEN** Orange painted black plastic shell has slot at one end and screw hole at other end, large black "N" and large white "H," Type II sheet metal frame, one piece black plastic brakewheel, black door guides fastened with rivets, black door latch, sintered iron truck side frames and knuckle couplers, 1957-60, Balint Collection.   20 30 50

24039 **D & R G** White unpainted plastic box car shell with plug door, "Rio Grande" and "INSULATED BAKERY GOODS" in black "Cookie Box" in orange-red, Type II or III sheet metal frame; shell has slot at one end, screw hole at other and side slots; it is fastened to frame by screw at one end and slot at other; one piece plastic brakewheel, sintered iron trucks with knuckle couplers, 1959.

(A) Type II sheet metal frame, Greenberg Collection.

               10 15 20

(B) Type III sheet metal frame, concave ovals on truck side frames, Stromberg Collection.   10 15 20

24043 **B M** Blue painted black plastic box car shell with opening doors, "B M 24043" in black, large black "M" outlined in white and large white "B," black door latch, sintered iron truck side frames with concave ovals, knuckle couplers, one piece brakewheel, 1957-60.

(A) Type II frame, door guide fastened with rivets, black unpainted doors, Balint Collection.   20 30 45

(B) Type III frame, black metal door guides pressed into shell, Newcomer and Patterson Collections.   20 30 45

24045 **M E C** Dark green sides, roof and ends, Type II frame fastened by screw slot; opening door, riveted door guides, one piece plastic brakewheel, "M E C 24045," "NEW 3-56" and other technical data in white; pressure sensitive paper label shows Maine Central tree logo, sintered iron trucks, knuckle couplers. Prototype illustrated as part of Olson rare box car plate, reportedly only a handful were manufactured. No Reported Sales

24047 **GREAT NORTHERN** Plug door box car, red painted black plastic shell, white "GREAT NORTHERN," five white dots on lower car sides; black sintered iron truck side frames, knuckle couplers, 1959.

(A) Paper adhesive label with goat and white lettered "GREAT NORTHERN RAILWAY," Type II frame, one piece brakewheel, Balint Collection. 50 75 100

(B) Paper decal with goat and white lettered "GREAT NORTHERN RAILWAY," Type III frame, no brakewheel.

               50 75 100

24048 **M St L** Red painted black plastic body with light white lettered "M St L 24048" and technical information; black paper label with "The Peoria Gateway" in semi-script white lettering, red painted black plastic opening door, black door guides that snap into frame and black latch on each side, one piece brakewheel, Type II frame, knuckle couplers, black sintered iron side frames, 1959-62.

(A) Type II frame, Newcomer Collection. 40 60 80

(B) Type III frame, Stromberg Collection. 40 60 80

24052 **UNITED FRUIT GROWERS EXPRESS** Civil War type stock car with plug door on one side and no door on other, yellow unpainted plastic shell, two sets of grates on each side; blue lettered "U.F.G.E." and "BANANAS" and two bunches of bananas; plug door simulated wood barn door, black plastic Pike Master trucks and couplers; Type III frame, two slots on each car side for frame, 1961, Newcomer Collection. 5 7 10

24054 **SANTA FE** Box car with opening door, red translucent or painted plastic, white lettered "AT S F" and "SL;" "Super SHOCK CONTROL" in white outlined box; black metal door guides pressed into shell, black latch, black plastic Pike Master trucks and couplers, Type III frame, one piece brakewheels.

(A) Red painted black plastic shell, 1962-64, Newcomer Collection.   20 30 40

(B) Red unpainted shiny plastic shell, black painted ladders and grab iron, 1966, Balint and Patterson Collections.   7 9 15

(C) Red painted dull red plastic shell, painted red letters, Patterson Collection.   7 9 15

(D) Red painted white plastic shell, Jones Collection.   7 9 15

[240]55 **THE GOLD BELT LINE** Yellow plastic Civil War type plastic body lightly oversprayed in red, adhesive backed aluminum label reads "THE GOLD BELT LINE" in black letters on gold belt with red area; Civil War type stock car with grates near each end on side; simulated barn type side door; intended to be Civil War ammunition car. Type III black painted sheet metal frame with plate on one end and one on each side; black sintered iron truck side frames with knuckle couplers or Pike Master trucks and couplers; As a new car design Gilbert designed the 240(55) to fit its current frame.the car comes with either two slots on each side or one slot on each side. The car comes with either a highly detailed plug door on one side and either an open door frame with detailed door or an open door frame with no door. Looking at the open door frame side of either car, the frame plate comes through the slots on the right side and through a slot at the left end. Looking at the closed side of either car, the brakewheel is on the right end of the catwalk. Both types of car have "PA-15D950-A" embossed on the inside of the roof.

(A) Two slots on each side, one slot at one end with the other end not pierced or slotted. On one side is a closed, highly detailed barn door with simulated boards forming a V. The point of the V points to the left side, and the V opens towards the right top and bottom corners. A simulated latch is seen on the right hand side of the door opening. The second side of the car has an open door frame with a simulated barn door to the left of the opening. The door does not have a latch. The door has a simulated V shaped design similar to that of the first side. There is a simulated latch on the right hand side of the door opening. The doors on both sides have simulated grab irons on the center near the bottom. "THE GOLD BELT LINE" appears on an adhesive label above "55" and to the right of the door on both sides. Looking at the open door side of the car, the frame plate comes through the slots on the right side, the end plates comes through the left end. The other two slots are not used; sintered iron truck side frames, Patterson and Newcomer Collections.   12 18 25

(B) One slot on each side of the car and one slot at the opposite end with the other end not pierced or slotted. The first side features a closed, highly detailed barn door with the point of the V to the left side; the V opens towards the right top and bottom corners. There is a simulated latch on the right side on the center bar. On the second side, there is an open door frame but no simulated door. "THE GOLD BELT LINES" appears on an adhesive label above the "55" to the left side of each side.   10 15 20

(C) Same as (A) but without "GOLD BELT" sticker, Pike Master trucks and couplers   10 15 20

24056 **B M** Blue plastic box car with opening doors, "B M 24056" in black and large black "M" outlined in white and large white "B," black door latch, Type III frame, shell fastened to frame by one slot on each side, one piece plastic brakewheel, press-in type door guides, opening door, Pike Master trucks and couplers, 1961.

(A) Blue painted black plastic shell, Walsh Collection.   20 30 40

(B) Unpainted blue plastic shell, Walsh and Patterson Collections.   30 45 60

24057 **MOUNDS** Civil War type stock car with plug door, simulated barn door and two stock grates on one side; other side has door opening but no door as well as two stock grates; white or ivory unpainted plastic shell with maroon "MOUNDS 24057" and red Mounds candy bar, black plastic Pike Master trucks and couplers, Type III frame with two slots on side with plug door, 1962.

(A) White unpainted plastic, Newcomer Collection.   5 7 10

(B) Ivory unpainted plastic, Stromberg Collection.   7 15 20

24058 **POST** Plug door box car, white or ivory unpainted plastic shell with "Breakfast Cereal" and logo in red and "Post" in white, Type III frame, shell with one slot on each side and one at end, black sintered iron truck side frames with knuckle couplers, or Pike Master trucks and couplers, one piece brakewheel, 1963-64.

(A) White shell, sintered iron truck side frames, knuckle couplers, Stromberg Collection.   5 7 10

(B) Ivory shell, sintered iron truck side frames, knuckle couplers, Stromberg Collection.   5 7 10

(C) Same as (A) but reads "Breakfast Cereals" with an "s," Stromberg Collection.   6 9 12

(D) Same as (A) but Pike Master trucks and couplers, Welter Collection.   6 9 12

24059 **B M** Blue sides, part of Hawkeye set with 21168 Southern loco, 1963, believed similar to 24056.   45 65 95

24060 **M St L** Existence confirmed by Patterson.   No Reported Sales

24065 **N Y C** Black plastic box, shell painted New York Central green with "N Y C 24065" and technical data in white, white paper label with "NEW YORK SYSTEM" in black and "CENTRAL" in white, all with sans serif face; two black metal door guides snap into shell, has black latch on each side, green painted black plastic opening door or plug doors, Type III sheet metal frame with plates through car sides and one end, one piece brakewheel and wheels with deep dish facing out.

24065 **N Y C** Reefer, same green as 24065 box with opening door, one piece plastic brakewheel, Pike Master trucks and couplers, Type III frame, same white lettering as box car, does not have sticker; white silk-screened lettering, Carnes Collection.

     No Reported Sales

See next entry for reefer version of 24065.

(A) Black sintered iron truck side frames with concave ovals, opening doors, knuckle couplers, Caples and Stromberg Collections.   20 30 40

(B) Black plastic Pike Master trucks and couplers, opening doors, Newcomer Collection.   20 30 40

(C) Same as (B) but plug doors, Carnes Collection.

     No Reported Sales

24065 **N Y C** Reefer style shell is same color and has white lettering as does 24065 N Y C box; has opening door, one piece plastic brakewheel, Pike Master trucks and couplers, Type III frame but does not have the sticker found on the box car version, Carnes Collection.   No Reported Sales

24066 **LOUISVILLE & NASHVILLE** Blue painted black or white plastic shell with plug door; "L & N," "24066" and technical data all in yellow; yellow logo D and F, Type III sheet metal frame with plates holding shell at one end and on sides, knuckle couplers, black sintered iron truck side frames with concave ovals, one piece plastic brakewheel, 1960.

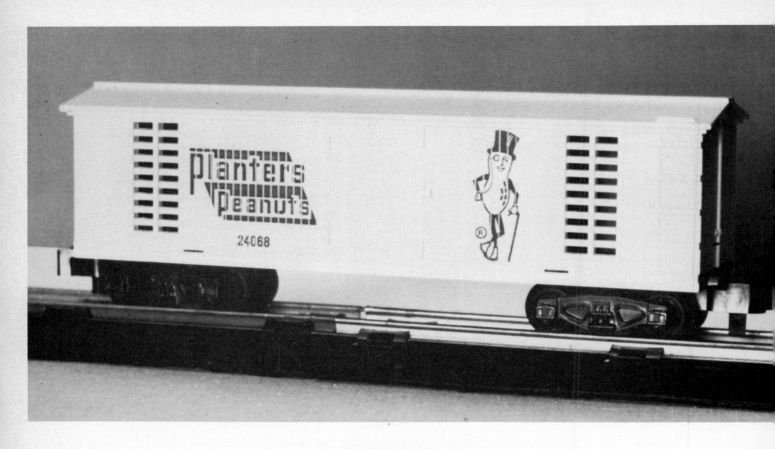

**The Very Rare 24068 Planters Peanut Box
from the DeMarco Collection**

(A) Blue painted black plastic shell with reinforcing "plate" on each lower corner, Manson and Balint Collections.

             50   75   100

(B) Blue painted white plastic shell, Stromberg Collection.

             50   75   100

24067   **KEYSTONE LINE** Box, "FASTEST ROUTE TO TOP PROFITS," black metal door guides held in place by rivets, black door latch, large black "K" inside of "C," orange unpainted plastic shell, no number on car, black sintered iron trucks, knuckle couplers, brakewheel, Type II frame, 1960, Walsh Collection.   500 800 1000

24068   **PLANTERS PEANUT** White unpainted plastic Civil War type stock car with two grates on each side near end; plug door on one side with blue "Planters Peanuts" surrounded by red panel area; blue Mr. Peanut, black plastic Pike Master trucks and couplers, Type III frame with two slots on each side for base plates; second side with plug door open and blue "p l" with small red area and blue Mr. Peanut, 1961. Only two currently known to exist, De Marco Collection.   500 700 1000

24076   **UNION PACIFIC** Stock car with open slats and opening doors, yellow painted black plastic shell, silver painted roof and ends, "U.P. 24076," in red or maroon with red or maroon line above and below; yellow painted black plastic doors; black door guides either fastened with rivets or pressed in; black door latch; sintered iron truck side frames with knuckle couplers or Pike Master trucks and couplers, Type II or III frames, 1957-60.

(A) Red lettering, Type II frame, door guides fastened with rivets, sintered iron truck side frames with concave ovals and knuckle couplers, Stromberg Collection. 12 18 25

(B) Red lettering, Type III frame, door guides fastened with rivets, sintered iron truck side frames with concave ovals and knuckle couplers; Stromberg Collection.

             12   18   25

(C) Maroon lettering, Type III frame, door guides pressed into sides, Pike Master trucks and couplers, Stromberg Collection.   7   11   15

24077   **NORTHERN PACIFIC** Stock car with open slats and opening doors; red painted black plastic shell, silver painted roof and ends, white "NORTHERN PACIFIC," aluminum plate with black outlined pig wearing hat with letters "N P" and "PIG PALACE" in black. One or two piece brakewheel, press-in black door guides, black door latch, sintered iron truck side frames with concave oval and knuckle couplers or Pike Master trucks and couplers; Type III frame; shell with one slot on each side, one slot at one end and screw hole at other end, 1959-62.

(A) Sintered iron truck side frames with concave ovals, one piece brakewheel, Newcomer Collection.   35 50 75

(B) Pike Master trucks and couplers, two piece brakewheel, Olson Collection.   35 50 75

(C) Same as (A) but two piece brakewheel, Stromberg Collection.   35 50 75

24402   **ILLINOIS CENTRAL** Reefer, similar to 24403, observed by Taylor.   No Reported Sales

LINES

REFRIGERATOR

Rath

THE RATH PACKING CO

R.P.R.X.
24426

24426 RATH PACKING

Swift

SWIFT
REFRIGERATOR LINE
SRLX
14950

14950 SWIFT

MOUNDS

NEW HAVEN
MOUX
24063

24000 NEW HAVEN

KO&G
KANSAS OKLAHOMA AND GULF

INSULATED

KO&G
00000

00000 K O & G

24045 MEC

C N R
REFRIGERATOR

CANADIAN
NATIONAL
C.N.
00000

00000 C N R

The Olson Collection

24403 **ILLINOIS CENTRAL** Plug door reefer, orange unpainted plastic shell with "IC" and "24403" in green and green diamond logo with "ILLINOIS CENTRAL," Type II frame, black sintered iron trucks with concave ovals, knuckle couplers; two dark green rectangles to left of door, no brakewheel, Newcomer Collection.

5 7 10

24409 **NORTHERN PACIFIC** Reefer, orange painted sides, brown painted roof and ends on plastic shell with opening doors, "NORTHERN PACIFIC" and "Main Street of the Northwest" in black script, white "NORTHERN PACIFIC" logo decal with red and black yin/yang symbol; black door guides, orange painted door with black trim and lettering; one piece brakewheel, sintered iron truck side frames, knuckle couplers, 1957-58.

200 300 400

24413 **AMERICAN REFRIGERATOR TRANSIT CO.** Reefer with opening door, orange painted sides and silver painted roof on black plastic shell; three paper decals: a red, white and blue Union Pacific shield but Union Pacific does not appear on decal, a red cog wheel with white "MISSOURI PACIFIC LINES" and red, white and blue "WABASH" flag with black staff and tassels silk-screened on car; black door guides pressed into shell or riveted to shell; black truck side frames, knuckle couplers, one piece plastic brakewheel, black plastic door with "Close & Lock Door Before Moving Car," Type II frame, 1957-60.

20 30 40

24416 **NORTHWESTERN** Reefer with black plastic shell painted dark green with yellow side band; "NORTHWESTERN REFRIGERATOR LINES COMPANY 24416" in black and adhesive backed paper label with yellow, red, black and white "NORTHWESTERN" logo; opening doors, one piece brakewheel, sintered iron truck side frames, knuckle couplers, black door guides, Type I or II frames; shell fastened to body by four pins or by screw at one end and slot at other end; 1957-59, Olson and Leonard Collections.

350 450 600

24419 **CANADIAN NATIONAL** Gray painted black plastic reefer shell with "CANADIAN NATIONAL" in dark red in two lines and underscored, gray paper label with "C N R" and "SERVES ALL CANADA" in red in red outlined box, green maple leaf, gray painted black plastic opening reefer door with red trim, grab irons and ladders and red lettering; one piece brakewheel, black metal door guides fastened with four rivets; Type II frame held to shell by plate and screw, wheels with deep dish facing out; sintered iron truck side frames, 1958-59, Newcomer Collection.

50 75 100

[24420] **SIMMONS CARLOAD BARGAINS SALE** Reefer with plug door, orange or white unpainted plastic with black circle around black lettering, one piece plastic knuckle couplers, sintered iron truck side frames, no brakewheel, 1958.
(A) Orange unpainted plastic, Walsh Collection.

200 300 450

(B) White unpainted plastic, Carnes Collection.

No Reported Sales

24422 **GREAT NORTHERN** Box car with plug or opening door, light green unpainted plastic body with plug door and "GREAT NORTHERN" in white serif face with white "GREAT NORTHERN" logo; body with screw hole and slot and slots on side, Type III frame, plastic Pike Master trucks and couplers, no brakewheel, deep rim wheels, Caples Collection. (Note similar car in next entry which is the more common.)
(A) Plug door, Caples Collection.

50 75 100

(B) Opening door, Carnes Collection.

No Reported Sales

24422 **GREAT NORTHERN** Reefer with plug door, light green unpainted plastic reefer body with plug door and "GREAT NORTHERN" in white serif face, white "GREAT NORTHERN" logo, body with screw hole and slot at ends, shell with slots in side, Type III frame that fastens with one end plate and one plate on each side, 1965-66 plastic Pike Master truck and couplers, no brakewheel; deep rim wheels, Caples Collection. (Note similar car in previous entry which is the more valuable!).

9 12 17

Also note that the illustrated car is shown with sheet metal truck side frames and knuckle couplers. The sheet metal truck side frames are believed to have been changed from the original Pike Master trucks.

24422 **GREAT NORTHERN** Reefer with opening door, light green painted black plastic shell, black door guides pressed into frame, black plastic one piece brakewheel, Pike Master trucks and couplers, Type III frame; See two previous entries for other versions, Balint Collection.

35 50 80

24425 **BAR** Reefer with opening door; black plastic shell painted red; "BAR," "24425" and "NEW 55" in white, paper label in red, white and blue with "BANGOR & AROOSTOOK RAILROAD" and "Serving NORTHERN MAINE" in white, Type III frame with plate through each car side; one piece brakewheel, sintered iron side frame trucks, knuckle couplers, black metal door guides pressed into shell, 1960, Balint Collection.

75 100 150

24426 **RATH PACKING CO.** Reefer with opening doors, black plastic painted orange on sides and ends, tuscan roof, two black metal door guides pressed into body shell, "REFRIGERATOR" and "R.P.R.X." in tuscan; Type III frame, sintered iron side frame trucks, knuckle couplers; Indian head paper pressure sensitive sticker in red and white with "Rath" in blue, 1960-61, Walsh Collection.

75 100 150

25013 **SEABOARD** Walking brakemen, same as 970, but numbered 25013, 1957, Carnes Collection.

200 300 400

25019 **OPERATING MILK CAR** 1957-60, white painted black plastic shell, Type V frame, one plug door on one side, two operating doors on other side, one piece plastic brakewheel; shell has slot at one end and screw hole at other; black door guides attached with rivets, "Gilbert's Grade A Milk Pasteurized 25019" in black and cow front profile in circle, knuckle couplers, sintered iron truck side frames with concave ovals; price includes platform, 1957-60, Stromberg and Patterson Collections.

20 30 40

25041 **ERIE** Operating box car, 1957.

No Reported Sales

25042 **ERIE** Operating box car, brown painted black plastic shell, Type V frame, sintered iron truck side frames with knuckle couplers, "ERIE 24024" in white, "Erie" decal, lettering identical on both sides, four small barrels, shell fastened to frame by four pins; door guides only on the side with two opening doors; door guides fastened by rivets; the second side has a plug door; one piece plastic brakewheel, 1957-58, Rudzinski, Balint and Walsh Collections.

30 50 75

25049 **D R G W** White unpainted plastic box car shell; shell with plug door; "Rio Grande" and "INSULATED BAKERY GOODS" in black; "Cookie Box" in orange-red; Type I sheet metal frame; with Smitty the Walking Brakeman; sintered iron truck side frames, knuckle couplers, 1958-60, Balint Collection.

30 45 60

[25056] **U S M** Two car set consisting of box car and rocket launcher. Box car has yellow body, "37 DIVISION" and "BUILT USA 56" and "USM LD. LMT. 10000" all in black on plug door side; on side with two operating doors: "USM LD. LMT. 10000 DANGER

OFF LIMITS 37 DIVISION BUILT USA 56;" metal door guides fastened with rivets, Type V frame with shell fastened to frame by four screws; one piece plastic brakewheel. Yellow flat car has 90° launcher and tool box similar to 969 flat launcher. Flat is lettered "37th DIV. ROCKET LAUNCHER," 1959. Both cars have to be connected and on track for the missile to be launched, both cars have sintered iron truck side frames and knuckle couplers, 1959 production. Newcomer and Welter Collections.

75	130	175

25057   **TNT** Exploding box car. This car and the 25061 have a special frame. The car has a five piece shell of black plastic; "TNT EXPLOSIVES CARRIER SERVICE DO NOT HUMP" in yellow and red and "DANGER 25057" in red; one truck has pick up shoe, 1960.

(A)   Silver top and ends, Balint Collection.   20   30   40
(B)   Green top and ends.   20   30   40

25061   **TNT** Exploding box car. This car and the 25057 have a special frame. The car has a five piece black plastic shell, "TNT EXPLOSIVES CARRIER SERVICE DO NOT HUMP" in red and yellow, and "DANGER 25061" in red; one truck with pick up shoe, 1961.   20   30   40

25062   **MINE CARRIER** Yellow sides, light brown or silver roof and ends, lettered "25062 MINE CARRIER," "EXPLOSIVES," "DANGER," "DO NOT HUMP THIS CAR." This is a spring loaded car that "explodes" when hit by a rocket, 1962-64.

(A)   Silver roof and ends.   15   22   30
(B)   Light brown roof and ends.   15   22   30

Civil War type box with Hayjector mechanism

25082 NEW HAVEN box with Hayjector mechanism

25081   **N Y C** Light green unpainted Civil War type stock car body with large faded white "N Y C 25081" and "NEW YORK CENTRAL" logo, hay bale unloading mechanism (called a "Hayjector") inside car; trip extends below car; black plastic Pike Master trucks and couplers, Type III frame with plate that fits into one slot on one car end and into one slot on each side of car; or Type IIIA frame; car shell is designed with two slots on each side to facilitate assembly, 1961-64.

(A)   Type III frame, Balint Collection.   5   10   15
(B)   Type IIIA frame, Stromberg Collection.   5   10   15

25082   **NEW HAVEN** Orange painted black or translucent red plastic box car body with opening door; black door guides press into shell; Type III frame with plate that fits into one slot at one end of car, and into one slot on each side of car; "N H 25082" in white with white line above and below; large black "N" and large white "H," haybale unloading mechanism inside car; black trip for mechanism extends below car; black plastic one piece brakewheel, Balint Collection.

(A)   Orange painted red shell, Balint Collection.   10   15   20
(B)   Orange painted black shell, Pike Master trucks and couplers, Stromberg and Welter Collections.   10   15   20

9700   **A.T.S.F.** Red plastic shell with black painted ends and roof; white "CAPY 149000 XL LD LMT 150200 LT WT 69800" on left side of door, white "EX W 10 5 H 14 0 EW 10 0 H 14 4 IL 50 6 IW 9 3 IH 10 6 CU FT 4920." Frame fastened to shell by one slot on each side, a slot at one end and a screw at other; sintered iron trucks with flat ovals, knuckle couplers, 1979.   10   15   20

PROTOTYPE BOX CARS

00000   **D & R G W** Prototype Rio Grande box car, silver band, yellow band separated by black line, silver roof and ends, black sintered iron trucks, knuckle couplers, two black door guides fastened with four rivets, hand lettering, Walsh Collection.

No Reported Sales

24000   **NEW HAVEN MOUNDS** Plug door box, prototype Type III frame, slots through sides, cream plastic shell with "MOUNDS" in red, black sintered iron trucks, knuckle couplers, Walsh Collection.   No Reported Sales

00000   **CANADIAN NATIONAL** Reefer, light blue body with black and red lettering "C N R SERVES ALL CANADA," black metal door guides above and below door; knuckle couplers; hand-lettered prototype, not put into production, Olson Collection.   No Reported Sales

24426   **THE RATH PACKING COMPANY** Reefer with yellow sides, black roof and black lettering "P.B.R.X. CAPY 100000 LB LMT 34000 LT LMT 18000; RATH BLACK HAWK," decal, prototype, not put into production, Olson Collection.   No Reported Sales

14950   **SWIFT REFRIGERATOR LINE** Reefer with tuscan body with white stripes above and below door; door guides painted white; hand-lettered "Swift, SRLX 14950," in white, prototype, not put into production, Olson Collection.   No Reported Sales

24045   **M E C** Dark green box car, same color as 922, M E C stands for Maine Central, black door guides above and below door, crudely hand-lettered in yellow; prototype; reported that a handful produced, Olson Collection.   No Reported Sales

00000   **K O & G** Reefer with blue sides and black roof, hand-lettered "K O & G KANSAS OKLAHOMA AND GULF DF INSULATED, SOONER.......THE SOUTHWEST" in white, prototype not put into production; Olson Collection.   No Reported Sales

24060   **NEW HAVEN MOUX** Light blue box car with red and white "PETER PAUL INDESCRIBABLY DELICIOUS MOUNDS," blue door guides below and above door, Pike Master couplers; similar to 24000 with light cream sides shown on another plate; the 24057 which is somewhat different was put into production, Olson Collection.   No Reported Sales

The Welter Collection

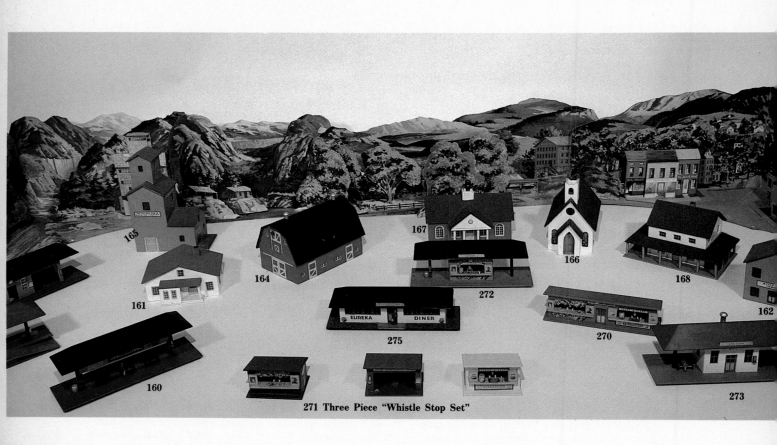

275 EUREKA DINER

271 Three Piece "Whistle Stop Set"

160 161 164 165 166 167 168 162 270 272 273

Chapter IX
ACCESSORIES

		Good	Very Good	Excel

21   **IMITATION GRASS 1949-50,** approximately a half-pound, in clear cellophane bag with white lettering, Newcomer Collection.   2   4   6

21A   **IMITATION GRASS 1951-56,** a half-pound, in clear cellophane bag with white lettering, Balint Collection.   2   4   6

22   **SCENERY GRAVEL 1949-56,** 22 ounces, Balint Collection; in white cellophane bag, Patterson Collection; in heavy printed paper bag, Olson Collection.   2   4   6

23   **ARTIFICIAL COAL 1949-56,** approximately a half-pound, white cloth bag, Newcomer and Balint Collections; plastic bag 3½ x 9", Stromberg Collection.   2   4   6

24   **RAINBOW WIRE 1949-56,** 25 feet of multi-strand four conductor wire, Patterson Collection.   2   4   6

25   **SMOKE CARTRIDGE 1947-56,** twelve small red plastic capsules in a box, Patterson Collection.   2   4   6

26   **SERVICE KIT 1952-56,** track cleaning fluid, oil, grease, brush, sanding sticks, commutator stick, tube cleaners, cloth, twelve-page manual in a box, Newcomer Collection.   2   4   6

27   **TRACK CLEANING FLUID 1952-56,** eight-ounce bottle, bluish liquid, Patterson Collection.   1   2   3

28   **TRACK BALLAST 1950,** approximately a half-pound, in white paper bag, Balint Collection.   1   2   3

28A   **TRACK BALLAST 1951-53,** white cellophane bag.   1   2   3

29   **IMITATION SNOW 1950,** white cellophane bag with yellow label on top, about four ounces.   4   6   8

29A   **IMITATION SNOW 1951-53,** reportedly "non-inflammable, non-toxic," approximately six to eight ounces in a white paper bag.   4   6   8

30   **HIGHWAY SIGNS 1949-50,** five yellow and three white metal signs, all with black lettering, mounted on blue cardboard insert in yellow box. VG and Excellent require box, Hawkins Collection.   5   12   20

30A   **HIGHWAY SIGNS 1951-52,** VG and Excellent require box; includes "Measured Mile, Stop, No Left Turn, Speed Limit, S Curve, R.R. and Parkway," top of box forms a display, Patterson Collection.   3   10   20

31   **RAILROAD SIGNS 1949-50,** eight white painted die-cast signs with black lettering mounted on blue cardboard insert in yellow box. Signs read, "SIDING 10 CARS, SLOW, W, HEAD CLEARANCE 4 FT., NO TRESPASSING R R PROPERTY, DANGER LIVE WIRES, OPEN SWITCH, ROAD CROSSING 100 YRDS.;" VG and Excellent require box, Hawkins Collection.   5   12   20

31A   **RAILROAD SIGNS 1951-52,** eight white painted die-cast signs similar to #31, mounted on blue insert inside yellow and blue box, VG and Excellent require box, Leonard Collection.   3   10   15

32   **CITY STREET EQUIPMENT 1949-50,** four green benches, two mail boxes, two fire hydrants mounted on blue cardboard insert in blue and yellow box. VG and Excellent require box and insert, Leonard Collection.   3   10   15

32A   **PARK SET 1951,** four green benches, one mail box, one trash container, two fire hydrants, four people in sitting position, VG and Excellent require box and insert, top of box forms a display.   10   20   30

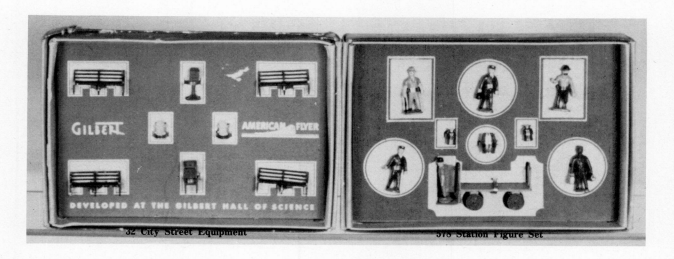

32 City Street Equipment   578 Station Figure Set

566[B] Whistling Billboard   561 Billboard Horn

566 Whistling Billboard   577 Whistling Billboard

561

759[B] Bell Danger Signal   760   760   759[A] Bell Danger Signal

592A Crossing Gate   23601 Crossing Gate

33 **PASSENGER AND TRAIN FIGURE SET 1951-52,** eight hand-painted, die-cast figures (conductor, trackman, flagman and three female and two male passengers), VG and Excellent require box and insert, Leonard Collection.   **10   20   30**

34 **RAILWAY FIGURE SET 1953,** "25 pieces bringing joy to the play world," includes six metal yard signs painted white with black lettering: "OPEN SWITCH, NO TRESPASSING R.R. PROPERTY, SIDING 10 CARS, DANGER LIVE WIRES, W, SLOW," green outfitted man with shovel has "EIRE" pressed into base; man with pick has blue pants and yellow shirt with "EIRE" pressed into base; gray outfitted man with post, "EIRE" pressed into base; green mail box; red fire hydrant; white "PAPER ONLY" trash can; gray outfitted man with pneumatic tool, "EIRE" pressed into base; blue outfitted man drinking from ladle with shovel and red bucket, "EIRE" pressed into base; gray outfitted man with mallet, "EIRE" and "FR" pressed into base; navy blue outfitted man pushes red wheel barrow; blue outfitted conductor with red flag; red outfitted woman and brown outfitted man sit on green bench; blue outfitted passenger with had and coat, "EIRE" and "HC" pressed into base; blue outfitted lady waving at departing passengers, "EIRE" pressed into base; green outfitted lady with pocketbook, "EIRE" pressed into base; brown outfitted passenger with over-night bag and coat, "EIRE" and "HE" pressed into base; set rests in clear plastic holder in blue box with yellow lid, Hawkins Collection; VG and Excellent require box.   **30   50   75**

35 **BRAKEMAN WITH LANTERN 1950-52,** three brakemen with blue overalls, gray hats, red lanterns, gray shirts, mounted on blue cardboard insert in yellow box, Hawkins Collection, VG and Excellent require original box.   **10   15   25**

40 **SMOKE SET 1953-55,** three pieces, funnel, capsule, brush; came with set.   **2   3   4**

50 **DISTRICT SCHOOL 1953-54,** illuminated, one room red painted country school, white outlined multi-paned windows, brass or chrome finished bell, red rectangular chimney; gray roof, green crackle painted sheet metal base, 6 7/8" long, 5¼" wide and 5" high, Newcomer Collection. (Also reported with red roof.)   **20   30   40**

100 **STEP DISPLAY 1948,** two sets of steps, each 60" long by 18" deep with three steps, 3" wide and 3" high (1948 dealer catalogue).   **No Reported Sales**

160 **STATION PLATFORM 1953,** brown grooved masonite base, three green benches, one seated female figure in green dress, silver painted trash barrel, mahogany stained wood posts, dark yellow billboard with three cardboard advertisements (PHILIP MORRIS Boy, RKO AND PHILIP MORRIS & CO.), vending machine, dark green plastic one piece hip roof, "VALLEY VIEW" in black letters on white field with red outline. Catalogue indicates that the station is illuminated but examined unit is not illuminated; made for Gilbert by Mini-craft, Hawkins Collection. (Also reported without VALLEY VIEW sign, Welter Collection.)   **20   30   40**

161 **BUNGALOW 1953,** one-and-a-half story building with plain white sides, front bay with two six pane windows and blue roof over bay, blue main roof, red chimney, illuminated, 8" long, 6" wide, 4" high.   **12   15   25**

162 **FACTORY 1953,** illuminated two-and-a-half story building with tan sides, brown windows, red square chimney, brown and yellow doors and red outlined "MYSTO-MAGIC COMPANY" sign. Three different roof elevations, two front doors, one small

and seven medium windows on front facade, 9¾" long, 4¼" wide and 5¾" high, illuminated, made for Gilbert by Mini-craft.   **30   45   60**

163 **FLYERVILLE STATION 1953,** scribed brown platform, waiting room and undercover waiting area, door, two windows, clock, schedule on green waiting room exterior facade, undercover area with bench, figure, vending machine, trash barrel, Chicklet advertisement and crumpled newspaper on floor; illuminated, aluminum painted roof ventilator, 11 7/8" long, 4" wide, 4 3/8" high, made for Gilbert by Mini-craft.   **20   30   40**

164 **RED BARN 1953,** red sides, yellow double crossbuck doors on overhead slide, crossbuck doors for hay loft, flanked by windows and with block and tackle above door, two small windows, two double small windows and two doors on each side, two roof ventilators, black gambrel roof, 10¾" long, 6 5/8" wide and 6 7/8" high; made by Mini-craft for A.C. Gilbert; Welter Collection.   **35   50   75**

165 **GRAIN ELEVATOR 1953,** tan sides, three distinct brown roofs, red outlined sign, "GOLDEN GRAIN ELEVATOR COMPANY," gray loading door, illuminated; made by Mini-craft for A.C. Gilbert, Welter and Balint Collections.   **30   45   60**

166 **CHURCH 1953,** white sides, dark green roof, simulated stained glass windows, wood toned door, white bell tower, illuminated, made by Mini-craft for A. C. Gilbert, Welter Collection.

   40   60   85

167 **TOWN HALL 1953,** two large arched white outlined windows flank each side of door, red sides, white pediment with windows supported by white pillars over front porch with clock, green roof with white cupola and bell, illuminated, 9¾" long, 6 5/8" wide and 6 7/8" high; made by Mini-craft for A.C. Gilbert, Balint Collection.   **30   45   75**

168 **HOTEL 1953,** two-and-a-half story building with covered porch supported by pillars on three sides, white sides, untrimmed windows, red square chimney, illuminated, 10" long, 6 7/8" wide and 5 7/8" high, two yellow doors with mustard color inserts, referred to as a "country hotel," made by Mini-craft for A.C. Gilbert, Balint Collection.   **30   45   60**

247 **TUNNEL 1946-48,** 11" long, without box   **1   2   3**
              with original box.   **7   15   20**

248 **TUNNEL 1946-48,** 14" long, without box   **1   2   3**
              with original box.   **7   15   20**

249 **TUNNEL 1947-56,** 11½" long with fiber constructed house and winding road,   **1   2   3**
with original box.   **3   6   13**

270 **NEWS AND FRANK STAND 1952-53,** manufactured by Mini-craft for Gilbert.
   (A) Blue paper covered sides, blue painted base and scribed roof, red and black decals with white backgrounds, "GILBERT NEWS COMPANY" over door, "FRANK & BEANS" over counter; "CIGARETTES..." under counter, red painted plastic door, two orange counters each with two orange shutters; basically a combined Newsstand and Refreshment Booth from a No. 271 set, exterior side signs read "RKO" and "PHILIP MORRIS," figures with red shirts, Caples Collection. Exterior rear signs read "PHILIP MORRIS," "OLD GOLD" and "RKO," Caples Collection.   **15   25   40**
   (B) Same as (A) but light blue exterior and figures with cream shirts, Caples Collection.   **15   25   40**

785 Coal Loader

752 Seaboard Coaler

741 Handcar and Shed

764 Express Office

789 Station and Baggage Smasher

779 Oil Drum Loader

271 **THREE PIECE "WHISTLE STOP" SET 1952-53,** The following pieces were made by Mini-craft for Gilbert; from Balint and Welter Collection; values are for all three items in original box.

         50 **75**

WAITING STATION

(A) Brown painted masonite sides, floor and scribed roof; does not have paper covered sides, has cardboard cutouts, "Presenting PHILIP MORRIS" and "RKO THEATRES..." on rear wall, "OLD GOLD CIGARETTES" and green "ADAMS Chicklets" inside. Sign over door reads "LOCAL TRAINS STOP ON SIGNAL" in green letters on white painted pressboard, "Life" magazine on floor. This piece is believed to have been sold under the Mini-craft label and not the Gilbert label, but it is listed here for comparative purposes and because of its interest to Gilbert collectors, Caples Collection.   **12** **15** **20**

(B) Brown paper covered masonite sides, brown painted smooth pressboard roof and base; cardboard cutouts similar to (A) but "LOCAL TRAINS STOP ON SIGNAL" is a red and black decal on white background; also has "Schedule" decal and wooden gum machine; silver painted barrel; newspaper copy reads "FIRST DRAFT CALL 20000" on floor, with female figure, Caples Collection.

         12 **15** **20**

(C) Brown painted masonite sides, floor and unscribed roof; does not have paper covered sides, has cardboard cutouts, "PHILIP MORRIS" on left outside wall, "RKO THEATRES..." on rear inside wall, "Presenting PHILIP MORRIS" on rear outside, yellow "Chicklets" on rear outside wall. Sign reads "LOCAL TRAINS STOP ON SIGNAL" in black on yellow board; "Draft call" newspaper on floor, American Flyer label on bottom, Stromberg Collection.

         12 **15** **20**

REFRESHMENT BOOTH

One piece white paper covered pressboard sides, paper taped together in rear; painted masonite roof and base; "OLD GOLD," "PHILIP MORRIS," and "RKO" cardboard cutouts. "FRANK & BEANS" and "CIGARETTES" are red and black decals with white backgrounds; dark yellow counter with "Pepsi-cola" barrel, two foot long hot dogs on grill; huge mustard bottle, cash register, two yellow shutters with "Pepsi" decals; Caples Collection.   **12** **15** **20**

NEWSSTAND

Green paper covered pressboard sides, green painted roof and floor; red, black and white decals read "GILBERT NEWS COMPANY" and "CIGARETTES..." Cardboard cutouts read "OLD GOLD," "RKO" and "PHILIP MORRIS..." Magazine cutouts above windows with yellow counter; man with blue shirt, on counter Daily News headline reads "N.Y. CRIME PROBE BLAST COURT," "AMERICAN FLYER" yellow and blue decal; small square cut base hole; Caples Collection. **12** **15** **20**

272   **GLENDALE STATION AND NEWSSTAND 1952-53,** gray grooved masonite base, one green bench, one silver barrel, blue painted newsstand, "GILBERT NEWS COMPANY," magazines and newspapers above dark yellow counter, Pepsi Cola keg, man with blue shirt, cash register, clock above counter, mahogany stained wood posts, dark gray plastic one piece hip roof, "GLENDALE" in black sans serif letters on white field with red outline; made by Mini-craft for Gilbert; Hawkins Collection.

         20 **30** **40**

273   **SUBURBAN RAILROAD STATION 1952-53,** gray grooved masonite base, waiting room with center door flanked by two windows, clock above door, one green bench on either side of waiting room, a woman on one bench, silver trash barrel, mahogany stained wood posts support one piece plastic hip roof, illuminated; "RKO Theater" paper label on side, "LAKE PARK" sign, Degano Collection.   **20** **30** **40**

274   **HARBOR JUNCTION FREIGHT STATION 1952-53,** made by Mini-craft for Gilbert.

(A) Brown scribed painted masonite and pressboard base, dark yellow painted masonite sides with green trimmed windows, "FREIGHT OFFICE" decal in red, blue and yellow over door; red painted masonite roof, illuminated, green wires, scale, hoist with chain and barrel along station end wall; pallets with barrel by station post; no man in window, Gilbert decal on bottom; Caples Collection.

         20 **30** **40**

(B) Same as (A) except red trim windows, a red man with blue shirt, Balint Collection.   **20** **30** **40**

(C) Mini-craft version, probably not sold by Gilbert, has dark brown scribed painted masonite and pressboard base, dark yellow painted masonite sides with red trimmed windows and doors in front and rear, "FREIGHT OFFICE" painted on wooden block; brown painted roof, dark red chimney with yellow cap; "PHILADELPHIA" crudely painted on block on roof. Listed to help differentiate Mini-craft from Gilbert, Caples Collection.   **20** **30** **40**

275   **EUREKA DINER 1952-53,** constructed from pressboard and masonite.

(A) Grass covered gray base, white paper covered sides, blue window panes, dark red lettered "EUREKA DINER" and "STEAKS & CHOPS," blue and orange front door; dark blue painted roof with silver painted turned wood chimney; sign on roof reads "EXCELLENT FOOD OPEN ALL NIGHT," two small square holes on base for support post on other items. Yellow label on base underside has blue lettered "AMERICAN FLYER MFD BY THE A.C. GILBERT CO" although the diner was actually manufactured by Mini-craft and a Mini-craft version exists. It is illuminated, has two attached green wires; man stands in doorway; Caples Collection.   **30** **40** **50**

(B) Similar to (A) but green windows; green and orange door and dark green roof, Caples Collection.   **30** **40** **50**

(C) Similar to (A) but red roof, red windows and doors.

         30 **40** **50**

(D) Mini-craft version, sold by Mini-craft not Gilbert, listed here to differentiate between the two, has removable blue roof with "EXCELLENT FOOD OPEN ALL NIGHT" on wood piece; detailed interior; sides not paper covered, large dark yellow painted blocks with "MINI DINER" beneath windows, "FISH & CHIPS TELEVISION STEAKS & CHOPS" above windows; Caples Collection.

         30 **40** **50**

450   **TRACK TERMINAL 1946-48,** for 0 gauge track. **20c** **30c** **40c**

453   **LAMP 1946-48,** three 18 volt clear bulbs. **60c** **1** **2**

460   **AMERICAN FLYER BULBS 1951, 1954,** assortment of 54 bulbs including Nos. 440, 441, 443, 444, 451, 453, 455 and 461, price includes box and complete set. **--** **20** **30**

520   **KNUCKLE COUPLER KIT 1954-56.**   **2** **3** **4**

541   **FUSES 1946,** for No. 10 inverter.   **1** **2** **3**

561   **DIESEL BILLBOARD 1955-56,** dark green base, white frame, Santa Fe Alco PA in foreground, steam engine on bridge in rear; diesel sound, lettered "AMERICAN FLYER" in white, Newcomer Collection.   **5** **9** **13**

561   **BILLBOARD HORN 1956,** Santa Fe Alco PA, PB, PA pulling a freight set across western desert landscape, green plastic perforated base; diesel horn mechanism, black lettered "AMERICAN FLYER Made By Gilbert," Balint Collection.

         12 **18** **25**

774[B] Floodlight Tower 23780 Gabe The Lamplighter 774[C] Floodlight Tower

751 Log Loader 596 Water Tower

566   WHISTLING BILLBOARD 1951-55.

(A)   Santa Fe Alco PA in foreground, steam engine in rear on bridge, light green base, white frame, diesel horn 1951-54, Patterson Collection.   6   9   13

(B)   Black steam engine in foreground, rolling countryside, black lettered "AMERICAN FLYER Made by Gilbert," Newcomer Collection, 1955.   6   9   13

568   WHISTLING BILLBOARD 1956, A.F. Challenger pulling hopper, gondola with load, box and tank, black plastic perforated base, nickel plate, steam whistle mechanism, black lettered "AMERICAN FLYER Made By Gilbert."   5   9   13

571   TRUSS BRIDGE 1955-56, stamped steel base, red, black or orange plastic girder sides; side forms a low arc, 10¾" long, 4¾" wide, Newcomer Collection.   2   4   6

577   WHISTLING BILLBOARD 1946-50, green stamped steel base with two rectangular black fiber feet, one at each end, riveted to base; two lights with slot through base to illuminate billboard, motor with whistle chamber, rubber stamped on base "Thursday NOV. 10, 1949," -- the date this particular piece was made; other pieces have other dates -- blue, yellow and green wires emerge from base, sign has sheet metal die-cast frame showing similing clown with red nose, red outlined mouth, red eyebrows and blue background, red lettering reads "RINGLING BROS. AND BARNUM & BAILEY" and blue lettering reads "The GREATEST SHOW ON EARTH." Lettering on yellow background, blue, yellow and red American Flyer decal on top surface, Yorkis Collection. (Also made before World War II.)   5   9   13

577 NL   WHISTLING BILLBOARD 1950, same as 577 but not lighted.   6   10   14

578   STATION FIGURE SET 1946-52, six figures -- yardman with peg leg holding white sign with black cross; blue uniformed porter with cream and brown bags; red cap; purple uniformed man with lantern; blue uniformed conductor, gandy dancer with sledge wearing tan overalls and blue shirt, rubber stamped on base "EIRE"; baggageman driving four-wheel green cart with four red or brass wheels; two shiny metal milk cans, one shiny metal barrel; mounted on blue cardboard insert in blue and yellow box. Excellent and VG require box, Hawkins Collection.   25   37   50

579   SINGLE STREET LAMP 1946-49, green or silver painted die-cast lamp with two screw binding posts on base.

(A)   Medium dark green, Newcomer Collection.   4   7   10
(B)   Silver, Newcomer Collection.   4   7   10
(C)   Light green, Welter Collection.   4   7   10

580   DOUBLE STREET LIGHT 1946-49, die-cast unit with two lamps, screw posts on base. Came one street light to a box, bulbs are packed in separate metal tin, bulbs are tear-dropped shaped and frosted white with die-cast finiales on bulbs.

(A)   Green painted, Balint Collection.   5   7   10
       with original box.   20
(B)   Silver plainted, Balint Collection.   5   7   10
       with original box.   20

581   GIRDER BRIDGE 1946-51, 53-56, stamped steel base, die-cast sides, 10" long, 4 5/8" wide and 1¾" high.

(A)   Silver finished, black "LACKAWANNA," 1951.   2   4   6
(B)   Black finished, white "LACKAWANNA," 1946-49.   1   3   4
(C)   Gray finished, black "AMERICAN FLYER," 1950, 1952, 1954 and 1956.   1   2   3
(D)   Black finished, white "AMERICAN FLYER," Stromberg Collection.   1   2   3

582   AUTOMATIC BLINKER SIGNAL 1946-48, yellow steel base with black top plate, red base for tubular steel shaft of crossing signal; black die-cast lamp heads with red alternately flashing lights; black and white X warning sign, "RAILROAD CROSSING." Track trip causes lights to flash when train passes. Base is 2 3/8 x 2 3/16", unit is 4 1/8" high; Leonard Collection.   15   25   40

583   ELECTROMATIC CRANE 1946-49, "grabs up load of steel by powerful electromagnet - hoists it high in the air - swings over car - lowers - and drops metal into car..." gray metal base, gray legs and deck, shiny metal platform, black moving deck, yellow house with red roof and black stack, green boom with red magnet; controller; blue, yellow and red "AMERICAN FLYER" decal on base, Newcomer Collection. (583 has a sequence reverse for motor with one button operation.)   20   40   55

583A   ELECTROMAGNETIC CRANE 1950-53, crane revolves left and right, string (cable) winds up and down, electromagnet picks up steel; gray or silver metal base, gray legs, deck and platform, black moving deck, yellow house with embossed rivet and window detail, red roof, black stack, green die-cast boom with red magnet; controller. 583A does not have a sequence reverse, but has two button operation. Balint Collection.   25   40   60

584   BELL DANGER SIGNAL 1946-47, green and silver painted die-cast base with pedestrian walkway and road; black base on crossing signal, tubular shaft, two alternately flashing red lights, X shaped crossing sign reads "RAILROAD CROSSING," watchman, bell mechanism; track trip causes lights to flash and bell to ring.   20   30   40

585   TOOL SHED 1946-52, gray painted sheet metal base, white painted embossed metal sides with red trim; door slides open, dark red bakelite roof; red sans serif lettered "TOOL SHED," white field, red outline, Newcomer Collection. Also found with light red painted black bakelite roof, Welter and Stromberg Collections.   7   10   15

586F   WAYSIDE STATION 1946-56, gray metal base with "AMERICAN FLYER" red, yellow and blue decal, yellow bench between post, one standing figure, one figure on green cart with brass wheels, with or without two milk cans and large barrel; green die-cast pillars and roof, or gray die-cast pillars and red roof (1946-49), two lights, 12" long, 5" wide and 3¾" high, Patterson Collection.   20   28   35

587   BLOCK SIGNAL 1946-47, gray base, 1¾ x 1¾", green two unit control box, tubular metal shaft, black ladder, green die-cast head; permits one train to follow another on single track without colliding, light flashes red and green; base 1¾ x 1¾, 5½" high; Leonard Collection.   12   15   25

588   SEMAPHORE BLOCK SIGNAL 1946-48, gray base, 1¾ x 1¾", green two unit control box, tubular metal shaft, black ladder, black die-cast head with finial; red, yellow and green lenses; red and white painted semaphore arm; permits two trains to operate on same track without colliding, has track trips; Jackson Collection.   15   25   40

589   PASSENGER AND FREIGHT STATION 1946-56, gray painted stamped metal base with yellow, blue and red "AMERICAN FLYER" decal; red and white painted embossed metal building with green plastic insert window panes, crackle green metal roof with red chimney, illuminated; "MYSTIC" name plates on each roof end, Patterson and Yorkis Collections.   10   13   20

590   CONTROL TOWER 1955-56, brown plastic base and stairs, three steps to black lower door, cream sides and windows with

103

769 Revolving Aircraft Beacon 769[A]

772[A] Water Tower   773[A] Oil Derrick   772 [D] Water Tower

simulated siding; illuminated, gray simulated roofing and siding beneath windows; black simulated shingle roof, brown chimney, base is 2½"square, 6½" high, sign on roof reads "CEDAR HILL JUNCTION." (Made by Bachman and very similar to the item marketed under their name.)   **12   17   25**

591   **CROSSING GATE 1946-48,** green painted die-cast base with silver finished pedestrian walkway and roadway; base 10 x 5¼"; yellow painted embossed sheet metal shack with dark maroon trim and roof; black die-cast gate post with white and black painted gates with red lantern; light shines through base to illuminate lantern; two screw posts on end; includes No. 707 track clip which automatically lowers gate when train approaches.   **10   15   25**

592   **CROSSING GATE 1949-50,** double arm gate with red plastic lantern; light shines through small hole in roadway, white or silver roadway and pedestrian walkway; red and white or light gray metal shed with green crackle painted roof and black stack; die-cast base with four screw posts and nuts, activated by No. 697 track trip, Caples Collection.   **10   15   20**

592A   **CROSSING GATE 1951-53,** double arm operating gate with red lantern, light shines through small hole in cream painted roadway, green grass; red and white metal shed with green crackle painted roof with black stack; paint often chips; red, yellow and blue "AMERICAN FLYER" decal; gate studied was rubber stamped "11-52" indicating manufacturing date. Many Gilbert American Flyer items come stamped with the manufacturing date which is very helpful in dating manufacturing changes. Other examples should show different dates; has two permanently connected wires, 8 7/8 x 2 7/8".
(A)   With pressed wood base, Caples Collection.   **10   15   20**
(B)   Die-cast metal base, Patterson and Welter Collections.   **10   15   20**

593   **SIGNAL TOWER 1946-54,** gray metal base with "AMERICAN FLYER" red, yellow and blue decal, doors open; originally came with track terminal.
(A)   White and red embossed metal sides, black painted metal exterior stairs, light green crackle finish roof with black chimney, doors open; came with track terminal, lighted, 7 5/8" high, Hawkins Collection.   **18   30   40**
(B)   Metal sides, brown painted metal exterior stairs, light green crackle finish roof with black chimney, doors open, Degano Collection.   **20   32   45**

594   **ANIMATED TRACK GANG SET 1946-47,** green stamped steel base, flagman moves forward as train approaches, while tampers move back and stop work. When train passes, tampers resume work; red tool box, yellow compressor wagon; track trip; 10 x 3¾ x 2½".   **250   375   650**
Note: There is a prewar 0 Gang Set which is difficult to distinguish from the 1946-47 version. This is the most desirable S gauge accessory and is extraordinarily rare; Leonard Collection.

596   **WATER TANK 1946-56,** fill pipe moves to horizontal position when button is pushed; has light green metal base, gray or black sheet metal leg supports, burnt orange or tuscan tank; "AMERICAN FLYER WATER TANK" on operating button, light on roof, yellow painted arrow or no arrow on black roof, blue, red and yellow "AMERICAN FLYER" decal on base.
(A)   Gray leg supports, yellow arrow, Caples Collection.   **10   15   20**
(B)   Black leg supports, no arrow, Balint Collection.   **10   15   20**

598   **TALKING STATION RECORD 1946-56,** one side has diesel horns and exhausts, the other steam locomotive whistles and piston sounds; for use in No. 799 station; 4¾" diameter. Record's train man calls out "New York, Philadelphia, Chicago and all points west; whoo, whoo, hiss, hiss, hiss; American Flyer through train, All Aboard - chug, chug," Patterson Collection.   **8   10   15**

599   **TALKING STATION RECORD 1956,** on first side train man gives instructions for car make-up, background noises (bell, whistles, etc.) are audible. Second side includes conversation between yard tower and conductor about freight hotbox problem; 4½" diameter; for use with No. 799 station; rarest of the records, Leonard Collection.   **5   9   15**

600   **CROSSING GATE WITH BELL 1954-56,** base painted with silver roadway and pedestrian walkway, white painted embossed shack with red trim, green crackle painted roof with black stack, black gate post with white and black gate; bell mechanism inside shack; light shines through roadway to illuminate lartern; 8 7/8" long by 1 7/8" wide, Balint Collection.   **10   15   20**

612   **FREIGHT AND PASSENGER STATION WITH CRANE 1946-51, 53-54.**
(A)   Green sheet metal base, 589 type illuminated station with white painted embossed sides and brown trim doors and window frames; green plastic window panes; tan roof, red chimney; crane has green base, gray rotating platform, yellow stamped embossed sides, red roof with black stack and green boom with black hook; control wheel on rear. (A similar crane but with different colors was made before the war.)   **25   40   50**
(B)   Gray sheet metal base, 589 type illuminated station with white painted embossed sides and red trim, and green windows and green roof with red stack; crane has green base, gray rotating platform, yellow painted embossed cab, control wheel on rear, red roof, black stack, green boom and black hook.   **25   40   50**
(C)   Same as (B) except black rotating platform, Balint Collection.   **25   40   50**

621   **HALF-SECTION STRAIGHT TRACK 1946-48,** 0 gauge, three-rail.*   **20c   30c   50c**

622   **HALF-SECTION CURVE TRACK 1946-48,** 0 gauge, three-rail.*   **20c   30c   50c**

668   **MANUAL SWITCH 1953-55,** left hand, not illuminated.   **4   6   8**

669   **MANUAL SWITCH 1953-55,** right hand, not illuminated.   **4   6   8**

670   **TRACK TRIP 1956,** when loco passes over trip, current passes through it to close contact and flows to an accessory. Does not have identifying letters, black fiber base, two screw posts and nuts, small metal rectangular box with adjustment screw, could be used to make non-derailing switches, Caples Collection.   **1   2   4**

680   **CURVE TRACK 1946-48,** 0 gauge, three-rail. *   **20c   30c   50c**

681   **STRAIGHT TRACK 1946-48,** 0 gauge, three-rail.*   **20c   30c   50c**

688   **SWITCHES 1946-48,** pair, 0 gauge, three-rail, remote.*   **20   30   50**

690   **TRACK TERMINAL 1946-56,** two spring clips, one with plate stamped "BASE POST."
(A)   Spring clips with Fahnstock clip (see-through hole).   **25c   50c   75c**

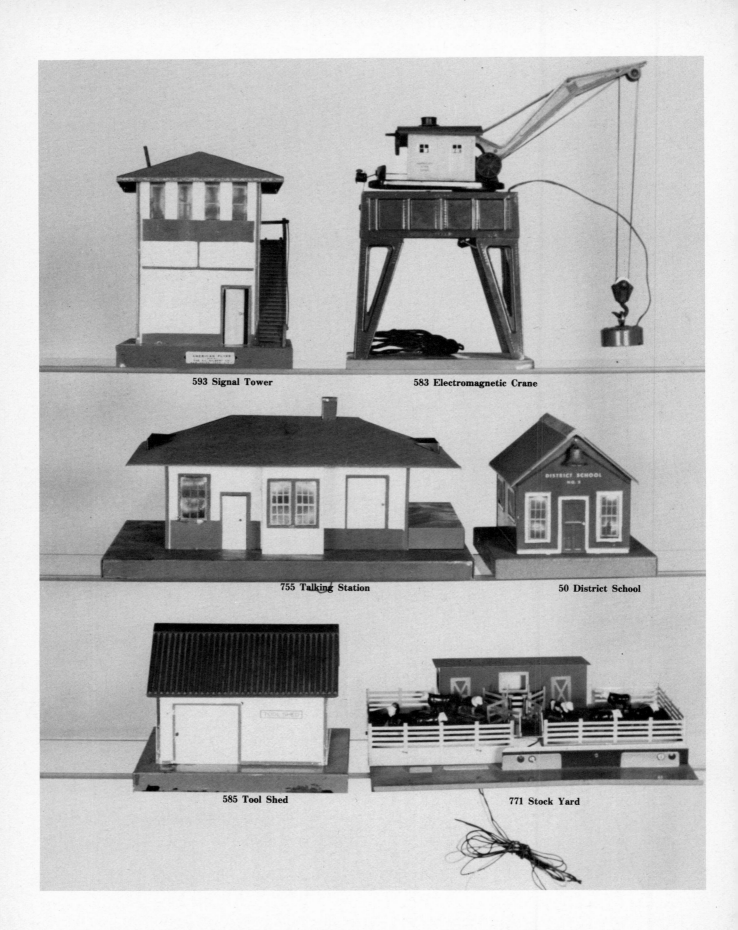

593 Signal Tower

583 Electromagnetic Crane

755 Talking Station

50 District School

585 Tool Shed

771 Stock Yard

(B) Spring clips with slots only (zip clip). 25c 50c 75c

691 STEEL TRACK PINS 1946-48, twelve pins in an envelope.
50c 75c 1

692 FIBER TRACK PINS 1946-48, four fiber pins in an envelope; hard to find but Gargraves makes a suitable replacement.
25c 50c 75c

693 TRACK LOCKS 1948-56, black metal spring clips hold adjoining track ties together, price for each, although came packaged with 26 locks. 2c 5c 7c

694 AUTOMATIC COUPLER TRUCK UNIT 1946-53, truck has two axles, four wheels and link coupler for converting 0 gauge cars to S gauge. 1 1.50 2

695 AUTOMATIC TRACK TRIP 1946, black base, track lock swivels on rivet, two metal sensing plates, metal rail flange plate held on by two rivets, two Fahnstock clips; reported to be extremely rare. 50c 2 5

695 REVERSE LOOP RELAY 1955-56, one piece green painted die-cast relay consisting of base, control box and tool shed; two piece fiber base, four rainbow wires; black rubber stamped "AMERICAN FLYER LINES" came in light tan box with red and white label and with two #707 and one #609 track trips and two fiber pins, Patterson Collection; also reported with three #707 track trips, Stromberg Collection. This is the less common of the two reverse loop relays. It also forms the base of the 761 semaphore. 10 15 20

696 TRACK TRIP 1955-57, black fiber base, rail flange clips, rail locking clip; see-through wire spring clip (Fahnstock clip), nickel or aluminum finish. Completes circuit from far side rail when wheel flange of rolling stock passes over it. It usually operates reliably, although sometimes it is necessary to push the retainer up to make better contact and to depress the black plastic shoe.
(A) Screw holds shoe, Caples Collection. 1 1.50 2
(B) Two rivets hold shoe, Caples Collection. 1 1.50 2

697 TRACK TRIP 1949-54, pressure operated switch for accessories; star wheel turns to adjust pressure; Posts 1 and 3 circuit completed by train passing, Posts 1 and 2 circuit opened by train passing, Caples Collection. 1 1.50 2

698 REVERSE LOOP KIT 1949-50, 52-54, in a two rail system with a reverse loop special wiring is required to prevent shorting. The 698 kit contains three #690 terminals, six fiber pins, one double pole, two wood screws, double throw switch, instructions and 120 inches of wire; price requires original packaging, Patterson and Stromberg Collections. 3 5 7

700 STRAIGHT TRACK 1946-56, 10" long, T-rail, four black ties.
15c 25c 35c

701 STRAIGHT TRACK 1946-56, half lengths, 5" long, T-rail.
15c 25c 35c

702 CURVE TRACK 1946-56, 10" long, twelve pieces form a circle with a 40 inch diameter, four black ties. 15c 25c 35c

703 CURVE TRACK 1946-56, half length. 10c 15c 20c

704 MANUAL UNCOUPLER 1952-56, black fiber top piece, black metal base, red lever.
(A) With "#704." 25c 50c 75c
(B) With "704." 25c 50c 75c

705 REMOTE CONTROL UNCOUPLER 1946-47, uncoupling unit integral with track section, large black plastic unit with two binding posts and black plastic uncoupling bar; button lettered "AMERICAN FLYER UNCOUPLER." 1 2 3

706 REMOTE UNCOUPLER 1948-56, black clamp-on type with black fiber top piece, black metal base, green or yellow box; either one yellow or one black wire fastened to unit or two binding posts, "AMERICAN FLYER UNCOUPLER" on gray or black plastic button; coil inside box pushes two control rails up.
(A) Green or yellow box, track flange clip, track locking clips, screw binding posts, with nine rivets including binding posts. 35c 50c 1
(B) Green box with track flange clip and track locking clip, seven rivets and wires fastened to unit. 35c 50c 1
(C) Green box with two studs and track locking clip with five rivets; wires fastened to unit. (We assume that the reduction in rivets on the box was an attempt to reduce costs.) 35c 50c 1

707 TRACK TERMINAL Black fiber with one spring clip stamped "BASE POST," used with accessories. 15c 25c 35c

708 DIESEL WHISTLE CONTROL 1953-56. 2 4 6

709 LOCKOUT ELIMINATOR 1950-55, black fiber base, two post and nut terminals, small rectangular metal box, small adjusting screw. Supplied low supplemental current so that a reverse unit would not sequence when main track current was off in block and motor was not turning, Caples Collection. Also reported with small rectangular bakelite box, no adjusting screw and with 690 and 707 track terminals and instructions, Patterson and Stromberg Collections. 1 2 3

710 AUTOMATIC TRACK SECTION 1946, one section of straight track the same length as a regular piece of track, with base and two inside rails for car pickup contacts on the action car to rub against. Used with earlier link couplers, Olson Collection.
50c 1 1.50

710 STEAM WHISTLE CONTROL Black bakelite box with silver four prong whistle generator tube; silver lever on switch slides back and forth with front of box in front of tube; produced "reasonable" approximation of steam whistle sound and is the more desirable of the two steam whistle controls made by Gilbert, Schneider Collection. 2 4 6

711 MAIL PICKUP Post on stand attaches to track; mail bag is hung on post; when lever on action car is activated it picks up bag; used with 718 and 719 mail pickup cars, Olson Collection.
2 4 6

712 SPECIAL TRACK SECTION 1949, operating car activator.(A) - (D) from Caples Collection.
(A) Black fiber base, screw terminal with nut; track flange holder; outside third rail pickup; track locking clip and six rivets. 50c 75c 1
(B) Same as (A) but Fahnstock "see-through" spring clip.
50c 75c 1
(C) Three piece metal unit, two spot welds, three rivets.
50c 75c 1
(D) Same as (C) but two spot welds; one rivet. Again, a fascinating pattern of detail reduction to limit costs -- see 706 for another example. 50c 75c 1

713 MAIL BAG HOOK 1953-55, with track terminal. 6 9 12

720 REMOTE CONTROL SWITCHES 1946-49, pair, black bakelite base has cutout area between turnout and motor unit and long

774[A] Floodlight Tower   796 Remote Control Sawmill

768[B] Oil Supply Depot

750[B] Trestle Bridge

rectangular box attached to main box for solenoid unit; manual auxiliary control lever; plastic caps over bulb for red or green illumination (caps usually melt),twin controller, Olson,Schneider and Patterson Collections.　　　　**10　15　25**

722A **REMOTE CONTROL SWITCHES 1950-56,** pair, black bakelite base is almost completely rectangular, no cutout area between turnout and motor as on 720. The solenoid mechanism is in a nearly square box; no manual auxiliary levers, colored cellophane lenses for red or green illumination, Schneider, Olson and Patterson Collections.　　　　**10　15　25**

722 **MANUAL SWITCHES 1946-51,** pair of left and right, not illuminated, with red and green switch flags to show direction the switch is thrown in, Patterson Collection.　　**3　5　8**

722A **MANUAL SWITCHES 1952-56,** pair of left and right, not illuminated.　　　　**3　5　8**

725 **CROSSING 1946-56,** 90°, black bakelite base, York Collection.　　　　**1　2　3**

726 **RUBBER ROADBED 1950-56,** straight, holds one section of straight track.
(A)　Gray rubber with six molded rubber ties and inserts for four metal ties, Patterson Collection.　**50c　75c　1**
(B)　Same as (A) but black rubber ties, Patterson Collection.　　　　**50c　75c　1**
(C)　1956, black rubber with 23 molded rubber ties (3/16" x 1 7/8") and inserts for four metal ties, Patterson Collection.　　　　**50c　75c　1**

727 **RUBBER ROADBED 1950-56,** curved, holds one section of curved track.
(A)　Gray rubber with six molded rubber ties and inserts for four metal ties, Patterson Collection.　**50c　75c　1**
(B)　Same as (A) but black rubber, Patterson Collection.　　　　**50c　75c　1**
(C)　1956, black rubber with 23 molded rubber ties (3/16" x 1 7/8") and inserts for four metal ties, Patterson Collection.　　　　**50c　75c　1**

728 **RE-RAILER 1956,** plastic unit with metal rails properly seats rolling stock wheels on rails; substitutes for one piece of straight track, 10" long.　　　　**1　3　5**

730 **BUMPER 1946,** illuminated, with screw base type bulb.
(A)　Bluish green plastic, Caples Collection.　**1　2　4**
(B)　Medium green plastic, Newcomer Collection.　**1　2　4**
(C)　Red, Newcomer Collection.　　**20　30　50**

731 **PIKE PLANNING KIT 1952-56,** plastic template, Dietzgen graph paper 10 x 15 x 12" and M3127 Instructions, Stromberg Collection.　　　　**8　11　15**

747 **CARDBOARD TRESTLE SET** Came in sheets to punch out and assemble, 26 trestles with 52 upright pieces and 54 cross pieces, designed to form a figure 8 or oval track layout. Comes with two extra cross pieces. The uprights start with four pieces one inch high and rise in groups of four every one-third of an inch until they reach five inches high. The cross pieces are brown grained to resemble wood, the uprights simulate gray stone, all pieces are printed on both sides, Balint and Patterson Collections.　　　　**4　8　15**

748 **OVERHEAD FOOT BRIDGE 1951-52.**
(A)　Gray painted pedestrian bridge, two twelve step units with square cutouts flanked by triangles, one horizontal span unit will span single or double track, 16" long, 13" wide, 7" high.　　　　**15　22　30**

(B)　Aluminum finished foot bridge, twelve steps with square cutouts when viewed from side, reportedly marked Colber.　　　　**15　22　30**

748 **GIRDER AND TRESTLE AND TOWER BRIDGE** Cardboard, Newcomer Collection.　　　　**20　30　40**

749 **STREET LAMP SET 1950-52,** three bronze finished plastic lamp posts 6 1/8" high; one post has a green "U.S.MAIL" box on it; a second has a red "Fire" box and the third is plain. Packed in a blue and yellow box with a removable nylon dome; prices for VG and Excellent require original box, Patterson Collection.　　　　**4　10　15**

750 **TRESTLE BRIDGE 1946-56.**
(A)　Aluminum finished stamped steel base and trusswork with much rivet detail, yellow painted embossed sheet metal tender house with roof and black stack and light, 17 3/4" long.　　　　**10　15　25**
(B)　Black painted stamped steel base and trusswork with much rivet detail, yellow sheet metal tender house with red roof and black stack and light, 17¾" long, black lettered "AMERICAN FLYER LINES" under window, 8¼" tall, 4¼" wide, Newcomer Collection.　**10　15　25**
(C)　Blue-gray metallic finish, may be five digit version, Welter Collection.　　　　**10　15　25**

751 **LOG LOADER 1946-50,** black or yellow bakelite base, red die-cast lattice piers, green sheet metal superstructure, yellow painted and embossed metal tender shed with red outlined windows and red bakelite roof. Electromagnet pulls log cradle up; log is grabbed by red metal spring clip and carried by cart up ramp; at top of ramp plunger unit presses against green superstructure and log falls into waiting car; brushless motor turns large black pulley which winds and unwinds cord causing cart to rise and descend black track; two button controller. Car not included. Action log cars 714, 717 and 917 could be used with the 751. The 751A solenoid is underneath and its location differs from the 751, Schneider Collection.　　**30　45　65**

751A **OPERATING LOG LOADER 1952-53,** similar to 751 but has steel base.　　　　**30　45　65**

752 **SEABOARD COALER 1946-50,** first button causes open bucket to descend to waiting loaded car; second button causes bucket to close on coal and carry coal bucket up into hopper; coal flows by gravity into car on adjacent track; two button controller; green painted stamped steel base, yellow painted metal machine shed, red outlined shed windows, dark red shed roof; gray painted metal loader structure; red outlined loader top windows on both sides; dark red loader roof, black sheet metal guides bucket up and down.　　　　**50　70　95**

752A **SEABOARD COALER 1951-52,** similar to 752 but operating door in loader hopper holds coal; when third button on controller is pressed hopper door opens and load flows into car; crackle green stamped steel base, yellow painted metal machine shed with red outlined windows and dark red roof; gray painted metal loader structure with red outlined windows at top and dark red roof; black sheet metal track guides black bucket up and down; track is laid through base; gray plastic controller with red, black and green buttons; Hawkins Collection. (Unconfirmed report of a 752A with a yellow base.)　　**40　60　85**

753 **SINGLE TRESTLE BRIDGE WITH BEACON 1952,** gray painted steel with rivet detail, Patterson Collection.　　　　**12　17　25**

748 Overhead Foot Bridges

748[A]   748[B]

23791 Cow-on-Track

787 Log Loader

23590 Control Tower

586F Wayside Station

GILBERT
AMERICAN FLYER
The A.C. GILBERT CO. • New Haven, Conn., U.S.A.
No. 23590 CONTROL TOWER
3/16" SCALE TRAINS

753 **MOUNTAIN, TUNNEL & PASSENGER SET** Cardboard, four pieces designed to go with #747 Trestle Set, photographic overlays of mountain scenery; consisted of two identical parts, Welter Collection.   7   12   15

754
DOUBLE TRESTLE BRIDGE 1950-52, steel bridge with aluminum finish, accomodates two trains with red airplane warning light on top, 24" long, 8½" wide and 5¾" high.
                                                                        17   22   35

755 **TALKING STATION 1948-58**, gray painted metal base, red and white painted embossed metal building with green paned plastic insert windows, elaborate record playing mechanism with brushless motor, worm drive and gear reduction, record beneath floor, speaker horn unit with needle, roof with red chimney, gray plastic controller "AMERICAN FLYER TALKING STATION," illuminated, 6" x 12" x 8". Record says: "New York, Philadelphia, Chicago; All points west; All aboard! Whoo, whoo. Hiss, hiss; American Flyer through train; Chug, chug," Patterson Collection
 (A) Crackle green roof, decal reads "MYSTIC STATION," red, yellow and blue "AMERICAN FLYER" decal on base, Patterson Collection.   15   22   30
 (B) Blue crackle roof, black sheet metal name plates on roof end reads in white serif lettering "MYSTIC," no decal on base, McCluskey Collection.   25   37   50
 (C) Pale green roof; Welter Collection.   15   22   30

758 **SAM THE SEMAPHORE MAN 1949**, Sam rushes out of shack, semaphore lowers and train stops when control button pressed, release button causes Sam to return to shack, semaphore to raise and train to start; green painted sheet metal box over shiny metal base, red and white painted embossed metal shed with green roof and black stack, red painted wood tool box; black semaphore pole with black ladder and black die-cast semaphore head with red, yellow and green plastic lenses, shiny metal plate on base reads "AMERICAN FLYER MFG BY THE A.C. GIBLERT CO. NEW HAVEN CONN. U.S.A.;" black, yellow, red and green wires emerge from base, 707 track trip; mechanism with single coil magnet and spring loading, Newcomer Collection.   7   10   15

758A **SAM THE SEMAPHORE MAN 1950-56**, green painted sheet metal box over shiny metal base, white painted and embossed metal shack with red trim, red window outlines and door; light green crackle painted sheet metal roof with black stack, red painted wood tool box; black painted metal tubing semaphore pole, black die-cast semaphore head with finial, red and white painted semaphore arm and red, yellow and green plastic lenses; Sam is reportedly named after one of Gilbert's managers. Sam came with a black plastic two button controller with white lettered "American Flyer Semaphore Man." The red button causes Sam to rush from the shack, the arm to fall and the passing train to stop. The green button causes Sam to return to his shack, the arm to raise and the train to resume its trip. The Fahnstock clip on the rear of the unit base provides a low voltage current so that the reverse unit does not sequence and the train is in essence stalled; includes 707 track trip. The mechanism has two coil magnets and no spring. These explanations were provided by Jim Sutter and Michael Newcomer.
 (A) Nickeled plate with black lettering on front. 15   30   45
 (B) Blue, yellow and red American Flyer decal behind tool box.
                                                                        15   30   45

759 **BELL DANGER SIGNAL 1953-56**, approaching train causes bell to ring and red lights on crossbuck to flash; includes track trips; 5" long, 2 7/8" wide and 5" high.
 (A) Crackle medium green painted die-cast base with two screw posts, brown sheet metal house with yellow outlined windows and trim, black roof with black stack, steel cross-buck post, two red flashing lights in green die-cast mounts, white sign with black lettered "RAIL ROAD CROS SING" with finial on post, nickeled identification plate.
                                                                        7   12   15
 (B) Black base, brown sheet metal shanty with yellow outlined windows and trim; green roof with black chimney; shiny steel crossbuck post, die-cast green lamp holders, with two red flashing lights, white crossing sign with black lettered "RAIL ROAD CROS SING," finial on post.   7   12   15
 (C) Dark green crackle painted base with two screw posts, reddish brown sheet metal house with yellow outlined windows and trim, light green roof with black stack, shiny steel crossbuck post, two red flashing lights in green die-cast mounts, white sign with black lettered "RAIL ROAD CROS SING," with finial on post, nickeled identification plate.   7   12   15

760 **AUTOMATIC HIGHWAY FLASHER 1949-56**, as train approaches red lights flash, after train passes lights go out; gray painted die-cast base with white lettered "AMERICAN FLYER MADE BY A.C. GILBERT CO. NEW HAVEN CONN., U.S.A.," two screw posts with nuts; shiny metal posts; two green die-cast lamp housings; white painted crossbuck with black lettered "RAIL ROAD CROS SING;" two 696 track trips; 4 7/8" high, base is 2 1/8" square.   6   9   12

761 **SEMAPHORE WITH TWO TRACK TRIPS 1949-56**, one piece light or dark green painted die-cast unit consisting of base, control box and tool shed, shiny metal post, semaphore with green, yellow and red lenses, yellow and black painted arm; two 697 track trips, came in tan box with red and white label and cardboard tag "CAUTION - Do not allow train to stand on track trip at any time or coil may become overheated M2620;" Hawkins Collection.   10   15   20

762 **2 in 1 WHISTLE 1949-50**, green sheet metal base with four fiber feet, white sheet metal billboard frame. Billboard depicts boy with huge ferris wheel and boxed Erector set, red lettered "ERECTOR," black lettered "THE WORLD'S GREATEST CONSTRUCTION TOY," two whistle sounds, one a distant train, one a nearby one, two button controller, one for each sound, probably the most desirable of the billboard whistles, Yorkis and Balint Collections.   7   14   18
 (A) With white painted die-cast frame; Welter Collection.
                                                                        7   14   18

763 **MOUNTAIN SET 1949-50**, three pieces of composition material totaling 29", each piece 7" deep x 6" high, can be used together to form a continuous mountain or separately with cuts for trucks.
                                                                        10   15   20

764 **EXPRESS OFFICE 1950-51**, green painted sheet metal base, gray painted embossed building with red outlined windows with green panes and door with red knob, dark green bakelite roof, illuminated, shiny metal plate with black lettering, Caples Collection.   30   40   60

766 **ANIMATED STATION 1952-54**, passengers move on platform as train stops, with 735 or 935 special coach; coach door and platform gate are opened and passengers board the train; green or gray painted stamped steel platform with black fiber liner, cream painted stamped steel waiting station with maroon roof, white sign with black lettered "GUILFORD," four handpainted metal figures, small cream sign at each end with "EXIT" in black letters, yellow passenger sheet metal bench, white picket fence with gates at each end, black plastic control button with black rotary knob and red buttons.   20   30   40

K766 Same as 766 but with 935 knuckle coupler car.   20   30   40

767 ROADSIDE DINER

767 **ROADSIDE DINER 1950-54,** green sheet metal base, yellow plastic sides and roof, red trim, lettered "STEAKS . CHOPS" on side, brick red doors, red smoke stack, white lettered "BRANFORD DINER GOOD EATS" on red background with sign held over roof by wire; hinged doors, large TV antenna, illuminated, white and black wires, 12 x 3 x 2½". The body is frequently chipped and missing an antenna.
(A) Yellow unpainted plastic.   **10 15 22**
(B) Yellow painted plastic.   **12 17 25**

768 **OIL SUPPLY DEPOT 1950-53,** green metal base, white painted embossed sheet metal pump house with red trim; two silver painted tanks.
(A) "SHELL" decals, "S.E.P.X. 8681" and "625." **18 28 38**
(B) "GULF" decals and "GRCX 5016, CAPACITY 100,000 LBS LT. WT. 489400," feedlines and hose, Gulf depot is harder to find, Excellent price requires original box which is lettered 7686, Newcomer Collection. **20 30 40**

769 **REVOLVING AIRCRAFT BEACON 1950,** red plastic base, gray plastic girders, black plastic ladder, red plastic top deck, silver finished revolving beacon with red and green lenses, light bulb with dimple, 12" high, 5" square base. Price includes bulb and rotating beacon, LaCalle Collection.   **6 8 10**

769A **REVOLVING AIRCRAFT BEACON 1951-56,** green plastic base; silver foil identification plate has black lettered "AMERICAN FLYER MFG. BY THE A.C. GILBERT CO. NEW HAVEN, CONN., U.S.A.;" gray painted stamped sheet metal girders, green plastic top deck and railing, gray plastic light socket with miniature screw threads, light bulb with dimple, revolving beacon pivets on bulb dimple, silver finished beacon with red and green lenses; white painted, embossed sheet metal shed with red trim; green wires emerge from base (dimple bulbs are available).   **7 9 14**

770 **BAGGAGE LOADING PLATFORM 1950-52,** green painted sheet metal base, green platform unit, yellow ramp unit, man with red shirt, yellow steps; when boxes are placed on loading ramp and the remote control button is pressed, the boxes are fed one at a time to man who lowers chute extension and sends box into car; die-cast boxes or milk cans with square base with simulated crimped steel bands, (used with 732 baggage car or 734 box car, not included), Stromberg Collection. **15 22 35**

770 **CARDBOARD TRESTLE SET** Set: thirty trestle upright, twenty-four banked trestle crossties, six long bridge crossties,

two long and two short bridge sides; fifteen trestles, forms a bridge at highest four trestles. Similar to 747 but banked, Welter and Balint Collections.   **8 12 17**

771 **STOCK YARD 1950-54,** green sheet metal base with pressed-up section to hold car activating plate; nickel finished plate reads "AMERICAN FLYER MFD. BY A.C. GILBERT CO. NEW HAVEN, CONN. U.S.A.," yellow sheet metal fence, black woven material lines yard, four brown and four black cows with white heads, each mounted on red brush type base. Brown metal shed with two yellow outlined simulated doors facing pen, with one yellow outlined window with plastic yellow lined insert between doors. Vibrator unit mounted inside of shed on steel bracket, green crackle painted sheet metal roof; gray plastic controller with rotary switch with black and red buttons. Controller has black sans serif lettered "AMERICAN FLYER STOCK YARD." Price includes 736 car with link couplers, Riley Collection. Also reported with black brush type base and black plastic controller, Patterson and Stromberg Collections. **15 22 35**

K771 **OPERATING STOCK YARD AND CAR 1950-54,** steers in pens mill about; when one exit gate is opened, cattle file up ramp into car; stock car unloads when exit door lines up with corral ramp; stock yard with cattle shed, price includes 976 car with knuckle couplers (knuckle version slightly more desirable). **17 27 37**

772 **WATER TOWER**
(A) 1950-52, gray plastic base and scaffold, black plastic ladder, red plastic storage tank, bulb in base heats oil type liquid in tube causing it to bubble; liquid sometimes solidifies and bubbling is adversely affected; metal cap often missing; two green wires are connected to bulb socket; metal plate reads "AMERICAN FLYER MFD. BY A.C. GILBERT CO..." although made by Colber Corporation, Irvington, NJ.   **9 14 19**
(B) Same as (A) but red plastic base and scaffold, gray tank, Welter Collection.   **9 14 19**
(C) Colber's is included to distinguish Colber's AF equipment from Colber's own (Colber label) products. Plate reads "THE COLBER CORPORATION," red plastic base, red railing around gray tank marked "COLBERVILLE," Caples Collection.   **7 12 15**
(D) 1953-56, green plastic base with white painted embossed metal shack with red trimmed green roof, dark gray painted steel scaffold, red and white checkerboard tank, Balint Collection.   **10 15 20**
(E) Same as (C) but not marked "COLBERVILLE," in Gilbert box, Welter Collection.   **10 15 20**

730 Bumper

730 Bumper

775 Baggage Loading Platform

773 OIL DERRICK 1950, 1951-52
(A) Red plastic base and tower with black plastic ladder. Ladder and tower sometimes warp; light in base heats oil type liquid in tube causing bubbling action; little silver plug on tube top, plate reads "AMERICAN FLYER MFD. BY THE A.C. GILBERT CO.," although made by the Colber Corporation; two green wires attached to bulb socket, 13¾" high, base 5" square, 1950, Caples Collection.
      10   15   20
(B) Same as (A) but gray base and tower, Welter Collection.
      10   15   20
(C) Same as (A) but "GULF" orange and blue sign, 1951-52.
      10   15   20
(D) Gray tower, red base, Colber plates, marketed by Colber, Caples Collection.
      5   7   10
(E) Same as (A) but no silver plug, Stromberg Collection.
      10   15   20

774 FLOODLIGHT TOWER 1951-56.
(A) Red square plastic base, gray girders, black metal central shaft, gray upper platform, four red lamp brackets each has black bulb holders and each lamp points to a different corner.
      10   15   20
(B) Gray irregular plastic base, white painted embossed shed with red trim and green roof, red painted sheet metal girders, black plastic upper platform, four floodlights face same direction.
      10   15   20
(C) Similar to (B) but silver finished upper platform, four silver lamp brackets, lamps supported by a black bracket, Patterson Collection.
      10   15   20
(D) Same as (B) but dark green upper platform, Balint Collection.
      10   15   20
(E) White plastic upper platform, Balint Collection.
      10   15   20

775 BAGGAGE LOADING PLATFORM 1953-55, crates are spring fed to baggageman who lowers chute extension and sends crates sliding into special box car (or into REA baggage car which functions well with this accessory). Black or green sheet metal base, green platform unit, yellow steps and ramp unit, die-cast or plastic man with red shirt; box car has link couplers; came with either crates or milk cans with square base, ramp with rollers in box car.
(A) Black sheet metal base, Schneider Collection.
      18   25   35
(B) Green sheet metal base, Welter Collection.
      No Reported Sales

K775 BAGGAGE LOADING PLATFORM 1953-55, crates are spring fed to baggageman (either die-cast metal or plastic) who lowers chute extension and sends crates sliding into box car (or into REA baggage car). Black sheet metal base, green platform unit, yellow ramp and steps, man with red shirt, car has conversion knuckle couplers with sheet metal side frames and split mount couplers. Ramp in box car does not have rollers. **18   25   35**

778 STREET LAMP SET 1953-56.
(A) One lamp with fire alarm box, one with mail box and one plain, Patterson Collection.
      5   7   10
(B) One lamp with fire alarm box, and two with mail boxes. The latter two are smaller in size and differ, Rudzinski and Welter Collections.
      5   7   10

779 OIL DRUM LOADER 1955-56, blue outfitted man on red three-wheel lift truck; truck rides on control arm over to green plastic barrel ramp; metal barrel chute allows shiny metal barrels to roll onto pickup chute and onto red truck; control arm conveys truck to platform side where barrel falls into waiting gondola; unit has tan plastic base with steps and ramp; bases vary in shade from light to dark tan; yellow and brown simulated stucco and wood plastic tender shed with barred windows, green plastic roof with simulated shingles; black plastic controller with rotary switch or push button with white lettered "AMERICAN FLYER OIL DRUM LOADER." Small metal plate with black lettering on plastic deck; two screw post terminals; four or five metal barrels, 8¾ x 3½ x 5½" high. 779 is one of the better functioning accessories and is found on Lionel as well as Gilbert layouts, Newcomer and Patterson Collections. **30   45   60**

780 RAILROAD TRESTLE SET 1953-56, 24 molded plastic trestles; 26 track locks, trestle rises to 4½" at its highest point.
(A) Orange plastic.
      1   2   3
(B) Black plastic.
      2   3   5

781 RAILROAD ABUTMENT SET 1953, simulated graduated concrete abutments -- 40 large (15/16"), 14 medium (5/8"), and 8 small (5/16"). Highest abutment is 3¾" and each is 2½"long and 1" wide, with 26 693 track locks, Stromberg Collection.
      10   15   25

782 RAILROAD ABUTMENT SET 1953, 48 extra abutment sections to extend trestle, 15/16" high. **5   12   20**

783 HI-TRESTLE SECTIONS 1953-56, twelve trestles, each 4.5" high for adding to and extending 780; includes twelve track locks.
      3   5   7

793 Union Station

784   **RAILROAD HUMP SET 1955,** see page 26.

784   **RAILROAD HUMP SET** Includes common items in a special package without their original packaging. Items are valued at their lower value: 3 No. 700 Straight Track, 2 No. 702 Curve Track, No. 730 Bumper, No. 678 Left or No. 679 Right Remote Control Switch, 6 No. 693 Track Locks, 6 Trestles, No. 706 Electric Uncoupler, with original packaging and original instructions, Olson and Balint Collections.   **25   40   50**

785   **COAL LOADER 1955-56,** first button causes clam shell bucket to descend black metal guide to loaded hopper car or coal tray; second button causes bucket with coal to close and ascend into top of structure; bucket opens and coal falls into hopper; third button causes coal to fall through chute into waiting hopper underneath building; green sheet metal base; six beige wood piers, rust primer colored truss work, beige metal superstructure; dark green outlined windows on both sides; red painted black plastic roof; black plastic controller marked "AMERICAN FLYER COAL LOADER" with red, copper and green buttons, blue or black metal coal tray, 14¼" high, base is 5" square; Hawkins Collection.   **45   70   90**

787   **LOG LOADER 1955-56,** cam action raises logs which are picked up by wire hooks, wire hooks hang from chair in which sits blue outfitted man, chair and logs ride up metal structure; stop unit causes log to fall into waiting car; tan plastic simulated wood base, gray metal legs and frame, black metal walkway and ladder, yellow plastic house with brown windows, red plastic roof and two screw terminal posts; "logs" are four pieces of half-inch dowl 5¼" long stained walnut; same man found on 779 barrel loader, Hawkins Collection.   **35   60   85**

788   **SUBURBAN STATION 1956,** gray plastic base with simulated decking; white plastic building with simulated wood siding, green double doors and green outlined windows; black train schedule board, green hip roof with red chimney; 10" long, 7¼" wide, 4¾" high; station has offset double doors and bay window; illuminated.   **7   10   15**

789   **STATION AND BAGGANGE SMASHER 1956,** 788 station with "Billy The Baggage Smasher" tirelessly trundling his load of freight back and forth across the station platform.   **25   40   65**

790   **TRAINORAMA** Scenic cardboard background units, original box required for Excellent price, Welter Collection.
       20   30   50

792   **RAILROAD TERMINAL 1954-56,** really a train shed; a simulated concrete plastic structure with four pillars on each side supporting frosted finished roof with simulated steel truss work. Includes three simulated concrete plastic ramps that can be moved. Shed accommodates two trains, removing the center ramp with allow it to accommodate three. The shed's design matches the 793, 794 and 799 station and they make a handsome pair. The 1954 catalogue describes the roof as clear but this version has not been confirmed.   **20   30   40**

793   **UNION STATION 1955-56,** simulated concrete structure with molding and cornice details; light tan plastic building has fourteen windows on each long side and four at each end; two interior lights with black and yellow wires; green painted metal roof with two black plastic ventilators riveted on; tower facade matches building, has two windows, with clock at 12:27 on green decal, maroon plastic step unit, door canopy and roof, with "AMERICAN FLYER LINES" pennant in red, white and blue on wooden shaft on roof; plastic window materials with green outlined panes, instruction sheet shows how tower could be placed at different locations on building to produce different effects; Hawkins Collection.   **20   35   50**

794 UNION STATION WITH TWO LAMPS 1954, same as 793 but with two lamps 5.5" high, one lamp with mail box and other with fire alarm box. Premium price cited for Excellent requires original packaging, otherwise, same price as 793 plus value of two lamps.   **25 35 55**

795 UNION STATION AND TERMINAL 1954, consists of 793 and 792 combined. Offered only one year, premium price cited for Excellent requires original packaging.   **40 60 100**

799 AUTOMATIC TALKING STATION 1954-56, 793 with stop and record units. With push of button, train stops in front of station; record produces hissing steam, piston chugs and trainmaster's voice. When record completed train resumes journey.   **20 40 60**

23021 IMITATION GRASS 1957-59, about a half-pound, shown as "21" in 1957 catalogue. Plastic bag, Olson Collection.   **4 7 15**

23022 SCENERY GRAVEL 1957-59.*   **2 6 10**

23023 IMITATION COAL 1957-59.*   **2 6 10**

23024 RAINBOW WIRE 1957-64, 25 feet of four conductor -- yellow, red, green and black wire.*   **2 6 10**

23025 SMOKE CARTRIDGES 1957-59, twelve plastic capsules per box. Claimed to be "Harmless if swallowed accidentally.." Box is stamped "No. 23025."   **3 4 5**

23026 SERVICE KIT 1957, 59-64, Track Cleaning Fluid, Oil, Grease, Brush, Sanding Sticks, Commutator Stick Tube Cleaners, Instruction Booklet, shown in the 1957 catalogue as No. 26. In red and white box numbered "No. 23026," Patterson Collection.   **3 7 12**

23027 TRACK CLEANING FLUID 1957-59, bottle, claimed to be "non-toxic, non corrosive."*   **1 2 3**

23028 SMOKE FLUID DISPENSER 1960-64, pocket size squeeze tube dispenser for both S and H0 smoking engines.   **1 2 3**

23032 RAILROAD EQUIPMENT KIT 1960-61, contains Straight Track, Re-Railer, Truss Bridge, Track Cleaning Fluid, Grease, Oil, and Instruction Manual in cardboard container.   **10 15 25**

23036 MONEY SAVER KIT 1960, 62, 64, twelve bottles of Track Cleaner and twelve bottles of American Flyer Smoke in counter display unit. Price requires display unit.   **10 22 30**

23040 MOUNTAIN, TUNNEL & PASSENGER SET 1958.   **No Reported Sales**

23249 TUNNEL 1957-64, similar to 249 but in box lettered "No. 23249."   **9 11 15**

23320 AMERICAN FLYER TRAFFIC MASTER 1960, U. S. Map, Line Indications, Selective Controls for Yard and Mainline, Railroad Line Selector and City Selector. Catalogued in 1960 Advance Catalogue but apparently not produced, Welter Collection.   **No Reported Sales**

23561 BILLBOARD HORN 1957-59, similar to 561 but box lettered "No. 23561."   **7 11 15**

23568 WHISTLING BILLBOARD 1957-64, similar to 568 but box lettered "No. 23568."   **7 11 15**

23571 TRUSS BRIDGE 1957-64, similar to 571 but box numbered "23571."   **3 5 7**

23581 GIRDER BRIDGE 1957-64.
(A) Aluminum finish, "AMERICAN FLYER" in black letters.   **3 4 5**

23586 WAYSIDE STATION 1957-59, similar to 586F but in box lettered "No. 23586," includes Redcap, porter and baggage car with man.   **10 15 20**

23589 PASSENGER AND FREIGHT STATION 1959, similar to 589 but came in box lettered "No. 23589."   **15 25 35**

23590 CONTROL TOWER 1957-59, same as 590 Tower but in red and white box lettered "No. 23590," Newcomer Collection.   **10 15 20**

23596 OPERATING WATER TANK 1957-58, same as 596 Tank but in box lettered "No. 23596."   **10 17 25**

23598 TALKING STATION RECORD 1957-59, for replacement of record in 799 or 23786; sounds include diesel horns, steam whistles, bells and pistons, 4¾" diameter.   **3 5 8**

23599 TALKING STATION RECORD 1957, replacement record for 799 or 23786. Train man on record gives train make-up instructions; whistles and bells sound. Other side plays conversation between freight conductor and control tower about hotbox problem, 4¾" diameter.   **6 10 20**

23600 CROSSING GATE WITH BELL 1957-58, same as 600 but in box lettered "No. 23600."   **5 7 10**

23601 CROSSING GATE 1959-62, gray plastic base, white plastic building with red windows, trim and doors; red roof and black stack; single arm gate with yellow and black diagonal stripes; not actuated by train; button must be pressed by operator. Gilbert supplied unit with button rather than track trip. This unit shown with and without roadway in catalogue. Sample observed without roadway. Confirmation requested of version with roadway.   **5 7 10**

23602 CROSSING GATE 1963-64, believed to be same as 23601. Confirmation requested.   **6 8 11**

23728 RE-RAILER Reported but not confirmed.   **2 3 4**

23750 TRESTLE BRIDGE 1957-61, same as 750 but in box marked "No. 23750."   **18 20 25**

23758 SAM THE SEMAPHORE MAN 1957, same as 758A but came in box marked "No. 23758."   **12 15 20**

23759 BELL DANGER SIGNAL 1957-60, same as 759 but in box marked "No. 23759."   **5 8 10**

23760 AUTOMATIC HIGHWAY FLASHER 1957-60, same as 760 but came in box marked "No. 23760."   **3 5 6**

23761 AUTOMATIC SEMAPHORE 1957-64, green painted die-cast base, tool chest, signal control box, fiber bottom, unit examined is rubber stamped in silver "May, 1960." (Date will differ on other items.) Black rubber stamped on base "American Flyer Lines." Shiny steel pole, black sheet metal ladder, black painted die-cast lamp unit, black sheet metal arm with green, yellow and red lenses, yellow paint on semaphore arm with nicely formed finial on top.   **8 15 25**

*We would appreciate more information describing this item.

23763   **BELL DANGER SIGNAL 1961-64.***   4   7   10

23764   **FLASHER SIGNAL 1961-64.***   3   5   7

23769   **REVOLVING AIRCRAFT BEACON 1957-64,** same as 769A but came in box marked "No. 23769." Also reported with plastic house similar to house of 23601; Welter Collection. 10   15   20

23771   **OPERATING STOCKYARD AND CAR 1957-61,** similar to K771 but box marked "No. 23771." K771 has sheet metal side frames while 23771 has die-cast side frames. Cattle must be precisely lined up and prodded; the car must be lined up and the gates must be opened by the operator to work properly. Even with such assistance, the cattle sometimes die inside the car and the car must be opened and manually removed, Schneider and Stromberg Collections.   **18   35   50**

23772   **WATER TOWER 1957-64,** same as 772 but box marked "No. 23772."   10   15   20

23774   **FLOODLIGHT TOWER 1957-64,** same as 774 but box marked "No. 23774."   10   15   20

23778   **STREET LAMP SET 1957-64,** same as 778 but box marked "No. 23778."   8   12   16

23779   **OIL DRUM LOADER 1957-61,** same as 779 but box marked "No. 23779."   **30   45   60**

23780   **GABE THE LAMPLIGHTER 1958-59,** Gabe climbs the ladder one step at a time, when he reaches the top the lights go on and off and Gabe slides down the ladder, 11½" high; black or green plastic base, aluminum finished metal tower, black or green top deck, four lamp floodlight; Gabe all in blue except for flesh color face; small all white plastic shed or white metal shed with red trim on base with green or red roof, black plastic controller with green, copper and red buttons with white lettered "AMERICAN FLYER LAMPLIGHTER." Red button turns light on; when button turned the light remains on; tiny copper colored red button in center causes Gabe to descend on ladder -- with each push of the button the catch is released and Gabe comes down one step; green button causes Gabe to climb one step. When Gabe reaches the top the light goes on and then off unless the red button is pushed and turned.
(A)   Plastic shed, Schneider Collection.   **45   65   90**
(B)   Metal shed, Rudzinski Collection.   **45   65   90**

23785   **OPERATING COAL LOADER 1957-60,** same as 785 but box marked "No. 23785," Balint Collection.   **45   65   90**

23786   **AUTOMATIC TALKING STATION 1957-59,** gray plastic base with simulated decking, white plastic building with simulated wood siding, green double passenger doors offset to side of green outlined bay windows; black train schedule board, green hip roof with simulated shingles, red chimney, 10" long, 7¼" wide and 4¾" high; with record playing mechanism and record, illuminated; Balint Collection.   **30   45   60**

23787   **REMOTE CONTROL LOG LOADER 1957-60,** same as 787 but box marked "No. 23787;" Balint Collection.   **35   60   85**

23788   **SUBURBAN STATION 1957-64,** same as 788 but box marked "No. 23788."   10   15   20

23789   **STATION & BAGGAGE SMASHER 1957-59,** same as 789 but box marked "No. 23789."   **20   40   60**

23791   **COW-ON-TRACK 1957-59,** when operator presses button Bossy wanders onto track, oncoming train comes to a halt, Bossy

returns to pasture and train resumes its journey. One piece green plastic base and pasture, black and white or brown and white cow.
(A)   Black and white cow, Newcomer Collection. 10   15   20
(B)   Brown and white cow, Balint Collection.   10   15   20

23796   **REMOTE CONTROL SAWMILL 1957-64,** reddish brown plastic base with elaborate wood grained simulation on top surface embossed "AMERICAN FLYER MFD. BY THE A.C. GILBERT CO. NEW HAVEN, CONN. U.S.A.," two screw binding posts on top deck of base, black plastic four-wheeled cart rides in channel, cart carries half piece of dowel approximately 2½ inches long with brass brads which clips into spring clip on cart, large silver plastic blade (not dangerous to fingers) attached to metal shaft, elaborate gearing process for converting power from brush type motor, motor unit and boom base located in cream colored plastic building with elaborate wood sheafing, four pane windows. Building is on two levels - on upper level is slot for loading wood on end; black plastic boom comes out of upper unit, four-wheel truck rides on boom, follows string up. Blue rubber flexible man with flesh colored face is fully dressed, including hat, and rides on boom sub-assembly. (Reproductions of men are available.) Wire unit mounts into moving chair unit beneath boom (reproduction wire unit available), gray plastic sawdust pile painted cream on one side (reproduction available) has two nibs that fit into corresponding holes on base of unit. Eight pieces of lumber believed to come with unit. Green plastic roof with elaborate ridges, one for each section since roofs differ in size, replacements are available. To the best of our knowledge, "23796" is exactly the same as "796" except that the box is marked "23796." Comes with black plastic button marked in white sans serif letters "American Flyer Sawmill" with yellow and black wire. It is very important that a buyer check that the sawmill equipment is complete. In particular the moving chair unit and the car are not available as reproductions, and their absence substantially reduces the value of the piece. Price assumes complete unit.   **60   90   125**

23830   **PIGGY BACK UNLOADER AND CAR 1959-60,** beige plastic ramp unit with three arches, two gun metal gray or black sheet metal ramp units; one unit assists in loading trailers on and off flat car; other ramp assists in moving trailers from plastic ramp to ground; red and blue trailers with "AMERICAN FLYER TRAINS" and "GILBERT HALL OF SCIENCE" in white letters. Two boys and large loco at one end from 1946-48 catalogue covers. Backing flat car with trailers into ramp causes trailers to load onto plastic ramp; trailers then can be transferred to ground. Trailers can be transferred from ground back to plastic ramp and then onto empty flat car, includes gray car with "MONON 24550" lettered in red, Welter and Balint Collections.   10   18   25

INTRODUCTION TO SCENIC PANELS

In 1965 Gilbert introduced All Aboard Scenic Panels. The panels are 17 x 17" pre-wired plastic modules which include track, landscaping and in some cases buildings. The sections are connected by the usual track pins and are held together by special track locks. These colorful but very fragile units were made in Portugal and had pre-drilled holes to accommodate scenery. In 1966 Gilbert manufactured the 1965 units but added a snow scene. The catalogue number for the entire snow scene of six panels is 20814.

26101   **SCENIC CURVE TRACK PANEL 1965-66,** hill divided by cut for track, stop sign, two fences, Pike Master curve track.
(A)   One street lamp, telegraph pole, three trees, Balint Collection.   3   5   8
(B)   Two street lamps, two brushes, snow scene, Stromberg Collection.   3   8   15

*We would appreciate more information describing this item.

26121 SCENIC STRAIGHT TRACK PANEL 1965-66.
- (A) Ranch house, lake, foot bridge, two piece picket fence, one large tree, stop sign, railroad crossing signal, street lamp, telegraph pole, Balint Collection. **5 6 10**
- (B) Marsh paint scheme, farm house, car bridge, manual uncoupler, railroad crossing sign, light, stop sign, small trees, one large tree, two picket fence units. **5 6 10**
- (C) Farm house, marsh, car bridge, two picket fence units, one large tree , stop sign, railroad crossing signal, street light. **5 6 10**
- (D) Same as (B) but lake rather than marsh, no uncoupler. **5 6 10**

26122 SCENIC STRAIGHT PANEL 1965-66, with remote whistle.
- (A) Colonial house, ravine, foot bridge, five trees, stop sign, railroad crossing sign, street lamp, control button, whistle mechanism inside house, Balint Collection. **7 10 12**
- (B) Similar to (A) but snow panel, Stromberg Collection. **7 15 20**

26141 SCENIC ELECTRIC RIGHT SWITCH PANEL 1965-66.
- (A) Remote control right switch with controller, plowed field, one picket fence, one street lamp unit, one railroad crossing signal, one telegraph pole. **7 10 12**
- (B) Similar to (A) but snow scene, Stromberg Collection. **7 15 20**

26142 SCENIC LEFT SWITCH PANEL 1965-66, left hand Pike Master remote switch with control, cultivated field, street lamp, railroad crossing signal, stop sign, telegraph pole, two trees.
- (A) Summer scene, Balint Collection. **7 10 12**
- (B) Winter snow scene, Stromberg Collection. **7 15 20**

26151 SCENIC CROSSOVER PANEL 1965-66, Pike Master crossover, lake, railroad bridge, billboard, tree, stop sign, railroad crossing signal, street lamp, telegraph pole.
- (A) Summer scene, Balint Collection. **7 10 12**
- (B) Winter snow scene, Stromberg Collection. **7 15 20**

26300 Pike Master STRAIGHT TRACK 1961-64, 10" long, 24 ties. **10c 25c 40c**

26301 Pike Master STRAIGHT TRACK 1961-64, short section, 4¼" long, 9 ties. **10c 25c 40c**

26302 Pike Master STRAIGHT TERMINAL TRACK WITH UN-COUPLER 1961-64, two spring clips for transformer wires; manual uncoupler. **50c 1 2**

26310 Pike Master CURVE TRACK 1961-64, 12" long, 26 ties. **10c 20c 35c**

26320 Pike Master RIGHT HAND REMOTE SWITCH 1961-64, with controller. **3 6 9**

26321 Pike Master LEFT HAND REMOTE SWITCH 1961-64, with controller. **3 6 9**

26322 Pike Master 90º CROSSING 1961-64. **1 2 3**

26323 Pike Master RIGHT HAND MANUAL SWITCH 1961-64. **2 4 6**

26324 Pike Master LEFT HAND MANUAL SWITCH 1961-64. **2 4 6**

26340 Pike Master STEEL TRACK PINS 1961-64, 12 per package. **40c 60c 80c**

26341 Pike Master INSULATING TRACK PINS 1961-64, 12 per package. **40c 60c 80c**

26342 Pike Master ADAPTER PINS 1961-64, 4 per package. **30c 45c 60c**

26343 Pike Master TRACK LOCKS 1961-64, 12 per package. **30c 45c 60c**

26344 Pike Master TRACK TERMINAL 1961-64. **20c 30c 40c**

26415 TRACK ASSORTMENT PACK 1960, 1962, counter display pack for stores; includes six terminals, six packages of track pins, six packages of fiber pins, 72 straight and 24 curve tracks, six half track, three crossings, three re-railers, twelve half straight track, price requires original packaging. **15 25 35**

26425 TRACK ASSORTMENT PACK 1960, straight track. **6 9 12**

26520 KNUCKLE COUPLER KIT 1957-64, two knuckle couplers, two rivets. **1 2 3**

26521 KNUCKLE COUPLER KIT 1957-58, 12 knuckle couplers for converting link coupler cars, with split rivets and tubing for punching out old link couplers, Stromberg Collection. **6 12 20**

26601 FIBER ROADBED 1959-62, straight, molded from composition material to resemble prototype roadbed; one section of traditional S gauge four tie track fits into track recesses. **15c 30c 50c**

26602 FIBER ROADBED 1959, 61-62, same as 26601 but for curve track. **15c 30c 50c**

26670 TRACK TRIP 1957-58. **2 4 6**

26671 ELECTRIC TRACK TRIP 1959, senses presence of train, completes circuit for accessory or switch, Stromberg Collection. **2 4 6**

26672 ELECTRIC TRACK TRIP 1960, senses presence of train, completes circuit for accessory switch. **2 4 6**

26673 ELECTRIC TRACK TRIP 1961-64, operates two trains on same track and prevents collisions. **2 4 6**

26690 TRACK TERMINAL 1957-59, black fiber base, metal spring clips to both rails; stamped "690." Can only be distinguished by original envelope marked "26690." VG and Excellent require original envelope. **50c 1.50 2**

26691 STEEL TRACK PINS 1957-60, 64, twelve per package. **30 50 70**

26692 FIBER TRACK PINS 1957-60, 64, four per package. **20c 40c 60c**

26693 TRACK LOCKS 1957-60, 64, twelve per package. **50c 75c 1**

26700 STRAIGHT TRACK 1957-64, believed to be identical to 700. **15c 25c 40c**

26708 ELECTRIC HORN CONTROL 1957, believed to be identical to
[708] 708. **2 4 6**

26710 STRAIGHT TRACK 1957-64, half section, believed to be identical to 701. **15c 25c 35c**

26718
[678] **REMOTE CONTROL LEFT SWITCH 1957,** believed to be identical to 678.   5   7   12

26719
[679] **REMOTE CONTROL RIGHT SWITCH 1957,** believed to be identical to 679.   5   7   12

26720 **CURVE TRACK 1957-64,** believed to be identical to 702.   15c   25c   35c

26726 **RUBBER ROADBED 1958,** half straight section.   50c   75c   1

26727 **RUBBER ROADBED 1958,** half curve section.   50c   75c   1

26730 **CURVE TRACK 1957-64,** believed to be identical to 702.   15c   25c   35c

26739
[710] **ELECTRONIC WHISTLE CONTROL 1957,** believed to be identical to 710.   50c   1   1.50

26742 **REMOTE CONTROL SWITCHES 1957,** pair of left and right with controller. The switches do not bear numbers. Boxes illustrated in catalogue show the number "702A." We need confirmation that boxes exist with "26742" printed on them.
No Reported Sales

26744 **MANUAL SWITCHES 1957-58,** pair of left and right, switches do not bear numbers. Boxes carry catalogue number "26744."   9   11   15

26745 **RAILROAD CROSSING 1957-64,** 90°, 10" long. This item does not contain any numerical identification and appears to be identical to 725. Only the box stamping differentiates the two.   1   2   3

26746 **RUBBER ROADBED 1957-64,** straight section that holds one piece of S gauge track. Appears identical to 726 roadbed, only difference appears to be the box, found in both gray and black rubber.   50c   75c   1

26747 **RUBBER ROADBED 1957-64,** curve section that holds one piece of S gauge track, appears identical to 727 roadbed except for the box. Found in black, not gray, rubber with wire or narrow ties, Welter and Rudzinski Collections.   50c   75c   1

26748 **AUTOMATIC RE-RAILER 1957-64,** black plastic unit that re-rails rolling stock; 10" long, substitutes for one piece of track. Item does not have number, except for box it is identical to 728 Re-railer.   1   2   3

26749 **BUMPER 1957-60,** green plastic unit snaps on end of siding; with recoil spring and warning light. Appears to be the same as 730, only difference is the box numbering. Excellent price requires original box.   1   2   3

26751 **PIKE PLANNING KIT 1957-59,** with template scaled to 1" per 1' and booklet "American Flyer MODEL RAILROAD HANDBOOK" and 10 x 15" graph paper.   5   8   12

26752 **REMOTE CONTROL UNCOUPLER 1957-58, 60-61,** black plastic base 1 7/8 x 4½", clamps onto T rail track; swivel clip forces unit against track; small black tool shed with gable roof covers mechanism; black single button control unit with red button lettered "American Flyer Uncoupler," Stromberg and Balint Collections.   1   1.50   2

26756 **BUMPER 1961-64,** with warning light and recoil spring; compatible with standard "S" track or Pike Master; how does this item differ from older style bumpers?   1   2   3

26760 **REMOTE CONTROL SWITCHES 1958-64,** with controller. Appear similar to 720 but came in box numbered "26760."   15   25   35

26761 **REMOTE CONTROL SWITCH 1958-64,** left hand unit.   7   12   17

26762 **REMOTE CONTROL SWITCH 1958-64,** right hand unit.   7   12   17

26770 **MANUAL SWITCHES 1959-64,** pair.   8   12   16

26781
[780] **RAILROAD TRESTLE SET 1957.** Box numbered "26871," same as 780, Balint Collection.   10   15   20

26782 **TRESTLE 1958-60,** more information needed.   1   3   5

26783 **HI-TRESTLES 1957,** twelve trestles, each 4½" high for adding to and extending highest elevated part of 26781 TRESTLES. Includes twelve track locks. Appears the same as 783, box numbered "26871," Balint Collection.   5   10   15

26790 **TRESTLE 1961-64,** more information needed.   1   3   5

26810 **POW-R-CLIPS 1960-64,** makes inconspicuous connection from transformer to track.   20c   30c   40c

27460 **LAMP ASSORTMENT KIT 1959, 1964.**   5   10   15

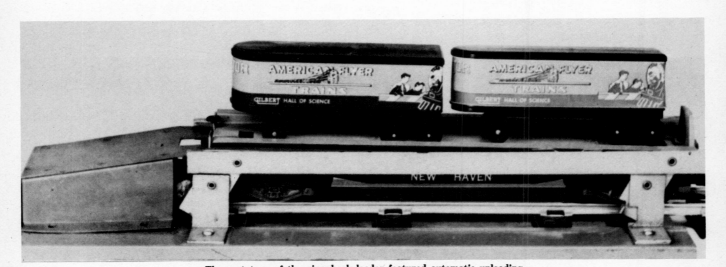

**The prototype of the piggyback loader featured automatic unloading.
However it was not made this way because of cost considerations. Photo
from the Walsh Collection.**

Chapter X

TANK CARS

TANK CARS

Gilbert used five basic tank designs over twenty years of S Gauge production. The single dome tank comes in three varieties:

(1) Single dome complete tank with four stanchions on the side and wrap-around handrails.

(2) Single dome complete tank with four stanchions on the side, wrap-around handrails and platform, such as the Chemical tank.

(3) Single dome tank with open bottom, six stanchions on the side; handrails do not wrap around the ends, such as the 24329 Hooker and 24316(D) Mobilgas.

Gilbert also produced a triple dome complete tank with four stanchions on each side and wrap-around handrails. Unlike Lionel, Gilbert did not produce a two dome tank car.

The general development of tanks is: first, cars come with Type A trucks and link couplers with thin shanks, embossed with "PAT NO. 2240137" and without weights. Cars are also found with Type B and C trucks with black or brass weights. Later cars are found with sintered iron truck side frames and knuckle couplers. The last issue of Gilbert tank cars comes with Pike Master trucks and couplers. Fundimension cars come with sintered iron truck side frames and knuckle couplers.

Development of the frame and the method of fastening the frame to the tank is very interesting. Both plastic and die-cast frames, but not sheet metal frames, were used. We have numbered the plastic frames Types I through IV. The first Gilbert tank cars in 1946 come with Type I plastic frames, which unfortunately frequently warped, were soon replaced by die-cast frames. Finally in 1957-58, plastic frames return and remain the mainstay for tankers until the end of Gilbert production. Fundimensions has continued to use plastic frames.

PLASTIC FRAMES

Type I plastic frames were made in 1946 and typical of frames manufactured during this period often warp. They are embossed "PA-10064" on the frame. The frames have air tanks and brake detail on the underside and fasten to the tank with a single screw. There are two square tabs on the tank which fit into matching square inserts on the frame's chassis. These frames have flat ends with two molded grab irons on each end. There is usually one two-piece brakewheel mounted through the frame.

Type II plastic frames were introduced about 1958 and have embossed information "PA 14D403." The frame has a one piece brakewheel at one end and two diamond shaped

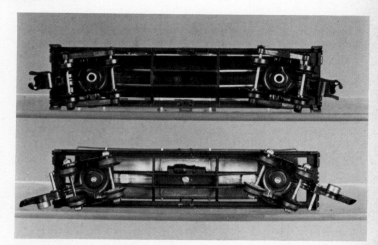

Top Shelf: Type IV Plastic Frame; Bottom Shelf: Type II Die-cast Frame

markers at the other. The frame ends have open plastic steps on each corner with two molded grab irons on each end. The frames fasten to the tank by a central round plastic guide and two snap-in projections from the base of the tank or with a screw accompanied by two square plastic guides. Steps are long with pierced risers. Frames usually come with sintered iron truck side frames and with cars numbered 24321, 24324, 24323 and 24309.

Type III plastic frames were made about 1960. They are embossed with "PA 15D692." Frame ends have two small discs and two small projecting plates, sometimes called grab irons, on each end. The frames are fastened to the tank by a screw and two square guides on the tank. The steps are long with pierced risers. These frames come with the 24316 Mobil tank, 24328 Shell, 24329 Hooker and 24330 Baker's Chocolate. The frame includes a cradle for the tank to fit into. This tank is open on the bottom. Type III frames usually come with Pike Master trucks and couplers and may or may not have a diamond shaped marker at one end and a one piece brakewheel, stand and a diamond shaped marker at the other end. The markers and brakewheels are pressed and glued into square holes in the frame. However some cars do not come with markers and brakewheels even though the square holes are there.

Type IV plastic frames were used in 1979 by Fundimensions and come with the 9100 tank. They are a continuation of the Type III PA 15D692 with new embossed lettering "AMERICAN FLYER R BY LIONEL R OF FUNDIMENSIONS TM," facing the track on the outside.

DIE-CAST FRAMES

Die-cast frames were introduced in 1946 when Gilbert discovered that plastic frames warped badly. The three known types of die-cast frames are readily identified by their end shape and steps.

Type I die-cast frames were made from 1946-51 and come with some of the 625 series cars. They have long steps at each of the four corners and have serrated ends with four teeth. They do not have brakewheels or diamond shaped markers. The frames are fastened to the tank by a screw and two square guides extending from the body of the tank. They come with Type A trucks and link couplers.

Type II die-cast frames were made from 1947-51 and come with some of the 625 series cars. The ends are serrated and have four teeth. There are short steps at each of the four corners, no brakewheels and no diamond shaped markers on the frame. The frames are fastened to the tank by one screw and two square guides extending from the tank body. They come with sheet metal trucks and link couplers. There are three large slots through the frame at each end.

Type III die-cast frames were made from 1952-57. They have short steps at each of the four corners. The frame is pierced at each end on the top surface with three slots. The ends are smooth with only a minor outline of the step frame; they do not have brakewheels or diamond markers. The frames are fastened to the tank by a screw and two square guides extending from the body of the tank. This frame comes with Types A and B trucks and link couplers. Cars with the numbers 925, 926, 910, and 912 usually have Type II die-cast frames.

625 **SHELL** The orange versions of this car are the rarest Gilbert tank cars. The black and silver versions are relatively common. Both versions are usually warped.

(A) Orange painted Type I black plastic tank with black dome cap and ends, shiny metal handrail wraps around entire tank, shiny two step ladders, a small "S.E.P.X. 8681" in black is underlined; also "CAPACITY 90000 LBS.;" frame is often warped, one two-piece brakewheel through one end, Type A trucks, link couplers with thin shank and embossed "PAT. NO. 2240137," no coupler weights; tank fastened to frame by screw, Leonard and Bargeron Collections. **300 400 500**

(B) Same as (A) but with "LT.WT. 40400 7-27." **300 400 500**

(C) Same as (A) but unpainted acetate plastic and "LT.WT. 40400 7-27," Newcomer Collection. **300 400 500**

(D) Black unpainted single dome plastic tank, wire handrail wraps around entire tank, shiny metal ladders, "S.E.P.X. 8681" underlined in white, Type I black finished die-cast frame and Type I plastic frame, Type A trucks, link couplers with thin shanks, no coupler weights and embossed "PAT. NO. 2240137," tank fastens to frame with screw, no brakewheel or diamond markers; circa 1946, Newcomer and Bargeron Collections. **5 8 12**

(E) Silver painted black plastic single dome tank, shiny wire handrail wraps around entire tank, shiny metal ladders on both sides, black "S.E.P.X. 8681," "CAPACITY 800000 LBS." "LT. WT. 40400 7-27," Type III black finished die-cast frame, embossed "PA 8955," Type A trucks, link couplers with thin shanks and no coupler weights, embossed "PAT. NO. 2240137," tank fastened to frame by one screw; tank embossed on end "AMERICAN FLYER MFD. BY THE A.C. GILBERT CO. NEW HAVEN, CONN. U.S.A.," circa 1946, no brakewheel or diamond markers, Caples Collection. **5 8 12**

(F) Same as (D) but link couplers with thick shanks, embossed "PAT. NO. 2240137," with brass coupler weights, Degano Collection. **5 8 12**

(G) Same as (E) but "GULF" label, Manson Collection. **6 9 15**

(H) Same as (E) but Type D trucks, black coupler weights, Bargeron Collection. **5 8 12**

Important Note: Reproduction orange 625 Shell cars have been made and are most readily distinguished by their bright shiny, new appearance.

625G **GULF** Silver painted black plastic single dome tank, "GRCX 5016 CAPACITY 100000LBS. LT.WT. 48900" in black; orange logo decal with blue "GULF," shiny metal handrail wraps around entire tank, shiny metal ladders on both sides; Type II die-cast black finished frame, no handrails or diamond markers, short solid steps and link couplers.

(A) Type B trucks, black coupler weights, Newcomer Collection. **5 7 10**

(B) Type D trucks, black coupler weights, Caples Collection. **5 7 10**

The Rare Celanese Chemical Tank Car

910 **GILBERT CHEMICAL** 1954, green painted gray or black plastic tank with center yellow band, single yellow dome, black platform and ladders, black finished handrail wraps around entire tank, large black lettered "GILBERT CHEMICALS," small black lettered "GATX 910 CAPY 100000 LBS. LT.WT. 47100" and "BLT 10-53;" black die-cast Type III frame, no brakewheel or diamond markers; tank fastened to frame by screw and two square plastic guides extending from tank body; sintered iron truck side frames and knuckle couplers. This car was originally intended to be the Celanese Chemical car and has, therefore, Celanese colors, Newcomer and Patterson Collections. **30 45 60**

912 **KOPPERS** 1955-56, black painted black plastic single dome tank with platform, dull black handrails and copper or nickel finished ladder; orange sans serif "KOPPERS" "CHEMICALS·PLASTICS" "K P C X 912" with line above and below; "KOPPERS" paper label with eight sides, light gray border and two red triangles; black plastic or black finished die-cast frame, sintered iron truck side frames, knuckle couplers.

(A) Type III die-cast frame with no brakewheel or diamond markers, small solid steps, Newcomer and Bargeron Collections. **10 20 35**

(B) Type II plastic frame with brakewheel, possibly diamond markers, large pierced steps, Newcomer Collection. Note that the car illustrated is missing its dome.) **10 20 35**

925 **GULF** 1953-56, silver finished black plastic tank, single dome, black handrails, shiny two step metal ladders; on left is "GRCX 5016 CAPACITY 100000 LBS. LT.WT. 48900," on right side is "GULF" orange decal with blue lettering; sintered iron truck side frames, knuckle couplers, no brakewheels, Patterson Collection.

625

625

625

625G

910

912[A]

912[B]

925

926[A]

926[B]

958[A]

24310

24313

24316

(A) Type III die-cast frame, Patterson and Bargeron Collections.   **3**   **5**   **8**

(B) Type II plastic frame, Bargeron Collection.   **3**   **5**   **8**

926   **GULF** 1955-56, silver painted black plastic three dome tank car, metal handrail wraps around entire tank, silver finished ladder; black underlined "GATX 33648," "CAPACITY 80000 LT.WT. 40700," orange circular logo with "GULF" in blue letters, different types of frames, die-cast truck side frames, knuckle couplers.

(A) Type III die-cast frame without brakewheel or diamond markers; frame is pierced at each end with three slots, small solid steps integral to body, tank fastened to body by screw and two square guides extending from tank, Balint and Newcomer Collections.   **10**   **15**   **20**

(B) Type II plastic frame with long pierced steps, brakewheel at one end, two diamond markers at other, tank fastened to body by screw, black railing wraps around tank, shiny ladders, Balint Collection.   **10**   **15**   **20**

958   **Mobilgas** 1957, catalogued as 24516 but car has "958" on side. Box may be marked "24516" or "24515." Confirmation requested with respect to "24516." Red single dome, plastic tank, black handrail wraps around entire tank, silver finished ladder, "W E O X 958" in white with line above and below, "CAP. 10000 LT.WT. 2450" and at other end "NEW 6-51 CU. FT. 1234" 'or "NEW 4-51 CU. FT. 1234," black die-cast frame without the diamond marker and brakewheel; with long pierced steps; tank fastens to frame by one screw, sintered iron truck side frames, knuckle couplers.

(A) "958" "NEW 6-51...," (box probably marked "24516" Newcomer and Schneider Collections.) Confirmation of "24516" box requested.   **7**   **10**   **13**

(B) "958" "NEW 4-51...," with a factory stamped box numbered "24515" which is crossed out and "958" written in pencil on the box, Bargeron Collection.   **No Reported Sales**

24305   **MONSANTO** Reported to exist, more details requested.   **No Reported Sales**

24305
KOPPERS 1957.

(A) "912" car inside a "24305" box, plastic frame, Walsh Collection.   **No Reported Sales**

(B) Car numbered "24305," plastic frame, Carnes Collection.   **No Reported Sales**

24306   **KOPPERS** 1957, probably a 912 car with a plastic frame inside of a "24306" box, confirmation requested.   **No Reported Sales**

24309   **GULF** Silver painted black plastic single dome tank with silver finished handrails and ladders, "G.R.C.X. 5016" in black which is underlined and "CAPACITY 100000 LBS" and "LT.WT. 48900;" black plastic frame with one or two diamond markers at one end and brakewheel at other, long pierced steps; sintered iron truck side frames, knuckle couplers, Patterson Collection.   **3**   **4**   **6**

24310   **GULF** 1958-60, silver painted black plastic single dome tank with silver finished handrails and ladders; "G.R.C.X. 5016 CAPACITY 100000 LBS LT.WT. 48900" in black, black plastic frame with brakewheel at one end and two diamonds on other, sintered iron truck side frames, knuckle couplers, orange logo with "GULF," Schneider Collection.   **10**   **15**   **20**

24313   **GULF** 1957-60, silver painted plastic three dome tank with black finished handrails and silver finished ladders; "G.A.T.X. 3364" in black and underlined and "CAPACITY 800000 LT.WT. 40700;" orange circular paper label with blue "GULF" logo, black

finished plastic Type II frame with one piece brakewheel at one end and diamond marker at other, long pierced steps; tank fastened to frame by central round plastic guide and two snap-in projections, sintered iron truck side frames, knuckle couplers, Newcomer Collection.   **10**   **15**   **20**

24316   **Mobilgas** Red painted black or white plastic single dome tank, with or without handrails and ladder, "W E O X 24316" in white with line above and below; "CAP. 100000 LT. WT. 2450" in white and at other end "NEW 4-57" and "CU.FT. 1234," knuckle or Pike Master couplers. Also reported with "NEW 4-51," -- see (F) below.

(A) Red painted black plastic tank, black plastic frame with brakewheel at one end and two diamond shaped markers at other end; black painted handrails and shiny metal ladders; base fastened to tank by one screw, sintered iron truck side frames, knuckle couplers, Caples Collection.   **10**   **15**   **20**

(B) Same as (A) but base fastened to tank by two blocks on tanks and nipple (from tanks), Caples Collection.   **10**   **15**   **20**

(C) Red painted white plastic tank, Type II plastic frame with one diamond marker at one end and one brakewheel at other end, Pike Master trucks and couplers, no handrails or ladder, Caples Collection.   **4**   **6**   **8**

(D) Red painted black plastic tank, Type III black plastic frame with brakewheel at one end and one diamond marker at other; shiny handrails and ladders, base fastened to tank by screw and two square plastic guides; long pierced plastic steps, sintered iron truck side frames, knuckle couplers, car has six stanchions on each side and railing does not wrap around entire tank. Black plastic frame includes cradle for tank; tank is open on bottom, 1960, Newcomer Collection.   **10**   **15**   **20**

(E) Same as (D) but Pike Master trucks and couplers.   **5**   **7**   **10**

(F) Red painted plastic tank, Type III black plastic frame, lettered "NEW 4-51," otherwise same lettering as main description; no handrailing, and end plates that hold handrails on side are not drilled, diamond warning at each end, brakewheel at one end only; Pike Master trucks and couplers, Santapietro Collection.   **5**   **7**   **10**

24319   **PENNSYLVANIA SALT** 1958, blue paint over silver paint on gray plastic or blue paint over black plastic single dome tank with black platform, black finished ladders; shiny handrail wraps around entire tank, yellow "LIQUID CHLORINE," "WYANDOTTE MICHIGAN," "PENNSYLVANIA SALT MANUFACTURING COMPANY," "24319" with yellow line above, "CAPY 10,000 LT WT 4320," yellow keystone with "PR" inside, black plastic frame with one piece brakewheel at one end and diamond marker at other; sintered iron truck side frames, knuckle couplers; tank fastens to frame by a single screw; Schneider, Bargeron, Newcomer and Balint Collections. (IMPORTANT: reproductions have been made; they have a sharply drawn keystone, originals have a poorly drawn keystone which lacks sharp edges. An original, also, according to Tom Austin, has a platform with four legs, each leg has a nipple which fits into receiving holes on the shoulder or projecting flanges of the tank body. Reproductions do not have holes on the shoulder or projecting flanges. Consequently the nipples have been cut off from the platform legs and the platforms glued in place. Holes are not visible on the shoulders of the tanks. If you are in doubt as to whether a car is a reproduction or an original, we urge you to secure professional advice. Reproductions currently sell for $40.)   **125**   **170**   **225**

24320   **DEEP ROCK** 1960, black plastic single dome tank, "DEEP ROCK" and "DRX 24320" in yellow, black plastic Type II frame

24319

24321

24323

24324

24325

24329

without diamond marker and brakewheel, tank fastened to frame by one screw. **100 130 170**

24321 **DEEP ROCK** 1959, black unpainted plastic single dome tank with or without handrails, "DEEP ROCK" and "DRX 24321 in yellow, black unpainted plastic frame without brakewheel or diamond shaped units, sintered iron truck side frames and knuckle couplers.
(A) With flat black finished handrails and shiny ladder, black unpainted plastic tank, black plastic frame with two diamond shaped markers at one end and one piece or no brakewheel at other end; long pierced steps, tank fastened to Type II frame with nib and two plastic snap-in girders, Patterson and Balint Collections. **10 20 30**
(B) Without handrails, ladders and platform; Type II plastic frame with no end markers or brakewheels, long pierced steps, tank fastened to frame by nipple and two plastic snap-in girders, Patterson and Newcomer Collections. **10 20 30**

24322 **GULF** 1959, silver painted black plastic single dome without handrails or ladder, black lettering, sintered iron truck side frames, knuckle couplers.
(A) With handrails. **No Reported Sales**
(B) Without handrails, silver painted black plastic tank, no ladders, platform, end markers or brakewheel, Type II frame, long pierced steps, tank fastens to frame by nipple and two blocks, Balint Collection. **10 15 20**

24323 **BAKER'S CHOCOLATE** White single dome plastic tank with gray platform, shiny handrails and ladders.
(A) White tank with white ends, gray platform, shiny

handrails, black ladder, plastic frame with two diamond markers at one end and a one piece brakewheel at other; lady with brown and white dress, red block with "SINCE 1780" in white, "CHOCOLATE ONLY AAR 203W SPECIAL GATC 2-9-54" in brown and on other side "GATX 24323 CAPY. 136000 LT. WT. 73700;" gray cap on dome, sintered iron truck side frames, knuckle couplers, Newcomer Collection. **75 125 150**
(B) White unpainted tank with gray painted ends, gray platform, shiny handrails, black ladder, Type II plastic frame with two diamond markers at one end and a one piece brakewheel at other end, lady with brown and white dress, red and black paper sticker with "SINCE 1780" in white, "CHOCOLATE ONLY AAR 203W SPECIAL GATC 2-9-54" in brown and on other side "GATX 24323 CAPY. 136000 LT. WT. 73700," painted gray dome cap, tank fastens to body by nib and two snap-in blocks, sintered iron truck side frames and knuckle couplers, Patterson and Balint Collections. **50 75 100**
(C) Same as (B) but white painted black plastic tank, Bargeron Collection. **50 75 100**

24324 **HOOKER** 1959-60, orange painted single dome, black plastic tank with black unpainted plastic center area; black ladder, platform, dome and dome cap; shiny railing wraps around entire tank, "HOOKER" in large sans serif face on left side; "NIAGARA FALLS N.Y. GATX 24324" in small white face, black HOOKER logo with black letters; logo is a paper label, black plastic Type II frame with one piece brakewheel at one end and one or two diamond shaped markers at other; tank fastened to frame by pressure fit with square tabs on tank, sintered iron truck side frames, knuckle couplers, Schneider and Newcomer Collections.
17 25 40

24325 GULF Silver painted black plastic single dome tank, "GRCY 5016" in black and underlined; "CAPACITY 100000 LBS. LT. WT. 548900" in black, orange paper label logo with "GULF" in blue.

(A) Type III frame with cradle, shiny side rails that do not wrap around tank, two diamond markers and one piece brakewheel, silver ladders, tank fastens to frame by screw, Pike Master trucks and couplers, Balint Collection.

          10   20   30

(B) Type II frame without cradle; no handrails, ladders, diamond markers or brakewheels on frame; long pierced steps are part of frame, sintered iron truck side frames with knuckle couplers, Newcomer Collection. **3   5   6**

24328 SHELL 1962-66, unpainted yellow plastic single dome tank, with black finished handrails that do not wrap around, six stanchions on each side, no platform; red "SHELL" and small red "CAPACITY 10,000 GAL LT LMT 120000 LBS LT WT 48,200 LBS," red and yellow sticker with shell motif; Type III plastic frame with black cradle for tank; brakewheel and diamond marker at one end and one diamond marker at other end, Pike Master trucks and couplers, tank fastened to frame by one screw, currently available new for $10.00, Bargeron and Patterson Collections. **3   5   7**

24329 HOOKER 1964-65, all orange unpainted plastic single dome tank with black finished handrails that do not wrap around tank, six stanchions on each side, ladder and platform; orange dome and cap; "HOOKER" in large white sans serif face, "NIAGARA FALLS N.Y. GATX 24329" in small white face; orange and white "HOOKER" logo; Type IV black plastic frame with cradle for tank, one brakewheel at one end and two diamond markers at other; tank fastened to frame by one screw through bottom, Pike Master trucks and couplers, Patterson and Newcomer Collections. **7   10   15**

[24329] HOOKER

(A) With platform, 1961, no information available.
          No Reported Sales

(B) Without platform, 1963-65, no information available.
          No Reported Sales

24330 BAKER'S CHOCOLATE 1961-62, White unpainted tank embossed "PA 15D691" with white ends, shiny handrails, black ladder, gray platform; Type III plastic frame with long pierced steps and cradle for tank with a diamond marker at one end and a diamond marker and brakewheel at other end; no lady; black "SINCE 1780," and brown "CHOCOLATE ONLY AAR 203W SPECIAL GATC 2-9-54" and on other end of same side "GATX 24330 CAPY. 136000 LT. WT. 73700," white dome cap, tank fastened to body by one screw, Pike Master trucks and couplers, Bargeron, Balint and Schneider Collections. **15   25   40**

9100 Gulf, 1979, Fundimensions production, white unpainted plastic single dome tank with shiny handrail on each side that does not wrap around tank, six stanchions on each including two dummy end stanchions; black finished stamped metal ladders, black plastic platform with two wire railings; "PA15D691" embossed inside tank; tank has open bottom; large orange lettered "Gulf," "WRNX 9100 CAPY 155000 LBS LT WT 107800 NEW" in small black face; black plastic Type IV frame with cradle; and push-in black plastic diamond marker at one end. At other end is one piece plastic brakewheel, stand and diamond marker, both units press into square holes in frame. "PA 15D692" is embossed on frame's inside surface facing the tank; the frame has four long pierced steps, one at each corner. Black sintered iron truck side frames, knuckle couplers, Greenberg Collection. **10   15   25**

9101 UNION 1980, Fundimensions production. **8   12   15**

The Gilbert exhibit at the 1939's World Fair.
Note the H0 and the old Chicago Flyer. Walsh Collection.

24568

24516

[928]

24579

The American Flyer Circus

643

643

[649] Circus Coach

Note That the Tractor is Missing from the Right Hand Flat Car.

Chapter XI

FLAT CARS

Broadly defined, flat cars include all cars with loads mounted on flat surfaces except searchlights, cranes and work cabooses. Over the years Gilbert made a variety of flat cars and a fascinating assortment of loads. Loads range from mundane girders and pipes to exotic Christmas trees and rocket fuels. Perennial favorites include jeeps, autos, racers and trucks. The most desirable loads are The Corvette and the Old Time Cannon followed by Circus Cars with Cages.

Flat car frames show considerable change and development. Immediate postwar cars (1946) come with plastic frames, embossed "PA 9952," which tended to warp. Gilbert consequently experimented with other materials and soon introduced die-cast frames. Their advantage is greater weight, their limitation is the hand work required to remove the flashing (residue casting) produced in the manufacturing process. It appears that only one type of die-cast frame was made for regular flat cars.[1] It is embossed "PA-9952," the same as the plastic frame, and provides one hole for a two piece brakewheel. Frames do not appear to have been primed, although they hold paint quite well which suggests that their surfaces were properly prepared before painting. The frame is 8 5/8 inches long end-to-end.

About 1953 Gilbert introduced stamped steel frames. Their advantages are less clean-up and less hand work as well as enough weight so that cars in a long train will track properly but not strain the engine. Stamped steel frames are usually rubber stamped on the side, not on the underside. About 1950 another innovation made news in frame design. Presswood was substituted for metal frames. One impetus for the substitution was a potential metal shortage, particularly zinc, caused by diversion of metals for the Korean War effort. One presswood car is embossed "No. 5" on the underside. When it became obvious that the war would not adversely affect the availability of essential metals Gilbert returned to metal frames. One characteristic of the wooden frames is that paint does not adhere as well.

Gilbert's flat car line evolves slowly: frequently a car would be offered for three or four years and then would be replaced by another. New entries were usually limited to one or two per year. It is important to understand that the 1946 line has its origins in the 1941 line. The 715 automatic Army unloading car is based on the 1941 472 Army unloading car. The 628 log car is a revision of the stamped steel 482 from 1941. In a similar fashion the 627 girder car has its origins in the 483 girder car. However, a new car concept the 717 log unloading car is added in 1946. This car, a modified Army unloader, which carries logs, provides the natural compliment to the new 751 log loader, an important new accessory.

The exact same line-up is offered in 1947. However,

Gilbert makes a number of important changes in individual items although their catalogue numbers do not change. Couplers were changed from thin shank to thick shank to solve breakage problems. Type A trucks with slots are replaced by Type B trucks without slots. Decal lettering is replaced by rubber stamp lettering. The pickup shoe for operating cars is changed from a "between the rails" pickup to "an outside" pickup. And most important, the troublesome plastic frames are replaced with die-cast frames for the 627 and 628. Hence in terms of improved car operations, 1947 is a very important year.

1948 marks the addition of a new 636 Erie depressed center car. The Erie is a handsome car with six-wheel trucks and carries a yellow cable reel. This design in revised form stays in the line until 1958, a very long sales period. 1948 also sees the introduction of brass coupler weights. The addition of weights keeps the link couplers securely fastened and substantially reduces random uncoupling.

1949 brings only one major change: the armored car on the 715 unloader is replaced by the Manoil coupe, a sign that war interests have declined and peace time pursuits should be honored. The 628 log car, the 627 girder car, the 717 log unloading car and the 636 Erie depressed center car continue in the line. Coupler weights are changed from brass to black making it possible to distinguish the 1949-53 black weight-thick shank coupler from the 1948 brass weight-thick shank coupler, from the 1947 thick shank-no weight coupler from the 1946 thin shank-no weight coupler. It also makes the car more attractive because the coupler weight blends with the link.

In 1950 the entire 1949 line is repeated. A major innovation includes the 643 circus car with tractor and two wagons. Circus car load variations are numerous and a true collector's delight; the details are presented later in this chapter. The 627 girder car receives a lettering change to "AMERICAN FLYER." This production marks the end of a car whose origins go back to the 483 girder car of 1941.

For 1951 the 715 car unloader, the 717 log unloader, the 628 log car, the 636 Erie depressed center reel car, and the 643 circus car are all carried on from 1950. Apparently a new log unloader, a 714 with a die-cast chassis, is also introduced, although there is considerable confusion about it. The catalogue pictures the 717 log unloader with a sheet metal chassis quite similar to the 715 auto unloader. However the illustration of the 717 is erroneously labeled 714. The text correctly listed the 714 and describes it as having a die-cast base. The description also gives its colors

---

[1] A different frame, PA 10358, was used for the depressed center cars.

as black and yellow which is not correct. These are 717 colors. The catalogue description gives its length as 9" which adds to the confusion since neither the 717 or 714 are nine inches long. Given the accurate and detailed text Gilbert provides, this error probably is not very serious!

In 1952 the old standbys: the 628, 636, 715 and 717 are offered and illustrated as well as the 643 circus flat which is being offered for the third year. The new 714 is correctly described and illustrated. Finally a major new car the 648 Track Cleaning car, is introduced. Mounted on a long depressed center chassis the car features two sets of wipers - the first applied fluid and the second wiped the rails clean. This is an interesting case of taking an existing chassis -- one used for the reel load -- and finding a new use for it.

1953 was a year of major change in the Gilbert line as the sheet metal trucks and link couplers are replaced by the sintered iron side frame trucks with knuckle couplers. Because of the need to provide continuity many cars are offered both ways. The link coupler, introduced in 1939 and a faithful peformer for many years, is phased out. This major change, the second in eight years that would make its previous production obsolete is handled very differently from the previous round. This time Gilbert makes available a simple, inexpensive kit for operators to update link coupler cars. The kit includes the necessary punch and replacement link and rivet. Gilbert not only provided a replacement coupler kit, it also offered many of the separately sold cars in both link and knuckle coupler versions. Hence we have our favorite 628 log car being offered with its new updated companion 928 (the lettering on the side of 928 is now in large letters); the 636 depressed center reel car is now still offered with its new version 936; 648 is offered with its new brother 948; 634 circus wagon is offered without a 900 series companion, probably because this was to be the last offering. The 915 unloading car is offered along with the favorite 615 auto unloader. The 714 log unloader link coupler car is joined in the line by a knuckle coupler version 914. The old sheet metal chassis 717 log unloader, dating from 1946 disappears from the line. Old Gilbert cars don't fade away and don't get melted down. Rather they end up on collectors' shelves.

In 1954 Gilbert prunes the large 1953 line and two of the six hundred series items are dropped: 628 and 636, leaving the knuckle coupler 928 and 936. Both link and knuckle versions are still offered for the other items: 714 and 914, 648 and 948 and 715 and 915. Either there were plenty of link 714, 648 and 715 left from last year or strong sales justified making more! 905 is added to the line replacing the 605 flat offered only in 1953. 905 is a sheet metal frame car that came with the starter set K5401T.

In 1955, the long running auto loader, the 915 gets a new load -- its second -- the Renwal gasoline truck which replaces the racer. The racer and truck load comes in many variations and these are listed under 915 in the detailed listings. Since Gilbert changes suppliers for the gasoline truck with Renwal replacing Tootsietoy we expect there is an interesting story behind this change. The 914 log unloading car is offered again as is the 936 depressed center flat. For 1955 Gilbert

updates the 936 with new "PENNSYLVANIA" roadname and Western Electric lettering on the reel. The 948 is still in the line keeping the tracks clean. The 928 log car is not offered in 1955 and ends a series that began before World War II.

1956 is a year of major innovation, new entries include: a new lumber car, 928 with stakes in New Haven markings, a 971 action car, a 971 Southern Pacific lumber unloading car featuring Joe and Moe, a 956 piggy back car with trailers advertising American Flyer Trains on a chassis with Monon markings, a 915 auto unloader and a 914 log unloader are continued into their fourth year.

1957 is a water shed year in the history of Gilbert. The installation of a new computer system leads to the renumbering of the line in a then unfamiliar five digit sequence. Our old favorites appear to take on new identities: the 948 track cleaning car is given catalogue number 24533, the 936 depressed center flat car is assigned 24519, the 956 piggy back becomes a 24536, the 928 with stakes becomes a 24516, the 915 becomes a 25033 and the 914 becomes a 25003 and last year's new entry, a 971, is catalogued as a 25016. However, these items are actually made with their old three digit numbers on their sides. The boxes are usually marked with the new five digit numbers! A brand new action flat car, the vertical missile launching car, appears with 969 on its side but is catalogued as a 25045. This missile car is prophetic as it signaled the development of an entire aerospace dimension to the model railroad industry, an innovation eventually followed by Lionel and Marx.

The five digit numbers in 1958 appear on the equipment and in the catalogue, and yet some items still have their three digit numbers on them: 24519 now appears on the side of the 936 depressed center car with reel, 24533 now appears on the side of the 948 track cleaning car, 24539 is now the New Haven flat with pipes, a new olive drab ROCKET TRANSPORT, 24553, carries two colorful rockets, 24536 replaces the 956 Monon piggy back, 24516 replaces the 928 stake car, the hard to find 25003 replaces 914 and 25016 replaces 971, 969 is replaced by the 25045 ROCKET LAUNCHER.

1959 represents the largest offering of new flat cars in all of Gilbert's and American Flyer's 50 years. Use of a flat car to carry diverse and interesting loads is a practice adapted by both Marx and Lionel at about this time. The flat car with load provides an inexpensive way to update the line and to generate more fan interest. 1959 also marks the formal observance of "the Gilbert Company's" 50th anniversary. This year brings in a unique two unit rocket launcher and box car. The box car is necessary for activating the rocket launcher. It did not meet with great popular acclaim however and is offered for only one year. Today, it is of course highly prized and brings a substantial price!

In 1959 Gilbert also introduces one of its more popular accessories, the 23830 Piggy Back Unloader. This accessory permits the operator to unload and reload two trailers on a specially outfitted flat car. The new flat car, 24550, is equipped with a special backstop that makes unloading/

24566   24574

905   909

928   928

956   [245]65

24553   24539

24556   24572

24575   24577

loading possible and replaces the 24536 which is not offered. Six flat cars are also carried on from 1958: the 25003 Log Unloading Car, 25016 Lumber Unloading Car, 24553 Rocket Transport Car, 24533 Track Cleaning Car, 24539 New Haven Flat with pipes, 25045 Rocket Launcher.

Two other popular cars make their debut in 1959: 24557 Jeeps and 24558 Christmas Tree. The trees come in a plastic bag to prevent unnecessary wear and tear in transit. Most were promptly displayed and very few people have their trees in unopened plastic bags! The car appropriately bears the Canadian Pacific roadname. Lionel management recognized a good idea when they saw it and in 1959 Lionel brought out its 6826 Christmas Tree Flat Car. The Gilbert and Lionel cars have both shown better than average appreciation! It would be fun to have a new American Flyer Santa Claus handcar!

The Jeep car is also offered in 1960 and 1961 and is popular among collectors. Military items seem to spark new interest -- particularly since we were not currently fighting any wars. An uncatalogued New Haven Flat, 24559 without a load is also made for an inexpensive Sears set that year only; it is a hard to find car. The 24556 Wheel Transport also appears for its only showing in 1959.

1960 is a year of consolidation after the great expansion of 1959. The 25003 Log Unloader is offered for the last time. (Recall that the 25003 developed from the 914, which in turn developed from the 714, which was first offered in 1951 or 1952.) The 25016 Lumber Unloading Car is offered in 1960 for the last time. The 24533 Track Cleaning Car continues a series that began with the 648. The long and successful sales career of this car is undoubtedly due to its apparently useful function on the layout. According to operators, however, the car gets mixed reviews for its operating efficiency! The 24539 New Haven with pipes is joined by the 24540 New Haven with pipes and both, as standard line items, provide inexpensive and playful cars; the pipes could be replaced with all kinds of other loads by imaginative, young engineers. The 25045 is sold for the last time and is joined by two updated Rocket Launchers, the 25059 and 25046. The new aerospace hardware receives Pentagon approval as their 45° launch angle substantially increases the liklihood of hitting the targets (compared to the 90° launch angle of the older unit). In fact the 45° angle creates a fine opportunity for practice and proficiency shots by apprentice missile controllers. To assist in this national endeavor, Gilbert thoughtfully provides a special target box car, the 25057. It explodes (or more accurately springs apart) when hit or even when a near hit occurs (at times the car would self destruct on its own command).

The aerospace industry was booming. The railroads and the model railroads both vied for their share of the toy space business. Gilbert, keenly aware of this latest public enthusiasm, offers at least three other related items: the 24574 Rocket Fuel Transport which gives the railroad its fair share of the hazardous traffic business and the 24577 Jet Engine Transport which mandates some high value traffic requiring special care. Another flat car which carries the

latest application of aerospace technology to land-based transportation is the 25515, Rocket Sled. The sled features four huge exhaust ports and a driver willing to eject with the slightest encouragement but it does not prove itself the model for future ground transportation. With its small motor, shared with slot cars, the rocket sled contributes more with its futuristic looks than its reliable performance. Gilbert engineers had an eclectic approach to transportation needs as demonstrated by their willingness to prepare young generals to fight 1860 style wars with the (245)65 Civil War Cannon Car. This car carries an unusually well detailed Civil War period cannon.

Flat cars offer something new in 1961 with the 24566 New Haven Auto Transport and five autos. The flat with Jeeps is issued again but with a new 24572 number. The Borden's milk car container, curiously mounted on the National Car Co. flat is offered in 1961 and continues in the line until the end of production in 1966. As such, the Borden's milk load dating back to the thirties has the longest track record of all Gilbert production. Through war and peace, through depression and boom times, Americans never outgrew their need for a milk car! The 24579 Multi-Purpose Flat, introduced in 1960, appears in the 1961 line to again offer lasting play value with its alternative loads. The last new and interesting load offered by Gilbert is the 24578 New Haven Flat with a Corvette. Today this flat car and load are much in demand.

PRODUCTION LISTING	Good	Very Good	Excel

Several flat cars come without catalogue numbers on them:

C & N.W. RY. With link couplers; see (628).

C & N.W. RY. With sintered iron truck side frames, see (928).

NEW HAVEN Flat with pipes, Pike Master trucks and couplers, see (24564).

"Borden's" Tank Unpainted black plastic frame, Pike Master trucks and couplers, see (24575).

Frame Black unpainted plastic, no load, Pike Master trucks and couplers, catalogue number not known.   1   2   3

65 F.Y. & P.R.R. See (245)65.

605   **AMERICAN FLYER LINES** Log load, gray painted sheet metal frame, not embossed on bottom, "AMERICAN FLYER LINES" in black, Type B stamped steel trucks, link couplers with black weights, six brown stained logs a half-inch in diameter, 7½ inches long, Sutter and Schneider Collections.   3   5   7

607   **AMERICAN FLYER LINES** Work caboose, see caboose chapter.

609   **AMERICAN FLYER LINES** Girder load, gray painted sheet metal or die-cast frame, embossed on bottom, stamped steel trucks, link couplers, orange painted die-cast girder fastened to frame by black steel straps.

(A) Gray plastic frame, 1946, embossed "PA-9952," Type A trucks, link couplers, embossed "PAT. NO. 2240137," no weights.   3   5   7

(B) White plastic frame, 1946, embossed "PA-9952" on underside, Type A trucks, link couplers, embossed "PAT. NO. 2240137," no weights.   3   5   7

(C) Gray metal frame, 1947-50, embossed "PAT. NO. 2240137."   3   5   7

627 AMERICAN FLYER LINES Flat orange painted die-cast bridge girders held to base by two sheet metal straps and two pins (from frame); "AMERICAN FLYER LINES" on frame side, die-cast frame painted gray.   **5   7   10**

627

627 C & N.W. RY. Flat with orange painted die-cast bridge girder fastened with two pins (from frame) as well as two black metal straps; "C & N.W. RY." and "42597" on frame side, one two-piece brakewheel (metal shaft and black die-cast wheel), "627" in black on girder.

(A) Unpainted light gray plastic frame embossed on underside "PA-9952" and "AMERICAN FLYER MFD. BY THE A.C. GILBERT CO. NEW HAVEN, CONN. U.S.A.;" "627" decal on girder; black decal on side reads "C & N.W. RY. 42597," Type A trucks, link couplers without weights, embossed "PAT. NO. 2240137," 1946, Greenberg Collection.   **6   9   12**

(B) White unpainted plastic frame, "627" on girder, black decal on side reads "C.& N.W. RY. 42597," Type A trucks, link couplers without weights, embossed "PAT. NO. 2240137," 1946.   **6   9   12**

(C) Bluish-gray die-cast frame with embossed "PA-9952," Type A trucks, link couplers with brass coupler weights, 1947-50, removable girder, one two-piece brakewheel at one end, girder rubber stamped "627" in black on one side and "AMERICAN FLYER LINES" on other side, Degano Collection.   **6   9   12**

(D) Same as (C) except Type C trucks with brass weights, Sutter Collection.   **6   9   12**

(E) Same as (C) except Type C trucks with black weights, Sutter Collection.   **6   9   12**

(F) Same as (C) except Type B trucks with brass weights, Yorkis Collection.   **6   9   12**

[628] C. & N.W. RY. Plastic, die-cast or pressed wood flat with six logs ½" in diameter x 7½" long, "C. & N.W. RY." on frame side.

(A) Gray plastic frame, "PA-9952 AMERICAN FLYER MFD. BY A.C. GILBERT CO. NEW HAVEN, CONN. U.S.A." embossed on underside; "C. & N.W. RY." on frame side; two piece brakewheel, Type A trucks, link couplers embossed with "PAT. NO. 2240137," no weights, Sutter Collection.   **5   7   9**

(B) White plastic frame, "C. & N.W. RY." on frame side; brakewheel, Type A trucks, link couplers, embossed with "PAT. NO. 2240137;" no coupler weights.   **5   7   9**

(C) Gray painted die-cast frame, embossed "PA9952 AMERICAN FLYER MFD. BY THE A.C. GILBERT CO. NEW HAVEN, CONN. U.S.A." on underside and "C. & N.W. RY." on frame side, one two-piece brakewheel, Type C trucks, link couplers, brass coupler weights, Sutter Collection.   **5   7   9**

(D) Gray painted pressed wood base, number does not appear on car, large letters, sintered iron truck side frames, knuckle couplers, one two-piece brakewheel, Balint Collection.   **10   20   30**

634 See crane and floodlight chapter.

636 ERIE Depressed center reel car; gray painted die-cast or pressed wood frame with a two piece brakewheel at each end; "ERIE 7210" in black on frame side with line above and below; "CAPY 27500 LD LMT 71400" "LD WT 106100 NEW 5-28" or same but "NEW 5-29" in black.

(A) Die-cast metal frame painted gray, six-wheel trucks with sheet metal sides, link couplers with black coupler weights, light yellow painted reel side with "AMERICAN FLYER 636 MFD. BY THE A.C. GILBERT CO. NEW HAVEN, CONN. U.S.A." in black, "NEW 5-28."   **6   9   12**

(B) Same as (A) but painted bluish-gray, reel side darker yellow with "NEW 5-29," Sutter Collection.   **6   9   12**

(C) Pressed wood frame, 1953.   **6   9   12**

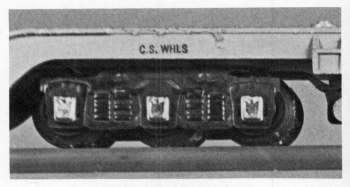

**The Special Six Wheel Trucks
Found on the 636 Depressed Center Car**

643 AMERICAN FLYER CIRCUS Two wagons and one truck tractor; tractors are both translucent green plastic with white, blue or green wheels; cages have green wheels and blue or yellow sides, red or blue ends, yellow or green roofs, red or blue bases, all in various combinations. Each cage contains one animal including (A) standing bear, (B) standing male lion, (C) upright gorilla, (D) rhinoceros, (E) pelican, (F) zebra, (G) female lion, (H) camel, Sutter, Petri, Leonard and Schneider Collections.

CAGE COLORS				ANIMAL / COLOR
Side	**End**	**Roof**	**Base**	
blue	red	green	red	pelican
blue	red	green	red	upright gorilla
red	blue	yellow	red	standing male lion
blue	red	yellow	red	female lion/red
red	blue	green	blue	rhino/blue
blue	red	yellow	red	pelican/red
red	blue	yellow	blue	gorilla/yellow
red	blue	green	blue	pelican/blue
red	blue	yellow	blue	female lion/yellow
red	blue	yellow	blue	male lion/yellow
blue	red	green	red	male lion/yellow
red	blue	yellow	blue	zebra/yellow
blue	red	green	red	rhino/yellow
red	blue	yellow	blue	camel
blue	red	green	red	zebra

"AMERICAN FLYER CIRCUS" in paper consists of a large white envelope (18" high x 10¼") with blue instructions printed on it. It includes twenty-three yellow tickets (2½ x 1½" approximately) with "AMERICAN FLYER CIRCUS" "ADMIT ONE" in red, plus four sheets:

Sheet 1: 19¾ x 18" Big Top;
Sheet 2: 19¾ x 18" Sides of main tent;
Sheet 3: 19¾ x 18" Circus wagons, maintenance and
Sheet 4: 19¾ x 18" Freak show, Animal tent.

The paper Circus complete is worth $100.*

(A) Yellow painted die-cast frame, one two-piece brakewheel, "AMERICAN FLYER CIRCUS" in red, Type C metal trucks, link couplers, wooden black painted block held on by two removable turned metal studs, black coupler weights, Newcomer, Yorkis and Petri Collections. Note, example shown has conversion couplers.

With two cages and truck tractor, Yorkis and Petri Collections.	...	60	80
Car only, with wooden block and two studs.	5	10	15
Car only.	3	6	8

(B) Yellow painted pressed wood frame, one two-piece brakewheel, "AMERICAN FLYER CIRCUS" in red, Type B sheet metal trucks, black coupler weights, link couplers, frame embossed "5," wooden black painted block with two removable studs, Newcomer Collection.

Car with two cages and truck.	...	60	80
Car with wooden block only.	5	10	15
Car only.	3	6	8

(C) Red painted die-cast frame, brakewheel, "AMERICAN FLYER CIRCUS,' sheet metal trucks, link couplers, wooden black painted block with two removable studs, Leonard Collection.

Car with two cages, truck.	...	60	80
Car with wooden block only.	5	10	15
Car only.	3	6	8

645   AMERICAN FLYER Work and boom car, see caboose chapter.

646   ERIE Floodlight, see crane and floodlight chapter.

Top 648,   Bottom 948

648   AMERICAN FLYER Track cleaning car, red or brownish-red painted die-cast depressed center frame, yellow painted wooden barrel at one end and yellow painted tool box at other, two two-piece brakewheels (example illustrated is missing one brakewheel), silver painted horizontal plastic tank with non-removable dome cap, "648 AMERICAN FLYER SERVICE CAR" in white on frame side, Type B trucks, link couplers (example shown has replacement knuckle couplers), two spring-loaded cleaning pads of replaceable felt, Sutter and Newcomer Collections.

(A) Red frame, Type B trucks, black coupler weights, Sutter Collection.   5   9   12

(B) Brownish-red frame, Type D trucks, black coupler weights, Sutter Collection.   5   9   12

714   LOG UNLOADING CAR Black die-cast frame with solenoid, one two-piece brakewheel, gray tilting platform holds three walnut colored logs, Type A and B trucks, link couplers, black coupler weights, 1951-54, Newcomer Collection.   10   15   20

715   AMERICAN FLYER LINES Auto unloading car, offered from 1946 through 1954 in a variety of frame and superstructure color combinations; with different truck and coupler arrangements, different loads (and we suspect different ramp-tilting mechanisms). The loads have attracted the most interest. There are Tootsietoy armored vehicles, Manoil coupes and Tootsietoy racers. The catalogues show armored cars first, in 1946-48, followed by Manoil coupes, 1949-52, and by the Tootsietoy racer, in 1953 and 1954. The car loads come in different colors and may have other differentiations as well. The railroad car comes with a special unloading track section with an inside pickup in 1946 only and with an outside rail pickup from 1947 through 1954. This popular car is also available with sintered iron truck side frames and knuckle couplers from 1953 through 1956 (as a "915").

(A) Black frame, red superstructure and yellow tilting ramp; superstructure fastened to base by four tabs and slots, two at each end, Type A trucks, no coupler weights, couplers embossed with "PAT NO. 2240137," white decal "715" and "AMERICAN FLYER LINES" on frame top. Tootsietoy armored car with white wheels, embossed on bottom. There is a current pickup mounted on the fiber shoe between the wheels with two brass contacts, 1946, Schneider Collection.   10   15   20

(B) Black frame, red superstructure, yellow tilting ramp, superstructure fastened to base by four tabs and slots, two at each end, Type A trucks, black coupler weights, "AMERICAN FLYER LINES" rubber stamped in white at both ends of frame top; no stamped or embossed lettering on frame underside, no number on deck, gray with brown camouflage "U S ARMY" armored car with solid black rubber tires embossed 'TOOTSIETOY MADE IN UNITED STATES OF AMERICA," current pickup arm goes through truck side frame to make contact with outer third rail, 1947-48, Type C trucks, black coupler weights, Sutter Collection.   10   15   20

(C) Black sheet metal frame, red superstructure, yellow tilting ramp, superstructure fastened to base by four tabs, solenoid wrapped in beige cloth-tape; Type A trucks, black coupler weights, "715" rubber stamped in white on frame top at one end and "AMERICAN FLYER LINES" at other; red and silver painted one piece Manoil coupe with silver grill and black solid rubber tires, and embossed "MANOIL NO. 707." Current pickup arm goes through the truck side frame to make contact with outer third rail, 1948-50, Petri and Schneider Collections.   10   15   20

(D) Gray frame, red superstructure, yellow tilting ramp; superstructure fastened to base by four tabs, black crepe tape on solenoid with thin ¼" masking tape; Type A trucks, black coupler weights, white rubber stamped "715" on frame top at one end and "AMERICAN FLYER LINES" at other, blue or red Manoil coupe with black wheels, red version embossed "MANOIL NO. 707." Current pickup arm goes through truck side frame to make contact with outer third rail, 1951, Schneider and Stromberg Collections.   10   15   20

---

* We would like to reprint Flyer's Paper Circus. If we receive 200 orders for the Paper Circus, at $10.00 a set, we will print it this year. If you would like to order one or more please send an undated check or your charge number (MC or VISA) with expiration date to Greenberg Publishing Co., 729 Oklahoma Ave., Sykesville, Maryland 21784. We will not cash your check or charge your account unless we have the orders by November 1980.

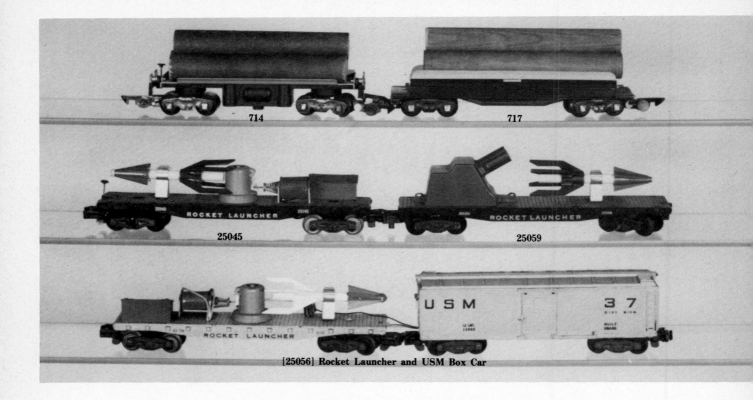

714   717

25045   25059

ROCKET LAUNCHER

USM 3 7

[25056] Rocket Launcher and USM Box Car

(E) Black frame, red superstructure, yellow tilting ramp; superstructure fastened to base by four tabs; current pickup from outside third rail, Type B trucks, black coupler weights, white "715" at one end of frame on top and "AMERICAN FLYER LINES" at other, blue and silver Manoil coupe embossed on underside "MANOIL MADE IN U.S.A. PAT PENDING #707," 1951; Sutter Collection.

                                 10   15   20

(F) Black frame, red superstructure and blue tilting ramp, superstructure fastened to base by four tabs, current pickup from outside rail, Type A trucks, black coupler weights, white "715" at one end of frame on top surface and "AMERICAN FLYER LINES" at other end; blue Tootsietoy racer #7 embossed on underside "TOOTSIETOY," rubber wheels, 1952, Stromberg Collection.

                                 10   15   20

(G) Black frame, red superstructure, yellow tilting ramp; superstructure fastened to base by four tabs, current pickup from outside rail, Type B trucks, black coupler weights, white "715" at one end of frame on top surface and "AMERICAN FLYER LINES" at other, silver Tootsietoy racer with black rubber wheels; racer made from cast metal; racer has no embossing on underside, 1953. This version is also offered with knuckle couplers as a 915.

                                 10   15   20

(H) Black frame, red superstructure, yellow tilting ramp; superstructure fastened to base by four tabs, current pickup from outside rail, sheet metal trucks, black coupler weights, "715" in white at one end of frame on top surface and "AMERICAN FLYER LINES" at other, Tootsietoy racer, 1954. Note that the 715 is still listed in the 1954 catalogue although knuckle couplers were being offered for the second year.

                                 10   15   20

The Manoil coupe has been reported in a number of colors: silver and red, red with black wheels, blue with black wheels, green, orange and silver and blue with black wheels.

717   **AMERICAN FLYER LINES** Log unloading car, black painted sheet metal frame and superstructure, yellow painted sheet metal tilting bin, three large logs 6 1/4" long x 13/16" in diameter, no lettering on side of frame.

(A) Fiber plate between wheels on one truck with two brass contacts to pickup current, Type A trucks, link couplers with narrow shank and embossed "PAT. NO. 2240137," 1946.   **6   9   12**

(B) Metal pickup shoe extends through truck side frame, Type A or B trucks. Example observed with Type A trucks, brass weights, rubber stamped "AMERICAN FLYER LINES" and "717" in white on respective ends of top surface, 1947-52, Newcomer Collection.   **6   9   12**

(C) Same as (B) but Type C trucks with black weights; logs are 5 1/2" long x 13/16" in diameter, Sutter Collection.

                                 6   9   12

905   **AMERICAN FLYER LINES** Gray painted stamped steel frame with six brown stained logs held in place by two black metal straps, one two-piece brakewheel, black sintered iron truck side frames, knuckle couplers, 1954, Newcomer Collection.

                                 5   7   9

907   **AMERICAN FLYER** Work and boom car, see caboose chapter.

909   **AMERICAN FLYER LINES** Shiny gray painted sheet metal frame, orange painted die-cast girder, one piece brakewheel mounted on sheet metal stanchion, "AMERICAN FLYER LINES 909" in black sans serif face on frame side, depressed areas for truck fastening rivets, sintered iron truck side frames, knuckle couplers, girder is fastened to frame by two black sheet metal straps. The logs are kept from side to side motion by small lips pressed into frame. The fastening method should be compared with some models of the 627 where pins, requiring an additional hand operation, hold the girder in place, Newcomer and Degano Collections, 1954. (Gilbert had found a way to reduce his costs!)   **5   9   12**

914   25003

915 wrong load   915

915   969

914   **AMERICAN FLYER LINES** Log unloading car, black or gray die-cast base with simulated pump mechanism with gray or silver tilting bin, sintered iron truck side frames, knuckle couplers, three mahogony stained logs, each 7/8" or 3/4" in diameter and 5 1/4" or 6 1/8" long, no lettering on frame side; "914" and "AMERICAN FLYER LINES" on top of bin, two wire railings at each end, one two-piece brakewheel.

(A) Black die-cast base, gray painted tilting bin, Newcomer Collection.   **7**   **9**   **14**

(B) Black die-cast base, aluminum unpainted tilting bin, 1957, Sutter and Newcomer Collections.   **7**   **9**   **14**

(C) Gray die-cast base, silver tilting bin, catalogued in 1956, confirmation requested.   **No Reported Sales**

915   **AUTO UNLOADING CAR** The 915 is the knuckle coupler version of the very popular 715 Auto Unloading Car. The 915 comes with several different frame and superstructure color combinations and different loads. All of the varieties listed below have sintered iron truck side frames and knuckle couplers. Cars with gray frames have black lettering and cars with black frames have white lettering. "AMERICAN FLYER LINES" appears at one end and "915" appears at the other end on the top surface. In 1957, the 915 came inside a box with 25033 printed on its end. "25033" was the new five digit catalogue number. A 915 with a 25033 box is worth more than a 915 with a 915 box.

The 915 comes with the racer in either blue, red or silver and the Renwal truck in red, purple, light green, turquoise or blue. The racer has rubber tires and resembles an XK Jaguar except for the grill; the Renwal truck has black plastic wheels and headlights and a chrome finished grill and bumpers..

(A) Black frame, red superstructure, yellow ramp, blue racer, 1953-54, Sutter Collection.   **10**   **15**   **20**

(B) Gray frame and superstructure, brown ramp, racer, 1955.   **10**   **15**   **20**

(C) Gray frame and superstructure, brown ramp, Renwal gasoline truck, 1955-56.   **10**   **15**   **20**

(D) Bluish-gray frame and superstructure, brown ramp, Renwal gasoline truck, 1955-56.   **10**   **15**   **20**

928   **NEW HAVEN** Log car, black finish die-cast frame with two piece brakewheel, "N H 928 NEW HAVEN CAPY 100000" in white on side, six mahogony stained logs held in place by two black metal straps, black sintered iron truck side frames, knuckle couplers, 1954, Newcomer Collection.   **5**   **7**   **10**

[928]   **C. & N.W. RY.** Log car, gray painted die-cast frame, one brakewheel, "C.&N.W.RY. 42597" in black, sintered iron truck side frames, knuckle couplers, logs held on by two black sheet metal straps, six logs, light stain. The lettering is heavier than that usually found on Gilbert cars. Frame is embossed "PA 9952 AMERICAN FLYER MFD. BY A.C. GILBERT CO. NEW HAVEN, CONN. U.S.A." Also reported with pressed wood base, embossed "No. 5" on underside, Sutter, Newcomer and Schneider Collelctions.   **4**   **6**   **8**

928   **NEW HAVEN** Lumber car, flat with eight stakes, four squared pieces of wood, 7¼ x 9/16 x 5/16," black unpainted plastic frame, embossed with "PA 9952" on underside, "NH 928 NEW HAVEN CAPY 100000" in white on sides, black sintered iron truck side frames, knuckle couplers, two piece brakewheel, 1956, Newcomer and Sutter Collections.   **5**   **7**   **10**

936   **ERIE** Depressed center car, gray painted die-cast frame, 1953-54, with embossed "PA 10358," one brakewheel at each end, brakewheels composed of metal shaft and die-cast wheel, "ERIE 7210" with underscore in black on frame side, six-wheel trucks with black finished sintered iron truck side frames, knuckle couplers; wire cable reel with yellow painted sides and black "AMERICAN FLYER LINES 936 MFD. BY THE A.C. GILBERT CO. NEW HAVEN, CONN. U.S.A." Also lettered either "NEW 5-28" or NEW 5-29," Sutter Collection.   **6**   **9**   **12**

636

936

936

936 **PENNSYLVANIA** Depressed center car with gray cable reel, tuscan painted die-cast frame with two piece brakewheel at each end, white lettered "BUILT BY GILBERT," "PENNSYLVANIA" with line over it, "CAPY 275000 LD LMT 271400 LT WT 105100" and "NEW 5-54" on frame side, six-wheel trucks with black finished sintered iron side frames, knuckle couplers, wire cable reel with gray sides and black "Western Electric," Newcomer Collection.　　　　　　　　　　　　　　15　25　35

945
AMERICAN FLYER LINES Tool and boom car, see caboose chapter.

948 **AMERICAN FLYER LINES** Track cleaning car, tuscan painted die-cast depressed center frame, shiny yellow plastic barrel at one end and yellow painted black metal tool box at other, two piece brakewheel at each end, silver painted black horizontal plastic tank with nonremovable dome cap, "948 AMERICAN FLYER LINES SERVICE CAR" in white on frame side, black sintered truck side frames, knuckle couplers, two spring-loaded cleaning pads, track cleaning solution is applied directly to felt pads, Newcomer and Stromberg Collections.　　7　11　15

956 **MONON** Piggy back car, gray unpainted or painted plastic frame, "BLT 1-56 CIL MONON" in red and red "M" inside circle, "LG 46-0," two piece brakewheel; two plastic trailers with red, white and blue image showing boys looking at the large engine. (This image is taken from the 1946-48 catalogue covers.) White lettered "AMERICAN FLYER LINES" on trailer sides, three axles under each trailer with smaller diameter wheels in the front, sintered iron truck side frames, knuckle couplers, two separate trailer brackets; does not work with unloader, 1956, Sutter, Newcomer and Bargeron Collections.　12　15　20

969 **ROCKET LAUNCHER** Black unpainted plastic frame, tuscan painted black plastic tool box, solenoid with red tape fabric

covering coil, gray die-cast rocket launch unit; red, white and blue rocket; red, green and blue rocket or red, yellow and blue rocket; shiny metal clamp holds rocket, two piece brakewheel; black sintered iron truck side frames, knuckle couplers; came in a box marked "25045" or rarely "25044," catalogued as "25045" in 1957; note that "969" appears on side. (Reproduction rockets are available.) In the absence of a box, the box is assumed to be a 25045.
(A) With 25045 box or no box, Bargeron, Schneider and Sutter Collections.　　　　　　　　　　　10　15　20
(B) With 25044 box, Sutter Collection.　　20　30　40

971 **SOUTHERN PACIFIC** Lumber unloading car, tuscan painted plastic frame, 1956, yellow "CAPY 100000 LT WT 39500" and "ACF BLT 11-53" and "SOUTHERN PACIFIC 971," metal superstructure holds eight pieces of lumber plus simulated piece, each piece is 1/16 x 7/16 x 5 11/16, two men in blue work outfits with red shirt/scarf and flesh colored faces and hands, sintered iron truck side frames, knuckle couplers. Comes in box marked "25015," Schneider, Bargeron and Newcomer Collections.
　　　　　　　　　　　　　　　　15　22　30

24516 **NEW HAVEN** Lumber car, flat with eight stakes, four square pieces of wood 7¼ x 9/16 x 5/16, black unpainted plastic frames, "NH24516 NEW HAVEN CAPY 10000" on side in white, black sintered iron truck side frames, knuckle couplers, 1957-59, two piece brakewheel, Sutter and Newcomer Collections.
　　　　　　　　　　　　　　　　　7　9　12

24519 **PENNSYLVANIA** Depressed center car with gray cable reel, tuscan painted frame with brakewheel at each end, white lettering on frame side, rare.　　　150　225　300

24533 **AMERICAN FLYER LINES** Track cleaning car, brown painted die-cast depressed center car with six-wheel trucks, sintered iron truck side frames, one two-piece brakewheel at each end, yellow plastic barrel at one end and yellow plastic tool box at other end, two spring-loaded cleaning pads.

(A) Large horizontal silver painted black plastic tank, 1957-64.
          6   9   12

(B) Two vertical silver painted black or white plastic tanks, 1965, Bargeron Collection.
          6   9   12

(C) One vertical white plastic tank, 1966.
          6   9   12

24536   **MONON** Piggy back car, gray unpainted plastic frame, "BLT 1-56 CIL MONON" in red, red "M" inside circle, "LG 46-0," two plastic trailers with red, white and blue image showing boys looking at large engine. (Image from the 1946-48 catalogue covers.) One piece brakewheel; the trailers have two axles in the rear and one axle in front and two separate trailer brackets; it does not work with unloader; sintered iron truck side frames, knuckle couplers, 1958, Bargeron Collection.   7   11   15

24537   **NEW HAVEN** Pipe flat car, black painted red plastic frame with "NH 24537 NEW HAVEN CAPY 100000" in white, eight metal stanchions; three silver finished plastic pipes, sintered iron truck side frames, knuckle couplers, Balint and Sutter Collections.   15   20   25

24539   **NEW HAVEN** Pipe flat car, black unpainted plastic frame with white "24539 NEW HAVEN CAPY 100000," eight metal stanchions, three silver plastic or orange cardboard pipes, sintered iron truck side frames, knuckle couplers.

(A) Silver pipes, 1958-59, sintered iron truck side frames, knuckle couplers, Newcomer Collection.   5   7   15

(B) Orange pipes, 1963-64.   10   15   20

24540   **NEW HAVEN** Pipe flat car, black unpainted plastic frame, white 24540 NEW HAVEN CAPY 100000," eight metal stanchions, may have been produced for a Sears set, rare.
   20   30   40

24550   **MONON** Piggy back car, gray unpainted plastic or gray painted black plastic frame, red "BLT 1-56 CIL MONON," red "M" inside circle, "LG 46-0," two black plastic trailers with red, white and blue image showing boys looking at large engine. (Image from the 1946-48 catalogue covers.) One piece plastic brakewheel; the trailers have two axles in the rear and one axle in front; comes with either two separate trailer brackets which would not work with the 23830 unloader or with a single end bracket (when it comes with the 23830 unloader); sintered iron truck side frames, knuckle couplers, 1959-64, price does not include the unloader, Sutter,Bargeron and Stromberg Collections.   7   11   15

24553   **ROCKET TRANSPORT** Olive drab painted black plastic flat car with two metal spring brackets, each holds one plastic red, white and blue rocket; one two-piece brakewheel, sintered iron truck side frames, knuckle couplers, white "24533 ROCKET TRANS-PORT 24533," "NEW 1-55," 1958-60, reproduction rockets are available, Sutter, Balint and Bargeron Collections.
   15   20   25

24556   **ROCK ISLAND** Wheel transport car, black unpainted plastic car with metal superstructure and four axles, each with two wheels, one metal post in each corner, one two-piece brakewheel, white "R I 24556 ROCK ISLAND CAPY 100000," sintered iron truck side frames, knuckle couplers, 1959, Sutter,Schneider and Newcomer Collections.   13   18   25

24557   **U.S. NAVY** Transport car, gray painted black plastic car with black metal superstructure with two metal olive drab jeeps. Jeeps are embossed: "JEEP TOOTSIETOY MADE IN USA;" one or two piece brakewheel, sintered iron truck side frames, knuckle couplers, 1959-61, black "24557 U.S. NAVY NEW 4-57," Sutter, Newcomer and Schneider Collections.   25   37   50

24558   **CANADIAN PACIFIC** Christmas tree car, tuscan painted black plastic, eight metal stanchions, one piece or two piece brakewheel, white "24558 CANADIAN PACIFIC BLT 10-30," sintered iron truck side frames, knuckle couplers, four conifers made from a fiber type of material around a metal wire or from a rubber type material, 1959-60.

(A) Fiber material on metal wire, two piece brakewheel, Newcomer and Balint Collections.   30   45   60

(B) Rubber type tree, one piece brakewheel, Sutter Collection.   30   45   60

24559   **NEW HAVEN** Flat car without load; black unpainted plastic, reportedly made for Sears as part of set 20059, "N H 24559 NEW HAVEN CAPY 100000" in white, 1959; sintered iron truck side frames, knuckle couplers.   10   15   20

24562   **NEW YORK CENTRAL** Flat car without load with four metal stakes, part of Set No. 20610, The Dispatcher; white "24562 NEW YORK CENTRAL" black plastic frame, 1960, sintered iron truck side frames, knuckle couplers, Balint Collection.
   7   11   14

[24564]   **NEW HAVEN** Flat car with pipes; black unpainted plastic, eight metal stanchions; four silver-gray plastic or orange cardboard pipes, "NEW HAVEN CAP 100000" in white, 1960, Pike Master trucks and couplers, Balint Collection.
   10   15   20

[245]65   **F.Y. & P.R.R.** Cannon car; tan plastic frame with wood simulated side frames (four scribed slats) and large brown cannon with black barrel, four inches long overall, yellow spoke wheels with black rims and hub; the cannon actually fires small pellets. (Reproduction sides and cannons have been made. Original cannons have hollow shanks and are embossed "JAPAN," replacement cannons have solid shanks.) Sintered iron truck side frames, knuckle couplers, 1960-61, Sutter, Balint and Newcomer Collections.   50   75   100

24566   **NEW HAVEN** Auto transport car, black unpainted plastic frame with white "NH 24566 NEW HAVEN CAPY 100000," blue plastic tractor with spare mounted on cab rear, silver plastic trailer with five autos: salmon, green, red, yellow and blue; trailer has eight wheels, Pike Master trucks and couplers.

(A) Black unpainted plastic frame with white "NH 24566 NEW HAVEN CAPY 100000," blue plastic tractor with spare mounted on car rear; silver plastic four-wheel trailer with five autos: salmon, green, red, yellow and blue; Pike Master trucks and couplers, 1961-65, frame embossed "PA 16D287-1."   10   15   20

(B) Gray unpainted plastic frame, 1961, "NH 24566 NEW HAVEN CAPY 100000" in black, Pike Master trucks and coupler.   100   125   150

(C) Same as (A) but red tractor, Sutter and Balint Collections.   10   15   20

24566   **NATIONAL CAR CO.** Auto transport car; black unpainted plastic frame with white "24566 NATIONAL CAR CO. BLT. 10-30," plastic tractor with spare mounted on cab rear; plastic eight-wheel trailer with five autos, 1961-65.   10   15   20

24572   **U.S. NAVY** Jeep transport car, gray unpainted plastic frame, black "24572 U.S. NAVY 24572," two olive drab jeeps, 1961.
   40   60   80

24574   **U S AIR FORCE** Rocket fuel transport, blue unpainted plastic frame with yellow "24574 U S AIR FORCE UNIT 11" with one piece plastic brakewheel; two silver painted black plastic vertical tanks; red metal bulkheads with solid front surface and pierced sides; bulkheads are lettered "DANGER HIGHLY

FLAMMABLE" "DO NOT HUMP," sintered iron truck side frames, knuckle couplers, 1960-61, Sutter, Newcomer and Schneider Collections. Reported with Pike Master trucks and couplers; confirmation requested.   **20   30   40**

24575   NATIONAL CAR CO Milk container car, black unpainted plastic frame with white "24575 NATIONAL CAR CO BLT 10-30," one piece brakewheel, two white unpainted plastic tanks with black "CAPY 40000 Bordens NEW 57 SPEC III," 1960-66, Newcomer Collection.   **7   10   14**

[24575] Milk container car, black unpainted plastic frame with no lettering, two white unpainted plastic tanks with black "CAPY 40000 Bordens NEW 57 SPEC III;" no brakewheels, Pike Master trucks, Pike Master couplers, 1965, still available new from Dan Olson; Bargeron and Balint Collections.   **4   8   12**

24577   ILLINOIS CENTRAL Jet engine transport, black unpainted plastic frame, white "24577 ILLINOIS CENTRAL BLT 57;" two silver painted plastic tank shaped containers with black "TURBO JET J-75 ENGINE RELEASE AIR BEFORE OPENING DO NOT DESTROY CONTAINER," 1960-61, 63-64.
(A) Pike Master trucks and couplers, Sutter and Newcomer Collections.   **9   12   18**
(B) Sintered iron truck side frames and knuckle couplers, one piece brakewheel, Balint Collection.   **12   18   25**

24578   NEW HAVEN Corvette transport car, black unpainted plastic frame, white "NH 24578 NEW HAVEN CAPY 100000," no brakewheel, gray figure, white grill; blue Corvette; comes unassembled with decals in a plastic bag, embossed "PA 16D408-1" on underside of car, wheels turn.
(A) Green-blue Corvette numbered "14" in red inside of circle, 1962-63, Leonard Collection.   **50   75   100**
(B) Blue Corvette numbered "81" in red inside of circle, 1962-63, Sutter and Leonard Collection.   **40   60   80**

24579   ILLINOIS CENTRAL Multi-purpose car, tuscan painted black plastic frame, eight black metal stakes, two red metal bulkheads, two silver painted plastic tanks lettered "THE LCL CORPORA-TION....," three pieces of lumber, four silver finished plastic pipes or four orange cardboard pipes; stakes and brakewheel come in separate package with instructions to cement brakewheel in slot on car; very difficult to obtain complete unit, 1960-61.
(A) Four silver plastic pipes, sintered iron truck side frames, knuckle couplers, Newcomer Collection.   **10   15   20**
(B) Four orange cardboard pipes, Pike Master trucks and couplers, Balint Collection.   **10   15   20**

25003   AMERICAN FLYER Log unloading car, black die-cast base embossed "PA 11436," aluminum bin tilts to dump logs, four walnut stained logs 5 3/16" long x ½" in diameter, "25003" in small numbers on side with fence; "AMERICAN FLYER" in black on side where logs roll off; sintered iron truck side frames, knuckle couplers, 1957-60, Walsh Collection.   **70   120   150**

25007   C.B & Q Coal dump, see hopper and dump car chapter.

25016   SOUTHERN PACIFIC Lumber unloading car, 1957-60, brown plastic frame, yellow lettering; black superstructure holds one large scribed wooden block, 7/8 x 11/16 x 5¾", two rubber men in blue work outfits with red scarves and flesh colored hands and faces, men unload lumber; one brakewheel, sintered iron truck side frames, knuckle couplers.   **20   30   40**

25025   C.B & Q Coal dump car, see hopper and dump car chapter.

25033 Truck Unloading Car 1957, cars numbered "25033" have not been found. The number appears in the 1957 catalogue and 25033

was applied to boxes containing some cars numbered 915. See 915 for more background.   **No Reported Sales**

25044   ROCKET LAUNCHER This number does not appear in the catalogue. It has been observed on boxes that contain the 969 ROCKET LAUNCHER, circa 1957, (see 969).

25045   ROCKET LAUNCHER Black unpainted plastic frame with "25045 ROCKET LAUNCHER 25045" in white, tuscan painted black plastic tool box, solenoid with red tape covering coil; gray die-cast rocket launch unit; red, white and blue rocket or red and white rocket; shiny metal clamp holds rocket, one or two piece brakewheel; black sintered iron truck side frames, knuckle couplers; (reproduction rockets available), 1957-60. It is reported that rockets numbered "969" are found inside boxes numbered "25045." These items are listed under "969;" Schneider, Newcomer, Stromberg and Sutter Collections.   **12   17   25**

25046   ROCKET LAUNCHER Black plastic unpainted frame, rocket launches at 45° angle from blue plastic launcher, rocket has red nose, white body and a small blue circle at the bottom of the rocket. One piece plastic brakewheel or no brakewheel; "25046 ROCKET LAUNCHER 25046" in white, twice on each side, sintered iron truck side frames, knuckle couplers, shiny metal bracket holds rocket; Sutter and Balint Collections.
                            12   17   25

[25056]   ROCKET LAUNCHER and USM Box Car, yellow frame, tuscan tool box, solenoid with red insulating tape; gray launch base, white and red rocket, shiny sheet metal clamp; yellow painted plastic box car with "US M LD LMT. 10000" in black and on other side of door "37 DIVISION BUILT USA 56," both cars with sintered iron truck side frames and knuckle couplers.
                            75   130   175

25058   SOUTHERN PACIFIC Lumber unloading car, tuscan painted black plastic frame, "SOUTHERN PACIFIC," and technical information " CAPY 100000 LT WT WT 39500 ACF BLT 11-53" in yellow; black sheet metal superstructure holds one large scribed block 7/8 x 11/16 x 5¾", two rubber men in blue work outfits with red scarves and flesh-colored hands and faces, one brakewheel, Pike Master trucks and couplers, 1961-64. Gilbert made three versions of this car: 971, 25016 and 25058. The change from 971 to 25016 is simply a change in the numbering system. The change from 25016 to 25058 indicates the change from sintered iron trucks on the 25016 to Pike Master trucks on the 25058, Schneider and Balint Collections.   **30   40   50**

25059   ROCKET LAUNCHER Black painted plastic frame with "25059 ROCKET LAUNCHER 25059" in white; blue unpainted launch unit; launch unit propels rocket at 45° angle, red, white and blue rocket, shiny metal clamp holds rocket, Pike Master trucks and couplers. The car is also reported to be marked "USAF" in the 1960-61 Defender Set, Balint Collection.   **10   15   20**

25071   AMERICAN FLYER TIE CAR Plastic frame with four stakes, simulated brown wooden bin sides, container holds ties; trackside trip causes ties to eject, plastic shed on rear, Pike Master trucks and couplers, 1961-64.   **7   11   15**

25071 Tie Car

25515 **U.S.A.F.** Rocket Transport, black unpainted plastic frame; "25515 U.S.A.F. BLT57" in white, sheet metal rack to keep rocket sled on car, Pike Master trucks and couplers or sintered iron truck side frames and knuckle couplers, no brakewheel. Yellow unpainted plastic rocket sled with red silk-screened nose, blue silk-screened lightening bolts on both sides, red and aqua oval with red arrowhead paper label on both sides. The motor is believed to have been made in Japan and was also used in Gilbert slot cars. The motor has a gear coming out of one end in direct drive to the gear on the drive axle. It is a simple unit and reportedly performs modestly at best. The rocket has five huge exhaust tubes at rear.

(A) Black plastic man ejects from rocket sled by use of uncoupler mechanism; Sutter, Caples and Yorkis Collections.   **20   30   40**

(B) Black plastic man glued into cockpit, Yorkis Collection.   **15   25   35**

The prototype of the American Flyer Circus set.
Note the B & O herald on the tender. Walsh Collection.

137

Chapter XII

CRANES AND FLOODLIGHTS

A crane is an important part of any model railroad. In fact a crane is a favorite car to add to the line, and with its control wheels and pulleys its play value is significant. Since American Flyer and Lionel produced a competitive but parallel line of cranes the development of Flyer's cranes can best be understood in comparison with Lionel's.

S Gauge has its origins in the late 1930's American Flyer 0 Gauge production. Conseuqently our comparison begins there. In 1939 Gilbert produced two very similar cranes, a die-cast 514 and a stamped steel 481; they are predecessors to the 1946 635 crane. All three -- the 514, 481 and 635 -- have a similar cab and boom. The 514 has a die-cast frame with three slots at each end while the 481 has a stamped steel frame. Both the 514 and the 481, of course, were designed for 0 Gauge track with wide frames, although their cabs are proportioned to 3/16th scale. When the 635 was introduced the frame was redesigned in plastic as were the other 1946 car frames. The new frame is proportioned correctly at 3/16th of an inch to the foot. Because the 635 frame warped it was soon refitted with a die-cast frame.

Lionel produced two competitive cranes in the late 1930s, a large sheet metal 2810 and a small sheet metal 2660. The 2660 is remarkably similar to Gilbert's 514 and 481. However the 2660 sold for $4.50 in 1941 while Gilbert's 514 cost $5.00 and the 481 cost $3.50. Hence, Gilbert's sheet metal version has a $1.00 price advantage while its die-cast version cost fifty cents more than Lionel's sheet metal version. In 1946 Gilbert's 635 retails for $4.50 as it does in 1947. In 1946 Lionel's 2560 (the 1946 version of the 2660), retails for $5.50. It is interesting to note that both manufacturers use separate price sheets in 1946 and do not include prices in their catalogues. This omission most likely reflects unsettled postwar price and cost constraints and permitted them to adjust prices to their true costs more easily. It may also relate to OPA price controls.

In 1946 Lionel replaces the large tin plate type 2810 crane with the more sophisticated and realistic 2460. The 2460 features a highly detailed die-cast chassis with a bakelite plastic cab and boom. This unit comes with six-wheel trucks with blind wheels (without flanges) on the center axle. The new 2460 crane with the updated small prewar crane as 2560 with new trucks, gives Lionel a decided advantage. However, since the equipment is not interchangeable the advantages are limited.

Gilbert continues to manufacture its die-cast base, sheet metal top 635 from 1947 through 1949. In 1950 Gilbert introduces the 644 crane and upgrades its line of cranes. The 644 is a highly detailed and impressive piece with a double paired block and tackle (compare to Lionel's single block and tackle). Flyer's 635 features six-wheel trucks similar to those

on the Hudson and U.P. tender but to achieve a cost savings and greater operating efficiency the center axle is now a dummy. As with Lionel's 2460 Gilbert uses a die-cast base and a plastic cab. As an added feature Gilbert offers a Jack Beam--designed by Maury Romer -- which can be extended beyond the track to support heavy loads. However, "there is nothing new under the sun." In the late 1930s Lionel made a track fastening device for its 2810 which accomplished the same task. Gilbert's, however, is prototypical.

Although Gilbert discontinues the 635 in 1949, its cab is used on the 583 crane and the 612 freight and passenger station. Gilbert's multiple use of dies and stampings is typical of toy train manufacturing, particularly of Marx production, and to a lesser extent of Lionel's. It is interesting to find that Lionel uses its crane cabs on its wreckers and on its tower-mounted yard cranes. Gilbert uses its crane cab as part of the 650 bridge which is sold until 1956! The 635 does not die in 1950. In 1953 it is resurrected as a 606, now as part of the GM switcher work train; it is altered, though, to price it competitively and give it more play value. The die-cast frame is replaced with stamped steel, the truck mounting is changed from screws to rivets and Gilbert, one more time, gives the consumer more bang for his buck.

The change to knuckle couplers begins in 1952 and 1953 with top of the line sets. In 1954 knuckle couplers are installed on the rest of the line. In 1954 the 606 crane is upgraded to a 906 with new trucks and couplers when it becomes part of the GM switcher work train set. In retrospect, then, we find that the attractive 1939 small sheet metal cab crane is offered as late as 1954 -- certainly a long run for a Gilbert crane.

Returning to the heavyweight "INDUSTRIAL BROWN-HOIST" 644, its prototype was made by the Industrial Brownhoist Company. Lionel's crane has a known prototype, the Bucyrus Erie. In 1953 the 644 crane makes the transition to knuckle couplers and becomes a 944. (In 1952 it comes as a 944 with one set.) However, because of the numerous link coupler outfits Gilbert continues to manufacture the link coupler version of the 644 until 1954. A careful examination of the 1953, 1954 and 1955 catalogues shows that the 944 appears with only a single block and tackle, although the double block and tackle had been promoted for the 644. 944s that have been observed have the double block and tackle feature.

In 1952 Lionel drops its six-wheel 2460 crane and replaces it with a similar but less costly 6460 with four-wheel trucks. Thus we see that from 1952 through 1957 Gilbert offers the only crane with a six-wheel simulated side truck, a clear marketing advantage.

In 1957 the 944 was replaced; it was replaced by a similar appearing 944 that is catalogued as a 24523. At this time, no cranes have been verified carrying the 24523 designation. We assume that the 944 was continued in 1957 and that the box was numbered 24523, however, this hypothesis awaits verification.

The 24543 made its debut in 1958 to replace the 944 which had been offered from 1953. 24543 continues the black plastic elaborately detailed cab and boom but substituted a simpler and longer flat car type plastic frame. Plastic frames were produced much more rapidly and without the expensive stripping costs of die-cast frames. The double block and tackle is now a single block and tackle. In the catalogue illustration the pulley that links the cable controlling the boom heights to the spool is still present. There is a short cable but the boom has a plate at the rear with wire supports. The crane is now marked "AMERICAN FLYER LINES" in large, bold letters on the frame and cab. The substitution of the much longer frame changes drastically the appearance of the crane and gives it a much sleeker and more modern but alas less realistic appearance! The simulated six-wheel trucks give way to less costly four-wheel trucks, following the example set by Lionel back in 1952.

In 1959, the crane again changes its catalogue designation and becomes a 24561. Gilbert substitutes a gray boom for the black boom and plugs the top of the cab. In 1960 the 24561 loses its sintered iron truck side frames and knuckle couplers and joins the Pike Master series, it is offered through 1961. In 1962 the crane becomes a 24569 and is offered through the end of production in 1966. The frame and boom are now unpainted light gray plastic instead of gray paint on black plastic. The stringing is in white instead of dark green. In 1966 the crane comes in the new "All Aboard" packaging.

	Good	Very Good	Excel

606 **AMERICAN FLYER LINES** Gray painted stamped steel base, with crane cab located slightly off center (on the base), yellow painted steel cab with "AMERICAN FLYER LINES" in black sans serif, one window and one door on each side; dark red roof with black chimney; gray metal brakewheel stand with plastic one piece brakewheel that fits into stand; a black die-cast hand wheel on the rear of the cab controls the boom height; the black die-cast hand wheel on the side of the boom controls the "cable" length; green painted die-cast boom; three piece pulley-frame-hook combination, "AMERICAN FLYER LINES 606" in black on frame side; Type A trucks, black coupler weights, boom is embossed "PA 9220." This car was offered as part of Set 53171 in 1953 with 607 Boom Car. See caboose chapter for the 607 Boom Car. Bargeron and Stromberg Collections. 10 15 20

[635] **C & N W RY** Gray painted die-cast base; "C & N W RY 42597" on base, light yellow or red painted sheet metal cab with two windows and one door on each side; "AMERICAN FLYER LINES" in black sans serif face, red roof, black stack; cab located on one end of chassis, green boom overlaps frame by about one inch; black die-cast hand wheel on the side of the boom controls "cable" length; black die-cast wheel on rear of cab controls boom height, three piece hook-pulley combination; Type B copper finished trucks with link coupler, black coupler weights; boom embossed "PA 9220;" frame embossed "PA 9952 AMER-

ICAN FLYER BUILT BY A.C. GILBERT CO. NEW HAVEN, CONN. U.S.A."
(A) Light yellow cab, 1948-49. 10 15 20
(B) Red cab, 1948. 10 15 20

635 **C & N W RY** Gray unpainted plastic base (1946) or gray painted die-cast base (1947-48), light yellow painted sheet metal cab with one door and one window on each side, "C & N W RY 42597" in black on frame's side; "AMERICAN FLYER LINES" in black sans serif face on the side of the cab; cab located towards center of frame, black die-cast hand wheel on cab rear controls boom height; black die-cast hand wheel on boom side controls "cable" length; three piece hook, pulley and frame combination, one two piece brakewheel.
(A) Gray plastic base, decal lettering on side of cab and side of frame; Type A trucks, link couplers, embossed "PAT NO...," frame is often warped. 15 22 30
(B) Gray painted die-cast frame, black rubber stamped lettering, Type A trucks, link couplers with no coupler weights, 1947-48. 7 11 15

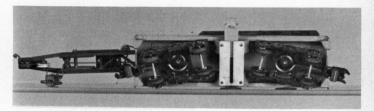

Note Extended Jack Beam

644 **AMERICAN FLYER** Gray painted highly detailed die-cast base embossed on underside "PA 11321," one piece white painted die-cast Jack Beam mounted beneath frame center. The beam can be extended beyond the track to provide stability when lifting heavy loads; black die-cast truck side frames, simulated six-wheel trucks with two axles and four wheels; red, brown or black plastic cab with "AMERICAN FLYER 644" in white sans serif face; two black die-cast wheels on one cab side; one wheel uses a cable and pulley to control boom height; the other controls the length of the block and tackle cable; black unpainted plastic boom with "INDUSTRIAL BROWNHOIST" in white sans serif face. Suspended from the boom are three fastening units: a three piece block with hook; a two piece pulley and mounting unit with three holes and a third cable with only a small hook. The three fasteners are found on the prototype. These fasteners work either separately or in conjunction with one another; link couplers, black coupler weights.
(A) Red unpainted plastic cab, black boom, 1950. 10 15 20
(B) Red unpainted plastic cab, no crank on control wheels, green boom, 1950, Stromberg, Bargeron and Balint Collections. 15 20 30
(C) Brown painted white plastic cab, cranks on control wheels, green boom, 1950-51, Petri Collection. 15 20 30
(D) Black painted white plastic cab, no cranks on control wheels, black boom, 1951-53. 15 20 30

906 **AMERICAN FLYER LINES** Gray painted stamped steel base with the crane's cab located slightly off center; yellow painted steel cab; "AMERICAN FLYER LINES" in black sans serif face on cab's side, one window and one door on each side of the cab; dark red roof with black chimney; gray metal brakewheel stand with one piece plastic brakewheel that fits into the stand; the black die-cast hand wheel on the rear of the cab controls the boom's height, the black die-cast hand wheel on the side of the boom controls the "cable" length; green painted die-cast boom; boom is embossed "PA 9220," three piece pulley-frame and hook combination; "AMERICAN FLYER LINES 906" in black on the

644

944

24561

906

[635]

side of the frame, die-cast truck side frames and knuckle couplers. The 906 is an updated 606 with knuckle couplers and carries on (to 1954) the basic crane design that originated in 1939! Gilbert believed in carrying on a good tradition! Newcomer and Bargeron Collections. This is also reported with sheet metal trucks and link couplers with black weights, LaCalle Collection.

7   11   15

944   AMERICAN FLYER Gray painted highly detailed die-cast base embossed on underside "PA 11321;" "AMERICAN FLYER 944" in black sans serif face on side of base; one piece die-cast Jack Beam mounted beneath frame center which extends beyond the track to provide stability when lifting heavy loads. Black die-cast truck side frames; simulated six-wheel trucks with four wheels, black painted cream plastic cab with "AMERICAN FLYER 944"

in white sans serif face; two black die-cast wheels on one side of cab, one wheel controls boom height through cable arrangement; the other controls cable with large hook; black unpainted plastic boom, boom lettered "INDUSTRIAL BROWN HOIST" in white sans serif face; suspended from boom are three separate fastening devices: a three piece large hook, a pulley-frame combination and a two piece mounting unit with three holes and a "cable" with a small hook; ..knuckle couplers, 1952-56, Newcomer, Balint, Stromberg and Bargeron Collections.

10   15   20

24523   AMERICAN FLYER Catalogue illustration shows a 944. We assume that the 944 was offered in 1957 and came in a box marked "24523." Verification requested.   **No Reported Sales**

24543 **AMERICAN FLYER LINES** Gray painted plastic frame with "AMERICAN FLYER LINES" in heavy black sans serif letters, frame embossed "#1" on bottom; black unpainted plastic cab in heavy white block sans serif face: "AMERICAN FLYER 24543;" two black die-cast control wheels on one side of cab; one wheel controls boom height through wire arrangement while the other controls block and tackle height. Half of cab roof is missing, a plate on rear with wire supports. Black sintered iron truck side frames, knuckle couplers, 1958 only. Stromberg and Balint Collections.   **10   15   20**

24561 **AMERICAN FLYER LINES** Gray painted or unpainted plastic frame; black sans serif "AMERICAN FLYER LINES," frame embossed "PA 16D287-1;" black painted black plastic cab with heavy white block sans serif "AMERICAN FLYER 24561;" two black die-cast wheels on one side of cab, one wheel controls boom height through cable arrangement while the other wheel controls the single block and hook; roof is closed (compare with 24543).

(A) Gray painted black plastic frame and gray painted black plastic boom sintered iron truck side frames, knuckle couplers, 1959, Newcomer and Stromberg Collections.
                    7   11   15
(B) Gray unpainted plastic frame, Pike Master trucks and couplers, 1960-61, Bargeron Collection.   **6   9   12**

24569 **AMERICAN FLYER LINES** Gray unpainted plastic frame, "AMERICAN FLYER LINES" in black sans serif face, frame embossed "PA 16D287-1;" black painted or unpainted black plastic cab with "AMERICAN FLYER 24569" in heavy white block sans serif face, two die-cast wheels on one side of cab and one wheel controls boom height through cable arrangement; other wheel controls the single block and hook. Gray plastic boom with "INDUSTRIAL BROWNHOIST" in black letters, 1962-66.
(A) Unpainted black cab, Stromberg Collection.   **7   11   15**
(B) Black painted black cab, Bargeron and LaCalle Collections.
                    7   11   15

[646]

[946]

[646]

634   934

934

Note Replacement Couplers on Row 3

Floodlights

Model railroads are related to real railroads in various ways -- both have engines, rolling stock, track-side industries, track, switches and the like. But model railroads differ significantly from real railroads in their proportions! Model railroads have much too little track relative to real railroads, too few box cars and too many floodlight cars! But floodlight cars are fun -- running your train in a darkened room or basement with the floodlight beam illuminating a miniature world is exciting drama. All the model railroad companies produced floodlight cars and these are probably second only to cranes in their appeal as add-ons to a growing railroad empire. Gilbert, in true form, produced an extensive and varied selection of this specialized car.

The Gilbert S Gauge floodlight story begins in the late thirties with the take-over of Chicago Flyer. In 1938, Gilbert continues the Flyer tin plate type 3213 with a stamped steel frame, stamped steel superstructure substantially raised above the frame, gigantic brakewheel assembly and railings the length of the superstructure along both sides with large stamped steel side frames and journals and an off-and-on switch. In 1939, Gilbert introduces the link coupler system and changes car numbers. The 1938 floodlight is reoffered as a 415 with new link couplers. (Note that the 1938 crane is a large and cumbersome piece that looks little like a crane. The modern crane appears in 1939.)

Many American Flyer cars were upgraded in 1939 and are offered as die-cast kits including a caboose, hopper, gondola, tank, box, cattle car and wrecker. However the floodlight is continued as the 1938 stamped steel car. In 1940 and 1941 the floodlight is offered as a 488; a 3/16" scale model in stamped steel. The 488 features a smaller and better proportioned brakewheel, handrailings on the main deck not on the superstructure; "AMERICAN FLYER" in one of the two embossed areas on the superstructure, no longer on the superstructure's side, and truck mounted link couplers, no longer frame mounted couplers going through a slot on the frame. The trucks change from the large center slot side frame to the finer detailed six-spring side frame truck and the off-and-on switch is no longer visible on the superstructure. For the postwar 1946 market, Gilbert upgrades the floodlight car with a highly detailed plastic frame, lowers the superstructure height to give a low slung appearance and remounts the handrails on the lowered superstructure. Since the superstructure is metal, it is easier to fasten the handrails to this part rather than to the plastic frame. The redesigned car includes new realistic roadname lettering on the side of the frame with the car's number and the "AMERICAN FLYER LINES" lettering is in a less conspicious embossed area on the superstructure. This new car is numbered 634.

1946 cars, as we have indicated, initially come with plastic frames as did a number of other Gilbert 1946 cars. Because of warping and other problems, die-cast bases were subsequently substituted. The floodlight car shares other characteristics of the 1946 line. Decal lettering is used rather than rubber stampings. Secondly, the most visible lettering is either a copy of prototype lettering or very suggestive of the style and form of prototype lettering. This realistic lettering is also seen on 1946 hoppers, box cars, tank cars and cabooses. Lionel offers comparable cars in 1938-42 and again in the immediate postwar period. Where Gilbert offers only one floodlight car each year, Lionel offers a large and a small series of floodlight cars. The smaller Lionel series, comparable in size to 3/16 scale No. 488, consists of the 620 with manual couplers and the 2620 with electric couplers. In 1940 the 620 sold for $2.75 while the 2620 sold for $3.75. Gilbert's 488 sold for $3.00 and featured electrically-operated couplers. The larger Lionel series was much more expensive: the 2820 sold for $5.50 while the 820 sold for $4.50. Gilbert offers more value to the consumer.

In 1946 Lionel drops both prewar floodlight series and offers a newly designed work caboose with a searchlight on its deck. This exceptionally handsome and well detailed die-cast car is offered through 1948. In 1949 and 1950 the work caboose is offered as a 6420. However a true floodlight car was introduced by Lionel in 1949. This finely detailed die-cast chassis car has a depressed center and large floodlight. The car has a simulated diesel generator unit in the depressed center of the chassis. The plastic generator unit is found in green, orange, maroon and tan.

The next year, 1950, Gilbert introduces a competitive floodlight car with a depressed center and generator. Gilbert's version features six-wheel trucks and has a long, sleek appearance. Lionel's version appears boxier and comes with four-wheel trucks. Gilbert charges $4.95 for its car, while Lionel charges $5.95. Lionel's version is 10 inches long while Gilbert's is 10½ inches long.

---

634 **C. & N.W.R.Y.** Gray or blue-gray die-cast or plastic frame with simulated wood decking; frame embossed "PA9952" on underside; "C. & N.W.R.Y. 42597" in black on frame underside, one two piece brakewheel with shiny metal shaft and black die-cast wheel; black sheet metal superstructure with two wire handrails riveted in place, decal, silver or white lettering on superstructure in embossed areas: "AMERICAN FLYER LINES" and "634;" die-cast lamp supports; yellow, silver or black die-cast lamp housing, lens held in place by wire retaining ring; link couplers.

(A) Medium gray plastic base, Type A trucks, link couplers without weights; embossed "PAT. NO. 2240137," yellow lamp housing, white decal, lettering on superstructure, 1946.   **9   12   18**

(B) Dark gray plastic base, Type A trucks, link couplers without weights and embossed "PAT. NO. 2240137," yellow lamp housing, white decal "AMERICAN FLYER LINES" at both ends of superstructure, 1946, Yorkis and Patterson Collections.   **9   12   18**

(C) Same as (A) but black lamp housing.   **9   12   18**

(D) Same as (B) but white plastic frame, Patterson Collection.   **9   12   18**

(E) Same as (A) but black lamp housing and white plastic frame.   **9   12   18**

(F) Same as (A) but light gray plastic base, Petri Collection.   **9   12   18**

(G) Gray painted die-cast base, Type B trucks, brass coupler weights, yellow lamp housing, Degano Collection.   **9   12   18**

24547, Stromberg Collection

(H) Same as (G) but Type C trucks, Degano Collection.
9 12 18

(I) Gray painted die-cast base, Type C trucks, black coupler weights, silver lamp housing.
9 12 18

(J) Gray painted die-cast base, Type A trucks, no coupler weights, yellow lamp housing, Yorkis Collection.
9 12 18

(K) White plastic base, Type A trucks, link couplers, without weights, and embossed "PAT. NO. 2240137," yellow lamp housing, silver stamped letters; Stromberg Collection.
9 12 18

[646] **ERIE** Gray painted depressed center die-cast frame, "L52 1 ¹⁄₃" and "ERIE 7210" in black with lines above and below; also "CAPY 275000 LD LMT 271400 LD WT 105100 NEW 5-29;" green, light green or red generator rides in depressed center; frame embossed "PA 10358," black painted die-cast lamp bracket, silver or chrome finished lamp housing; two two-piece brakewheels, six-wheel trucks with stamped steel sides and nickel journals; link couplers with black coupler weights. Also comes with "NEW 5-28" rather than "NEW 5-29."

(A) Green painted die-cast generator, silver finished lamp housing, 1950, "NEW 5-29," Balint Collection.
9 15 20

(B) Light green plastic generator, chrome finished lamp housing, 1950.
9 15 20

(C) Green unpainted plastic generator, silver finished lamp housing, "NEW 5-29," 1951-52; Stromberg and Schneider Collections.
9 15 20

(D) Same as (C) but chrome finished lamp housing.
9 15 20

(E) Red painted black plastic generator, silver finished lamp housing, "NEW 5-29," Schneider Collection. 9 15 20

(F) Red painted black plastic generator, silver finished lamp housing, "NEW 5-28," Petri Collection. 8 12 16

(G) Green painted white plastic generator, silver finished lamp housing, "NEW 5-29," Petri Collection.
9 15 20

934 **C. & N.W.RY.** Light gray or deeper blue-gray painted die-cast frame, frame is embossed PA9952 on underside; black stamped steel superstructure with two nickel finished handrails riveted in place; "C & N W RY 42597" in black on side of frame; one two-piece brakewheel; "934" and "AMERICAN FLYER LINES" in white on embossed areas of superstructure; black die-cast lamp support brackets; silver painted lamp housing; dark black finished sintered iron truck side frames, knuckle couplers, 1953-54, Newcomer Collection. (The number 934 also appears on an unlighted red caboose in 1955!) 7 11 15

934 **SOUTHERN PACIFIC** Brown painted die-cast frame with simulated wood decking, frame embossed "PA9952" on underside; "SOUTHERN PACIFIC 934" and "CAPY. 100000 LT. WT. 39500 ACF. BLT 11-53" in white on side of frame, one two-piece brakewheel with metal shaft and die-cast wheel, black painted sheet metal superstructure with two handrails riveted in place; "AMERICAN FLYER" and "934" in silver in embossed areas on superstructure; black die-cast lamp support bracket with two screws through support into aluminum finished die-cast lamp housing; lens held in place by wire spring; dark gray sintered iron truck side frames, knuckle couplers, 1954, uncatalogued, Degano Collection. 8 12 16

946 **ERIE** Gray painted depressed center die-cast frame with embossed "PA 10358" on underside; "L52 1½" and "ERIE 7210" in black with line above and below on side of frame; "CAPY 27500 LD LMT 271400 LT WT 105100 NEW 5-29 or "NEW 5-28;" red or green painted cream plastic or red or green unpainted cream plastic generator which rides in depressed center; black painted die-cast lamp bracket, silver painted lamp housing, two two-piece brakewheels, six-wheel trucks with sintered iron truck side frames, knuckle couplers.

(A) Red painted plastic generator, "NEW 5-28," Balint Collection.
10 15 20

(B) Red painted plastic generator, "NEW 5-29," Patterson and Balint Collections.
10 15 20

(C) Green painted plastic generator. 10 15 20

(D) Red unpainted plastic generator, "NEW 5-29," Stromberg Collection.
10 15 20

(E) Green unpainted plastic generator, "NEW 5-28," Patterson Collection.
10 15 20

[24529] **ERIE** Gray painted die-cast base, depressed center base frame, "L52 1½" and "ERIE 7210" in black with line above and below on side of frame. Also, "CAPY 27500 LD LMT 271400 LT WT 105100 NEW 5-29" in black; yellow plastic generator rides in depressed center; black die-cast light brackets, silver painted lamp housing; two two-piece brakewheels, six-wheel trucks with sintered iron truck side frames, knuckle couplers, 1957-58.
10 15 20

24547 **ERIE** Brown painted black plastic yellow diesel, silver painted lamp housing, part of the "KEYSTONE ROCKET FREIGHT" Set, No. 20425; Stromberg Collection. 100 150 200

24549 **ERIE** Brown painted black plastic frame, "ERIE 24549" in white on frame side with gray, black or white die-cast lamp support brackets, gray, black or white lamp housing; black, red or yellow generators, black sintered iron truck side frames, knuckle couplers or Pike Master trucks and couplers.

(A) Yellow generator and silver light, black die-cast lamp support brackets, black sintered iron truck side frames, knuckle couplers, Stromberg, Bargeron and Balint Collections.   8   12   16

(B) Red generator with silver light.   8   12   16

(C) Yellow generator, dull brown paint, steel lamp support bracket, unpainted white plastic lamp housing, Pike Master trucks and couplers, currently still available new for $10.00, "PA-16D287-1" frame, Bargeron, Stromberg and Balint Collections.   5   7   10

(D) Yellow generator, shiny brown paint, steel lamp support bracket, unpainted black plastic lamp housing, Pike Master trucks and couplers, currently still available new for $10.00 "PA-16D287-1" frame, Stromberg, Bargeron and Balint Collections.   5   7   10

24549 ERIE

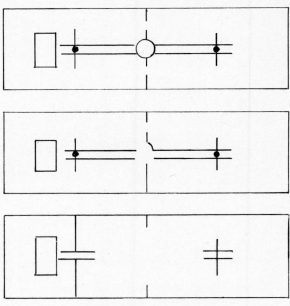

Three different plastic frames found with the 24549[A].

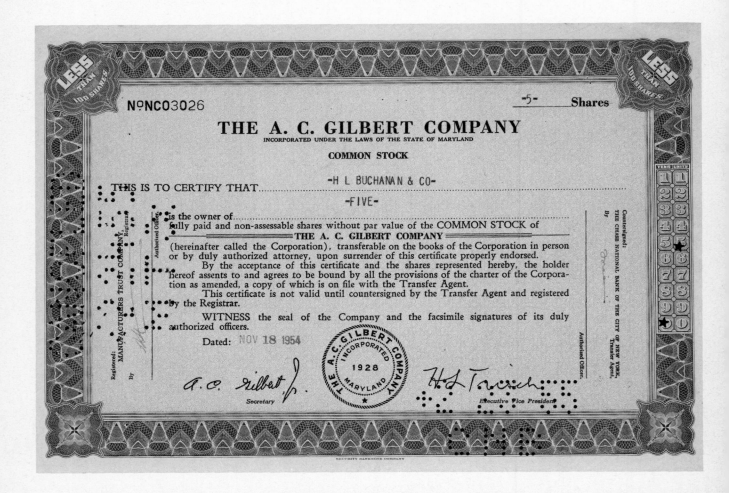

Chapter XIII

PASSENGER CARS

THE DEVELOPMENT OF THE PASSENGER CAR

Gilbert's 1946 line is a continuation and revision of its prewar 0 Gauge designs. Two different lines of plastic cars are introduced in 1946: a heavyweight car with roof ventilators and a streamlined, more modern appearing car with smooth sides and roof. Both lines are realistic copies of cars of the New York, New Haven and Hartford Railroad. The heavyweight design is introduced first in 1939 for the top-of-the-line Northern loco with a 521 Baggage Club Car and a 524 Pullman. An Observation is not offered. The 521 and 524 are die-cast and have remarkable detailing. They come with six-wheel sheet metal side trucks and link couplers. However, the die-casting process which created such magnificently detailed rolling stock also produced extremely heavy cars. Youthful engineers consequently encountered operating difficulties. Gilbert also introduces a slightly smaller and less attractive sheet metal version of the heavyweight series in 1941. They are the 496 Pullman and the 497 Observation which are not continued after the war.

The 1946 streamlined series originates in 1941 with a 494 Baggage Car and a 495 Coach. These cars feature the distinctive rounded roofs of the 1946 cars but have embossed sides where the "AMERICAN FLYER LINES" and catalogue numbers are rubber stamped. The distinctive white outlined windows appear on the 495 coach. These cars are offered in red, green and blue. Unfortunately the blue is not continued after the war.

In 1946 both the heavyweight and the streamlined series are manufactured in bakelite for the first time. The bakelite cars are distinctive because of their thick shells. Bakelite is made from a plastic powder which is compressed into a solid by heat and pressure inside dies. According to Maury Romer, the dies used to make the heavyweight die-cast series are reused with minor alterations for the bakelite cars. The bakelite heavyweight cars, to the best of our knowledge are produced with bakelite plastic chassis (or bases). As we indicate in the descriptions that follow, these chassis are embossed with three numbers, one for each die used in the molding operation. Hence if you want a four step pullman, one combination of dies is used; if you want a car with only two steps and rounded ends, another combination is used. This combination approach, preplanned when the dies were made, resulted in a tremendous savings in production costs.

The thinner bodied cars are made from a different kind of plastic. This plastic uses a liequid base which is injected into a mold and is known as injection molding. It is less expensive and Gilbert adopts it. Consequently, today, we find cars with thick (bakelite) and thin shells (injection molded). A person knowledgeable about plastics can easily detect the differ-

ent tactile and smell qualities between bakelite and injection plastics. In fact, in the Gilbert plant you could smell the difference! (Today, if you apply a cigarette lighter or match, you can also smell the difference, although we hardly recommend such a test!)

It should be noted that in continuing the heavyweight cars, Gilbert used shells designed for 0 Gauge track. Consequently these shells are almost 3/8" too wide.

The next stage in development of the passenger line is production of extruded aluminum passenger cars. These cars were originally intended to be injection molded plastic but there were insufficient funds for the die work. The funds allocated for 1950 development were used primarily in the design and construction of dies for Alco diesels and the GP-7. Consequently Mr. Romer and his staff had a problem -- how to produce matching streamlined aluminum cars for their new Santa Fe Alcos. Mr. Romer decided that extruded aluminum was the solution. Extrusion dies are relatively inexpensive when compared to injection molds.

The extruded aluminum was purchased in fifteen foot lengths and was then sawed to length. After which the windows were punched out and the bottom of the car trimmed. These cars filled market needs but were very heavy and had minimal detail. Hence in a year or two as money became available for tooling, new injection dies were made to produce the lighter and more detailed plastic cars. (In 1952, when Gilbert introduced the plastic series, Lionel adapted and stayed with extruded aluminum for its deluxe passenger cars.) The design of the injection plastic streamlined cars was based on a Budd design. Mr. Romer went to Philadelphia and personally visited the Budd executive offices where he was given blue prints and photos. These designs were modified modestly and the cars slightly shortened. Illustrations of the Budd prototype cars can be found in the **Car Builders Cyclopedia.**

The Frontiersman train also has a very interesting history. As Mr. Romer tells it he had been visiting Ed Alexander's train museum in Yardley, Pennsylvania, where he saw an old-time train that Mr. Alexander had built from scratch, except for a Gilbert Atlantic chassis used to power the train. Since Gilbert management had been talking for some time about adding an old timer, Mr. Romer saw an excellent opportunity to use Alexander's design work. He asked Mr. Rath, the Gilbert sales manager, and one of his salesmen to visit Mr. Alexander's museum. Mr. Rath was obviously impressed because he bought Mr. Alexander's model and took it back to New Haven. It became the basis for the Gilbert old timer. The train was turned over to the drafting department to provide their model for drawing up blue prints for the tooling department. Since Alexander had constructed the passenger coaches in a three piece assembly, the draftsmen also drew it this way and the tool makers followed suit and made the tools this way. These cars are a striking departure from the previous Gilbert passenger car design and because of the three piece assembly cost considerably more to manufacture. The prototype, formerly owned by Romer, is now in the Edward Leonard Collection.

SPECIAL SETS

This chapter recounts the history of the most popular and longest running Gilbert set, the Santa Fe, and then reviews a number of other prominent sets. The history of Gilbert's Santa Fe passenger set chronicles the major changes in Gilbert's postwar development and reflects both its high points and vicissitudes.

The Santa Fe story begins with exuberant growth in 1950 as the market expands and sales soar. The set becomes more elaborate and more cars are added; at the same time manufacturing changes, i.e., the substitution of plastic for aluminum passenger car shells and the change from link to knuckle couplers, reduce costs and improve performance.

In 1950 the Santa Fe comes with the "War Bonnet" color scheme; it is an unusually attractive design that catches the fancy and imagination of boys and their parents. It is not surprising to find that Lionel enjoys the same superior sales performance from their Santa Fe diesel introduced in 1948 and their Santa Fe streamlined set introduced in 1952.

Gilbert's Santa Fe set consists of the new 360 PA unit with twin motors and a matching 361PB unit. Both units come with black "Santa Fe" lettering along the lower side and the "360" with "Santa Fe" decal on its nose. They also sport wire handrails along the sides in the middle as well as along the ladders. There are three extruded aluminum cars: 660 Baggage, 662 Vista Dome and 663 Observation. The loco also contains a built-in electronic horn. This is the "top-of-the-line" set in 1950 and sells for $62.50. Today, in excellent condition this set brings $150. This set scooped Lionel's by two years -- Lionel's aluminum streamliners did not appear until 1952.

In 1951 Gilbert retains the Santa Fe "Deluxe Streamliner" as its top-of-the-line set (No. 5108W), but features the new 364 PB unit with air chime whistle and the double motored PA 360. Here begins the first of a long line of refinements and improvements. Otherwise this is the same as the 1950 version (and brings $150 in excellent condition).

In 1952 Gilbert revised the 5108W Santa Fe set by changing from extruded aluminum passenger car shells to plastic shells with aluminum finishes. However, the car numbers and the set number remain unchanged and to think that only one phrase in the catalogue gives away this major improvement! According to the copywriter the engines are "pulling the aluminum-finish luxury car effortlessly." (In 1951, the engines are "pulling its realistic all aluminum luxury cars.")

Although Gilbert is not completely candid, they do produce a better running train in 1952 because the lighter cars perform in a superior manner! Pulling plastic cars, the top-of-the-line 1952 set, worth $150 today, is an excellent value when compared to the cost of new trains.

Gilbert makes several major changes on their 1953 "Chief." The former 1952 PA, PB combination with three cars becomes a magnificent three engine PA, PB, PA with four chrome finished cars. This magnificent train is seven and a half feet long and is priced at a new high price for Gilbert of $71.50. The set features Gilbert's new knuckle couplers, and the PA units for the first time have couplers on their front ends. The change in couplers and composition means new numbers. The set is now called a No. K5375W and the engines are numbered 470 (PA with two motors), 471 (PB unit) with air chime whistle, and 472 (PA dummy unit); the cars are numbered 960, "COLUMBUS" Baggage and Club; 961 "JEFFERSON" Pullman; 962 "HAMILTON" Vista Dome and 963 "WASHINGTON" Observation.

In 1953 Gilbert capitalizes in part on the 1952 switch from aluminum to plastic shells. The dramatic weight reduction made possible a substantially longer and more impressive train without requiring a change in motors or power supplies although Pull-mor traction tires were added. This impressive train compares very favorably in its sleek appearance with Lionel's Santa Fe streamliner and brings $275 in excellent condition.

In 1954 Gilbert reissues "THE CHIEF" as set No. K5375W, a three unit diesel with four revised coaches.[1] Again the copywriter clues the careful reader to a change: "four scale model streamlined passenger cars of the latest design...." The cars have attractive red stripes added to their sides and also have a number change, an "R" is added to their previous number where "R" indicates red stripe. The addition of the red stripe did not require a change in the injection molds. Hence a relatively low cost cosmetic change dramatically improves the appearance of the cars. The "COLUMBUS" Baggage-Club car is now 960R, the "JEFFERSON" Pullman is catalogued as 961R, the "HAMILTON" Vista Dome as 962R and the "WASHING-TON" Observation as 963R. Finally a satin finish replaces the earlier chrome finish. In 1955 Lionel makes a similar change in their streamlined passenger cars and add maroon stripes to the new Congressional Set. The price of the top-of-the-line set reaches a new high of $75. Today the 1954 set with red trimmed passenger cars brings $325.

In 1955 Gilbert introduces "THE NEW CHIEF PASSENGER" as Set No. 5580H. The $74.95 passenger set relinquishes its place at the top-of-the-line to a sister freight set priced at $84.95. "Diesel Roar," a major new feature is added to the set, it is a decent approximation of the sounds of a diesel locomotive. Now the triple unit diesel comes with a 470 PA with dual motors, 471 PB with air chime whistle and 473 PA dummy unit. For the first time a black and white Santa Fe logo decal appears on the cab side beneath the windows. Also the lettering "SANTA FE" replaces the

[1]In both 1953 and 1954 the nose decal reads "CHIEF" and the lettering along the lower side reads "AMERICAN FLYER LINES."

The Silver Flash Set

477

478

960

961

962

963

lettering "AMERICAN FLYER LINES" along the side; on the nose decal the lettering "SANTA FE" replaces "CHIEF" even though the name "CHIEF" is highlighted as part of the set's name. In these lettering changes, Gilbert returns to the markings of 1950-52.

1955 also marks a change in the composition of the four passenger cars. The set now consists of one 960R Baggage, two 962R Vista Domes and one 963R Observation. Today this set is worth $325.

1956 sees a new milestone in the history of "THE CHIEF." The three unit engine now pulls a remarkable consist of FIVE cars including a 960R Baggage, two 962R Vista Domes, one 961R Coach and one 963R Observation. The engine markings continue as they were in 1955 and the PA units are numbered 470 and 473 and the PB unit is continued as a 471. This set is today worth $375.

1956 is the first year of a Flyer eight unit train. At the same time the handsome, new NORTHERN PACIFIC eight unit train is also introduced. Again, set prices rise, and this year's new high is $81.95 for Set No. 5683RH. Considering the price we expect that the operator is usually Dad. (We will discuss this set in detail later in the chapter.)

For many people 1956 marks the apex of Gilbert train production. Not only are there two magnificent eight unit passenger trains, but the catalogue itself is a spectacular production; certainly its extremely high gloss coated paper cover suggests the extravagance within. 1956 also marks the first time that Gilbert produces a single engine Santa Fe set. As the older Santa Fe sets move up in price, a market opens up for a less deluxe version. (Lionel in 1955 recognized this potential market and brought out a single motored version, 2243, of its deluxe twin motored F-3.) So in 1956 Gilbert issues The "EL CAPITAN" (No. 5640TBH) with a single motored PA 462 with three coaches 961R, 962R and 963R. The deluxe features -- an electronic horn and diesel roar -- of course are not included. This set is worth $150 today in excellent condition with its original boxes.

In 1957 Gilbert changes its numbering system and replaces the familiar three digit 900 series with a strange and disconcerting five digit system. This change, intended to aid the computerization of inventory, did not work out as anticipated. The Santa Fe set (No. 20083), now known as the "SUPER CHIEF," is illustrated in the 1957 catalogue with its old numbers: 470, 471 and 473 for the engines and 960 Baggage, two 962 Vista Domes, 961 Pullman and 963 Observation for the passenger cars. However, the set listing describes the three engines as 21902 and the cars as 24773 Baggage and Club, two 24813 Vista Domes, one 24793 Coach and 24833 Observation. The engines are later described by the factory as 21902, 21902-1 and 21902-2. The set WAS NOT produced with the new numbers on the engines and cars. However, the boxes that the items come in are marked with them. The 1956 single motor stripped down set is not carried in 1957 because of disappointing 1956 sales. The eight unit 1957 set today brings $350.

In 1958, the "SUPER CHIEF" set No. 20083 is continued unchanged with the 1957 consist, at the same price of $84.50.

Gilbert offers the buyer of a set a substantial savings as the individual pieces have a total list price of $223.55.

In 1959 after nine years, the longest Gilbert run of any set, the Santa Fe is dropped. the new top-of-the-line passenger set for 1959 is the 20535 Pony Express Set offered at $67.50.

In 1960 the Santa Fe set reappears as "The Chief" but in much less plumage. Now offered as set No. 20620 there is only a single motored PA 21927 with a plastic drive gear and a two position reverse pulling three cars: 24773 Columbus, 24813 Hamilton and 24833 Washington. Gilbert charged $44.95 for the set whereas one in excellent condition brings $200 today. "The Chief" is produced through 1961 and 1962 as Set No. 20735, the last of Gilbert's Santa Fe "CHIEFS." By 1961 Gilbert's decline is much in evidence and the 1962 catalogue sadly marks its last listing and the end of the line for "THE CHIEF." Today this set in excellent condition brings $150.

Gilbert produced several other name passenger sets that are highly prized by collectors: the Northern Pacific, the Pony Express Union Pacific and the Missouri Pacific.

The Northern Pacific set is introduced in 1956 as the "VISTA DOME NORTH COAST LIMITED," Set No. 5685RH. It consists of a three unit diesel: PA 490 with dual motors, 491 PB with Diesel Roar and Electronic Horn and 493 PA unpowered. There are five passenger cars: 900 Baggage, 901 Coach, two 902 Vista Domes and a 903 Observation. Some Gilbert enthusiasts rate this eight piece set as the single most desirable set -- others feel that the 1958 Missouri Pacific deserves this honor. In any case, an eight piece Northern Pacific set in excellent condition with original boxes will easily bring $900., and sometimes $1000.

The Northern Pacific set is catalogued in 1957 with the new five digit numbers. The set, now numbered 20370 is less impressive and contains only two PA units, the 490 with two motors (catalogued as 21916) and the unpowered 492 with electronic horn and Diesel Roar. It has four rather than five passenger cars. They are catalogued as 24706 Combine, 24703 Coach, 24709 Vista Dome and 24713 Observation, but actually come numbered 900, 901, 902 and 903 respectively. We suspect that some boxes may be numbered with the five digit catalogue numbers and your confirmation is requested. This set in excellent condition in original boxes brings $450.

The set was last offered in 1958 as "The North Coast Limited." It consists of a single PA 21551 with a single motor, traction tires, plastic steps integral to the shell and four unlighted cars: a 24843 Combine, 24846 Pullman, 24849 Vista Dome and a 24853 Observation. The set also includes a Billboard Horn, uncoupler, 50 watt transformer and 16 track sections. The catalogue points out that, if purchased individually, the train items would total $86.75 but that the set price is only $49.95. Today this set in the original boxes in excellent condition brings $450.

The Pony Express set, 20525, is offered for two consecutive years, 1959 and 1960. It has the same 21925 and 21925-1PA units in striking yellow and gray livery with two motors with Pull-mor power (traction tires), a bell which

The Late Northern Pacific Set

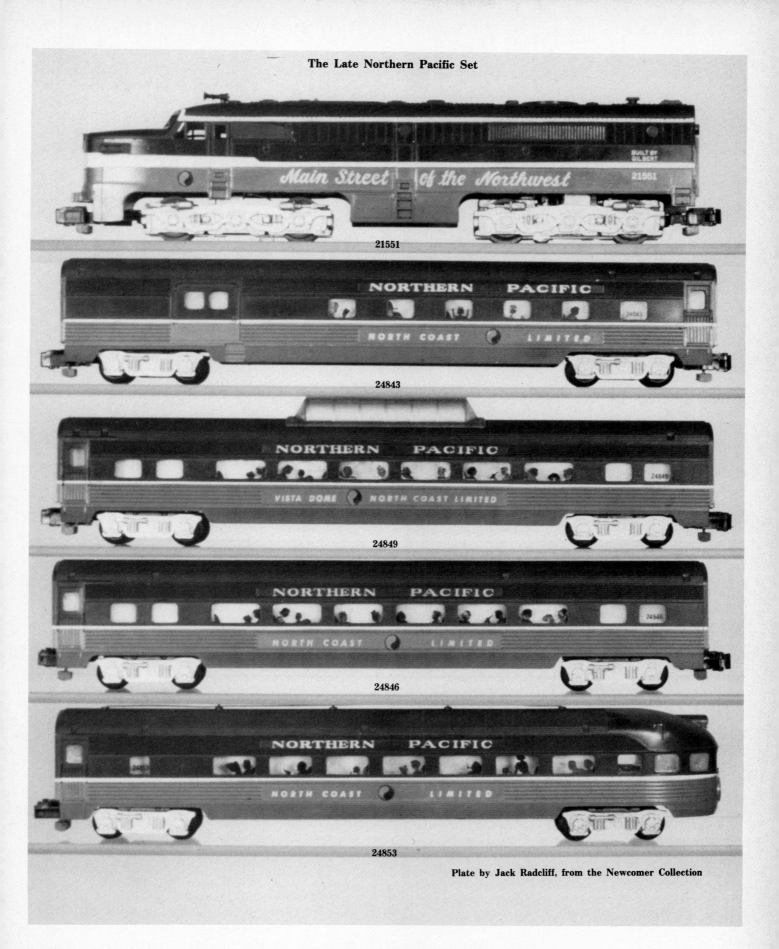

21551

24843

24849

24846

24853

Plate by Jack Radcliff, from the Newcomer Collection

rings as the engine moves slowly in or out of the station and four illuminated cars, the 24837 Star Dust Combine, 24838 Dream Cloud Coach, 24839 Columbia River Vista Dome and 24840 Moon Glow Observation. This top-of-the-line passenger set is offered with transformer and track for $67.50 in 1959 and $69.98 in 1960. Today this handsome set in the original boxes brings $775.

In the view of many Gilbert enthusiasts the Missouri Pacific 1958 set is **THE SET**. The Mo-Pac Flyer or Eagle passenger set has a dramatic blue, silver and yellow color scheme. As a 1958 premium set it comes with two Alco A units, 21920 and 21920-1, with dual motors, electronic diesel horn and Pull-mor traction tires. Four handsome cars complete the set, a 24856 EAGLE HILL Combine, 24859 EAGLE LAKE Coach, 24863 EAGLE CREEK Vista Dome and 24866 EAGLE VALLEY Observation. The cars are lighted. Lionel's competitive set in 1958 is the double unit Santa Fe with four extruded aluminum passenger cars. Lionel's set which does not include a transformer sold for $100. Clearly Gilbert has a substantial price advantage over Lionel and in the view of Gilbert enthusiasts offers much more value! Today, in the opinion of many, this set is the single most valuable Gilbert passenger set and brings $1000. in excellent condition in the original boxes. The Mo-Pac Eagle passenger set then disappeared from the line for four years to reappear in 1963 as set 20767. The motive power is limited to one Alco PA with a single motor, 21920-1, with four cars, 24856 EAGLE HILL, 24859 EAGLE LAKE, 24863 EAGLE CREEK and 24866 EAGLE VALLEY Observation. The catalogues state that both the 1963 and the 1964 sets are illuminated. However our review panel reports that the passenger cars observed by them are not illuminated. The 1963 set is listed as "less than $60.00." The 1964 catalogue only hints at the price but indicates that the engine is available for separate sale at $24.98. Sadly, the Mo-Pac Eagle is the last passenger set offered by Gilbert. Today the 1963-64 set brings $450.00. More details on car and loco variations can be found in the diesel and passenger car sections.

There are three other much-sought-after passenger sets. The easiest to acquire is the satin finished Comet with its one 466 PA unit with a single motor and three aluminum finished plastic cars with a blue stripe through the windows; 960 Columbus Baggage and Club Car, 962 Hamilton Vista Dome and 963 Washington Observation. The set is offered as K5334T in 1953 and 1954 and as 5335TBH with horn and Pull-mor traction tires in 1955. With its original boxes and in excellent condition it currently sells for $160.

The Silver Rocket set is also a favorite of collectors. It consists of two PA units, a 474 and 475, in a silver and green finish and four matching cars with green stripes through their windows. Three of the cars are 962G Hamilton Vista Domes, the fourth is a 963G Washington Observation. The set is catalogued in 1953 and 1954 as K5364W and features two motors in the 474 PA unit and an air chime whistle. In 1955 it is numbered 5570H and features Pull-mor traction tires. Today this set brings $275. with its original boxes in excellent condition.

The Silver Flash is the most difficult set to find. It consists of a 477 double motored PA unit in brown and aluminum finish, a matching 478 PB unit, plus three matching aluminum finished plastic cars with a brown stripe through the windows. The cars are the 960C Columbus Baggage and Club Car, 961C Jefferson Coach and 963C Washington Observation. This set if in excellent condition with its original boxes is worth $400.

CIVIL WAR SETS

As the centennial celebration of the Civil War approached, Gilbert, Lionel and Marx each produced "old timers." Gilbert's contribution to this solemn political anniversary was a passenger set (No. 20550) headed by the "FRANKLIN" and a freight set (No. 20655) headed by the "WASHINGTON." The engine in both sets has the same injection molded shell but each is decorated in different paint schemes. To confuse matters both sets are given the same name, the "FRONTIERSMAN." The passenger set is offered first and is catalogued from 1958 through 1960. It consists of the (210)88 Franklin, (247)20 Coach, (247)30 Baggage and (247)40 Combination, is relatively common and easy to obtain in its original, attractive packaging and today brings $125.

The freight set comes later, first appearing in 1960 and available through 1962. It consists of a (21089) WASHINGTON pulling a (245)65 CANNON Car with removable field piece and "plank" sides, (240)55 AMMUNITION Box Car and (247)50 SUPPLY and TROOP Car. This is much less common than the passenger version and is currently bringing $325. plus in excellent condition in the original box.

MILITARY SPACE SETS

The U.S.-U.S.S.R. military space competition of the late 1950s is reflected in the toy train world. Gilbert, Lionel, Marx and Kusan all produced military-space theme sets. Gilbert's entries include two different "Defender" sets with three different set numbers offered over four years from 1959 through 1962. In 1959 the set is No. 20525 and consists of a (21)234 C & O GP-7 with ringing bell, 24557 Jeep Transport, 25057 USMC Detonation Car and USMC Rocket Launcher, 24549 Floodlight and yellow and silver AMERICAN FLYER Caboose. Today this set is worth $325. in excellent condition.

In 1960 the set is renumbered No. 20625 and consists of a (21)234 C&O GP-7 with ringing bell, 24577 Jet Engine Transport, 25046 Rocket Launcher, 25515 Rocket Sled with Flat Car, 24574 Rocket Fuel Car and 24631 yellow and silver AMERICAN FLYER Caboose. In 1961 and 1962 the set is numbered 20740 with the same consist. This set, offered through 1962, is worth $275. in excellent condition. As far as military space competition on the tin plated rails is concerned, the U.S. had an unstoppable lead by 1962!

CIRCUS SETS have a long tradition in the toy train world. Ives in 1928 introduced a standard gauge train complete with special cars and numerous paper accessories.

[247]30

247[40]

247[20]

Lionel waited until 1935 to introduce its first and only circus set, the Mickey Mouse Circus. This set consists of an inexpensive clockwork engine, three tin lithographed cars and myriad paper accessories. The Lionel Set has dramatically appreciated. Finally, in 1950, Gilbert made its contribution to tin plate circus history with its "CIRCUS TRAIN."

The Gilbert train consists of a red 353 streamlined steam loco and matching tender, two 643 yellow flat cars with one truck, each pulling two circus wagons and 649 yellow coach lettered "World's Greatest Show!!" Numerous variations of these items exist. (To learn more about them refer to our detailed listings under locos, flats and passenger cars.)

The best - at least for one author, are the paper accessories, the main tent, side shows, animal cage, portal, ticket booth, colliope, hot dog stand, wagon, clowns, trainers, three kings, spectators and a packet of tickets. The red 353 engine is rarely found in excellent condition, and the paper cutout accessories, if present, are often ragged. Hence, this set brings a handsome price -- $600. -- if in excellent condition and if the cutouts are present; and only $350. if excellent but missing the paper cutouts. In good condition without the paper the set is worth $125. (If AF enthusiasts show sufficient interest the publisher will reprint the Circus Set cardboard cutouts.)

1950 is a banner year for lovers of Gilbertiana paper. In addition to the Circus Set, Gilbert offers the No. 5001T Farm Set. It includes an undistinguished 300AC Atlantic loco and four frequently seen cars: 640 gray hopper, 639 yellow "AMERICAN FLYER" box, 641 red "AMERICAN FLYER" gondola and red 638 "AMERICAN FLYER" caboose. However, its great appeal is its cardboard building set which consists of a farm house, garage, shed, hen house, barn and farm implements including mower and wagon. The rolling stock without the cardboard is worth $50. or less, if in excellent condition. When the cardboard cutouts are present and if in excellent condition, the value jumps to $250.

Probably the most unusual special set that Gilbert made is the 1963 "GAME TRAIN" (No. 20800). This set, a royal fiasco as a marketing venture, is potentially gilt edged as far as collectors are concerned. It consists of a L2001, Casey Jones loco with tender, a "Buffalo Hunt" light green gondola, a "Freight Ahead" red caboose and includes a "22 x 15" U.S. map game board, railroad track market sections, city cards, buffalo cards, loco markers, flagmen, freight revenue chart, ten sections of Pike Master track and a transformer. It provides for three different games, all with catchy names: "Race with Casey Jones," "The Buffalo Hunt" and "Freight Ahead." Complete, in excellent condition with its box, this set even though it is hard to sell brings with patience $75.

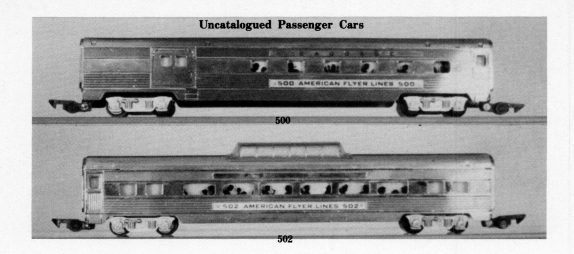

500

502

		Good	Very	Excel
			Good	

20 See (247)20.

30 See (247)30.

40 See (247)40.

50 See (247)50.

500 **AMERICAN FLYER LINES** Combine, streamlined series, chrome or silver finish, sheet metal trucks, black coupler weights, usually with "500" on each side; also reported with "500" on one side and "600" on other side; same as plastic 660 but with different number; illuminated, not catalogued, 1952 production, Balint, Patterson and Manson Collections.

		Good	Very Good	Excel
(A)	Chrome finish.	50	75	125
(B)	Silver finish.	50	75	125

501 **AMERICAN FLYER LINES** Coach, streamlined series, chrome or silver finish, link couplers, black coupler weights; usually "501" appears on each side but Patterson reported one with "501" on one side and "601" on other, illuminated, not catalogued, 1952 production, Balint, Patterson and Manson Collections.

(A)	Chrome finish.	50	75	100
(B)	Silver finish.	50	75	100

502 **AMERICAN FLYER LINES** Vista Dome, streamlined series, chrome or silver finish, "502 AMERICAN FLYER LINES 502" on riveted plate centered below dome, "PULLMAN" above window, silhouetted people, aluminum finished die-cast trucks, link couplers with black coupler weights; came with Silver Streak Set, matches 500 and 501, illuminated, not catalogued, 1952 production, Balint, Patterson and Manson Collections.

(A)	Chrome finish on black plastic shell, Petri Collection.	50	75	100
(B)	Silver finish.	50	75	100

503 **AMERICAN FLYER LINES** Observation, streamlined series, chrome or silver finish, link couplers with weights, came with Silver Streak Set, matches 500, 501 and 502, illuminated, not catalogued, 1952 production.

(A)	Chrome finish.	50	75	100
(B)	Silver finish.	50	75	100

649 **CIRCUS COACH** Yellow with "AMERICAN FLYER CIRCUS" in red letters above red outlined windows and "WORLDS GREATEST SHOW!!" beneath windows, red outlined handrails,

illuminated, came with 353 engine and 643 flats with loads.

		Good	Very Good	Excel
(A)	Yellow painted cream plastic shell, brass weights, Type B sheet metal trucks with six embossed springs, sheet metal frame; substantially thicker plastic shell than (B), Yorkis Collection.	20	30	40
(B)	Light yellow unpainted plastic shell, black weights, Type C trucks with undifferentiated, embossed springs, die-cast frame with steps, substantially thinner plastic shell than (A), frame marked "PA-10454-A," thin ridge at both ends of frame, Yorkis Collection.	20	30	40
(C)	Same as (A) but yellow paint over green paint on cream plastic shell, Caples Collection.	20	30	40
(D)	Same as (B) but frame marked "PA-10454," thick ridge at both ends of die-cast frame, with steps, Caples Collection.	20	30	40
(E)	Same as (A) but with red cast underframe and steps.	20	30	40
(F)	Same as (B) except yellow-orange unpainted plastic shell, Petri Collection.	20	30	40

650 **NEW HAVEN** Pullman, matches 651, seven double windows flanked by one small window at each end; "NEW HAVEN" in white sans serif letters, white outlined windows with different outline thicknesses, link couplers, some illuminated, some not; plastic shells are found with thick or thin sides.

(A)	Green unpainted plastic shell, plastic frame, no coupler weights, 1946, Type B trucks. Note: the plastic shell and/or frame are frequently warped.	20	30	40
(B)	Red unpainted plastic shell, plastic frame, no coupler weights, 1946, Type A trucks, die-cast journals, silver lettering, Sutter Collection. Note: the plastic shell and/or frame are frequently warped; windows not white or silver outlined; embossed "PA 10084-A, PA-10084," Sutter and Passman Collections.	20	30	40
(C)	Green unpainted plastic shell, die-cast frame, no coupler weights, 1947, Type B trucks.	10	15	20
(D)	Red unpainted plastic shell, die-cast frame, no coupler weights, 1947, sheet metal trucks.	10	15	20
(E)	Green unpainted thin plastic shell, sheet metal frame, not illuminated, "NEW HAVEN" lettering is 2 3/16" long; Type B trucks with three embossed spring areas with faintly detailed springs, no coupler weights, 1947.	10	15	20
(F)	Green painted cream plastic thick shell, die-cast frame, "PA-10454-A," with steps and thick frame ends; thick lettered "NEW HAVEN" 2 1/16" wide, brass coupler			

weights. Type B six spring sheet metal trucks, illuminated, 1948.   **10   15   20**

(G) Same as (F) but frame "PA-10454-A" with thin frame ends, 1948.   **10   15   20**

(H) Red unpainted thin plastic shell, die-cast frame with steps and thin ends, "PA-10454-A," thick outlined white painted windows; "NEW HAVEN" 2 3/16" wide, sheet metal side frames with Type C trucks with two embossed spring areas with no spring differentiation; brass coupler weights, illuminated, 1948.   **10   15   20**

(I) Same as (H) but frame "PA-10454," 1948.   **10   15   20**

(J) Green unpainted plastic shell, sheet metal frame, Type B trucks, black coupler weights, 1949-53.   **10   15   30**

(K) Same as (J) but Type A trucks, Sutter Collection.   **10   15   30**

(L) Green unpainted thin plastic shell, die-cast frame with steps and thick ends "PA-10454," thickly outlined white painted windows, illuminated, "NEW HAVEN" is 2 1/2" wide, sheet metal truck, frames with Type C trucks, two embossed spring areas with no spring differentiation; black coupler weights, 1949-53, one paper light diffuser.   **10   15   20**

(M) Same as (L) but frame embossed "10454-A," Stromberg Collection.   **10   15   20**

(N) Same as (K) but "NEW HAVEN" is 3 3/16" wide, has slotted sheet metal truck frames with Type C trucks, two embossed spring areas with little spring differentiation, 1949-53.   **10   15   20**

(O) Same as (M) but Type B trucks, fogged celluloid in windows, no paper diffuser, brass coupler weights, 1948, Stromberg Collection.   **10   15   20**

(P) Red unpainted body, sheet metal frame, "NEW HAVEN" is 2 3/32" wide, Type B trucks, paper light diffusers, black coupler weights, 1949-53, Stromberg Collection.   **10   15   20**

(Q) Same as (K) but "NEW HAVEN" is 2 3/16" wide, 1949-53.   **10   15   20**

Some of the above descriptions are less complete than others. We would very much appreciate receiving more information on these pieces. We also believe that other variations exist and hope you will use the form at the back of this book to tell us about them.

NEW HAVEN Baggage, matches 650, two large plug doors on each side; "NEW HAVEN" above doors in sans serif white letters; "RAILWAY EXPRESS AGENCY" on lower side between doors; all observed pieces unlighted; link couplers; plastic shells are found with thick or thin sides.

(A) Green unpainted plastic shell, plastic frame (these are often warped), no coupler weights, Type B trucks, 1946.   **20   30   40**

(B) Red unpainted plastic shells, plastic frame (these are often warped) no coupler weights, Type A trucks, 1946, silver lettering, nickel journals, Welter Collection.   **20   30   40**

(C) Same as (B) but die-cast journals, Welter Collection.   **20   30   40**

(D) Green unpainted thick plastic shell, die-cast frame, "PA-10454," with thin ends, black sheet metal trucks with slots and two embossed spring areas without differentiation. (This is a Type A because of slot and Type C because of no differentiation), no coupler weights, "NEW HAVEN" is 2 1/16" wide, 1947.   **10   15   20**

(E) Red unpainted plastic shell, die-cast frame, brass coupler weight, Type B trucks.   **10   15   20**

(F) Same as (D), die-cast frame, "PA-10454-A," Type C black sheet metal trucks with two embossed spring areas with no differentiation, black weights, 1949-53.   **10   15   20**

(G) Same as (F) but one Type A truck and one Type B truck, brass weights, Stromberg Collection.   **10   15   20**

(H) Red unpainted thick plastic shell, die-cast frame, "PA-10454-A;" thin frame ends, Type C black sheet metal trucks with two embossed spring areas with no differentiation, black weights, "NEW HAVEN" is 2 1/16" wide, 1949-53.   **10   15   20**

652   **PULLMAN** Heavyweight series based on New Haven passenger cars with six-wheel trucks with stamped steel side frames. This car came with red or green painted or unpainted plastic shells. The shells are either thin or thick plastic. The cars are all illuminated and have white paper liners to diffuse and soften light; the shells are elaborate with ventilators and other surface details. The car sides differ from each other as did those of the prototype. There are fourteen windows on one side with the window pattern: one, two, one, two, two, two, two, one and one with a door at each end. The windows come with and without shades. On the first side the windows with and without shades are: one-no shade, two-shade, one-no shade, two-shade, two-shade, two-shade, two-shade, one-shade, one-no shade. The second side has twelve windows all with shades: one, two, two, two, two, one, two with a door at each end, 1949-53.

(A) Thick green unpainted plastic shell; black plastic base marked PA-10067 PA-10067A PA 10067B," two sheet metal short trucks each with coil and leaf springs; the trucks have a coil spring with five segments, a three leaf spring, another leaf spring and a coil segment with five leaves. We call this a "six spring truck." There are six flanged wheels on each truck. The car has an operating door on each end of each side with a window on the door. The window has a yellow divider through the door window. "652" in white on center of car side beneath windows in fine numerals, Caples Collection.   **12   17   25**

(B) Dark olive green paint on light green plastic shell, "PULLMAN" in block serif letters which are different from the elegant thickening and thinning that characterized (A), "632" in heavier white stamped lettering than (A), centered on car side beneath windows, copper finished short metal trucks as well as black finished metal trucks, two of each with same spring design, same plastic underchassis with same part number as (A); same window pattern as (A) above.   **12   17   25**

(C) Polished red plastic shell, "PULLMAN" in sans serif letters above window and "652" at each end; red painted metal doors with springs on each side, same window pattern as two previous green cars including absence of shades in what are presumed to be bathrooms. The short trucks show the same spring pattern as do (A) and have a black finish; brass coupler weights, illuminated, Caples Collection.   **12   17   25**

(D) Green painted plastic, "PIKES PEAK" in white large letters below window, "652" on both ends of side, "PULLMAN" on upper left and right sides of car, Welter Collection.   **12   17   25**

(E) Red unpainted bakelite "652" centered beneath windows, short trucks, black coupler weights, black plastic base, opening doors, Stromberg Collection.   **12   17   25**

(F) Green painted plastic, long truck.   **12   17   25**

(G) Red painted black plastic shell, same lettering as (C), brass coupler weights, opening doors, Stromberg Collection.   **12   17   25**

(H) Red painted white plastic shell, plastic base, sans serif "AMERICAN FLYER LINES" above windows, "PULLMAN" above windows at each end, "652" below windows, "PIKES PEAK," centered beneath windows, plug doors, Stromberg Collection.   **20   30   40**

(I) Red painted red thick plastic shell, "PULLMAN" centered above windows and "652" in white centered below

Heavyweight Passenger Cars

953

952

652

654

954

654

978

154

windows, black bakelite base embossed "PA 10067 PA 10067A PA 10067B," four steps, Wade Collection.

12   17   25

653   **PULLMAN** Actually a combine but lettered PULLMAN above windows in white. This car matches 652 and 654 and came with them in passenger sets and was available separately. It is a model of a 1930 heavyweight passenger coach. On the first side the car has a green or red painted metal baggage door which opens, and plastic window material with yellow lines simulating venetian blinds followed by four double windows all with window shades, followed by the bathroom window, followed by the passenger door which opens. On the other side, the order is reversed; the passenger door is followed by a bathroom window, followed by four double windows, followed by the baggage door. The car is illuminated and has a paper liner which diffuses the light and produces a very soft subtle effect.

The roof has four ventilators on one side and six on the other. This is the same roof pattern observed on the 652 and represents Gilbert's dedication to realism. The base of the combine has part numbers, "PA 10067, PA 10067A, PA 10067B," which appears the same as that of the 652. However the base is different since the 653 does not have steps at one end while the 652 has steps at both ends. The PA number was not changed but it is possible that the die for the base was changed without changing the PA number. This was indeed the case as according to Maury Romer, the base die had three sections with removable end sections. The removable end sections allowed addition of sections with and without steps. Hence the middle section with the die numbers for the three parts remained unchanged while new end sections were inserted! The car is found in red or green painted plastic and red or green unpainted plastic. The number "653" is found on the middle of the side or on both ends of the side; it is found with long and short metal trucks with six wheels, all came with link couplers.

(A)   Red painted red plastic, long sheet metal trucks, no coupler weights, "PAT. NO.," link couplers.   **12   17   25**
(B)   Green painted light green plastic, long sheet metal trucks, no coupler weights, "PAT. NO.," link coupler, "653" on center of side.   **12   17   25**
(C)   Red painted red plastic, short sheet metal trucks, brass coupler weight, link couplers, "653" on center of side, Yorkis Collection.   **12   17   25**
(D)   Green painted green plastic, short sheet metal trucks, brass coupler weight, link couplers, "653" on center of sides, Yorkis Collection.   **12   17   25**
(E)   Red unpainted bakelite, short sheet metal trucks, brass coupler weight, "653" on center of sides.   **12   17   25**
(F)   Same as (E) but "653" on both ends of each side.   **12   17   25**
(G)   Same as (E) but black weights, opening doors, Stromberg Collection.   **12   17   25**
(H)   Green unpainted plastic, short sheet metal trucks, brass coupler weight, "653" on center of sides.   **12   17   25**
(I)   Same as (G) but "653" on both ends of each side.   **12   17   25**
(J)   Same as (C) but "653" on ends of sides, Wade Collection.   **12   17   25**

654   **PULLMAN** Actually an Observation but lettered "PULLMAN" in white, serif letters above windows on both sides. This car comes in both red or green painted plastic or red or green unpainted plastic. It comes with "654" centered on the side beneath windows or on both ends of each side. It always came with link couplers although several different kinds of link couplers are seen. The car has an observation deck with brass railing and name plate with black American Flyer decal with white lettering. It comes with two different kinds of six-wheel trucks: 2 1/4" long and 1 5/8" short.

As we have remarked earlier, Gilbert went to unusual lengths in the immediate postwar period to build prototypical equipment with authentic window and roof ventilator configurations. Furthermore, it is less expensive to build symmetrical cars, i.e., cars with the same window and ventilator arrangements on each side, but Gilbert was true to the prototype. The window arrangement of the 654, from the front end of the train, shows twelve windows on the first side: two small windows, two medium, two large, two medium/large, one medium/large and three medium/large, all with window shades. The second side of the car has ten windows: one medium/large, one medium/large, two large, two large, one medium/large and three medium/large. The roof ventilator patterns are also different on the first side: three small, two large, one small, one large, one small, one large, one small, one large, one small, one large, one small and one large. On the second side, from the front end are: three small, two large, one small, one large, one small, one large, one small, one large, one small, one large, one small and one large. The car is illuminated and has a paper liner which diffuses the light and produces a soft, subtle effect.

Lionel equipment in contrast had symmetrical sides and less expensive die-cast costs. Of course the irony is that Flyer's realism probably went unnoticed by most if not all boys and even goes unnoticed by collectors today. The least we can do today is give Gilbert credit for his efforts and the authenticity of his equipment.

(A)   Red painted red plastic, long sheet metal trucks, no coupler weights, "PAT. NO.," link couplers, "654" centered on side.   **12   17   25**
(B)   Same as (A) but dark green painted green plastic.   **12   17   25**
(C)   Red painted plastic, short sheet metal trucks, brass coupler weight, "653" on center of side.   **12   17   25**
(D)   Same as (C) but green painted green plastic.   **12   17   25**
(E)   Red unpainted bakelite, short sheet metal trucks, brass coupler weight, "653" on center of side.   **12   17   25**
(F)   Same as (E) but highly polished green unpainted plastic.   **12   17   25**
(G)   Red unpainted bakelite, short sheet metal trucks, brass coupler weight, "654" on both ends of each side.   **12   17   25**
(H)   Same as (G) but silver platform railing, black weights, Stromberg Collection.   **12   17   25**
(I)   Same as (A) but green unpainted plastic.   **12   17   25**
(J)   Green unpainted plastic, short sheet metal trucks, nickel journals, brass coupler weights, Sutter Collection.   **12   17   25**

655   **SILVER BULLET** Coach, chrome or satin aluminum finish, black lettering, sans serif "American Flyer Lines" above windows, "655" at both ends of the car on each side, "SILVER BULLET" decal with blue lettering and gold field underneath windows on both sides, sheet metal base with provision for light, but not illuminated, seven double windows flanked by two small windows, flanked by two doors on each side, no steps, link couplers, Circa 1953. The Silver Bullet was a beginner set; in the passenger version there are two coaches numbered 655 with link couplers or 955 with knuckle couplers and an engine and tender. One of the satin finished cars observed was badly scratched and could be scratched through the finish from both sides. The light coming through the scratch revealed a cream colored plastic rather than grayish-white. Our observations of the underlying plastic color are most likely consistently distorted by the paint on the other side. We have no solution to this reporting problem since the people who are generous enough to share their collection with us could not be expected to scrape a car's finish. However, since we are consistent in observing all cars, observers using the same process will get the same results.

(A)   Chrome finished white plastic, Type D trucks, Petri and

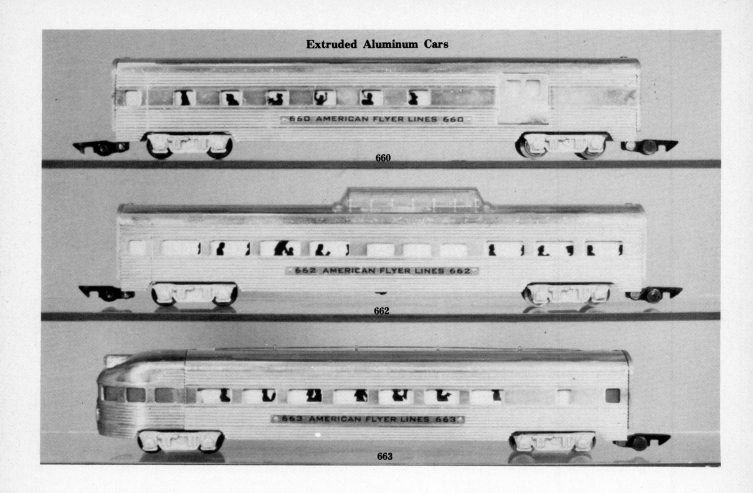

Balint Collections.   **10   20   30**
(B) Same as (A), Type B trucks, Stromberg Collection.
     10   20   30
(C(Satin aluminum finished gray plastic.   **8   15   25**
(D) Satin aluminum finished green plastic, Type D trucks, Stromberg Collection.   **10   20   30**

655   **AMERICAN FLYER LINES** New Haven type, smooth roof coach, similar to 655 Silver Bullet shells, "AMERICAN FLYER LINES" over windows, "655" centered below windows, 1953.
(A) Green painted plastic.   **10   15   20**
(B) Red painted plastic.   **10   15   20**

660   **BAGGAGE AND CLUB CARS** Streamlined series, first appeared in 1950-51 with extruded aluminum shell. According to Maury Romer, Gilbert had intended that this car and the matching cars in the series be made from plastic and match the Santa Fe diesel. However, most of the allocated tooling funds were used to develop the Alco PAs which left insufficient funds for the plastic injection molds. Hence the much less expensive aluminum extrusions were utilized. The extruded aluminum cars were heavy -- to heavy -- and the cars did not pull well. When funds were available in 1952 the cars were retooled for injection plastic molding. The lighter weight plastic shells permitted substantially longer trains and probably cost less too, once the tooling was paid for. Both the plastic and aluminum cars have symmetrical window and door arrangements. The plastic and aluminum cars had different passenger doors. On the aluminum car the passenger door is indicated only by a vertical groove through the car side, while on the plastic car it is fully developed. The cars also differ in their lettering. The cars are illuminated

and come with link couplers with black weights and aluminum finished die-cast passenger trucks.
(A) Extruded fluted aluminum shell, die-cast ends held by screws through roof; "660 AMERICAN FLYER LINES 660" on plate riveted beneath windows; plate extends 1 1/16" beyond windows; no lettering above windows; silhouetted people; separate baggage door insert; black sheet metal base without ridges embossed "PA 11225;" four-wheel trucks with aluminum finished die-cast sides; groove runs vertically through side separating last non-silhouetted window from silhouetted windows, Newcomer Collection.
     15   22   30
(B) Chrome finished black plastic shell: "660 AMERICAN FLYER LINES 660" centered below window on riveted plate; black sheet metal base; "BAGGAGE" above windows; fully developed passenger door on each side, silhouetted people, Newcomer Collection.   **12   17   25**
(C) Lacquer type chrome finished black plastic shell, black sheet metal base with ridges, fully developed passenger door on each side, same lettering as (B), Caples Collection.
     12   17   25

661   **PULLMAN** Streamlined series, matches 660. (See 660 for background.) Both the aluminum and plastic cars have symmetrical sides. The aluminum cars have a simulated door followed by two small, six large with silhouettes and two small windows. The plastic cars have two small windows followed by six large with silhouettes, followed by two small windows followed by a well detailed door with window; aluminum finished truck sides, interior illumination.
(A) Extruded aluminum fluted shell, die-cast ends held by

661

screws through roof, "661 AMERICAN FLYER LINES 661" on plate riveted to side beneath windows, plate is not centered beneath windows, no lettering above windows, black sheet metal base without ridges, base embossed "PA 11225 AMERICAN FLYER MFD. BY THE A.C. GILBERT CO. NEW HAVEN, CONN. U.S.A.," vertical groove through side, Newcomer and Stromberg Collections.   **15   22   30**

(B) Chrome finished black plastic shell, "660 AMERICAN FLYER LINES 660" off center slightly on riveted plate beneath window; black sheet metal base, "PULLMAN" above windows, fully developed passenger door on each side, Newcomer Collection.   **12   17   25**

(C) Lacquer type chrome finished black plastic shell, black sheet metal base with ridges, fully developed passenger door on each side, same lettering as (B), Caples Collection.   **12   17   25**

662   VISTA DOME Streamlined series, matches 660. (See 660 for background.) Both the aluminum and plastic cars have symmetrical sides. Doors on the aluminum cars are simulated by a groove, they have a small window, four large windows with silhouettes, three medium windows and three large windows with silhouettes. The plastic cars have two medium windows, six large windows with silhouettes and two medium windows and a fully developed door with window. The domes are a separate piece of plastic on both the aluminum and plastic cars and are off-center on the roofs of the aluminum cars and centered on the plastic cars. The car lettering differs, they are illuminated and come with link couplers with black weights and aluminum finished die-cast passenger trucks.

(A) Extruded aluminum shell, die-cast ends held by screws through roof, "662 AMERICAN FLYER LINES 662" on plate riveted to side beneath windows, black sheet metal base without ridges, base embossed "PA 11225," Newcomer Collection.   **15   22   30**

(B) Chrome finished black plastic shell; "662 AMERICAN FLYER LINES" on riveted plate beneath windows; black sheet metal base with ridges, "PULLMAN" above windows, fully developed door, Newcomer Collection.   **12   17   25**

(C) Lacquer type chrome finished black plastic shell, black sheet metal base with ridges, fully developed passenger door, same lettering as (B), Caples Collection.   **12   17   25**

663   OBSERVATION Streamlined series, matches 660, 661 and 662. (See 660 for background.) Both the aluminum and plastic cars have symmetrical window and door arrangements. The aluminum car has one small simulated window in door, one small window, several large windows with silhouettes and three small windows on each side. The plastic cars have a fully developed door with a small window followed by a small window, seven large windows with silhouettes and three small windows. Both

cars are illuminated and have radio antennas on the roof, illuminated drumheads, red tail lights, link couplers with black coupler weights and aluminum finished die-cast passenger car trucks. The base for the observation differs from that of the Pullman and Combine in that it has a rounded end, is about a half-inch shorter and is embossed "PA 11225A" rather than "PA 11225."

(A) Extruded aluminum shell, large die-cast section forms tapered end; plastic drumhead reads "AMERICAN FLYER LINES," no lettering above windows; flat sheet metal base embossed "AMERICAN FLYER MFD. BY THE A.C. GILBERT CO. NEW HAVEN, CONN. U.S.A. PA 11225A."   **15   22   30**

(B) Chrome finished black plastic shell, "663 AMERICAN FLYER LINES 663" on riveted plate beneath windows, "PULLMAN" above windows; black sheet metal base with ridges, Caples Collection.   **12   17   25**

(C) Lacquer type chrome finished black plastic shell, black sheet metal base with ridges, same lettering as (B), Caples Collection.   **12   17   25**

718   MAIL CAR 1946-54, "NEW HAVEN" "718" and "RAILWAY EXPRESS AGENCY" in white and centered on each side, non-illuminated; white, red and/or green plastic mail bags labeled "AMERICAN FLYER LINES." Also came with mail pickup pole and button; price includes only car and two mail bags. The car has a mail pickup arm of stamped metal which is activated by a solenoid. The car would either pickup or drop off a bag.

(A) Red painted thick cream plastic shell, sheet metal base, copper anodized sheet metal trucks with two embossed spring areas, each with three springs, one truck with slot for power pickup arm, black weights, Caples Collection.   **10   15   20**

(B) Green unpainted thick plastic shell, "PA 10089," die-cast base "PA-10454-A" with thin ends, one black sheet metal truck with two embossed spring areas, each with three springs and two slots, one with power pickup arm, black weights, other with two embossed areas without spring differentiation.   **10   15   20**

(C) Unpainted thick red plastic shell; die-cast base "PA 10454," Type A trucks, black coupler weights, red pickup arm, Yorkis Collection.   **15   25   40**

(D) Unpainted thick red plastic shell, die-cast base "PA 10454-A," Type A trucks, black coupler weights, black pickup arm, Welter Collection.   **10   15   20**

(E) Light red painted plastic shell, stamped steel base.   **10   15   20**

732   OPERATING BAGGAGE CAR 1951-54, packing crates load through left door, crates then move down roller bars where blue man with flesh colored face and hands pushes crates out of right door; mechanism powered by trackside pickup. Also can be used with 770 Baggage Loading Platform. Operating side reads "732" at both ends, non-operating side "AMERICAN FLYER" without

The Lightweight Streamline Cars

951

651

650

650

955

955

955

serifs and "732" between doors; link or knuckle couplers, NEW HAVEN smooth roof style body; catalogue illustrations show different lettering than described above and it is likely that these versions exist, confirmation requested.

(A) Green unpainted thick plastic shell, die-cast frame, "PA-10454-A" with cut-off end and extra ovals to accommodate mechanism, one sheet metal truck with pickup arm through slot, two embossed areas with three springs each (six spring type), other truck the same but no slot or pickup arm; black coupler weight, Greenberg Collection.

        15   25   35

(B) Green painted thick white plastic shell, die-cast frame, metal operating door, Type B trucks, Stromberg Collection.

        10   15   25

(C) Unpainted thick red plastic shell; die-cast frame, Type C trucks, metal operating door, Stromberg and Balint Collections.

        10   15   25

(D) 1951 and 1952 catalogue illustrations, operating side, "NEW HAVEN" centered above and between doors, "AMERICAN FLYER" lower and between doors.

No Reported Sales

(E) 1953 catalogue illustration, operating side, no lettering between doors: "AMERICAN FLYER LINES" to left of left door; "732" on side near both ends near bottom.

No Reported Sales

735   **ANIMATED STATION COACH** New Haven type car with one small window at each end flanking seven double white outlined windows. Came with 776 Animated Station. Passengers "walk" from station through car and back to station, car came with either knuckle or link couplers and is lettered either "NEW HAVEN" or "AMERICAN FLYER LINES" above windows, numbered "735" below windows. Car is maroon painted black plastic or red unpainted plastic. Car has either Type B sheet metal or die-cast trucks, 1952-54.

(A) "NEW HAVEN" above windows, maroon painted red plastic, Stromberg Collection. 15 22 30

(B) "AMERICAN FLYER LINES" above windows, maroon painted red plastic, Patterson Collection. 15 22 30

(C) Same as (A) but red unpainted plastic, Welter Collection.

        15   22   30

900   **NORTHERN PACIFIC** Combine, 1956, black plastic shell painted olive green on lower third, white line beneath windows and painted dark green above line, baggage door with two windows, six large windows of which five have silhouettes, "900" in sixth window, door with window, knuckle couplers, silver finished die-cast passenger trucks; came as part of a highly desirable set 5685RH with a 490, 491, 493, 901, two 902s and 903s. White lettering below windows on smooth area "NORTH COAST LIMITED" with red and black yin yang logo between "COAST" and "LIMITED," illuminated, either with or without number in windows, black or dark green plastic shell, sheet metal base with two ridges, one between each truck and light socket, six screws fasten base to shell, known to come with or without number in windows. 50 75 100

901   **NORTHERN PACIFIC** Coach, 1956, see 900 for background, matches 900 except for side arrangement, door with window, two small windows, six large windows, two small windows, black, light or dark green plastic shell, with same base as 900, known to come with or without numbers in windows.

        50   75 100

902   **NORTHERN PACIFIC** Vistadome, 1956, see 900 for background, matches 900 except for side arrangement and dome, side arrangement is same as 901, white lettering on lower side reads "VISTA DOME" (then yin yang logo) "NORTH COAST LIMITED," black, light or dark green plastic shell with same

base as 900, with or without numbers in windows, large 5/32 or small 1/8 inch numbers on sides, Stromberg Collection.

        50   75 100

903   **NORTHERN PACIFIC** Observation, see 900 for background, matches 900 except for side arrangement; arrangement is door with window, one small window with "903," seven large windows, three medium windows, amber yellow translucent drumhead on rear with "AMERICAN FLYER LINES," red light on rear roof top glows when interior bulb is lighted, black base with rounded end, with or without numbers in small window.

        50   75 100

918   **MAIL CAR** 1953-56, New Haven type body, white sans serif lettering "AMERICAN FLYER LINES" or "NEW HAVEN" centered between and above two doors, "918" between doors and "RAILWAY EXPRESS AGENCY" between and below doors centered on each side, non-illuminated, knuckle couplers, white, red or green plastic bags lettered "AMERICAN FLYER LINES," with mail bag pickup stand and button marked "AMERICAN FLYER MAIL PICKUP." Same solenoid action as 718.

(A) "AMERICAN FLYER LINES" above windows, maroon painted gray plastic, sheet metal frame, die-cast trucks with flat area inside oval except for one side of one truck with concave oval, Balint Collection. 10 15 20

(B) Same as (A) but both sides of pickup truck with concave ovals, Stromberg Collection. 10 15 20

(C) "AMERICAN FLYER LINES" above windows, red painted black plastic, sheet metal frame, die-cast trucks.

        10   15   20

(D) "NEW HAVEN" above doors, red plastic car.

        15   22   30

951   **BAGGAGE** 1953-56, New Haven type car, two baggage doors, four-wheel die-cast trucks, knuckle couplers, "AMERICAN FLYER LINES" in sans serif letters above doors, "RAILWAY EXPRESS AGENCY" and "951" in sans serif letters between doors; matches 955 (B) and 955 (C).

(A) Green unpainted plastic shell, sheet metal frame base, Balint Collection. 10 15 20

(B) Red unpainted plastic shell, sheet metal frame.

        10   15   20

(C) Green painted white plastic shell, sheet metal frame, Petri Collelction. 10 15 20

(D) Red painted black plastic shell, sheet metal frame, Petri Collection. 10 15 20

(E) Green painted black shell, sheet metal base, flat ovals on truck sides, Stromberg Collection. 10 15 20

(F) Maroon painted black shell, Stromberg Collection.

        10   15   20

Introduction To 952-953-954

These cars were developed from the 652-653-654 cars of 1946-1953. The earlier cars came with link couplers and had three different types of bases: die-cast metal, plastic and sheet metal. The 652 series were based on New Haven heavyweight cars and were fairly accurate scale models showing the same side differentiation as shown on the prototype.

In particular the window size and number vary as do the ventilator size and number. Although the plastic shells appear similar Gilbert did change them. The relationship of the floor to the shell was changed during the course of 652 production. Later 652s are similar to the 952 series. In the early 652 series, the floor extends under the vestibule while for later 652s and 952s the floor does not.

The most obvious change was the change from link couplers and sheet metal trucks to knuckle couplers and die-cast truck side frames. Gilbert retained the distinctive six-wheel configuration which marked these as premium cars. The new truck side frames exhibited more detail than do the 652 series sheet metal frames. Careful examination of early 652 shells reveal many more rivets than appear on later 652 and 952 shells.

The doors which opened and operated with a spring mechanism on the 652 series were plug doors on the 952 series.

The observation platform which had plug windows on the early 654s, and fully pierced windows on later 654s, is fully pierced on the 954s.

The bases were extensively redesigned for later 652 cars and for the 952 series. We assume that the redesigns were intended to reduce costs, particularly assembly time.

The 953 BAGGAGE AND CLUB CAR evolved from the 653. The window and ventilator patterns of the 653 were carried over unchanged to the 953. The 653's large baggage door and passenger doors both operated while the 953 had plug doors. Early 653s had a floor under the vestibule while the 953, as was true of second series cars, did not have a floor under the vestibule.

952 **PULLMAN** 1953-56, heavyweight style car, painted or unpainted plastic shells with sheet metal, plastic or die-cast base, illuminated, six-wheel trucks with highly detailed die-cast side frames with knuckle couplers, different window and ventilator patterns on each side: fourteen windows and six ventilators on one side, and twelve windows, four ventilators on the other side with or without window silhouettes, yellow window shades except on end windows on fourteen window side; non-operating doors (in contrast to 652 operating doors); black rectangular boxes beneath car.
  (A) Green painted white plastic shell, "PULLMAN AMERICAN FLYER LINES PULLMAN" above windows, "952 PIKES PEAK 952" beneath windows in sans serif block letters, die-cast base, no silhouettes, fourteen windows on one side; twelve windows on other side, Balint Collection.
                                                                     15   22   30
  (B) Same as (A) but green paint over red paint over white plastic shell, with plastic base.   15   22   30
  (C) Red painted cream plastic shell; "PULLMAN AMERICAN FLYER LINES PULLMAN" above windows in black sans serif and in same face beneath window "952 PIKES PEAK 952."   15   22   30
  (D) Same as (C) but with silhouettes in window, Balint Collection.   15   22   30

953 **BAGGAGE AND CLUB CAR** 1953-56, the 953 evolved from the 653 Baggage and Club Car and matches 952 and 954. (See the Introduction to 952 series for background.) 953 has one plug baggage door, five pairs of medium sized windows with yellow shades, one small unshaded window and one passenger door on each side with twin shades. Above windows, "AMERICAN FLYER LINES," in white sans serif lettering and beneath windows in same face "NIAGARA FALLS;" "953" on the sides in white at each end and parallel with NIAGARA FALLS. The car is illuminated and has a white paper liner to diffuse the light; black finished passenger car die-cast truck side frames, six-wheel trucks, knuckle couplers.
  (A) Green painted white plastic, black plastic base with embossed "PA-10067, PA-10067A, PA-10067B," Caples Collection.   20   30   40
  (B) Same as (A) but die-cast frame.   20   30   40
  (C) Red painted cream plastic shell, plastic frame.
                                                       20   30   40
  (D) Tuscan painted plastic shell, die-cast frame. 20   30   40

  (E) Same as (C) but with silhouettes, Balint Collection.
                                                       20   30   40

954 **OBSERVATION** 1953-56, this car evolved from the 654 Observation and matches the 952 and 953. (See the Introduction to the 952 series for background.) 954 shared the same window and ventilator pattern as the 654; it had twelve windows on one side and ten on the other. See the 654 for a more detailed analysis. The frame and vestibules of 954 differed from those on the 654. The 954 had white block sans serif "AMERICAN FLYER LINES" above windows and "GRAND CANYON" in a similar typeface below the windows. "954" in white on the side toward each end. Brass railing with drumhead reads "AMERICAN FLYER" on round black decal with white lettering, six-wheel trucks with black painted die-cast passenger side frames, knuckle couplers, illuminated. The car had one fixed passenger door on the side; the window and door at the rear of the car were pierced and had plastic windows. It made a very attractive appearance as it ran down the main line. (This is a change from the usual 654. Some 654s have been observed, however, with pierced windows and door.) The car had three steps, similar to the 654. To provide sufficient clearance for the rear passenger truck, the steps from the observation railing have a diagonal cut-away that at first glance looks like a modeler's hand-filed improvement. Observed examples do not have silhouettes in the windows although silhouettes have been reported.   15   25   35

955 **COACH** 1954, New Haven style car with seven sets of double windows, one small window at each end, "AMERICAN FLYER LINES" above windows; knuckle coupler, not illuminated.
  (A) Satin silver finished plastic shell, "SILVER BULLET" on decal beneath window, die-cast frame, "955" on each end of each side, came with Gilbert's lowest priced passenger set "THE SILVER BULLET" (K5406T).   15   20   30
  (B) Green painted plastic shell, "955" centered beneath windows, came with "THE ARROW" (K411T), matches 951(A), white outlined windows and handrails, sheet metal frame, Patterson Collection.   15   20   30
  (C) Tuscan painted black plastic shell; "955" centered beneath windows, came with "THE MOUNTAINEER" set, people silhouetted in windows, sheet metal frame, matches 955(B), concave ovals, Stromberg and Patterson Collections.
                                                       15   20   25
  (D) Red painted black plastic shell, people silhouetted in windows, sheet metal frame, white outlined windows and handrails, Balint and Petri Collections.   15   25   35

The 960 series (960, 961, 962 and 963) evolved from the 660 passenger cars. The 660 series began as extruded aluminum cars and rapidly evolved into injection molded plastic cars. The 960 series continued the basic 660 plastic shell without changes. The shell's base in the 660 series and the 960 series was fastened with screws through the base.

960 **COLUMBUS** (Combine), aluminum or chrome finish on black or white and possibly other color plastic fluted shells, with or without color band passing through windows from passenger door at one end to edge of the baggage door; and from the other edge of the baggage door to the car's end; black sans serif "AMERICAN FLYER LINES" above windows on flat car surface and black sans serif "960 COLUMBUS 960" below windows on metal plate; thickness of lettering varies across cars; the car shell is fluted and highly detailed with roof vents, four small rectangular indents and other parts -- a masterful piece of plastic die work. The cars had more surface detail than the extruded aluminum cars because plastic injection molding lends itself to detail. American Flyer had used extruded aluminum in some of the 660 series passenger cars. The 960s

Passenger Car Frames

The top two rows are 960 series cars with ridges down the center of the floor and six sheet metal screws fastening the shell to the floor.

The bottom two rows are 660 series extruded aluminum cars with flat metal bottoms that slide into channels on the sides.

were illuminated with silhouetted figures in the windows and had aluminum finished die-cast truck side frames with four-wheel trucks. These cars have knuckle couplers and a black sheet metal base with ridge through center; broken by the light socket. The base is fastened to the shell by six machine screws and two plastic posts. Stamped into base was "AMERICAN FLYER MFD. BY THE A.C. GILBERT CO. NEW HAVEN, CONN. U.S.A."

(A) Chrome finish without color band, black plastic shell.
            20   30   35
(B) Same as (A) but white plastic shell, Stromberg Collection.
            20   30   35
(C) Aluminum finish without color band, black plastic shell.
            18   25   30
(D) Same as (C) but aluminum finish over chrome finish on black plastic shell.   20   30   40
(E) Aluminum finish with blue band, black plastic shell, part of Comet Set.   30   40   50
(F) Aluminum finish with green band, black plastic shell, part of Rocket Set, Balint Collection. 20   30   40
(G) Aluminum finish with dark red band, black plastic shell, part of Santa Fe Set.   15   22   30
(H) Aluminum finish with brown band, black plastic shell, Patterson Collection.   30   40   60
(I) Aluminum finish with brown band, white plastic shell, also reported with "962" in window, Fazenbaker Collection.
            30   40   60
(J) Aluminum finish with orange band, black plastic shell, part of New Haven Set, Balint Collection. 20   30   40

961 **JEFFERSON** (Pullman), aluminum or chrome finish on black, white and possibly other color plastic fluted shell; with or without color band passing from passenger door to far end of same side; black sans serif lettered "AMERICAN FLYER LINES" above windows on flat car surface and black sans serif lettered "961 JEFFERSON 961" below windows on metal plate; thickness of lettering varies across car; the car shell is fluted and highly detailed with roof vents, four small rectangular indents and other parts — — a masterful piece of plastic die work. The car is illuminated and found with silhouetted figures in the windows; with aluminum finished die-cast truck side frames and knuckle couplers. The black sheet metal base has a ridge through

its center broken by the light socket; the base was fastened to the shell by six machine screws and two plastic posts. Stamped into base was "AMERICAN FLYER BY THE A.C. GILBERT CO. NEW HAVEN, CONN. U.S.A." Matches 960, 962, 963. (See 960 for background on this item.) Note that chrome finish pieces tended to chip and/or become discolored with age.

(A) Chrome finish without color band, black plastic shell, Stromberg Collection.   20   30   35
(B) Aluminum finish without color band, black plastic shell.
            20   30   35
(C) Aluminum finish with blue band.
           Not Produced
(D) Aluminum finish with green band, black plastic shell, part of Rocket Set.   20   30   40
(E) Aluminum finish with dark red band, black plastic shell.
            15   22   30
(F) Aluminum finish with brown band, white plastic shell.
            30   40   60
(G) Aluminum finish with orange band, black plastic shell, New Haven Set.   20   30   40
(H) Same as (B) but aluminum finish over chrome finish on black plastic shell.   20   30   40
(I) Same as (F) but black plastic shell. 30   40   60

962 **HAMILTON** (Vistadome), aluminum or chrome finish on black plastic fluted shell with or without color band passing from one end through windows to passenger door at other end. Vestibules were integral to car. The car was illuminated and had silhouettes in the windows in a window pattern of two small, six large and two small which is replicated on the other side. The plastic Vistadome was applied as a separate piece. Black sans serif lettering above windows reads "AMERICAN FLYER LINES" and black sans serif lettering below windows on a nickel finished metal plate riveted to the side reads "962 HAMILTON 962." The car had aluminum painted die-cast truck side frames with four wheels and knuckle couplers. There was a sheet metal base with a ridge running on the center of the base. Stamped into base was "AMERICAN FLYER MFD. BY THE A.C. GILBERT CO. NEW HAVEN, CONN. U.S.A."

(A) Chrome finish on black plastic shell, without color band, Stromberg Collection.   20   30   35
(B) Aluminum finish on black plastic shell without color band.
            20   30   35
(C) Aluminum finish on black plastic shell with blue band, part of Comet Set, Balint and Newcomer Collections.
            30   40   50
(D) Aluminum finish with green band on black plastic shell, part of Rocket Set, Balint and Newcomer Collections.
            20   30   40
(E) Aluminum finish with dark red band on black plastic shell.
            15   22   30
(F) Aluminum finish with brown band, black plastic shell.
            30   40   60
(G) Aluminum finish with orange band on black plastic shell, Stromberg Collection.   20   30   40
(H) Same as (B) but aluminum finish on chrome finish on black plastic shell.   20   30   40
(I) Same as (F) but black plastic shell. 30   40   60

963 **WASHINGTON** Observation, matches 960, 961, and 962; chrome or aluminum finished black or other color plastic fluted shell. The side view shows a door, small window, seven large windows with silhouettes and three small windows. There is a tail light above the rectangular windows on the rear of the car and a drumhead that reads "AMERICAN LINES FLYER" beneath these windows. The car is illuminated and had a radio antenna on the roof fastened with three stanchions. There were four small rectangular indents on the car side where the side joined the roof. There was only one knuckle coupler and the car

962

962

962

962

962

962

962

had aluminum finished die-cast four-wheel truck side frames. The sheet metal base was held to the shell by six machine screws and two plastic posts. The base had a ridge running down the center, broken by a light socket. The observation's floor differed from those of coaches and combines because of the observation's rounded end and its bulge at the rear for the drum headlight. The car is found with and without color bands. If bands are present, they run from the door on one side to and including the end of the car and back to the door on the other side. Car has thin black block lettering, "AMERICAN FLYER LINES," above windows on milled area and "963 WASHINGTON 963" on nickel plate attached to sides by pins beneath the windows.

(A) Chrome finish without color band on black plastic shell, Stromberg Collection.   **20   30   35**

(B) Aluminum finish without color band on black plastic shell.   **20   30   35**

(C) Aluminum finish with blue band on black plastic shell, part of Comet Set, Stromberg Collection.   **30   40   50**

(D) Aluminum finish with green band on black plastic shell, part of Rocket Set, Stromberg Collection.   **20   30   40**

(E) Aluminum finish with red band on black plastic shell.   **15   22   30**

(F) Aluminum finish with brown band on black plastic shell, part of Silver Flash Set.   **30   40   60**

(G) Aluminum finish with orange band on black plastic shell, part of New Haven Set, Stromberg Collection.   **20   30   40**

975   **ANIMATED STATION COACH** .1955, New Haven type car, with one small window at each end flanking seven double white outlined windows. Came with K766 Animated Station. Passengers "walk" "with help" from station through car and back to station. Sometimes they refuse to walk! Came with knuckle couplers; lettered "AMERICAN FLYER LINES" above windows, "975" centered below windows, all sans serif. Car was dark red painted black plastic, had die-cast trucks with concave ovals, Stromberg Collection. (See 735 for link coupler version.)   **15   22   30**

978   **GRAND CANYON** 1956, action car; when train stops, brakeman on rear platform leans out to check cars ahead, when train starts up again he returns to post; man operated by a solenoid mechanism; car used same shell as 954 except that the steps were not tapered, the platform fencing ends so that the man can lean out over the steps. The base had been modified with a cutout for mechanism. Tuscan painted black plastic shell, blue dressed brakeman carrying a red lantern, drumhead on brass railing reads "AMERICAN FLYER LINES;" car is illuminated; figures silhouetted in windows, Balint and Patterson Collections.   **30   55   80**

24703   **NORTHERN PACIFIC** Coach, part of the NORTH COAST LIMITED Set in 1957, its first year as a five digit number. There have been no confirmed reports of a coach numbered 24073. Probably the 1957 coach version was made with its 1956 number, "901," on its side. Since there are reports of other five digit 1957 items having three digit 1956 numbers while their boxes carry "correct" 1957 five digit numbers, it is likely that this was the case. If a boxed 24703 does exist and it contains a "901" the combination of the box and coach would bring a substantial price.   **No Reported Sales**

24706   **NORTHERN PACIFIC** Baggage and Club Car; probably a "900" in a box marked "24706" from 1957. (For background see 24703.)   **No Reported Sales**

24709   **NORTHERN PACIFIC** Vista Dome, probably numbered "902" in a box marked "24709" from 1957. (For background see 24703.)   **No Reported Sales**

24713   **NORTHERN PACIFIC** Observation, probably numbered "903" in a box marked "24713." (For background see 24703).   **No Reported Sales**

24720   **COACH** Frontier type, yellow unpainted sides and ends, black unpainted dull or shiny finish plastic roof and base, lettered above windows in bold Barnum letters "F.Y. & P.R.R." These letters stand for "Fifty Years of Progress in Railroading." At both ends is a closed window pattern "20" and at the right side facing the viewer on a lower wood scribed panel in sans serif block is "American Flyer Lines" in three lines; brakewheels at both ends of the car; not illuminated, black painted die-cast truck side frames which are the same mold as those used on the streamlined passenger cars and knuckle couplers. This car's construction was quite different from other American Flyer S gauge passenger cars. Most Flyer passenger cars had a one piece plastic side and roof assembly which fastened to a separate base. The 24720 however was made of three plastic parts: a roof with studs, yellow sides and a base. Machine screws went through the base and attached to the roof stud extensions. The car had wire reinforcing struts on its underside on both sides. Matches (247)30, (247)40, and (247)50.

(A) Dull finish roof, Stromberg and Newcomer Collections.   **12   22   30**

(B) Shiny finish roof, Stromberg Collection.   **14   25   35**

24723   **BAGGAGE** 1957, probably numbered "951" in a box marked "24723." (For background on the general problem see 24703.) Confirmation requested.   **No Reported Sales**

[247]30   **OVERLAND EXPRESS** Baggage, lettered above windows in black Barnum letters:"F.Y. & P.R.R." Beneath windows in black Barnum lettering is "OVERLAND EXPRESS." The number "30" appeared on each side at each end. The car does not have symmetrical sides. On the first side are a door with or without cross bracing, two small windows, a blank area and a door opening without door. On the second side is a small window, a door, with or without cross bracing, two windows, a blank area and a door opening without door, black plastic brakewheels on ends. Otherwise similar to (247)20 which it matches and came with as part of the Frontiersman Sets of 1959-61. In the 1960 catalogue two versions are shown: one with a paper label "OVERLAND EXPRESS" on green background and one without decal and with item number "24730" in small type. We have only observed the first one. The decal has a green circle with a red triangle inside with the words "Overland Express" in white.

(A) Door with cross bracking, Petri Collection.   **12   22   30**

(B) Door without cross bracing.   **12   22   30**

24733   **PIKES PEAK** Catalogued in 1957 and appeared with "24733" on its side, in a box (1957) numbered "24733." Walsh Collection.   **100   150   225**

24739   **NIAGARA FALLS** Catalogued in 1957 with "24739" on its side, Balint Confirmation.   **100   150   225**

[247]40   **BAGGAGE EXPRESS** Combine, generally matches (247)20 and (247)30, unpainted yellow plastic sides and ends; black unpainted plastic roof, black unpainted plastic base, black plastic brakewheels, both ends. With black Barnum "F.Y. & P.R.R." above windows and centered on side. "40" appears at each end of each side; "BAGGAGE EXPRESS" flanks door; plug side door with window with or without cross bracing; "door" on other side is simply an opening; not illuminated; stove pipe which is often broken. Part of Frontiersman Passenger Set 20550 in 1960 but not included in 1959 set of same number.

(A) Door without bracing, Petri Collection.   **12   22   30**

(B) Door with bracing (simulated wood inscribing and cross bucks).   **12   22   30**

[247]50 **BAGGAGE EXPRESS** Combine, similar to (247)40 but in different color as it came with the Washington Freight Set. 20655 rather than the passenger set. Red painted yellow plastic sides and ends; black plastic roof, black unpainted plastic floor, wire reinforcing struts under the car on each side; this car has the same shell as (247)40(B) with simulated wood inscribing and cross bucks on door. There is a smokestack on the roof which is easily broken; came with a light mounting hole in the base but none known to be equipped with lights. "F.Y. & P.R.R." and "BAGGAGE EXPRESS" in yellow on sides and yellow outlined windows.

In the FRONTIERSMAN Passenger Car Series, Gilbert produced baggage and combine cars with door openings but without doors. The question then arises, were these intended to be operating units? Or, was the opening intended to enhance play value so that youthful engineers could add figures and interiors to these cars? Or, was it an oversight that became too expensive to rectify? We ask our readers for their views on these questions. The FRONTIERSMAN passenger cars are apparently the only passenger cars that we have observed without paper liners. Although some of the inexpensive Gilbert passenger cars such as the SILVER BULLET were not illuminated, they still had paper liners. **30 45 60**

24773 **COLUMBUS** Combine, catalogued in 1957-58; 60-62, aluminum finished black plastic body with red stripe across side through windows, knuckle couplers, black sans serif lettering above windows, "AMERICAN FLYER LINES," and on smooth area beneath windows "24773 COLUMBUS 24773;" aluminum finished die-cast passenger trucks, illuminated; window patterns: six medium sized windows with silhouettes. Matches 24793, 24813 and 24833 which came with it in the SUPER CHIEF Set in 1957-58, Patterson Collection. **30 45 60**

24776[A] **COLUMBUS** Combine, catalogued in 1957 as separate item, aluminum finished black plastic streamlined body with red stripe through window, lettered "AMERICAN FLYER LINES." Possibly appeared with "960," the 1956 number, on its side with a box printed with the 1957 number "24776." It should be noted that Gilbert also catalogued 24773 in 1957 and that it appears to be the same car. Since the 24773 has been seen and described, it may be that 24776 was never made. Catalogued with what we call 24796(A), 24816(A) and 24836(A), none of which are known to exist. **No Reported Sales**

24776[B] **COLUMBUS** Combine, catalogued in 1959 both as a separate item and as part of THE BANKERS Set 20520; the orange striped version of streamlined set lettered in black sans serif face "AMERICAN FLYER" above windows and on smooth area beneath windows "24776 COLUMBUS 24776;" aluminum finished die-cast passenger trucks, knuckle couplers, illuminated, silhouettes in windows; six medium sized windows on each side, aluminum finished black plastic shell. (The car examined had a peculiar feature -- on the window silhouette material, by the window closest to the passenger door, is the number "24843," which is the number of the Northern Pacific combine. Was the wrong silhouette used? Or, did Gilbert consistently put incorrect numbers in car windows? Hawkins Collection. **30 45 60**

24793 **JEFFERSON** Pullman, catalogued in 1957-58, 60-62, aluminum finished streamlined plastic body with red stripe across side through windows; knuckle couplers, above windows "AMER-ICAN FLYER LINES" and on smooth area beneath windows "24793 JEFFERSON 24793" in black sans serif lettering, aluminum finished die-cast passenger trucks, illuminated; window pattern: two small, six large with silhouettes, two small; matches 24773, 24813, and 24833 which came with it in the SUPER CHIEF Set. **30 45 60**

24794 **JEFFERSON** Pullman, aluminum finished plastic streamlined body with orange stripe through windows; knuckle couplers; above windows "AMERICAN FLYER LINES" and on smooth area beneath windows "24794 JEFFERSON 24794;" in black sans serif lettering; aluminum finished die-cast passenger trucks, illuminated; window pattern: two small, six large with silhouettes, two small; Rechenberg Collelction. **500**

24796[A] **JEFFERSON** Pullman, aluminum finished plastic streamlined body with red stripe through windows; catalogued in 1957 as separate item. Possibly appeared with "961," the 1956 number, on its side with a box printed with the 1957 number, "24796." However, it should be noted that Gilbert also catalogued 24793 in 1957 which appears to be the same car. Since examples of the 24793 are reported on, it may be that 24796 was never made. Catalogued with what we call 24776(A), 24816(A) and 24836(A) with red stripe, none of which are known to exist. **No Reported Sales**

24796[B] **JEFFERSON** Pullman, catalogued in 1959, aluminum finished streamlined black plastic body with orange stripe across side through windows; knuckle couplers, above windows "AMER-ICAN FLYER LINES" and on smooth area beneath window "24796 JEFFERSON 24796" in black sans serif lettering, aluminum finished die-cast passenger trucks; illuminated; window pattern: two small, six large with silhouettes, two small; matches 24776(B) and 24836(B). **20 30 40**

24813 **HAMILTON** Vista Dome, catalogued in 1957, 58, 1960-62, aluminum finished streamlined black plastic body with red stripe across side through windows, broken by passenger door, knuckle couplers, above windows "AMERICAN FLYER LINES" and on smooth area beneath windows "24813 HAMILTON 24813" in black sans serif lettering, aluminum finished die-cast passenger trucks, illuminated, window pattern: two small, six large with silhouettes, two small, Stromberg Collection. **20 30 40**

24816[A] **HAMILTON** Vista Dome, catalogued in 1957 as separate item, red striped version of streamlined passenger set; possibly appeared with "962," the 1956 number, on its side with a box that carried the 1957 number "24816." However it should be noted that Gilbert also catalogued 24813 in 1957 which appears to be the same car. Since examples of 24813 are reported on, it may be that 24816 was never made. Catalogued with what we call 24776(A), 24796(A) and 24836(A) with red stripe, none of which are reported to exist. **No Reported Sales**

24816[B] **HAMILTON** Vista Dome, catalogued in 1959 both as a separate item and as part of THE BANKERS Set 20520. This car matches 24776(B), 24796(B) and 24836(B). It is the orange striped version of the streamlined passenger car "AMERICAN FLYER LINES" above windows and on smooth area beneath window "24816 HAMILTON 24816" in sans serif very heavy black letters, aluminum finished die-cast passenger trucks; illuminated, window pattern: two small, six large with silhouettes, two small windows. Note that the shell is fastened to the base by six metal pins and two plastic posts. **25 37 50**

24833 **WASHINGTON** Observation, catalogued 1957-58, 60-62, aluminum finished streamlined black plastic body with red stripe across side through windows; knuckle couplers, above windows "AMERICAN FLYER LINES" and on smooth area beneath window " 24833 WASHINGTON 24833" in black sans serif lettering, aluminum finished die-cast passenger trucks, illuminated, window patterns: two small, six large with silhouettes, two small. Matches 24773, 24793, 24813 which came with it in the SUPER CHIEF Set. **25 30 40**

24836[A] WASHINGTON Observation, catalogued in 1957 as a separate item, red striped version of streamlined aluminum finished plastic passenger car; possibly appeared with "963," the 1956 number, on its side with a box that carried the 1957 number, "24836." However, it should be noted that Gilbert also catalogued "24833" in 1957 which appears to be the same car. Since examples of 24833 are known to exist, it may be that 24836(A) was never made. 24836(A) was catalogued for separate sale with what we call 24776(A) and 24796(A), none of which are known to exist. **No Reported Sales**

24836[B] WASHINGTON Observation, catalogued in 1959 both as a separate item and as part of THE BANKERS Set 20520. It matches what we describe as 24776(B), 24796(B) and 24816(B). This is the orange striped version of the aluminum finished plastic streamlined passenger cars. It comes with very heavy sans serif black lettered "AMERICAN FLYER LINES" above windows. On smooth area beneath window it is lettered "24836 WASHINGTON 24836," aluminum finished die-cast passenger trucks, illuminated, window pattern: two small windows, six large windows with silhouettes and two small windows. Note that the shell is fastened to the base by six metal pins and two plastic posts. **25 35 50**

24837 UNION PACIFIC Star Dust Combine, 1959-60, black plastic shell with gray painted belly and roof, yellow painted sides, red lines on side near belly and roof, gray lines above and below windows; highly detailed shell with four small roof indents, small "retractable" stairs beneath gray painted baggage door, and steps beneath passenger door, side view shows passenger door with window, six windows, five of which have people silhouettes and the sixth only the number 24843. Gray painted baggage door with two windows; gray finished die-cast passenger trucks, knuckle couplers, "Star Dust" in red script flanked by "24837" in red on smooth area beneath windows, came with 24838, 24839 and 24840, Newcomer, Patterson and Stromberg Collections. **50 80 110**

24838 UNION PACIFIC Pullman, 1959-60, black plastic shell with gray painted belly and roof, yellow painted sides, red lines across side near belly and roof, gray lines above and below windows; highly detailed shell with four small roof indents and fluting on sides; side view shows passenger door with window, two small windows, six large windows with silhouettes, and two small windows, no number in windows, knuckle couplers, "Dream Cloud" in red script flanked by "24838" in red on smooth areas beneath windows, came with 24837, 24839 and 24840, Newcomer and Stromberg Collections. **50 80 110**

24839 UNION PACIFIC Vista Dome, 1959-60, black plastic shell with gray painted belly and roof, yellow painted sides, red lines across side near belly and roof, gray lines above and below windows; highly detailed shell with three small roof indents, same side view as 24838 Pullman, separate plastic dome fastened by melting plastic tab from dome inside of car to roof; knuckle couplers, illuminated, "Columbia River" in red script flanked by "24838" in red on smooth area beneath windows. Came with matching 24837, 24838 and 24840, Newcomer and Stromberg Collections. **50 80 110**

24840 UNION PACIFIC Observation, 1959-60, black plastic shell with gray painted belly and roof, yellow painted sides, red lines across side near belly and roof, gray lines above and below windows, highly detailed shell with four small roof indents, roof fluting does not continue over last three windows; illuminated round drumhead and red tail light on roof and illuminated interior; knuckle couplers. "Moon Glow" in red script flanked by red "24840" on smooth area beneath windows; side pattern, from front, passenger door, small window, seven large windows with

silhouettes, three medium windows; radio antenna on roof fastened by three rivets, came with a matching 24837, 24838 and 24839, Stromberg and Newcomer Collections. **50 80 110**

24843 NORTHERN PACIFIC Combine, 1958, not illuminated, plastic shell with gray-green painted belly and lower side; dark green upper side and roof; white line across side below windows; highly detailed shell with four small roof indents, small "retractable" stairs beneath two-tone green painted baggage door and steps beneath passenger door; side view shows passenger door with window, six windows of which five have silhouettes and one has only the number "24843;" two-tone green painted baggage door with two windows; silver finished die-cast passenger trucks, knuckle couplers, "NORTH COAST LIMITED" in white beneath window, "NORTH COAST" in sans serif block lettering and "LIMITED" in italics; red and black yin yang decal separates "NORTH COAST" from "LIMITED." Came with 24846, 24849 and 24853. **60 80 '110**

24846 NORTHERN PACIFIC Pullman, 1958, not illuminated, plastic shell with gray-green painted belly and lower side; dark green upper side and roof, white line across side below windows, highly detailed shell with four small roof indents and side fluting; side view shows passenger door with window; two small windows, six large windows with silhouettes and two small windows; last small window with number "24846;" white lettering and decal similar to 24843, knuckle couplers, silver finished die-cast passenger trucks. Came with 24843, 24849 and 24853. **60 80 110**

24849 NORTHERN PACIFIC Vista Dome, 1958, plastic shell; painted gray-green and dark green. Matches description of 24846 pullman except that number in small window is "24849" and white lettering beneath window on smooth area reads, "VISTA DOME NORTH COAST LIMITED" with yin yang decal between "DOME" and "NORTH," plastic dome fastened to one fluted roof. **60 80 110**

24853 NORTHERN PACIFIC Observation, 1958, not illuminated, plastic shell painted gray-green and dark green; white line across side below windows, highly detailed shell with four small roof indents; radio antenna on roof, round drumhead, red tail light on roof, knuckle couplers, "NORTH COAST LIMITED" in which with yin yang decal separating "COAST" and "LIMITED," "LIMITED" in italics, "NORTH COAST" in sans serif block lettering; "24853" in first small window. Came with 24843, 24846 and 24849. In 1958, the car came with metal steps and a plastic drumhead. In 1964, it had plastic steps and a paper drumhead. **60 80 110**

24856 EAGLE HILL Missouri Pacific combine, silver finished plastic shells with thick blue stripes on side framed by two thin yellow stripes, white "24856 EAGLE HILL 24856" beneath windows, "THE EAGLE" above windows. Combine is part of the Missouri Pacific set issued in 1958 and again in 1964. The set includes the 24856 plus 24859, 24863, 24866 and a dual motor 21920 and 21920-1 with horn in 1958 but a single motor 21920 in 1964. The 1958 version has a blue painted stripe passing through the doors and the base is attached to the shell with six machine screws. In 1964, the blue stripe does not pass through the door and the base is attached to the shell with four rivets. The 1964 set has the sad distinction of being the last passenger set made by Gilbert.
(A) 1958 model, Balint Collection. **50 100 150**
(B) 1963-64 model, Walsh Collection. **40 90 120**

24859 EAGLE LAKE Missouri Pacific coach, matches 24856; "24859 EAGLE LAKE 24859" below windows and "THE EAGLES" above windows, both in white.
(A) 1958. **50 100 150**

(B) 1963-64.   40 90 120

24863   **EAGLE CREEK** Missouri Pacific coach, matches 24856; "24863 EAGLE CREEK 24863" below windows, "THE EAGLES" above windows, both in white.
(A) 1958 version.   50 100 150
(B) 1963-64 version.   40 90 120

24866   **EAGLE VALLEY** Missouri Pacific observation, matches 24856; "24866 EAGLE VALLEY 24866" below windows, "THE EAGLES" above windows, both in white.
(A) 1958 version.   50 100 150
(B) 1963-64 version.   40 90 120

24867   **AMERICAN FLYER LINES** Combine with red stripe, not illuminated, part of 1958 set that came with 21813 M & St. L.   25 50 75

24868   **AMERICAN FLYER LINES** Observation, matches 24866.   25 50 75

24869   **AMERICAN FLYER LINES** Coach, matches 24866.   25 50 75

And you thought that making trains was a man's job. Photo from the Walsh Collection.

Chapter XIV

HOPPERS AND DUMP CARS

Gilbert offers five basic hopper car styles. The first, a 632, comes with a die-cast body and is a carry-over of the prewar 508. In addition, the 716, an operating car, comes with a sheet metal frame and bin. It is also a carry-over from the early forties 0 Gauge line.

Over the postwar period, Gilbert built three styles of plastic hopper bodies: two are short hoppers and one is a long, deluxe version. The short hoppers show a frequent Gilbert characteristic -- evolution toward a less expensive construction technique. Gilbert offers a limited number of roadnames in the first ten years of S Gauge production. In the mid-fifties, however, roadnames begin to proliferate as do those of Lionel. Thus, in the first ten years of S Gauge, an operator has a choice between a Lehigh, New England, Wabash or a Virginian, and in later years he could haul commodities in a B&O, a CB & Q, CRP (Jersey Central, C & E I (Chicago and Eastern Illinois), Santa Fe, Domino Sugar or a Peabody.

We include dump cars with hoppers since they often carry the same commodity. Gilbert offers a narrow selection of dump cars: it is C B & Q or else! However, the C B & Q is catalogued in four different numbers and comes in four versions. The first, the 719, has sheet metal trucks and link couplers; the second, the 919, has die-cast trucks and knuckle couplers; while the third, a 1957 five digit 25007, or so it was catalogued, is only known to appear with the three digit number 919. Two more five digit C B & Qs -- a 25025 and 25060 -- were then issued. The 719 and 919 have a gear-operated side dump mechanism, while the five digit units have a gravity operated mechanism with an automatic catch when the dump body returns to a horizontal position.

The Domino Sugar hopper is the rarest and most valuable of the hoppers. Produced in 1963-64 this car usually has end-of-the-line Pike Master trucks and couplers but because of the car's scarcity they hardly deter collectors. A few Domino Sugar hoppers do exist with sintered iron truck side frames and knuckle couplers. It would be interesting to know how Domino Sugar sweetened Flyer's pie for producing this car. The other notable hopper is the C & E I. What story explains why Gilbert chose a little known road to be replicated in quantity? Yet, the present scarcity of the C & E I indicates that few were actually manufactured.

Gilbert offers one automatic hopper, the 0 Gauge prewar 474 updated as an S Gauge 716. It is only offered through 1951. From that time on automatic action for coal is only available with C B & Q dump cars: the 719, 919, 25007, 25025 and the 25060.

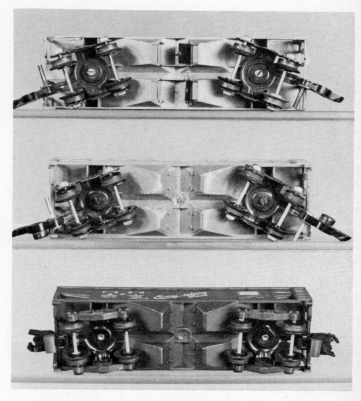

Hopper Underbodies:
Top Row: 632 Virginian with Sheet Metal Doors;
Middle Row: Type I Plastic Body with Screw Mounted Trucks;
Bottom Row: Type II Plastic Body with Rivet Mounted Trucks

HOPPER AND DUMP CAR LISTING

		Good	Very Good	Excel
VIRGINIAN See 632.				
624	**C R P** Similar to 24209, Carnes Collection.	**No Reported Sales**		

[632] **VIRGINIAN** Gray, blue-violet or cream painted die-cast body with"VIRGINIAN" in sans serif black face; no other letters or numbers; Type A trucks, link couplers with narrow shanks and embossed "PAT. NO. 2240137," no coupler weights. This is a continuation of the prewar 508 but with new trucks and lettering for 1946. It is the only die-cast freight car offered in 1946. The black sheet metal bottom doors open and close; the trucks are screw-mounted and the die-cast body is embossed "PA 9180."

(A)	Blue-violet, Sutter Collection.	15	22	40
(B)	Gray, Patterson and Newcomer Collections.	15	22	40
(C)	Cream, Walsh Observation.	**No Reported Sales**		

632 **L N E** Gray or black Type I unpainted plastic or gray painted die-cast body; "LNE 632" in white and in white outlined circle

632 LNE

632 LNE

632 LNE

640 AMERICAN FLYER

640 AMERICAN FLYER

640 AMERICAN FLYER

921 C B & Q

801 B & O

924 CRP

940 WABASH

24203 B & O

24209 CRP

24213 WABASH

24219 WESTERN MARYLAND

716   919

"LEHIGH NEW ENGLAND" with red smaller circle; "CAPY 100000 LBS. LD. LMT. 123800 LBS. LT. WT. 452000 LBS. NEW 5-39" in white, all with link couplers.

(A) Lighter gray plastic, Type A trucks, no coupler weights, coupler embossed with "PAT. NO. 2240137."   2   3   5
(B) Darker gray plastic, Type A trucks, brass coupler weights, Greenberg Collection.   2   3   5
(C) Light gray plastic, Type D trucks.   2   3   5
(D) Same as (B) but Type B trucks, black coupler weights.   2   3   5
(E) Black plastic, Type A trucks, no coupler weights, 1946, coupler embossed with "PAT. NO. 2240137," Stromerg Collection.   5   8   10
(F) Gray painted die-cast body, Type A trucks, no coupler weights, no red small circle, embossed "PA 9180," operating hatch covers, Yorkis Collection.   20   30   50
(G) Same as (B) but Type A trucks, no coupler weights, Sutter Collection.   2   3   5
(H) Bluish gray painted plastic "PA 12D155" body, Type B truck, black coupler weights, truck weights, Sutter Collection.   2   3   5
(I) Gray painted plastic "PA12D155" body, Type D trucks, black coupler weights, Sutter Collection.   2   3   5
(J) Same as (F) but bluish gray painted die-cast body, Sutter Collection.   20   30   40
(K) Very light gray plastic, almost white, Type A trucks, black coupler weights.   5   7   10
(L) Same as (A) but brass coupler weights, Stromberg Collection.   2   3   5
(M) Same as (B) but no coupler weight, Stromberg Collection.   2   3   5
(N) White plastic body, Type B trucks, Walsh Collection.   10   15   20

640   **AMERICAN FLYER** Type I or II plastic body; also die-cast body, unpainted gray plastic in three shades: light, medium and dark; white or black lettering; Type A, B or C trucks, with brass or black coupler weights or without coupler weights; 1949-53.

WHITE LETTERING "AMERICAN FLYER" in sans serif face, all Type I plastic unless otherwise indicated.

(A) Medium gray plastic body, Type B trucks, black coupler weight, Greenberg Collection.   2   3   5
(B) Same as (A) but truck weights embossed "PA 11304," Caples Collection.   2   3   5
(C) Same as (A) but Type C trucks, Caples Collection.   2   3   5
(D) Dark gray unpainted plastic body, Type C trucks, black coupler weight.   2   3   5
(E) Same as (D) but Type B trucks, Sutter Collection.   2   3   5
(F) Medium gray plastic body, Type C trucks, brass coupler weights, Sutter Collection.   2   3   5
(G) Black unpainted plastic body, Type C trucks, black coupler weights.   **No Reported Sales**
(H) Purple die-cast body, Carnes Collection. **No Reported Sales**
(I) Light gray unpainted plastic body, Type B trucks, black coupler weights.   2   3   5
(J) Same as (A) but Type C trucks, and truck weights, Stromberg Collection.   2   3   5

BLACK LETTERING "AMERICAN FLYER," 1949-53.

(A) Medium gray unpainted Type I plastic body, Type B trucks, black coupler weight, Newcomer Collection.   3   4   6
(B) Light gray unpainted Type I plastic body, Type B trucks, Black coupler weight, Newcomer Collection.   3   4   6
(C) White unpainted Type I plastic body, Type C trucks, black coupler weight, truck weights.   12   25   35
(D) Light gray painted Type II black plastic body, Type B trucks, black coupler weights, Sutter Collection.   3   4   6

640   **WABASH** Type II black painted black plastic body, white lettering "WABASH," black coupler weights, Type D trucks, 1953, Petri Collection.   9   14   18

716   **AMERICAN FLYER LINES** Sheet metal operating hopper; top hinged flap is opened by solenoid mounted through frame. Solenoid is powered by either a special shoe mounted on one truck for inside rail pickup or by picking up current through truck side frame from outside third rail. The inside rail pickup shoe was powered by a special bakelite track section with two inside rails.

(A) Red painted sheet metal hopper with black decal lettering in embossed areas: "AMERICAN FLYER LINES" in three lines in small, sans serif lettering in one area and "716" in other. Truck mounted pickup shoe unit. Shoe has two brass pads which contact special track unit. Black painted stamped sheet metal frame, nickel finished ladders on each end, one two-piece brakewheel; Type A trucks, link couplers with "PAT NO. 2240137." A continuation of prewar operating hopper; has relatively wide frame designed originally for 0 track and overhangs trucks considerably, 1946, Greenberg Collection.   6   9   12
(B) Same as (A) but "AMERICAN FLYER LINES" in both lettering areas on both sides; no numbers on car, Stromberg Collection.   6   9   12
(C) Similar to (A) but pickup lever goes through truck side frame to contact outside third rail, "AMERICAN FLYER LINES" and "716" are either rubber stamped or a decal on the superstructure, Type C trucks, link couplers, brass coupler weights, 1947-50.   6   9   12
(D) Red painted sheet metal hopper, gray painted sheet metal frame. Pickup lever goes through truck side frame to contact outside third rail, 1951.   7   11   15

719   **C.B.&Q.** Coal dump car; black die-cast base, maroon painted sheet metal or plastic bin; link couplers, black coupler weights, Type B trucks, lettered "C B & Q 719 CAPY 30 CU.YD. LD LMT 108100LB. LT WT 60100 LB," a pickup lever through truck side frame activates solenoid mounted to frame, solenoid pin pushes through frame under bin, Stromberg and Schneider Collections.   6   9   12

801   **B & O** Type II black plastic body with "B & O" in large white face and "B & O 801" in small white face in two lines with white lines above and below; white dot and technical data "NEW 10-52" in white; black sintered iron truck side frames, knuckle couplers, 1956-57, Newcomer Collection.   6   9   12

24225 Santa Fe   24221 C & E I

24216 UNION PACIFIC   24230 PEABODY

919 **C. B. & Q.** Coal dump, black die-cast frame; tuscan painted plastic superstructure tilts; sintered iron truck side frame, knuckle couplers, 1953-56, Newcomer Collection.
- (A) "CAPY 38 CU YD LD LMT 106000 LB LT WT 58100 LB" in white, Newcomer Collection.   7   12   15
- (B) "CAPY 30 CU YD LD LMT 108100 LB LT WT 60100 LB" in white, Patterson Collection.   **10**   **15**   **20**

921 **C. B. & Q.** Tuscan painted Type II black plastic body with coal load; "Everywhere West" in white script, rectangular "Burlington Route" logo, "NEW 11-47" in white; black sintered iron truck side frames, knuckle couplers, 1953-56, Newcomer and Bargeron Collections.   5   7   12

924 **C R P** Gray or bluish-gray Type II black plastic body with one piece hatch cover, one or two piece brake unit at each end; "FOR BULK CEMENT ONLY" in black, "JERSEY CENTRAL LINES" logo of Liberty with torch, black sintered iron truck side frames, knuckle couplers, 1953-56.
- (A) Gray, Newcomer and Sutter Collections.   5   7   9
- (B) Bluish-gray, Sutter Collection.   5   7   9

940 **WABASH** Black unpainted Type II plastic body, white letters, sintered iron truck side frames, knuckle couplers, Balint Collection.   5   8   10

24203 **B & O** Black unpainted Type II plastic body, "B&O" in large white letters, "B & O 24203" in small white face with white line above and below; white technical data includes: "NEW 10-52," dark gray sintered iron truck side frames; knuckle couplers, white dot to left of technical data, 1958, 1963-64, Newcomer and Bargeron Collections.   5   7   10

24206 **C. B. & Q.** Brown painted black Type II plastic body, black plastic cover with simulated coal load, sintered iron truck side frames, knuckle couplers; 1958, Balint and Patterson Collections.   15   25   40

24209 **C R P** Gray painted black Type II plastic body, one piece hatch cover; one piece brakewheel at each end; Type II body, "FOR BULK CEMENT ONLY" "JERSEY CENTRAL LINES" in black, logo of Liberty with torch, dark gray truck side frames, knuckle couplers, 1957-60, Balint and Newcomer Collections.   **12**   **20**   **25**

24213 **WABASH** Black unpainted Type II plastic body, "WABASH" in large white serif block letters; white lettered technical data, white oval data block, dark gray sintered iron truck side frames, knuckle couplers; 1958-60.

- (A) Black unpainted body, Balint and Sutter Collections.   **10**   **15**   **25**
- (B) Black painted black plastic body, Patterson Collection.   **10**   **15**   **25**

24216 **UNION PACIFIC** Tuscan painted black plastic body, Type III body, one piece plastic brakewheel, yellow-gold "UNION PACIFIC" and "ROAD OF The Streamliners," technical data includes "BLT 10-47;" black sintered iron truck side frames, knuckle couplers, 1958-60, Bargeron, Stromberg, Balint and Leonard Collections.   **12**   **18**   **24**

24219 **WESTERN MARYLAND** Tuscan painted black plastic body, Type II body, "WESTERN MARYLAND" in white with four white bars on each side; technical data includes "NEW 4-53," black sintered iron truck side frames, knuckle couplers, no brakewheel location, 1958-59; Leonard, Balint and Patterson Collections.   **12**   **20**   **30**

24221 **C & E I** Gray painted black Type II body, "C & E I" in very large red face on the side and "24221" in small face with line above and below; red oval logo with "C & E I," red technical data includes "NEW 10-45," sintered iron truck side frames, knuckle couplers. (C & E I stands for Chicago and Eastern Illinois), 1959-60, no brakewheel location, Patterson, Leonard and Sutter Collections.   **25**   **35**   **50**

24222 **Domino SUGAR** Yellow painted bone or black plastic hopper with cover; Type II body, "American Sugar Refining Company" in blue and "ASRX 2422" with line above and below, Pike Master trucks and couplers, also sintered iron side frame trucks and knuckle couplers, 1963-64. It is reported that these cars were closed out to dealers for 50 cents in 1966!
- (A) Yellow painted bone hopper, Balint Collection.   **50**   **75**   **100**
- (B) Yellow painted black hopper, Pike Master couplers, Stromberg Collection.   **50**   **75**   **100**
- (C) Yellow painted black hopper, sintered iron truck side frames, knuckle couplers, Walsh Collection.   **50**   **75**   **100**

24225 **Santa Fe** Red painted or unpainted plastic body, Type II body, gray plastic insert gravel load, "Santa Fe," "24225" and "NEW 11-50" in white; black sintered iron truck side frames, knuckle or Pike Master couplers, 1960-65.

   (A) Orange red painted plastic, sintered iron truck side frames, Caples Collection.   6   9   12

   (B) Red painted plastic, sintered iron truck side frames, Caples Collection.   6   9   12

   (C) Unpainted red plastic, Pike Master trucks and couplers, Sutter and Balint Collections.   6   9   12

   (D) Red painted black plastic, Pike Master trucks and couplers, Patterson Collection.   6   9   12

24230 **PEABODY** Cream or bone Type III plastic body, "PEABODY COAL COMPANY" in green, green logo resembles a lump of coal and grass, "PCCX 24230" and "BLT 5-51" in small face, sintered iron truck side frames and knuckle or Pike Master couplers and trucks, 1961-64.

   (A) Cream unpainted plastic body, sintered iron truck side frames and knuckle couplers, Sutter and Schneider Collections.   25   35   50

   (B) Bone painted cream plastic body, Pike Master trucks and couplers, Bargeron, Balint and Patterson Collections.   12   15   25

25007 **C. B. & Q.** Dump car, 1957, it was probably issued with a "919" on its side and came in a box printed "25007" on the end. Confirmation requested.   **No Reported Sales**

25025 **C. B. & Q.** Dump car, black die-cast base, base embossed with some brake detail and dump mechanism; tuscan painted sheet metal bin; black sintered iron truck side frames, knuckle couplers; 1958-60, "CAPY 30 CU YD LD LMT 108100 LB. LT. WT. 60100LB, C B & Q 250 25" on bin's side, Patterson Collection.   20   30   45

25060 **C. B. & Q.** Dump car, black die-cast base, base embossed "MADE BY A.C. GILBERT CO.," maroon painted plastic bin that dumps; "CAPY. 30 CU YD LD LMT 108100" "LT WT 60100" in white on side , knuckle couplers, sintered iron truck side frames, 1961-64, Balint Collection.   20   30   45

FUNDIMENSIONS PRODUCTION

9200 **B & O** Black unpainted plastic body, Type II body, one piece removable black plastic coal load, "B & O 9200" and "Chessie System" in large yellow face. Chessie System cat logo, yellow technical data including "NEW 9-72;" "AMERICAN FLYER R BY LIONEL R OF FUNDIMENSIONS TM" embossed on bottom, black die-cast truck side frames, knuckle couplers, 1979. Greenberg Collection.   5   10   20

SMITTY and Gabe absorbed in deep thought over one of their whistling, smoking choo-choos which remain popular choice with grownup fans.

Chapter XV

TRANSFORMERS

		Good	Very Good	Excel

1 25 watt transformer, 1951-52, black metal oval case.
50c / 1 / 2

1b 50 watt transformer, 1956.
1 / 2 / 4

1 1/2 45 watt transformer, 1953, black metal oval case.
1 / 2 / 3

1 1/2 50 watt transformer, 1954-55, rectangular front, curved rear, bakelite case.
1 / 2 / 3

2 75 watt transformer, 1947-52, rectangular black painted steel case.
1 / 2 / 4

2B 75 watt transformer, 1948, same as 2 but with circuit breaker.
2 / 4 / 6

4B 100 watt transformer, 1949-53, rectangular black painted sheet metal case.
2 / 5 / 9

4B 100 watt transformer, 1954, bakelite case with rectangular front and rounded rear.
2 / 5 / 9

4B 110 watt transformer, 1955, otherwise same as 1954.
2 / 5 / 9

5 50 watt transformer, 1946, 60 cycles; black oval sheet metal case, no circuit breaker.
1 / 2 / 4

5A 50 watt transformer, 1946, 25 cycles; black oval sheet metal case, no circuit breaker.
50c / 1 / 2

5B 50 watt transformer, 1946, 60 cycles; black oval sheet metal case, nickel top, circuit breaker.
2 / 4 / 6

6 75 watt transformer, 1946, 60 cycles; black oval sheet metal case, no circuit breaker.
1 / 2 / 4

6A 75 watt transformer, 1946, 25 cycles, black oval sheet metal case, no circuit breaker.
50c / 1 / 2

7B 75 watt transformer, 1946, 60 cycles, black oval sheet metal case, nickel top, circuit breaker with red pilot light.
2 / 4 / 6

8B 100 watt transformer, 1946-52, green and red pilot lights, red metal lever with black wood extension circuit breaker with reset button, oval sheet metal case with nickel top plate.
6 / 10 / 12

9B 150 watt transformer, 1946, dual control, black rectangular metal case with nickel top plate, circuit breaker with reset button, green and red pilot lights, two red metal knobs with wood handles.
10 / 15 / 20

10 D.C. invertor, 1946, converts D.C. to A.C.; black rectangular sheet metal case with fuse.
3 / 5 / 7

11 Circuit breaker, 1946, with red pilot light and reset button.
3 / 5 / 7

12B 250 watt transformer, dual control, green and red pilot, 1946-52, rectangular metal case with nickel top plate, circuit breaker with reset button, metal knobs with wood handles.
15 / 25 / 33

13 Circuit breaker, 1952-55.
3 / 5 / 7

14 Rectiformer, 1947, 1949, 150 watts, 60 cycles, combination rectifier-transformer that produces low variable D.C. voltage and low fixed A.C. voltage.
8 / 12 / 15

15 Rectifier, 1948-52, converts low voltage A.C. to D.C., reverse switch, two sets of binding posts, 4 amp capacity.
5 / 7 / 10

15B 110 watt transformer, 1953, bakelite case with rectangular front and rounded rear, "Dead Man's Control," green and red pilot lights.
10 / 15 / 20

16 Rectiformer, 1950.
3 / 5 / 7

16B 190 watt transformer, 1953, bakelite case, "Dead Man's Control," green and red pilot lights.
15 / 22 / 30

16B 175 watt transformer, 1954-56, bakelite case with rectangular front and rounded rear, "Dead Man's Control,"
green and red pilot lights.
15 / 22 / 30

17B 190 watt transformer, 1952, bakelite case with rectangular front and rounded rear, "Dead Man's Control," green and red pilot lights, volt and amp meters.
15 / 22 / 30

18B 190 watt transformer, 1953, bakelite case, dual controls, "Dead Man's Control," green and red pilot lights.
20 / 30 / 40

18B 175 watt transformer, 1954-56, bakelite case with rectangular front and rounded rear, dual controls, "Dead Man's Control," green and red pilot lights.
20 / 30 / 40

19B 300 watt transformer, 1952-55, bakelite case with rectangular front and rounded rear, dual controls, "Dead Man's Control," green and red pilot lights, volt and amp meters.
30 / 45 / 60

30B 300 watt transformer, 1953-56, bakelite case with rectangular front and rounded rear, dual controls, "Dead Man's Control," one green and two red pilot lights, two volt meters, two circuit breakers.
35 / 50 / 70

22004 40 watt transformer, 1960-64, came with various low priced sets; never described in catalogues.
1 / 2 / 3

22020 50 watt transformer, 1957-64, rectangular end with three binding posts, rounded end with plastic controller on top: on side is red, white and blue "AMERICAN FLYER LINES" logo, has built in circuit breaker. Catalogue illustration describes it as "No. 1 TRANSFORMER," lettering not confirmed.
1 / 2 / 3

22030 100 watt transformer, black case with rectangular end with three binding posts and rounded end with controller; on side is red, white and blue "AMERICAN FLYER LINES" shield logo, built in circuit breaker; catalogue illustration shows a "NO. 4B TRANSFORMER," lettering not confirmed.
2 / 4 / 6

22035 175 watt transformer, 1957-64, black bakelite case with gently rounded end with foot pad containing three binding posts; top surface has "American Flyer" in white semi-script face, speeds run from 0 to 120; a new type directional switch marked "ON OFF ON," permits train to be stopped and started without reversing direction. The transformer supplies a small current to keep the reversing unit coil from sequencing, even when the speed control is turned completely off. Circuit breaker button pops up when circuit overloads. Pushing button down resets breaker and closes circuit.
15 / 22 / 35

22040 110 watt transformer, 1957-58.
6 / 9 / 12

22050 175 watt transformer, 1957-58.
10 / 15 / 20

22060 175 watt transformer, 1957-58, dual controls.
10 / 15 / 20

22080 300 watt transformer, 1957-58, dual controls.
20 / 30 / 40

22090 350 watt transformer, 1959-64, black bakelite case, dual controls and dual circuit breakers, each with reset button; direction control includes a circuit that maintains a small current flow so that when train stops enough current flows to prevent the reverse unit from sequencing; two sets of three posts, "AMERICAN FLYER" in raised white painted letters (in informal script) on case.
20 / 30 / 40

Johnathan LaCalle at the controls of his Gilbert layout

EPILOGUE

Paul G. Yorkis

When I was growing up in Haverstraw, New York, my brother and I shared two Lionel 0 Gauge freights, one steam and one diesel. We had a small layout in the basement complete with Plasticville buildings, Tootsietoy cars and trucks, and here we spent many hours playing with the trains and took turns serving as engineer, trainman, police officer and mayor.

While I was very pleased with the setup, I vividly remember asking myself why Lionel trains ran on three rail track when the real railroads had just two rail track. The West Shore Division of the New York Central System was four blocks from my home, and I witnessed the introduction of the sleek diesels to take the place of the big black, very impressive steam locomotives. I often sat on a bank overlooking the tracks and dreamed of places the trains were going to and, for a while, even wished that I could work on the railroad. Even with my good imagination, I could not understand why Lionel trains had to have three rail track.

Finally, sometime around 1953, I remember going to the Lionel train shop which was located on the top floor of what I believe to have been an old freight station -- turned Gulf gas station. I asked the owner why Lionel trains had to run on three rail track. I was given an explanation which seemed reasonable. He also told me that if I wanted trains that ran on two rail track I should buy American Flyer. As I recall, no store in Haverstraw carried American Flyer S Gauge; and, additionally, my brother, older and bigger, wanted to keep Lionel.

Well, soon afterwards we moved from Haverstraw and the Lionel layout became mine. We moved again and again once more, and in the process my Lionel trains and I separated.

In 1971, now married and living in Maryland, the train collecting and operating bug bit once again. I started looking around for hobby shops to check out what was available. It seems that over a period of eighteen years, the good old hobby shop got replaced by the big discount department store. Needless to say, American Flyer was not available so instead of going back to Lionel I purchased H0. In the mid-seventies I switched from H0 back to Lionel and then expanded my collection to include Flyer, Standard, 0, and S Gauges. Train collecting, restoring, operating and repairing has become a very serious hobby for me and, for that matter, my family.

In late 1977 my family and I were visiting some friends, Jim and Judy LaCalle. Jim knew of my interest in trains and pulled out a box of American Flyer which he had had as a child. I know how much I wanted a layout like the "real" trains when I was his son Jonathan's age, so rather than purchasing them from him I suggested that he fix them up and build a layout together with his son.

After taking inventory of what he had and after discussing with Judy and Jonathan the general ideas about the layout, the LaCalle family attended a train meet as my guests. It was at this meet, after talking with the LaCalles and many other S Gauge enthusiasts, that it became obvious to me that my original question as a child about two rail track was a good one. In terms of the quality, variety, realism, play value, cost and space required for an extensive layout, S Gauge was and is the collector's and operator's

Another view of the LaCalle layout showing Plasticville buildings with Gilbert trains.

delight.

Jim as a child had always wanted switch tracks for his layout; but as Christmas came and went, Santa was never able to deliver. Jim was very pleased to learn that at train meets, yard sales, flea markets, and through other collectors, everything he wanted was still available.

The LaCalles now operate an 8' x 20' layout featuring three trains, passenger and freight, steam and diesel, and, oh yes, eight pair of switches. Their rolling stock includes eight engines, ten passenger and eighty freight cars traveling through a community of American Flyer, Lionel, Marx and Plasticville buildings and accessories and Matchbox and Hot Wheels cars and trucks. The accompanying photos show different scenes designed and executed by Jonathan.

As for my own collection, I have chosen to collect items with great play value like log dump cars, cattle cars and the tie-jector. My layout for American Flyer consists of six American Flyer layout panels, complete with the original signs and buildings; and my trains "run on two rail track just like the real trains do."

Bruce Greenberg

Gilbert's sale program focused on realism. Gilbert strove to offer greater realism than its arch rival Lionel. Gilbert admen pursued this concept with a vengeance. Gilbet equipment was "scale length," not just scale proportioned, and horrendous line cuts of "other toy trains" were shown to prove how misproportioned the others were.

In fact one of the unanticipated consequences of the Gilbert "hard sell" were and are (still) heated debates by the tens and possibly hundreds of thousands of boys and men on the merits of Gilbert versus Lionel trains. The memory of the arguments is still fresh in the minds of Gilbert enthusiasts and to a lesser extent of Lionel enthusiasts thirty years later. I remember my childhood Lionel trains (also long gone but replaced many times over) and my best friend John's flyer equipment. John and I used to argue about whose trains were "more realistic" and although John clearly won on two rails, I convinced myself that coupler realism was just as important. In any case it was never "I'd rather fight than switch;" our parents had too much involvement; although feelings did and do peak when Flyer-Lionel comparisons are made.

Gilbert fans still believe that their's is the superior product and that eventually the world will come around. As a lover of toy trains, whether they be Marx, Lionel, Gilbert or you name it, I prefer (my solution to the dilemma) to point out that beauty lies in the eyes of the beholder -- particularly that there is beauty (of a kind) in a stubby die-cast Scout for a train-hungry youngster) or in a Marx Commodore Vanderbilt. It is a matter of understanding what is intended. If the Scout set or the Marx windup or the Casey Jones brings joy and sparks that magic in the ten year old boy that will lead him to appreciate our iron horses or sleek sided diesels and to want to build another train layout, then these are great trains indeed! And who today can deny that American Flyer trains are recognized as the best mass marketed scale equipment produced during the 1950s.

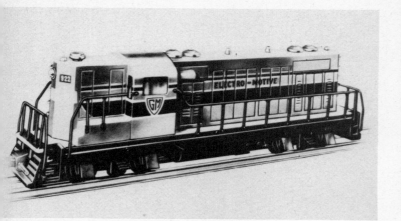

The GP-7 prototype 922; from the Walsh Photographic Collection.

The brakeman leaves the caboose to operate the semaphore. Invented by Gabe but not put into production. Walsh Collection.

Colber supplied many Gilbert accessories; from the Walsh Photographic Collection.

Keystone Camera developed a special promotion with Gilbert. This is a copy of Keystone's promotional literature. Walsh Collection.

PRESIDENT'S REPORT

To Our Stockholders:

1961 was not one of our more notable years from the standpoint of sales volume and profits. One serious financial set-back was a credit loss explained later, attributed to a sale made in 1960.

The uncollectibility of the account was not determined until mid-1961 following a meeting of several other creditors and our respective attorneys. Three other large suppliers suffered similar losses.

The decline in sales last year, as I mentioned in my letter of December 22nd, can in great part be attributed to the lessening interest in electric trains by today's youngsters.

Fortunately, the diversity of our toy lines prevented this decline from becoming more serious. Our Auto-Rama car race sets and transportation system, for example, continue to show a healthy sales growth. And early this year our coverage of the toy transportation world will be rounded out with the introduction of the American Flyer Championship Model Airplane line.

The Gilbert name remains the acknowledged leader in science toys. The rapid growth in popularity of this category has brought many new competitors into the market, some of them giant corporations who have never made toys before but who are using science sets as a part of their long range institutional promotion programs.

This past year our new Zoom electric microscope sets were well received. Erector, the only all-steel construction toy in the United States, remains a best seller. For 1962 the entire line has been revised to feature new and exciting space and science models. Other improvements are covered later in this report.

By far the biggest news of all, and a major milestone in the 52 year history of your company, has been our new association with the Wrather Corporation of California.

As I reported in previous letters, the common stock of my late father's estate, together with that owned by myself and the rest of the family holdings, were sold to the Wrather organization, a leader in the growing field of recreation and leisure time activities.

This joining of forces promises a bright future for your company, which has been a leader in educational toys for more than a half century and whose name is pre-eminent with trade and consumer alike.

The talents of the Wrather organization will provide a major boost to our product development, advertising, promotion and acquisition programs. While your company will continue as a separate non-integrated corporation with me as president, Jack Wrather and his associates, in concert with my top executives, hold great promise for an exciting and growing future. Many far-reaching and basic improvements are already underway, although major and significant results are not expected until 1963.

In personnel, there has been one notable change. Herman L. Trisch, my father's right hand man for most of his 42 years with the company, retired at the end of 1961.

As Vice President in charge of sales and, later, as Executive Vice President until 1954, he contributed much to the early growth of the company.

In the past few years he was most helpful as a special sales assistant to Harvey Rath, currently Vice President for Sales, and to me.

The rest of the management team, without whose special talents and support an organization of our size could not be operated, also deserves recognition. While the last few years have been difficult and often discouraging, I look forward with optimism and enthusiasm to bright and rewarding years ahead.

Respectfully submitted,

A. C. Gilbert

President

New Haven, Connecticut
February 14, 1962